CW01637688

Studia Persica

n. 3

Matteo Compareti

THE ELUSIVE PERSIAN PHOENIX

Simurgh and pseudo-simurgh in iranian arts

with an appendix by Larisa Yu. Kulakova

Paolo Emilio Persiani

Casa Editrice Persiani

piazza San Martino 9/C
40126 Bologna

Tel. (+39) 051/9913920
Fax (+39) 051/19901229

e–mail: info@persianieditore.com
www.persianieditore.com

We would like to thank Mr. Houshang Dadgostar
for supporting the publication of Studia Persica vol. 3

Cover art: elaboration of a mosaic from Edessa.
Studio Alex Mazzucato Mezzocolli ©

Editorial staff: Loris Di Bella, Marta Paone, Maria Vella

Contents

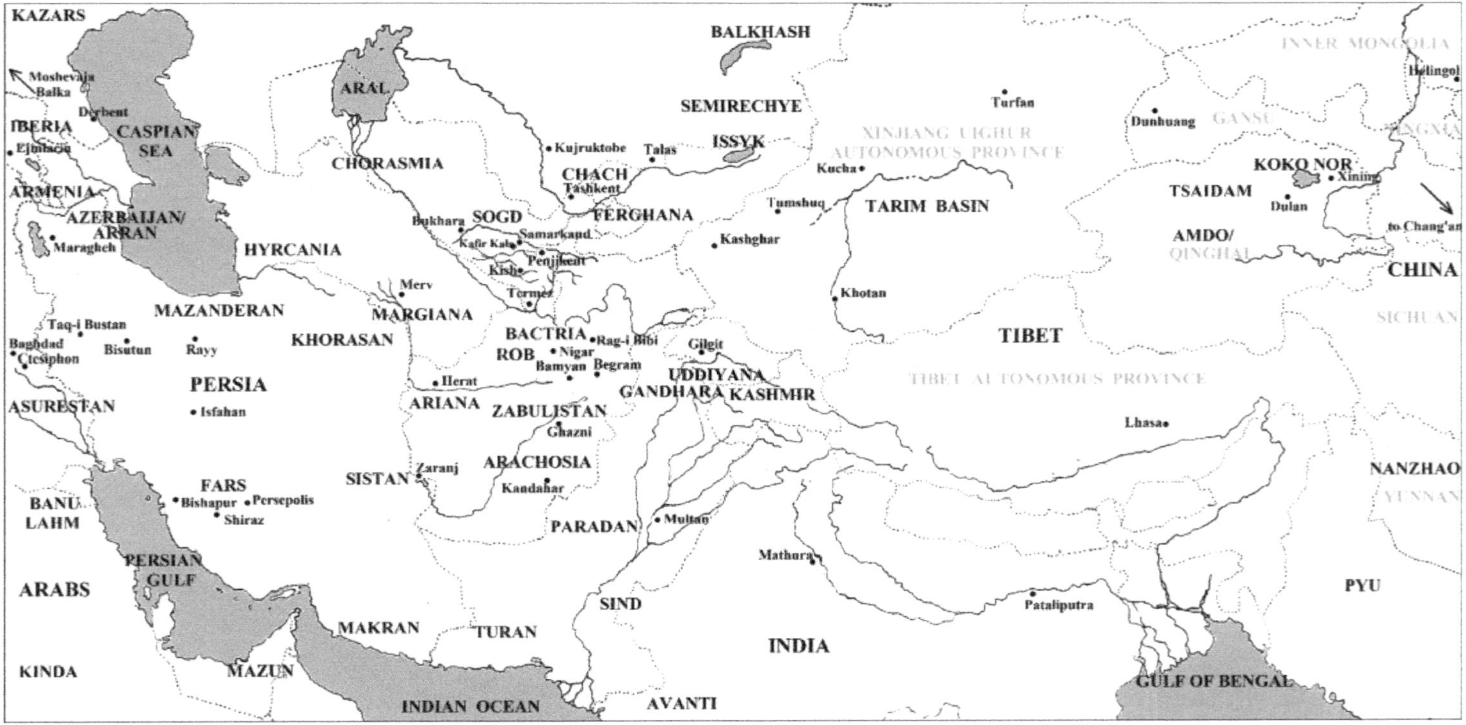

Map of historical regions, ancient sites, and modern cities mentioned in the text.

Acknowledgments

Many ideas expressed in the present study from the point of view of visual arts have been suggested after discussing the topic throughout the years – some even when I was still a student – with Boris Marshak. Some of his most recent studies already presented the base for the identification that I propose here. As recognized by Marshak himself,[1] his ideas about the *simurgh* were already expressed by Alessandro Bausani in 1978.[2] The two great Iranists formulated their hypotheses independently but, unfortunately, none of them presented a specific study on the *simurgh*.

Other friends and colleagues who greatly helped to see the fulfilment of the present study are Gianroberto Scarcia and Simone Cristoforetti. On the occasion of an international conference in honor of Boris Marshak held in 2008 in St Petersburg, those Italian colleagues presented some interesting researches that, starting from not easily accessible manuscripts, could once more support my hypothesis on the identification of the *simurgh* in Iranian arts.[3] Furthermore, it is very clear that Bausani and Marshak were aware of those manuscripts.

For the transcription of terms in other languages such as Middle Persian, Sogdian, Arabic, Farsi, Armenian, Russian, etc. I did not use diacritics that recur only in quoted studies and in the bibliography exactly as presented by the original authors. Whenever possible, I have tried to render specific signs according to English pronunciation although vowels respond better to Italian pronunciation. Therefore,

1 Marshak 1998, 85.

2 Bausani 1978a.

3 Cristoforetti, Scarcia 2013.

for example, the text will report Verethraghna and not *Vṛθrayna*, Mithra and not *Miθra*, Tishtrya and not *Tištriya*, etc.

The term "Iranian" that I used many times throughout this study does not refer necessarily to modern Iran, but also peoples such as the Bactrians, Sogdians, Chorasmians, etc. who shared the same culture and, to a certain degree, religious and linguistic ties with the (ancient) Persians. In his lectures at UC Irvine, Touraj Daryaee proposed to introduce the term "Iranic" that exists in other languages and could be compared to the case of Turkish and Turkic in English. For example, in Italian "iraniano" means "man from (modern) Iran" or, as an adjective, anything related to Iran. On the other hand, "iranico" refers, in more general terms, to ancient and modern peoples who spoke or still speak languages that are related to Persian. Therefore, as Daryaee proposed, we could say that Bactrian, Sogdian, Chorasmian, etc. are ancient "Iranic" languages while Farsi, Kurdish, Pashto, Ossetian, etc. are modern "Iranic" languages.

Several colleagues and friends have contributed to the completion of this study. First of all I would like to thank Simone Cristoforetti professor at the Department of Studies on Asia and Mediterranean Africa, Venice University "Ca' Foscari" for his kindness in discussing with me many passages in Persian texts which preserved precious information about the *simurgh*. Pavel Lurje, Head of the sector of Central Asia, the Caucasus and Crimea, Senior Research Fellow of the Oriental Department of the State Hermitage Museum and, since 2006, Director of the Russian archaeological expedition in Penjikent, has always helped me with unpublished material and new information about his fieldwork in Tajikistan and the museum collection at the State Hermitage. I owe him the invitation to go to Tajikistan in 2016 and visit Penjikent and the museums at the site, Dushanbe and modern Penjikent. This experience was decisive for my research on Sogdian art. Pavel Lurje's help was very important also for the inclusion of the appendix by Larisa Kulakova that appears at the end of this book. I am grateful to Larisa and Pavel for their work on unpublished and hardly accessible material at present preserved in the storage of the State Hermitage and for their decision to present the results of their investigations in a book on the Iranian phoenix/*simurgh*.

During the academic year 2013/2014 I was invited as visiting research scholar at the Institute for the Study of the Ancient World in New York (ISAW, NYU) while in 2015/2016 I have taught pre-Islamic Iranian arts at the Department of Near Eastern Studies, University of California, Berkeley (UC Berkeley). In that period, I had access to many American libraries and my investigations greatly improved. My warmest thanks to Guitty Azarpay (UC Berkeley), Judith Lerner and Sören Stark (ISAW, NYU) for their invitation and valid suggestions. My colleague Sara Peterson, professor at SOAS University of London, Art and Archaeology Department, made useful comments and looked after better English. Obviously, any mistakes or errors in this study should be considered solely mine.

My sincere thanks are also due to Li Sifei, Sha Wutian and Ge Chengyong for their kind invitation and constant support during my staying at the School of History and Civilization of Shaanxi Normal University (Xi'an). Li Sifei did most of the translations of Chinese sources and studies that were extremely useful for this book, especially for the part concerning the *fenghuang*.

Stra (Venice), March 2021

Introduction

The present study brings together a series of articles on the mythical bird of Persian tradition called *simurgh* (Middle Persian *senmurv*, Avestan *saena marega*) which I have published on several occasions. Those papers were mainly attempts to show that the very first approach to pre-Islamic Persian fantastic creatures by Kamila Trever – rarely challenged by scholars of Sasanian art – has been based on very weak evidence that deserves revision.

Between the two world wars, in a period particularly fortunate for Iranian studies, the Russian scholar Kamila Trever proposed to identify the flying dog with a peacock tail so widespread in (late) pre-Islamic Iranian arts as the *senmurv* of Middle Persian literature. Trever published her hypothesis in 1933 and 1937. Later on, her ideas were presented on several occasions for example in a French article in 1964. The original 1937 booklet in Russian was translated into English in 2005.[4] Trever adopted the ideas already expressed some time earlier by Nikolaj Marr on the identification of the *senmurv*/*simurgh* with the fantastic *paskuj* of the Georgian translation of the *Shahnameh*.[5] Although her identification did not appear to be unequivocally convincing for everyone, her hypothesis started to cross the borders of USSR to be reported uncritically by scholars interested in these kinds of fantastic creatures. The association of different ancient Middle Persian or Islamic period texts and the observation of art objects attributed to the Sasanians (224-651) and pre-Islamic Sogdiana has enabled the formulation of precise hypotheses.

The name of the creature deserves special attention. Already in the *Avesta* [*Yt.* XII, 17 and *Yt.* XIV, 41], a fantastic bird called *saena*

4 Trever 1937; Trever 1964; Trever 2005.

5 Marr 1918, 2081.

or *saena marega* (literally "*saena* bird") is mentioned (etymologically related to the Sanskrit *śyena*, literally "falcon").[6] During the Sasanian period, it would have become *senmurv* in Middle Persian (or Pahlavi), while *simurgh* is the Neo-Persian (or Farsi) name: quite obviously, both the Middle Persian and the Neo-Persian forms point to the same fantastic bird. It is very important to clarify this point because, in recent times, several scholars added some more confusion to the problem in regarding the *senmurv* and *simurgh* as two distinct creatures.[7] This assertion is clearly indebted to the hypothesis formulated by Kamila Trever[8] and reminds us of the "two fantastic animals *senmurv* and *simurgh*, iconographically different but sharing the same etymology".[9]

Islamic texts such as the national epic of the Persians (the *Shahnameh* or "Book of Kings") and Zoroastrian treatises (that, in any case, have all been written down only after the Islamization of Iranian lands) give some descriptions of the *senmurv/simurgh*. This creature was a giant bird that lived in a tree (possibly on top of a mountain) in the middle of the mythical Vourukasha Sea.[10] It was associated with birth (and re-birth that means immortality), fire, and music. Its connection with the pre-Islamic Iranian god of time Zurvan offers a clear parallel with the association between the phoenix and the god of time Aion, the Greco-Roman counterpart of Zurvan.[11] A reflection of this association can be observed on coins of Antoninus

6 Mayrhöfer 1956-76, III, 385.

7 Gierlichs 1993, 26; Charritat 2001; Leclerc 2001.

8 Trever 2005, 166.

9 Curatola, 1989, 51; cf. p. 43 on the Islamic iconography – i.e. the *simurgh* – "turned away from the universal prototype of the hippocampus" – i.e. the *senmurv*). On the same line "the *sēnmurv*, literally *sēn* 'dog' and *murv* 'bird' is a popular motif in Sasanian art": Gyselen 2009, 160. And again "the term *sēnmurv*, literally meaning dog-bird": Gyselen 2010, 228.

10 Christensen 1941, 66.

11 Scarcia 2003, 16; Compareti, Scarcia 2012, 224-226, 241; Grosserez 2013, 37-45. On the association between the phoenix and Helios, see: Sbordone 1935.

Pius mint in Alexandria in 138-139 CE reproducing on the reverse a haloed phoenix together with the inscription "Aion" in Greek.[12] In addition, the mountainous habitat of the *simurgh* reminds one of the Mount Casius in Syria where the phoenix lived that was confused with the nest of the Arabic *'anqa* on Mount Qaf.[13] According to al-Jahiz (eighth-ninth centuries) the *'anqa* that was "depicted on the carpets of kings" was called *simurgh* in Persian "as if one said that it alone was thirty birds".[14] The *Shahnameh* undoubtedly mentions the top of a high mountain as the dwelling place of the *simurgh*, a giant and aggressive bird that could carry elephants, crocodiles and leopards into the clouds [Khaleghi-Motlagh v, 24].[15] A fragmentary mural painting excavated at the site of Qarakhanid Samarkand also presents the image of a colossal bird of prey on the top of a mountain with a human head at its base. Unfortunately, the head of the bird was completely lost. The identification of this unusual painting was made possible thanks to the parallel offered by some poems of Hakim Suzani Samarqandi (twelfth century) explicitly mentioning the protecting *farr* (glory) associated with the shade of the *homa* or *'anqa*.[16]

12 Bisconti 1979, 30. Despite the rayed nimbus that accompains the phoenix on Roman coins, this bird had no explicit solar but rather royal connotations to be associated with the emperor and dynastic succession: Lecocq 2001.

13 The Greeks and the Romans called it Casius while the Semitic peoples called it Zaphon: Van den Broek 1972, 63-65; Scarcia 2010.

14 Bivar 2009, 4.

15 This description of the *simurgh* is very similar to the story reported by Marco Polo [CLXVII] about Madagascar where giant "griffin birds" lived. They were used to abduce in the sky elephants to let them fall down. Once the elephant was dead, they could eat them. According to some scholars, these "griffin birds" could be identified with the *rukh* of Arab legends: Grossato 2004, 120. Another Venician traveler, Antonio Pigafetta (1492-1531), gave a very similar description of *Garuda* that lived in Java (Indonesia): Grossato 2004, 132.

16 Karev 2003, 1724-1726. The human head seems to be part of another creature with the body resembling a turtle or some other animal with scales. Something similar can be observed in fourth-fifth century Sogdian paintings on a column from Erkurgan, not far from Kish (modern Shahrisabz). Above the object or creature

Some confusion with the Iranian concept called *xwarenah/xwarrah/farr(eh)* so important for the present study emerges already in this specific point. In fact, *farr* definitely had some connections with the mountains not only among Iranians but among Central Asian Turks as well.[17]

The most important story about the *simurgh* in Persian written sources is featured in the *Shahnameh* by Firdousi (late tenth-early eleventh century). I refer here to the *Shahnameh* in the D. Khaleghi-Motlagh edition in Persian (Costa Mesa-New York 1988-2001) that is the most commonly accepted one among scholars at present. When the noble Sam abandoned his little son Zal on the mountains because he was born with white hair, the *simurgh* saved and took the child in its nest. This part of the story suggests some maternal characteristics of the *simurgh* that was sometimes represented in Islamic book illustrations in its nest together with two cubs. Later on, Zal went back to his father's court after obtaining a magic feather of the *simurgh* to be burnt in order to summon the bird for help. The *simurgh* became in fact the protector of Zal and his family [Khaleghi-Motlagh I, 41-157].

Gianroberto Scarcia dedicated several studies to Zal and his characteristics such as albinism and his pagan motherland in eastern Iran (Sistan, Zabulistan). In his opinion, the figure of Zal in Persian mythology originated from the Iranian god of time Zurvan who, as observed above, was traditionally associated with the *senmurv/simurgh*.[18]

---

with scales in those paintings there is something looking like a caduceus of Hermes embellished with spread wings and snakes. However, according to some scholars, there would not be just spread wings and snakes but also birds: Mode 1989, 242; Sulejmanov 2000, figs. 78-79; Abdullaev 2011, 313-315. A creature at the base of the mountain where a bird (*fenghuang*?) stands can be observed when photographed under ultraviolet rays in a Western Han Chinese silks that was excavated in *kurgan* 6 at Noin Ula, Mongolia (see fig. 88 of this study): Riboud 1977; Elikhina 2009; Elikhina 2019.

17 Gnoli 1982.

18 Scarcia 1965; Scarcia 1991; Scarcia 2002; Shahbazi, Cristoforetti 2009;

It is worth observing that in a Sogdian fragmentary Buddhist text [P 8, 41-42] recovered in Dunhuang (China), Zurvan's representation was superimposed on the figure of Indian Brahma. For this reason, in the Sogdian version of the *Vessantara Jataka* [VJ 908-922], Zurvan had a beard evidently to identify him as an old man exactly like in Indian traditional representations of the creator god. His name too had some connection to oldness and one mysterious eastern Iranian deity that was recorded in Islamic and Chinese sources as Zun/Zhun/Zur.[19] In Indian religious traditions, the symbolic animal or vehicle (Sanskrit *vahana*) of Brahma was the swan (Sanskrit *hamsa*) that could have been confused with many other (magic) birds in India or abroad. It is not clear why and on which basis the Sogdians had started to adopt the Indian religious iconography to represent their own deities, but it appears to be at least since the sixth century CE.[20] However, in the case of Zurvan, Sogdian "magi" (priests) and artists operated a very precise choice regarding the iconography of Brahma and his symbolic bird. Recent studies on Sogdian epigraphic seal impressions from Kafir Kal'a produced some interesting arguments in order to identify Zurvan as a deity with two heads resembling the Roman god Janus. Parallels offered in Sasanian sphragistic seems to confirm Sogdian representations. Unfortunately, those objects are all

---

Compareti, Scarcia 2012, 236-246.

19 Wikander 1949-1950, 324-329. Nicholas Sims-Williams (1996, 657-648) proposed to identify the deity painted in a rock-cut niche at Nigar also called Dukhtar-i Nushirwan (Afghanistan) with a possible image of Zhun. Theophoric names of pre-Islamic rulers of the kingdom of Rob (eighty kilometers south of Samgan) that are attested in several written documents would confirm the relevant position of this deity: Sims-Williams 1997, 19. It is however worth noticing that at Nigar there were possibly other deities. In the line drawings of Nigar paintings published by Klimburg-Salter (1989, pl. LXXXVII, fig. 114), it is possible to observe fragments of at least two more arches that probably framed more deities beside the presumed Zhun. Some coins from Gozgan, in the west of Bactria-Tokharistan, are inscribed with the name of a local ruler called Zhulad that means "given by Zhun": Rezakhani 2017a, 180 n. 10.

20 Compareti 2009a, 177-178; Grenet 2010.

very small and just limited to human busts with inscriptions but no other attributes with the exception of some animal heads above the crown of the Janus-like deity identified with Zurvan.[21]

Other Islamic texts mentioned the *simurgh* and, at least since the period of Mongol dominion over Iran, it began to be frequently represented in book illustrations. Some of these texts had the *simurgh* as the main and almost exclusive protagonist such as in *'Aql-i sorkh* "The Red Intellect" and *Safir-i Simurgh* "The Calling of the Simurgh" by Shihab al-Din Sohravardi (1154-1191). In the famous mystical poem *Mantiq al-Tayr* "The Conference of the Birds" by 'Attar (ca. 1145-1221), the author plays on the similarity between the name *simurgh* and the Persian word for "thirty birds" (*si murgh*). A large group of the world's birds, who represent different human qualities, set off in search of the king of the birds (*simurgh*). Many of them drop out along the way. When the surviving thirty birds arrive in the land of the *simurgh*, they learn that their journey has been about seeing themselves for who they are.[22] Clearly, 'Attar did not write a poem on the *simurgh stricto sensu* but just used it as a pretext to discuss human self-awareness; nevertheless, it is worth noting that he knew that the *simurgh* was a bird and not something else.

In recent times, the *simurgh* never stopped to fascinate modern scholars and artists. In his essay *Manual de zoología fantástica* (later *El Libro de los seres imaginarios* "The Book of Imaginary Beings", 1957), Jorge L. Borges gave a description of the *simurgh* according to Gustave Flaubert *La tentation de Saint Antoine* (1874) that is to say, a magnificent reddish bird with four wings, a peacock tail, and a small human head.[23] It should not be ruled out that Maurits C. Escher later adopted just this description of the fantastic bird for his famous print *Other World* (1947). Such a work by Escher contributed to shape the

21 Grenet 2013, 204-206; Bogomolov 2020.

22 De Blois 1998; Saccone 1999, 111-121; Zambon 2001, 231-232.

23 Borges, Guerrero 2006, 192. See also: Zambon 2001, 231-232.

usual perception of this fantastic "Persian bird" at the wide public until our days.

As it will be observed below, the description of the *simurgh* as a human headed bird more similar to the sirens of Ulysses as represented sometimes in Classical art, was already included by some ancient Muslim authors in their literary works.

Chapter 1
The Persian phoenix/*simurgh* in written sources

Every ancient culture had its own cosmic bird that shared common characteristics, the most important ones being the giant size, some association with fire, and longevity. They are usually mysterious creatures and very vague descriptions are given in ancient literary texts. Just to mention some of these fantastic birds that had called the attention of scholars because of their possible association with the phoenix, here are some specimens: the ancient Egyptians had the *benu*; the Arabs the *'anqa* or the *rukh*; the Jews the *hol*; the Yezidi *Melek Ta'us*; the Indians *suparna* (or *Garuda*); the Tibetans *khyung*; the Hungarians *torul*, etc. Most of the information about these magic birds is included in folk tales, legends, fables, and epic. They rarely appear in historical documents and usually concern legendary aspects of heroes or relevant people. According to the tenth chapter of the *Gesta Hunnorum et Hungarorum* by Simon de Keza (thirteenth century), for example, "the coat of arm of King Attila, which he was accustomed to wear on his own shield, had the representation of the bird which in Hungarian is called *torul*, with a crown on its head".[24] Ancient Iranians (especially Persians) were not an exception. The magic bird of Iranian mythology was called *senmurv* in Middle Persian or *simurgh* in Persian.

The ancient Slavs represent a specific case in this list because one of the deities of their pre-Christian pantheon was named *Simar'gl*. Its aspect is not completely clear but, according to some scholars, this

24 Róheim 1954, 5. Curiously enough, one scholar associated the funeral of Attila with the Iranian concept of *farreh* that, as it is going to be explained below, was intimately connected with the *simurgh* bird: Borzsák 1990.

deity was represented as a bird.[25] Moreover, it is not excluded that *Simar'gl* was an Iranian borrowing specifically rooted in the figure of the Iranian *senmurv/simurgh*, although not every scholar agrees on this point.[26]

Biblical sources also mentioned the phoenix. The Jewish *hol* appears in the Midrash on Genesis as the only animal that refused to eat a piece of the forbidden fruit that Eve offered to Adam and all the other animals in the garden of Eden. For this reason, God has granted its immortality.[27] According to the Babylonian *Talmud*, the phoenix has been resting somewhere in the ark of Noah for a very long time after the Great Flood.[28] Other Jewish sources used the Greek phoenix in association with the *hol*, *chalkidry*, and other birds that had some connections with immortality and the sun.[29]

Associations between birds belonging to different cultural milieu were normal and could have been advanced not only by contemporary scholars but also by ancient observers. For instance, it would be worth noting that in modern Armenian the word for peacock is *siramarg*, with very small dialectal variants. This term too seems to be a clear Iranian borrowing from *senmurv/simurgh* because of the tight relationships between Armenia and Persia both in pre-Islamic and Islamic periods.[30] As it will be observed below, there are points of contact between the peacock and the phoenix in literary texts and visual arts.

---

25 Lelekov 1978, 23-32.

26 Trever 2005, 174-175; Compareti 2006, 190-191; Compareti, Cristoforetti 2012; Álvarez-Pedrosa 2014, 66- 67.

27 Ginzberg 1995, 49; Van den Broek 1999. The main scene in the floor mosaic of the Huarte church, Syria (fifth century, today in the Apamea Museum) is an image of Adam with his name in Latin above him and all the animals around. The phoenix appears on the right and it is recognizable because of the rayed halo around its head: Amad 1988, fig. 6.

28 Albrile 2000, 80 [*Sanhedrin* XI, 3, ed. Goldschmidt, t. 7, 488].

29 Grossato 2004, 95-102; Kulik 2009, 315-325.

30 Russell 1987, 308-309.

Also for the *simurgh* there has been much speculation among scholars; therefore, a short summary would be useful. All the following information can be found in a fundamental article on the *simurgh* by Schmidt[31] that, however, presents major methodological problems and, in the light of some more recent publications, should be considered with great caution. As reported in the introduction, already in Avestan language a fantastic bird called *saena marega* is mentioned; it became *senmurv* in Middle Persian, while *simurgh* is the Neo-Persian form. Islamic texts described the *simurgh* as a fantastic bird and sometimes represented it in book illustrations.

But let us to come to the representation of the *simurgh* in Iranian art following the risky identification by Kamila Trever. In her opinion, the *senmurv* (and the *simurgh*) would have been a winged composite creature with the head and paws of a dog and a peacock's tail. Despite several doubts raised by some scholars (including Schmidt) who criticized Trever's identification, her theory persisted for a very long time. In his review of Trever's original publication in Russian, Toll criticized her methodology in several parts but accepted the idea that the *simurgh* in pre-Islamic time was a composite winged creature.[32] Many other students of Sasanian iconography entirely based their observations on Trever hypotheses.[33] Only recently, her identification has been proved problematic and new ideas on the real iconography of the *simurgh* have been produced. In brief, the *simurgh* has always been represented as a fantastic bird, and the hybrid creature with wings, a dog-face, and peacock's tail should be rather regarded as a representation of *farr*/*farreh* that is, "glory" or "charisma".[34]

---

31 Schmidt 1980a. See also the review by Gignoux 1981. For a very long discussion on the *simurgh* that started from Marr's and Trever's identifications, see: Bertel's 1997, 154-289 (reviewed in Pistoso 2007).

32 Toll 1942.

33 Harper 1961; Riboud 1983; Romano 1994; Ierusalimskaja 1995; Grossato 2004; Movassat 2005, 95-98; Soudavar 2010; Gasparini 2014, 120; Rezakhani 2017a, 174-175.

34 Bausani 1978a; Marshak 1998, 85, Marshak 2002a, 140-141; Marshak 2002b,

Exactly as occurred with the phoenix, the *simurgh* too was probably confused by ancient authors with other fantastic birds that can be found in Persian myths. The Arabic *'anqa* became the normal substitute for *simurgh* (and phoenix) in Arab translations of Rustam's adventures or the *panchatantra* in place of *Garuda*.[35] In Arab literature there is also a romance called *Kitab al-'anqa* telling the story of a young woman called al-'Anqa who was kidnapped before her marriage by the *'anqa* bird and transported in South-East Asia. Only the brave future husband would be able to rescue her. In this story, the *'anqa* is described as a *jinniya* that is a female *jinn* (genie),[36] a group of mysterious creatures that were very often mentioned in the Koran like the one of the famous Aladdin lamp story. At least two passages of the Koran explicitly associated *jinn*s and fire [xv, 27 and lv, 15]. Exactly like the *simurgh* in the *Shahnameh*, *jinn*s too could be friendly or hostile towards humans.[37]

Without entering too deeply into the question, one can consider briefly another aspect of the *simurgh*, that is, its connection with the concept of *farr*(*eh*) (Avestan *xwarenah*, Middle Persian *xwarrah*), which could be translated as "glory", "fortune" or "charisma" and was essential for every Iranian king in order to rule, and heroes to fight monsters, and deities too possessed it. *Farr*/*farreh* had very strong connections with kingship and was sometimes described as a luminous aura around the body of ancient Iranian kings and heroes. It is a very problematic term that has been keeping scholars very busy for a

---

37; Compareti 2006. Among the experts in other fields of studies who accepted or mentioned this new identification, see: Treadwell 2008, 376-377; Gagetti 2012, 96-100; Canepa 2014, 4-5; Bollók 2015, 62, n. 20; Russell 2016; Riccioni 2019, 183; Gasparini 2020, 41.

35 De Blois 1998.

36 Bivar 2005, 19; Bivar 2009, 9. The Chinese-style *'anqa* is also the giant bird that is transporting a person in a fourteenth century illustration in one album in the Topkapi Museum, Istanbul [Hazine 2152, fol. 64 a]: Ettinghausen 1957, fig. 11.

37 Bausani 1955, note 100 to *sura* vi.

long time from the linguistic point of view too.[38] Both in Zoroastrian (or Mazdean) and Islamic Persian literature, this Iranian charisma can take several forms, and, among these, also the shape of a bird.[39]

In the Avestan myth, the *xwarenah* turned away from Yima in the form of the *vareghna* bird, which has been identified with a falcon because of some references in Middle Persian literature and representations on second century CE Kushan coins.[40] According to the *Bahram Yasht* [XIV, 35], the feathers of the *vareghna* bird had healing properties exactly like those of the *simurgh*.[41] Another important bird in Zoroastrian religion that was associated with Yima as well is the *karshiptar*. We know of it as the propagator of Zoroastrian religion only from written sources and it has never been identified in visual arts.[42] Possibly, the only companion of the *simurgh* explicitly mentioned in Middle Persian Zoroastrian texts is the *chamrush* bird,

---

38 Lentz 1973; Skjærvø 1983; Jacobs 1987; Lubotsky 1998; Gnoli 1999; Shenkar 2014, 131; Shavarebi, Qaemmaqami 2016, 263-266. On the connection between the idea of *xwarrah*, kingship, and its reflection on the Iranian *sada* festivity, see: Cristoforetti 2003, 314-316.

39 Shenkar 2014, 132. As Shenkar stressed in his book, several scholars proposed to identify many decorative elements appearing in pre-Islamic Iranian arts with manifestations of *xwarrah* without any real evidence, which should be supported by written sources. Abolala Soudavar (2003; 2010) published several studies on this aspect of *xwarrah*.

40 Stricker 1964; Grenet 2012. Patricia Crone proposed a parallel between the glory of Yima abandoning him in the shape of a bird and Abu Muslim who, according to some Islamic sources, escaped death by turning into a white dove: Crone 2012, 335. On the possible hidden reason(s) that caused *xwarrah* to abandon Yima, see: Lentz, 1962; Krasnowolska 1998, 86.

41 Pirart 1999, 473, 504-506. Bahram (Avestan Verethraghna) was the Zoroastrian god of war and victory who manifested himself to the Prophet Zoroaster ten times in different forms. His seventh manifestation was a magnificent bird, most likely a raven [XIV, 19].

42 Redard 2012. One expert of Chorasmian art proposed to identify it in representations of composite bird images from Koykrilgan Kala (Uzbekistan) that, however, could just be representations of the so-called *grilli*: Rapoport 1977, 62-67.

whose main function is to peck the enemies of Iran as if they were grains.[43] In this case too, its large size is implicit because it is represented as a bird of prey that could eat people. One last bird attested in Persian literature is the *homa*, whose name is clearly connected with kingship; yet, even if it also could remind of the phoenix, its ornithological identification is doubtful.[44] According to some passage of the *Shahnameh*, the Iranian glory/*farr* was contained in the feathers of the *homa* bird. There are no specific studies devoted to this important bird, described in the *Shahnameh* as "the bird of royal fortune (= *farr*)" or "whose feathers symbolize *farr*".

Feathers represented the main decorative element on the crown of Persian kings in Islamic arts. On the contrary, the single feather is completely absent from Sasanian crowns and could have been introduced into Persia during the Islamic period or even from abroad.[45] According to the fabulous text *Tahmuradnameh* mentioned by Barthélemy d'Herbelot de Molainville in his *Bibliothèque orientale* as quoted by Arthur Christensen,[46] "the *simurgh* or *'anqa* took Tahmuras in the land of *jinns*. The *simurgh* predicted what was going to happen to Tahmuras and gave him some of its feathers [in order to summon the bird for help]. Tahmuras embellished his crown with these feathers and the greatest warriors [of Iran] did the same after him. The *simurgh* itself helped Tahmuras in his fights against the demons". This legend is perhaps the origin of the decorative feathers on headgears in Islamic times. The feathers on Islamic headgears do not indicate any specific bird because no texts mentioned that specific aspect of their illustrated part. Clearly, the descriptions of all

43 Boyce 1975, 43.

44 Curatola 1989, 51. The recent identification of the *homa* bird with the griffin reproduced on some Achaemenid column capitals is just based on popular beliefs. That same creature became the *logo* of Iran Air.

45 Roux 1982, 27-57; Adamova 2008, 27. On the wings of Sasanian crowns and their implication with the *xwarrah* that was contained in them, see: Piras 2004, 193; Compareti 2010.

46 Christensen 1917, 214-215.

these birds are generic in nature and it is mainly the *simurgh* which is undoubtedly portrayed in Islamic book illustrations. However, the iconography of the *simurgh* also presents some problems.

Very important information about the *senmurv/simurgh* can be found in Persian written sources of the Islamic period. The most detailed story about the *simurgh* is the so-called Sistani cycle in the *Shahnameh* by Firdousi. An entire part of the *Shahnameh* describes the genealogy of the great hero Rustam whose family came from eastern Iran or Sistan.[47] The *simurgh* "kidnapped" and suckled the hero Zal, abandoned as a baby because of his albinism, which his father Sam regarded as a demonic trait. The fact that the *simurgh* was able to nurse Zal has been possibly at the origin of the mammalian features that have been attributed to this fantastic bird.[48] Once Zal grew up strong and healthy with the help of the *simurgh*, he joined his contrite father and ruled in eastern Iran, precisely in the region of Zabulistan, in modern south-eastern Afghanistan, around Ghazni. The family of Zal represented a cadet branch of the mythical Kayanids who ruled Iranian lands in very ancient times.[49] Both Zal and his son Rustam were protected by the *simurgh* and they were able to summon it in case of need just by burning one of its feathers.

Zal was educated as an Iranian nobleman and later he married Rudabeh, the daughter of the king of Kabul and the granddaughter of the demonic Zahak. Rudabeh had serious problems while giving birth to their son Rustam and was at risk of dying. At that point, Zal burnt one feather of the *simurgh* (or part of it) and evoked the magic bird, which then suggested to Zal that he should deliver Rustam by caesarean section. The feather had healing properties (like those of the *vareghna* bird) and Zal used it to cicatrize the caesarean section together with some herbs according to the instructions of the

47 S. Gazerani dedicated an entire volume to this subject. However, that author did not pay much attention to the figure of the *simurgh*: Gazerani 2015.

48 Cristoforetti, Scarcia 2013, 340-341.

49 Christensen 1932.

simurgh. This saved mother and child. Lastly, during Rustam duel with Isfandyar, Zal again evoked the *simurgh* in order to heal his son's wounds and obtain more advice about the way to win Isfandyar invulnerability. The *simurgh* was initially reluctant to tell Rustam how to kill Isfandyar because it knew that whoever was going to slay that Kayanid hero was irremediably damned. When the duel started again, Rustam was able to kill Isfandyar after shooting a special arrow in his eyes.

Isfandyar was the representative of the Kayanid dynasty and the champion of Zoroastrians while Rustam's family preferred to preserve its ancestral pagan religion rooted in eastern Iranian traditions.[50] Both heroes share common characteristics in the *Shahnameh* despite the absence of any hint at Rustam's reluctance to accept Zoroastrianism [Khaleghi-Motlagh III, 76-174]. In one of his (anachronistic) adventures (precisely the fifth), Isfandyar even killed the *simurgh* and its two offspring [Khaleghi-Motlagh V, 240].[51] One could then imagine that many *simurgh*s populated ancient Iranian lands or at least two – one good and one bad, one male and one female[52] – although this does not seem to be the case. This is just one example of the numerous problems in the text by Firdousi who collected ancient stories and legends from different epic Iranian traditions. According to folkloristic versions of the *Shahnameh*, the *simurgh* told Rustam about its hostility towards Isfandyar because that hero killed "his wife". Nothing like this can be found in official versions of the *Shahnameh* although there are several hints to the ambivalent nature of the *simurgh*.[53] Experts of Mesopotamian culture and art proposed a parallel between the ambivalent *simurgh* and the bird *anzu* of Sumerian mythology that

50 Yarshater 1998; Davis 2007, 56-61.

51 One page of the dispersed "1341 Inju'id *Shahnameh*" painted in Shiraz illustrates Isfandyar's killing of the *simurgh* that is curiously represented in non-Chinese style: Sims 2012, cat. 16.

52 Casartelli 1891, 83; Christensen 1941, 67; Mo'in 1964, 21-22.

53 Schmidt 1980a, 18.

later influenced the Akkadian Epic of Etana. The *anzu* bird (probably an eagle) too could appear in some stories as positive and in others as negative.[54] Mesopotamian elements will occur very often during this investigation on Iranian mythical birds.

Not all descriptions of the *simurgh* in the *Shahnameh* and other Islamic sources represent a problem. Despite its magic properties, the *simurgh* was just a bird and not a composite creature. According to Trever's hypothesis, the *senmurv/simurgh* was a composite creature in pre-Islamic literature and visual arts but it became a colossal bird in book illustrations of the Islamic period. As already noted, Trever's idea have met with the favor of scholars and students of Sasanian art for a long time. Some scholars who followed Trever, focused just on the dog head of that composite creature. This transformation from "monster" to bird would have taken place at the time of the Arab invasion of Persia and Central Asia because of the repulsion for dogs by Muslims. Briefly, the Arabs superimposed their own phoenix (the *'anqa* bird) to the figure of the original Iranian composite creature.[55] Apart from the fact that the dislike of Muslims for dogs is not that obvious, the idea just exposed could be considered valid only for the canine component of that composite creature while it does not explain in any way the disappearance of the peacock tail. There could be then further chronological problems connected to the first representations of the *'anqa* in Islamic book illustrations that do not seem to antedate the *simurgh*.

Many scholars accepted Trever's idea without substantial objections although the textual analysis presents several anomalies. Trever based most of her ideas on very problematic passages in Avestan and Middle Persian texts that seem to connect the *senmurv/simurgh* to

54 Aro 1976; Dalley 2016, 255. Despite the attempt of one scholar to connect the Etana myth to the famous decorations of the Hasanlu "golden bowl" (ca. thirteenth century BCE), it was demonstrated that there are not enough elements to propose any clear parallel with this specific myth: Francfort 2008, 176.

55 Khakimov 2012, 20.

the bat: *Wizidagiha i Zadspram* [III, 65], *Bundahishn* [XXIV, 27], etc. However, one passage of the *Bundahishn* [XIII, 23-24] included the bat in the family of birds and added that only the bat and the *senmurv* have milk to suckle their young and they both fly in the night.[56] Three aspects suggest a bat: because it can fly like a bird, has teeth like a dog and lives in holes like rats. In another passage [XIX, 18], the *Bundahishn* states that the *senmurv* is a bat.[57] This equation probably suggested to Trever that the *senmurv* had three natures too and looked like a bat although her argument was based on unclear morphological characteristics of a real animal (bat) and a fantastic creature (*senmurv*). Zoroastrian written sources were based on superficial observations that considered the bat as a bird evidently because both animals have wings and can fly.[58] Also in Islamic zoology as deduced from the *Kitab al-Hayawan* "Book of animals" of al-Jahiz (776-868), the bat (and the ostrich too) always represented a problem because its shape (*sura*), nature (*tabi'a*), and the presence of wings (*jinah*) pointed at including this animal in the group of birds.[59]

It is also worth noting that in his translation of the *Bundahishn* and some other Middle Persian texts in English, Edward William West had already rendered the *sen* bird (which he expressely associated to the *saena marega*, *senmurv* and *simurgh*) as "griffon" [XIV, 11; XXIV, 11] or "griffon bird" [XIV, 23-24].[60] Even though Trever based

56 Pliny reported very similar characteristics for the bat in his *Naturalis Historia* [X, 81].

57 The passage XIX, 18 is translated like this by E. West while D. Agostini and S. Thrope more recently rendered it in a quite different way: The Sēn bird and the bat are described in detail in another chapter [XXIV, 27]. It is in any case worth observing that the *senmurv* and the bat are mentioned together. Domenico Agostini kindly supplied me with useful information about his work on the *Bundahishn*.

58 Compareti, Cristoforetti 2012, 247; Russell 2016.

59 Raggetti 2008, 194.

60 West 1880, 47, 50, 89. See also the *Bundahishn* translation by Agostini and Thrope who preferred to render the animal under exam simply as "Sēn bird" [XIII, 10], [XIII, 23], and [XXIV, 27].

her observations on direct sources, it is probable that she (and N. Marr as well) knew the hypothesis of a magic bird also composed by parts of other animals as already expressed by E. West. In any case, it seems that between the end of the nineteenth-beginning of the twentieth century, pioneer-experts of Iranian studies and Zoroastrian texts considered the *senmurv/simurgh* as a composite creature.

Medieval Arab and Persian texts could be useful for the study of mythological creatures. Simone Cristoforetti has studied very interesting texts from the Islamic period that suggest a different identification for the composite animal commonly called *simurgh/senmurv* by Trever.[61] Two passages studied by Cristoforetti are particularly interesting for the representation of fantastic creatures. In the early tenth century, the Arab author Mas'udi [*Muruj al-dhahab wa ma'adin al-jawhar* "The golden meadows and gem mines" II, 282] wrote that the Sasanian sovereign Khusraw II Parwiz (590-628) had nine personal seals, one of which presented the image of something called *Khurasan khurra*, literally "glory of Khorasan," a region intended here to mean "east," "orient." In fact, Ernst Herzfeld used the Latin expression *gloria Orientis* to describe it.[62] Some centuries later, between the end of the eleventh and the beginning of the twelfth centuries, the great Muslim scholar Biruni (who was quoting Iranshahri in his table on the festivals of the Persians: *Qanun: maqala* III *bab* XI = vol. I: 258-260) described those *Khurasan khurra* as "flying foxes" that appeared in antiquity on the occasion of a "spring festivity" and represented

61 Cristoforetti, Scarcia 2013, 341.

62 Herzfeld 1938, 157. However, Herzfeld proposed to identify the *Khurasan khurra* as a deity and specifically the goddess Ardokhsho who occurred quite often on Kushan coins. H. Bailey (1971, 65) refused such an identification. Bivar rendered the passage by Mas'udi in a slightly different way. He translated: "The second seal had a bezel of cornelian (*almās*). Its engraving was (the words) *Khurāsān khurra* and its ring was of gold. With it were sealed the memoranda (*al-tadhkirāt*)": Bivar 1969, 32. This is just one possible interpretation although the text by Mas'udi suggests that *Khurasan khurra* was referred to a seal on a golden ring that was embellished with an image and inscription or just an image.

the wellness of the Kayanids [vol. I: 260].[63] These descriptions by the two Muslim authors point to the representation of *khurra* (a variant of *farr/farreh*) as a winged creature with a fox's head that had some connections with the Orient to be possibly intended here as eastern Iran (Khorasan or, we could assume, Sistan). Some more evidence on the association between the winged composite creature and *farr*(*eh*) could be found in Middle Persian literature as well.

In the Middle Persian text *Karnamag i Ardashir i Papagan*, the first Sasanian king Ardashir (224-242) was explicitly associated with a manifestation of *xwarrah* that was following him in the shape of a very controversial creature whose aspect cannot be determined since all Pahlavi manuscripts (written during the Islamic period) present a corrupted form of arameogram (Persian *hoshvaresh*) to describe it [ch. VII. 11-24].[64] That same episode about the trials of the first Sasanian king can be found in Firdousi's *Shahnameh* written in Farsi (Persian or, better, Neo-Persian language). Scholars expected to find a description of the *xwarrah* following Ardashir as a ram (*barre* in Neo-Persian, Middle Persian *warrag*) but this is not the case since Firdousi always used the very problematic term *ghorm*.[65] There are other episodes dealing with the creature called *ghorm* associated with *xwarrah* in the *Shahnameh* and other Islamic period Persian texts. For example, in his second trial Rustam and his horse Rakhsh are going to die in a desert when suddenly a *ghorm* appears and leads them to a water source [Khaleghi-Motlagh II, 24-25]. The authors of the catalogue of the David Collection (Copenhagen) identified an early fourteenth century illustration of Rustam washing Rakhsh as the representation of that hero's second trial [19/2006].[66] Unfortunately, the

---

63 Cristoforetti, Scarcia 2013, 341 on the basis of the Russian translation by Halidov (1959).

64 I refer to F. Grenet most recent translation (2003). Other modern translators noticed some problems in reading this term: Chunakova 1987, 91.

65 Cristoforetti, Scarcia 2013, 344.

66 Meyer, Wandel 2016, cat. 15.

ghorm (described as a ram in the caption) does not occur in the David Collection image nor in other similar illustrations of the *Shahnameh* such as the one in the Metropolitan Museum [Rogers Fund, 69. 74. 8].[67] The only enigmatic presence in those illustrations is the round object decorated with a human face (shield? helmet? *gorgoneion*?) hanging on the upper left corner. The *ghorm* could appear and guide those who lost their way in other literary works of the Islamic period. In the *Darab nameh* (an eleventh-twelfth century Persian romance), Queen Homay, who was the daughter of Bahman and granddaughter of Isfandyar, could find her way through terrible mountains just by following the *ghorm* sent by God to help her.[68]

As Grenet himself recognized, the term "*warrag*" is almost illegible in all the manuscript editions of the *Karnamag*. However, the assertion that "il [Firdousi] parle incontestablement d'un «bélier» (*bare*)" to render the word "*warrag*" in the *Karnamag* cannot be considered correct.[69] In his review of Grenet's translation, Gherardo Gnoli was not completely satisfied about the point concerning the *xwarrah*/*farr*.[70] Grenet proposed to identify the figure of the ram embellished with a ribbon and, sometimes, a necklace in Sasanian art as a representation of *xwarrah*. He considered a human figure with a ram head in a Sasanian seal in the Boston Museum of Fine Arts as a previously unknown representation of *xwarrah*.[71] In addition, D. Bivar too considered the beribboned ram with a necklace that embellished some inscribed late Sasanian seals and seal-impressions as a symbol of *xwarrah* despite the absence of any clear caption. A problematic

67 Simpson 1979, 193, fig. 78.

68 *Darab nameh* 1977, 328.

69 Grenet 2003, 43. Frantz Grenet probably relied on the same literary parallel proposed long before by Jacques Duchesne-Guillemin (1979, 382).

70 Gnoli 2006.

71 Grenet 2013, 204. Some scholars, who mainly followed the problematic description of *xwarrah* as a *ghorm* in the *Karnamag*, identified the ram as a symbol of glory among Saka, Scythians and Sarmatians. Shenkar 2014, 138.

reading of the *Karnamag* that once more identified the animal following Ardashir symbolizing the *xwarrah* as a ram constituted his main argument.[72] Neither Bivar nor Grenet considered the possibility that the *ghorm* could be something else.

It is not easy to decide what the *ghorm* looked like. Actually, in Farsi *ghorm* can mean "male mountain goat" although in some written sources it is described as a composite creature, for instance, in a unique *Shahnameh* manuscript at present in the British Library [Ms. C. III 24] dated 1217 CE. In that text, the *ghorm* is explicitly described as the creature representing the glory that was following Ardashir: it had "the wings of the *simurgh*, the tail of a peacock, the head and hooves of Rakhsh". Moreover, in a Persian text composed in Mughal India (*Kitab-i mustatab-i Buhayra*), the creature following Ardashir is described as a "flying dog" (*sag-i rawan*) rendered as "*ghorm-i zhiyan*".[73]

Other Middle Persian (but also Avestan) sources can be very useful in order to propose a concrete shape for the abstract concept of *xwarrah*. According to a list prepared by Michael Shenkar, *xwarrah* could appear as fire in the *Mihr Yasht* [x, 27], *Wizidagiha i Zadspram* [v] and *Denkard* [VII, 2.7]; a *vareghna* bird (falcon?) in the myth of Yima [*Yt.* XIX, 34]; a ram in the *Karnamag* (but, as observed above, this identification is problematic); and an enigmatic flying creature in *Denkard* [816, 13] and *Pahlavi Rivayat* [XXII, 10].[74] One passage of the *Zamyad Yasht* (that was entirely dedicated to *xwarenah*) described the "glory" as escaping from Turanian enemies of Iran riding a horse [*Yt.* XIX, 56]. This description might imply some bodily form.[75] Also in the *Bahram Yasht* [*Yt.* XIV, 41] there is a problematic part that was

72 Bivar 2006, 10.

73 Cristoforetti, Scarcia 2013, 342.

74 Shenkar 2014, 132.

75 Pirart 1992, 79-80.

transmitted by ignorant copyists. As it was suggested, in fact, an original animal (possibly fantastic) was confused with clouds.[76]

In Persian literature of the Islamic period and specifically in the *Shahnameh* there are several references to *xwarrah/farr(eh)* as a nimbus or luminous aura that legitimated kings of the Kayanid Dynasty and heroes of the Iranian epos.[77] This concept of divine splendor could have some precise parallels in the description and possible representations of the Mesopotamian *melammu*.[78] According to linguistic studies, the term included the root of "burning" and could be associated to the Indian concept of *tejas* that is "the majesty of a great sovereign, fiery energy, and vital power".[79]

Just as in the problems in the *Karnamag*, the word that described a manifestation of *xwarrah* as a flying creature in *Denkard* and *Pahlavi Rivayat* was written in a corrupted form that expert philologists proposed to reconstruct in different ways. According to one hypothesis, that term could be rendered in origin as *tannin* (arameogram *TNYN), literally "sea dragon," that is another composite creature.[80]

76 Pirart 2006, 67. Copyists and translators have been facing very similar problems since ancient periods practically everywhere. A clear parallel for this situation happened in the second century BCE Hellenistic Alexandria for those scholars who started the problematic translation of the Bible in Greek (*Septuagint*) and, specifically, for some terms that pointed at real or fantastic animals, especially *tannin* and *leviathan*: Angelini 2018, 90-92.

77 Shenkar 2017, 57. There is quite an extensive literature about *farr* as light or splendor in Persian texts of the Islamic period. Scholars focused especially on the *Shahnameh*. As Shenkar observed, there is a curious description of *farr* in the Tarikh-i Sistan as "the light above the ears of the king's horse": Shenkar 2014, 134. According to Gherardo Gnoli, *xwarrah/farr* is a luminous principle that resides in generating waters and could be also associated to the human (and animal) sperm: Gnoli 1962.

78 Cassin 1968; Emelianov 2010.

79 Gonda 1956, 35-36; Gnoli 2002, 1-6-107.

80 Henning 1947, 42; Bailey 1971, XXXIII, 30; Shenkar 2014, 133. The dragon *tannin* (plural *tanninim*) occurs in the Bible and Ugaritic texts. It could be connected to the ancient Mesopotamian myth of Marduk killing Tiamat that was described

This emended term, possibly referring to a fantastic creature, definitely presents a solution to many figurative problems and constitutes a precise parallel with Sogdian art to be discussed below. It could also be considered a perfect alternative to every translation of that passage in the *Karnamag* already attempted in the past.

Scholars such as D.D.P. Sanjana[81] and C.F. Horne[82] preferred to translate the creature following Ardashir in the *Karnamag* as "eagle" because, in their opinions, a bird of prey could better represent the appearance of *xwarrah* in a concrete form.[83] Experts in Zoroastrian texts have always been very skeptical about the identification of *farr* with a "dragon" (or *tannin*) since this kind of creature was usually considered in its monstrous negative exception.[84] Arbitrary deductions and translations definitely contributed to add more confusion for the textual description and artistic representation of magic birds, abstract concepts and composite creatures.

---

as a dragon. It is sometimes referred to the *leviathan* in the Bible and other dragon-like creatures: *rahab* and *peten*: Angelini 2018, 30-32. In one occurrence, the term *tannot* (connected to the same Semitic root of *tannin*) is referred to "sea monster" in the Bible where it is usually indicated to point at desert animals such as the jackal or birds of prey. The confusion between the dragon and a bird of prey in the Bible could remind one of a similar phenomenon in the Iranian sphere: Angelini 2018, 29. The Greek name of the vulture *gips* is graphically very close to *grips* (griffin) that was another composite creature: Angelini 2020. Curiously enough, *tannin* could have been at the basis of the Greek name for the tuna fish *thunnos*: Heider 1999. Around the eleventh century, Arabic astronomical-astrological terms such as *ra's al-tinnin* ("head of the dragon") and *dhanab al-tinnin* ("tail of the dragon") referred to the lunar nodes and eclipses that started to appear in Byzantine astronomical treatises: Kuehn 2011, 139; Pirtea 2019, 354. It is described in Zakarya ibn-Muhammad ibn-Mahmud al-Qazwini's *'Aja'ib al-mahluqat wa ghara'ib al-maujudat* "The Wonders of Creation and the Oddities of Existence" (thirteenth century): Berlekamp 2011, 77-87.

81 Sanjana 1896, 16-18.

82 Horne 1917, 225–254.

83 Compareti 2009-2010; Cristoforetti, Scarcia 2013, 342.

84 Schmidt 1980a, 59-60; Hintze 1999, 85-86.

Other problematic interpretations associated with the manifestation of *xwarrah* as a protection for Ardashir can be found in at least two more passages of the *Karnamag*. In both cases, the *xwarrah* assumed the aspect of an animal, probably an onager [ch. VIII, 7] and a bird (rooster or eagle)[85] [ch. X, 7]. In his recent translation of the *Karnamag*, Grenet translated the problematic passage *xwarrah i Kayan *pad dur* as "the glory of the Kayanids that was far away". However, he admitted that, from a mere graphic point of view, the same passage could be read *xwarrah i Kayan *pad gor* "the glory of the Kayanid [in the shape of an] onager". In fact, to accept the manifestation of *xwarrah* as an onager, one should expect the form **pad gor kirb*.[86] However, at least two more translators of the *Karnamag* preferred to accept the appearance of the *xwarrah* of the Kayanids as an onager because that reading is actually possible.[87]

The wild ass (*Equus hemionus* or *Equus onager*) that still lives in protected Iranian and Central Asian national parks was considered ambivalent in ancient Persian traditions exactly like other equidae. According to Jewish, Christian, and Islamic legends, the Queen of Sheba had one or both legs of a donkey (or goose or goat) that she kept covered under her clothes. King Solomon was curious about this and used a trick to see her legs. It is unfortunately impossible to say if Zoroastrians too were aware of the donkey-legged woman story because it is not given to know when these legends started to circulate.[88]

The onager was a highly esteemed prey for royal hunters and Rustam too was a great onager-hunter. According to the *Bundahishn* [XXIV, 19-21], a giant three legged and horned ass called *xar i se pay* lived in the ocean and helped the god Tishtrya to transform water

85 Chunakova 1987, 78, 100.

86 Grenet 2003, 124.

87 Antia 1900: 28; Pagliaro 1927, 39. The Russian translation too has "the glory of the Kayanids that was far away" although it reports in a note the onager option: Chunakova 1987, 96.

88 Pennacchietti 2000, 226-236.

from the sea into rain. Its description and possible connection with the unicorn and the *ridya* of Talmudic tradition clearly points at a magic animal.[89] Some copper Arabo-Sasanian coins presented on the reverse the image of an equine that scholars preferred to identify with an onager. In fact, the horse was usually represented in a kind of heraldic position with one lifted front leg.[90] The *Shahnameh* reports also the episode of the demon Akvan who had the shape of an onager and killed the horses of Kay Khusraw. Only Rustam was able to defeat it with a trick.[91] Despite some ambivalence, the onager was an important animal that appeared in epic and religious Iranian traditions.

It should be assumed that, according to written sources, manifestations of *xwarrah* included a plethora of forms (fire, light, bird, dragon, onager)[92] while the *senmurv/simurgh* was exclusively a giant (and magical) bird. It should not be ruled out the possibility that also the ram was another manifestation of *xwarrah* although such an identification has not been proved and it is just based on one reading of the *Karnamag* that still presents several problems. The Avestan god of war and victory Verethraghna manifested himself to Zoroaster in different animal and human forms. Among the animal manifestations, the ram was the eighth form.[93] The ram was also one of most popular animals on seals of Zoroastrian priests (magi)[94] and occurred in Middle Persian literature such as in the story called *Draht i Asurig* or "Babylonian Tree".[95] This animal had very important symbolic meaning in early Omayyad Persia and, in fact, it continued to be represented on

89 Panaino 2001; Kiperwassert, Shapira 2008; Norozi 2017; Scarcia 2018, 66-67.

90 Gyselen 2000a, 64.

91 Christensen 1941, 62-63.

92 Touraj Daryaee proposed to add to this list also the bull with a human head usually called *gopatshah* that started to appear on Arabo-Sasanian coins mint in Persia in the Omayyad period: Daryaee 2015, 47.

93 Pirart 1999, 493-497.

94 Gyselen 1995.

95 Brunner 1980; Maciuszak 2006.

copper Arabo-Sasanian coins for a long time.[96] In at least three eighth century Sogdian paintings from Penjikent (Tajikistan), the ram is the symbolic animal of a local goddess who usually appears together with a god sitting on a camel.[97] Even more remarkably, a god sitting on a rug above two rams leaning back to back occur on some Sogdian ossuaries from Yumalaktepa, Shahrisabz (ca. seventh century) together with other possible psychopompic deities.[98] It should not be ruled out the possibility that the ram as a symbol of a Sogdian goddess was actually a goat. This animal was sometimes associated to Ishtar in the Near East and, in Anatolia, to another goddess: Shaushka. The two deities have been already superimposed in very ancient times.[99] However, superimpositions of Zoroastrian deities on Mesopotamian, Greek or Indian gods in Sasanian and Sogdian religious iconographical sphere are not that straightforward nor easily established. Such an occurrence associated with pre-Islamic Sogdian deities connected to the ram suggests a more cautious approach to the problem. It should

96 Gyselen 2000a, 65.

97 Shenkar 2014, 84, 138-139, figs. 128-130. According to F. Grenet (1993, 157-159), the goddess with rams could be Ashi. This same couple could be the one represented in some burnt wooden friezes from Kujruktube, Otrar Oasis (southern Kazakhstan), where Sogdian immigrants have lived at least until the second half of the ninth century: Bajpakov 1992, 41-42; Bajpakov 1998, 248-256. A goddess sitting on a ram occurs also on Sogdian terracotta statuettes from Afrasyab: Meshkeris 1989, fig. 163.1.

98 Berdimuradov, Bogomolov, Daeppen, Khushvatkov 2008. Psychopompic deities in Zoroastrian texts usually are Mithra, Rashnu and Sraosha. Rashnu could be easily identified on the Shahrisabz ossuaries in which the central god is weighing the soul of the dead on scales (*psychostasy*) while Mithra could be the one sitting above a harnessed riderless horse on the right. At this point, one could think at Sraosha for the god sitting above the rams on the left although such an identification (although not impossible) does not seem completely convincing. In fact, Zoroastrians possibly associated Sraosha to a rooster: Shenkar 2014, 145. Grenet identified the harnessed riderless horse above our presumed Mithra as a sacrificial animal that a priest wearing a Zoroastrian mask (*padam*) was going to kill in front of a square object: Grenet 1993a, 61-65.

99 Danmaville 1962.

not be excluded that more than one Zoroastrian (especially Sogdian) deity had the ram (or the goat) as his/her symbolic animal.

The so-called *senmurv* actually points to the representation of *xwarrah* in figurative arts as well. Its mistaken identification with the magical bird of Iranian mythology should be reconsidered. For this reason, the name "pseudo-*senmurv*" or "pseudo-*simurgh*" should be preferred for the composite creature of pre-Islamic arts while the real *senmurv*/*simurgh* has always been described and represented as a colossal bird. This is what one can possibly observe in eighth century Sogdian mural paintings from Penjikent and definitely in Islamic book illustrations that, in many cases, presented clear captions.

Several museums include in their collections art objects embellished with pseudo-*senmurvs* that have been uncritically attributed to Sasanian Persia in the past (especially textiles, silver vessels, and glass). None of these items comes from controlled excavations and it cannot be ruled out that they probably represent the result of post-Sasanian, Central Asian or Byzantine production.[100] A completely different typology of pseudo-*simurgh* can be observed on a silver gilt dish in the Ny Carlsberg Glyptotek in Copenhagen[101] and one of the silver vessels found in the Kuri Kale grotto in Iran.[102] Another similar dish is at present kept in the Reza Abbasi Museum in Tehran but it could be actually a modern forgery.[103] The fantastic winged creature

---

100 *Sasanian Silver* 1967, cat. 72, 75; Whitehouse 2005, cat. A.1, E.18; Harper 2006a; Marshak 2006a; Compareti 2009b; Aimone 2020, 178-233.

101 Poulsen 1960.

102 Rahimi 2004, fig. 1.1.

103 Another doubtful golden object in a private collection that was published in a Swiss catalogue several years ago, presents also a griffin-like creature with wings, paws, and a peacock tail resembling those of pseudo-*simurghs*: *Trésors de l'ancien Iran* 1966, cat. 720. A brass jug kept in the British Museum presents another variant of the pseudo-*simurgh* that, in this case, has two horns above its head. The scholar who published a catalogue of these objects considered it to be a genuine Islamic metalwork from ninth century Iran or Iraq: Ward 1993, fig. 26. Very similar horns appear on the head of another unexcavated early Islamic bronze statue allegedly

on these objects seems to be a parrot with lion's paws. Despite the fact that some of the silver vessels from the Kuri Kale present Middle Persian inscriptions, all these objects should be probably dated to the post-Sasanian period. Since the Ny Carlsberg Glyptotek silver dish does not come from controlled excavations neither, any chronological attribution would be highly hypothetical, the only possible parallel being offered by the post-Sasanian Kuri Kale silver vessels. Actually, very few pseudo-*senmurvs* can be considered authentically Sasanian. Examples of pseudo-*senmurvs* appear twice on textile decorations in the late Sasanian rock reliefs of the larger grotto at Taq-i Bustan that, however, represents the most controversial pre-Islamic Persian rock relief and will be discussed below.

Trever considered mainly the passage in Zoroastrian literature about the elements that compose the *Simurgh* as terrestrial (the dog and the rat) and aerial (the bird): these same elements could have been reflected in the parts of the animals composing the fantastic flying creature of her study. She added the aquatic element too because of the observation of Iranian (not necessarily Persian) silver vessels in the collection of the State Hermitage Museum. The dog (or bat or fox) part was considered to be the terrestrial element, the wings to be associated with air and the fishy tail to water. Such a division appears

said to come from the Helmand River region (Afghanistan) that, however, should be identified as a dragon (of Tish?): Harper 1978, fig. 35c. As Harper (2006a) and Marshak (2006a) had already observed some time ago, most of the silverware considered Sasanian should be critically approached and another chronology or even attribution proposed. This is particularly true for specimens of toreutics in the National Museum of Iran, Tehran (Godard 1962, pl. 121), the Römisch-Germanisches Zentralmuseum (Miks 2012) and private collections (*Sasanian Silver* 1967, cat. 37). One silver plate from the Idemitsu Art Gallery (Tokyo) presented for the first time in the well-known catalogue *Sasanian Silver* (1967, cat. 1) and embellished with a hunting king riding a harnessed horse has one isolated pseudo-*simurgh* on the saddle. According to Boris Marshak (who informed me in a private letter), this object is "a modern forgery". The same plate was published in a Japanese book on the Shoso-in storehouse of the Todai-ji Temple (Nara) where the hunting king was identified with Shapur II (309-379): Hayashi 1975, fig. 84.

immediately problematic since the fishy tail is absent while its shape calls to mind the one of a peacock or, in any case, feathers and not scales.[104] Parallels between the *senmurv* and the bat or the *Khurasan khurra* and a flying fox could actually point at the same thing. As Curatola and Cristoforetti suggested, the flying fox mentioned by Biruni could actually be a kind of large fruit-eating bat that lives in India and can be kept in captivity (*Pteropus vampyrus*, *Pteropus giganteus*, *Pteropus poliocephalus*, etc.).[105] It seems therefore that both *senmurv* and *Khurasan khurra* (that is *xwarrah*) could be assimilated to the bat. However, as it will be demonstrated in the next part of this study, when the *xwarrah* started to be represented in seventh century CE Hunno-Turkish and Sogdian coins (figs. 12-13), it was actually the composite creature that Trever identified as the *senmurv*. On the contrary, the latter was always represented as a bird in Islamic book illustrations (figs. 43-52) and, possibly, in eighth century Sogdian paintings (figs. 34, 104). There are no clear representations of the *senmurv* in pre-Islamic Persian art.

Trever's identification has been accepted among scholars for a very long period of time. Schmidt was the most active in considering the problem of the *simurgh* in visual arts and texts. Despite some problems that he detected in Trever's identification, Schmidt never openly opposed her original ideas and, for this reason, his studies cannot be considered accurate.[106] Different aspects of the same problem has been considered in 1978 on a special issue of an Italian journal called "Oriente Moderno". However, the authors of that issue did not opposed Trever's hypothesis: they enriched it with some visual and literary material rooted in the cultures of the Caucasian region and Islamic Persia. Giovanni Curatola was one of those authors who followed Trever and pointed at some association with the Armenian

104 Trever 1964, 163; Trever 2005, 170.

105 Curatola 1989, 34-35; Marshak 1998, 85; Compareti, Cristoforetti 2012, 247; Cristoforetti, Scarcia 2013, 341.

106 Schmidt 1980a; Schmidt 1980b; Schmidt 2002.

vishap and *arlez*. According to Curatola, the "dog-bird" prototype already discussed by Trever (that was, in any case, indebted to Hellenistic models and also inherited by Christian art) has been "abandoned" at a certain point in Persian book illustrations.[107] In that same issue of Oriente Moderno, Bausani observed that a creature described similarly to the hybrid under examination could be approached to an auspicious event associated to the Persian New Year celebration to be found in a very important written source: Biruni.[108]

Marshak knew about Bausani's observations and he added some more evidence rooted in pre-Islamic Iranian arts in order to propose a convincing identification. His conclusions completely disagreed with Trever because he proposed to identify the flying creature with a dog head with "the glory of the Kayanids" that is to say the Sasanians.[109] However, Marshak still considered the flying creature in front of Rustam in a famous eighth century Sogdian painting from Penjikent (the so-called "Blue Hall") as an evidence that Trever's theory could have been partially true for Central Asian arts (fig. 34). In fact, the flying creature in front of Rustam is not exactly the same like the Sasanian version of that fabulous monster on the garments of the king at Taq-i Bustan (figs. 10-11) nor in Afrasyab paintings (fig. 31).[110]

As it will be observed below, Marshak's interpretation is correct but it could be further enriched in the light of new archaeological discoveries and very interesting recent publications.

107 Curatola 1978.

108 Bausani 1978a.

109 Marshak 1998, 85; Marshak 2002a, 140-141.

110 Marshak 2002b, 37.

Chapter 2
Simurgh and pseudo-*simurgh* in visual arts

Kamila Trever identified several fantastic creatures that belonged to very different cultural milieu with the *senmurv*/*simurgh* of ancient Iranian mythology. In her opinion, those creatures could be traced back to the same prototype that was rooted in pre-Islamic Persian and, possibly, even in Scythian art. Recent studies, which include textual, numismatic, archaeological, and art historical investigations, helped to shed new light on the correct identification of composite creatures uncritically considered in the past to be purely pre-Islamic Persian (specifically Sasanian) creations.

Not only written sources but visual arts too point at the winged dog with a peacock tail as a symbolic representation of *farr* and not the *simurgh* of Iranian mythology. Moreover, a Central Asian and not Persian origin is highly probable for the composite creature, as some evidence to be produced below seems to suggest. Written sources and some ancient paintings from pre-Islamic Central Asia and Islamic Persia seem to confirm that all descriptions and representations of the *simurgh* point to a bird. There is not much evidence about the popularity of this bird in pre-Islamic Persian art while it is in book illustrations of the Ilkhanid period that it started to be represented more and more frequently.

In this section, I will try to trace the origin, diffusion, and fortune of the composite creature that for a long time has been confused with the representation of the real *simurgh* of Iranian mythology.

2.1 Classical composite creatures

It is highly probable that the iconography of the pseudo-*simurgh* derived from an elaboration of the Hellenistic *ketos* (plural *kete*) that was a dog-fish initially introduced in Central Asia (and possibly Persia and India as well) after the Greco-Macedonian invasion of the Achaemenid Empire.[111] This kind of creature was very popular in luxury arts of the northern Black Sea region and originally had very strong funerary connotations. In the decorative frieze on a wooden sarcophagus from the necropolis of Gorgippa, Russia (third century BCE) at present kept in the State Hermitage, some scholar identified Nereids carrying the weapons of Achilles. This seems to be very probable since Thetis, the mother of Achilles, was a Nereid usually depicted riding a sea monster (fig. 1).[112] The possibility that Scythians were responsible for the introduction of the *ketos* as far as Pazyryk in southern Siberia should not be ruled out.[113] Luxury arts could have been the main means of transmission of Greek art in Persia and Central Asia although coinage too should not be neglected. In fact, silver coins reproducing the head or entire body of *ketos* and other creatures

111 Ierusalimskaja 1995; Riccioni 2016.

112 Polidovich, Shamina 2018.

113 Boardman 1997, 735; Polos'mak 2015, figs. 20-23; Varenov, Cheremisin 2020. The iconography of the *ketos* was used by Scythian artists to represent generic, evil dragons such as in the scene represented in the comb from the Haimanova Tomb, Ukraine (fourth century BCE): Polidovich 2019. The northern shores of the Black Sea were also important for the interactions between local "Scythian" people, Greek settlers and the Achaemenid Empire: Treister 2017. According to some scholars, the griffin had a very similar history. From the Mesopotamian-Egyptian-Greek point of interaction, it entered China via Central Asian people such as the Scythians: Hayashi 2000; Zhang, Xu, Wu, Qiu 2013. Other animals had an even more complicated history. The dragons at Tillya Tepe (first century CE) included Chinese, Greek, Indian and, obviously, local elements: Boardman 2003. Some birds on trees woven on a silk textile from Pazyryk *kurgan* 5 (3rd century BCE) have been specifically identified as Chinese phoenixes (*fenghuang*): Schiltz 1994, 284-288.

on the obverse have been minted in ancient western Anatolia at least since the sixth century BCE (fig. 2).[114]

Despite some hypotheses that the *ketos* originated as a Greek creature,[115] Mesopotamian components should not be underestimated in general terms.[116] It is unclear when Mesopotamian zodiacal iconographies entered Greek culture[117] but they could already be found on seal-impressions in late Seleucid Uruk.[118] The capricorn sign was shaped on the goat-fish (*suhurmashu*) that accompanied the Babylonian and Assyrian (originally Sumerian) god Ea and had apotropaic functions.[119] The famous "Gemma Augustea" in the Kunsthistorisches Museum in Vienna and other first century BCE-first century CE Roman art objects and coins clearly reproduce a capricorn shaped as a Mesopotamian goat-fish (fig. 3).[120] Curiously enough, the capricorn in the Gemma Augustea seems to fly in the air in front of the Roman Emperor as it is doing in some much more ancient Old Babylonian seals in the British Museum and other collections (fig. 4).[121] In Greek art too, animals such as birds with a necklace in their beak sometimes fly in front of important people.[122] It does not seem that the capricorn-like animal ever appeared in that position on Greek vase paintings. That creature, positioned in front of an important person, seems to be a symbol to exalt or glorify him. Even though the decoration of the Gemma Augustea was not much represented in Greco-Roman art, it is interesting to observe that some "official western" example

114 Kagan, Kritt 1995.

115 Boardman 1987.

116 Shepard 1940, 4-9; Childs 2004.

117 Van der Waerden 1953.

118 Wallenfels 1993.

119 Bausani 1978b, 279-281; Ornan 2005a, 125-127.

120 Dwyer 1973. The goat-fish was a very popular subject on Roman magic seals that were supposed to keep away bad luck and demons: Vitellozzi 2010, 92.

121 Collon 2005, fig. 170.

122 Li forthcoming 2021.

existed. As it will be observed below, the Sogdians appreciated this ancient "formula" and reproduced it in medieval funerary monuments and mural paintings.

The *ketos* could be represented as the vehicle of nereids, maenads or other minor aquatic deities in Greco-Roman arts[123] (fig. 5) but it presented negative connotations since it was also the monster that had to devour Andromeda in the myth of Perseus (fig. 6) and, according to some traditions, even one of the creators of Medusa and her terrible sisters, the Gorgons (and Graeae).[124] It appeared also as a pure decorative motif although its connection with water (and despite its wings) was always clear. In the "Casa del Tramezzo di Legno" in Herculaneum, the main internal decoration was a frieze that included *kete* and dolphins (fig. 7).

Ketos-like monsters were considered to be *psychopompi*, namely creatures that accompanied the soul of the dead in the underworld according to Classical culture and art. Non-composite animals conceived as *psychopompi* by the Greco-Romans were horses (the main transportation of warriors) and dogs that were associated with the god of the underworld, Hades, and chthonic Hekate. This goddess was explicitly associated to dogs that could be perceived in ancient Greek religion as good or demonic creatures.[125] According to Classical authors, some rivers were flowing in the underworld and, for this reason, psychopompic animals such as horses (*hippocampus*) and dogs started to be represented with characteristics of fish or dolphins although they kept the wings that can be confused with fins.[126] They have been adopted to represent Christian scenes in a funerary context mainly on sarcophagi to represent the Biblical *leviathan* since

123 Barringer 1998, 111-120.

124 Angelini 2010.

125 Johnston 1990, 134-142.

126 Bausani 1978b, 277; Favaro 2008; Scarcia 2018, 29-51. Among the composite sea creatures in Latin literature there was also the *pistris* or *pistrix*: Angelini 2018, 119.

the third century CE. Later, they started to be accepted also beyond the borders of the Roman-Byzantine Empire such as in the Caucasus and possibly the Iranian world.[127] In a very rich study on sea creatures in Biblical and ancient Greek traditions, Anna Angelini pointed at a very interesting parallel between the *ketos* and the idea of the passage into the underworld. In fact, this creature should have been actually conceived as a tomb in ancient times because whoever entered his mouth and belly could not come back to life.[128]

Wings on aquatic creatures represent a very interesting topic for the study of fantastic and monstrous animals. They could be considered completely out of place although, as already observed above, the fins of fishes could be confused with wings. There is however another more convincing explanation that was discussed in a penetrating article by Alessandro Bausani.[129] He observed that some symbolic animals of the zodiac presented aquatic characteristics because when ancient Mesopotamian people first studied and iconographically defined the constellations in the third millennium BCE, they were ideally positioned in the winter part of the sky. This part was dedicated to Ea (Sumerian Enki) who was the main Mesopotamian water deity and, as already observed above, his symbolic animal has been the goat-fish at least since the Kassite period (sixteenth-twelfth centuries BCE). Later on, the positions of those constellations changed for an observer on Earth because of the phenomenon called precession of the equinoxes. The symbol of *Aries* had assumed aquatic elements in very ancient Mesopotamia but was later transformed into a "normal" ram when that constellation started to coincide with spring and not winter anymore. One could assume that something similar happened with animals that in origin did not have wings. Ancient artists who very often were also expert astrologers possibly decided for some changes that were later transferred to the Greeks and many others. Actually, this

127 Compareti, 2006; Compareti 2009-2010.

128 Angelini 2018, 143-144.

129 Bausani 1978b, 282.

is just a simplified version of an extremely complex and long process that definitely included Egyptian and other local components.[130]

This already complicated situation cannot be considered complete without some hints to the artistic production of the Indian Subcontinent. According to some scholars, the presence of composite animals in India were adopted from Achaemenid art,[131] while others have proposed Greek models.[132] Indian written sources such as the *Vishnudharmottara Purana* [III, 52] presented explicit associations between *ketos* and *makara* that is a kind of "Indian dragon" usually related to water.[133] Persian art in the Achaemenid period had very strong Assyrian components that can be detected especially in the representation of composite creatures on seals and seal-impressions.[134] Such Assyrian components could have reached India before the coming of the Greco-Macedonians. For example, the peacock, which was originally an Indian bird, must have been introduced to the Mesopotamian region in ancient times. On the other hand, Greek art and culture had a strong impact in Bactria and Gandhara. So-called Gandharan "toilet-trays" present very often Greek composite creatures like *kete* and even Greek mythological scenes or deities (fig. 8).[135] Recent studies on Parthian seal impressions from Nisa (Turkmenistan) revealed extremely popular subjects such as nereids, *kete*, tritons, and other typical Greek composite creatures that have

130 Van der Waerden 1953.

131 Guy 2007, 18.

132 Boardman 1983; Czuma 1986, 60-61.

133 Manassero 2014, 100.

134 Garrison 2013, 571-574.

135 Boardman 1983; Stančo 2012, 160-173. Winged sea monsters appear also in Gandharan seal impressions: Ur Rahman, Falk 2011, 151-152. Composite winged creatures resembling *kete* are represented in Mathura art of the Kushan period (first-second century): Czuma 1986, cat. 9; Trivedi 1998-99, figs. 90A-E. Fantastic creatures with the back part of their body represented as plants or vegetal elements in Indian art could be considered genuine Gupta (fourth-sixth century) creations: Bhattacharya 2010.

been rightly related to Bactrian and Gandharan specimens.[136] Typical Greco-Roman *kete* that included fish-bull, winged fish-ram, winged fish-lion and winged fish-horse as represented in arts or described, for example, by Pliny in his *Naturalis Historia* [IX, 7] and Aelian in his *De Natura Animalium* [16, 18] embellished also Sasanian seals.[137]

The case of the dog as a psychopompic animal presents some further problems. The dog is another of those animals that could be considered positive or negative. Superimpositions of very different animals are not rare in Classical arts as it can be found in a passage by Aeschylus where the eagle that was sent to torment Prometheus was also called the "dog of Zeus" [*Prometheus bound*, 1021-1022][138] while, in another passage, the watchdogs of Zeus were the griffins [*Prometheus bound*, 802-805].[139] The Greek poet Lykophron (fourth century BCE), called the sea monster that swallowed Heracles "dog of Triton" [*Alexandra*, 31-37] with a probable association with the *ketos*.[140] This could be considered a reflection of the "positive" or, better, faithful nature of the dog. In its negative acceptation, there could be some implication with the wolf that is a wild dog or Cerberus that is the monstrous dog of Hades.[141] Despite their totemic importance for some ancient peoples (such as the Latins), wolfs terrified men who attributed to them supernatural powers connected to the underworld, darkness, and lycanthropy. Infernal dogs appear sometimes in Etrus-

136 Manassero 2014.

137 Ritter 2010, pl. XIV; Gyselen 2016, 88. Two unexcavated pseudo-Sasanian silver plates in the National Museum of Iran and the Wyvern Collection present an aquatic scene with four *ketos*-like creatures in the central part: Aimone 2020, 202-203. In a personal communication, Boris Marshak argued that the plate in the Tehran museum was not Sasanian.

138 Ajello 1978, 311-312; Compareti, Scarcia 2012, 240.

139 Angelini 2020.

140 In her study on sea creatures in Greek and Biblical traditions, Anna Angelini identified the head of the *ketos* with a wild boar despite this interesting passage of Lykophron that she knew well: Angelini 2018, 135, 139, 153, 155.

141 Woodford, Spier, 1992.

can vase paintings in the act of invading the world of living through passages in the shape of cylindrical wells from where warriors try to expel them back.[142]

It is not by chance that the *ketos* and our pseudo-*simurgh* present strong canine features. These expressed pretty well their ambivalence from an iconographical point of view as well. In addition, according to Zoroastrian precepts, the dog was a positive animal and had very clear funerary functions.[143] Its barking was considered a powerful repellent against demons like a crowing cock. The *Bundahishn* [XXIV, 48-49] expressely associated the dog and the rooster to the psychopompic god Sraosha.[144]

After becoming extremely popular in the new "Asian milieu," the *ketos* and other psychopompic creatures probably started to be re-elaborated in Bactria or Sogdiana by local artists who maintained in a first instance its funerary (and, possibly, canine) touch. Images of this re-elaborated *ketos* are archaeologically attested in Chorasmia, a Central Asian region that was never invaded by Alexander the Great.[145] Sixth-seventh century tombs that belonged to powerful Sogdian immigrants in China (the so-called "Sino-Sogdian" funerary monuments) present sometimes winged horses with a fish tail among their decorations. Creatures like this embellished at least one seventh century terracotta ossuary found at Ulkantoytepa, in the region of Tashkent.[146] It could be imagined that in Sogdiana, probably starting from the late seventh-early eighth century, these fantastic creatures were not anymore limited just to the funerary sphere but were adapted to represent typical Iranian concepts such as the charisma

142 Elliot 1995.

143 Andrés-Toledo 2013.

144 Subtelny 2011, 203. The rooster had apotropaic functions in Roman art and it was sometimes combined with a triton-like creature as a symbol of the Biblical God in special magic "gnostic seals": Vitellozzi 2010, 52-57; Cosentino 2013.

145 Minardi 2016.

146 Compareti 2019a, 78 n. 15.

and divine protection. They can be seen very often in front of deities, heroes and rich merchants in many paintings at the site of Penjikent (fig. 78).[147] This mechanism is still quite obscure and, in fact, it is not clear why the Sogdians adopted Hellenistic elements (possibly rooted in more ancient Mesopotamian traditions) and did not appropriate, for example, Central Asian models such as the personification of *farr* (Pharro/Pharo in Bactrian) that has been well-known in Kushan art since the second century CE and presented very strong Greek traits as well.[148] In the post-Kushan period, composite creatures do appear in Bactrian art such as, for example, on some inscribed seal-impressions that are part of a private collection.[149]

This slightly modified "Iranian" *ketos* (our pseudo-*simurgh*) was probably re-imported some centuries later into the "West", that is to say Persia, the Caucasian region, the Byzantine Empire, and, finally, the Omayyad Caliphate from Central Asia. Persian Zoroastrians possibly maintained its original symbolic value but it is not completely clear if Christians and Muslims did the same. It is most likely slightly before this stage of the process that the *ketos* underwent further transformations that rendered it more similar to the pseudo-*simurgh*. No Central Asian examples of the modified *ketos* observed above present a typical peacock tail, curly wings or other details that were going to be observed some time later in Sogdian art at Afrasyab (ca. 660) and Taq-i Bustan rock reliefs (ca. 600).[150] For this reason, one further

147 Azarpay 1975; Shenkar 2014, 139. Flying creatures exalting the most important person of the scene in Sogdian paintings never appeared in representations of fables usually positioned at the lower register of private houses in Penjikent.

148 Shenkar 2014, 135-137. A Sogdian Manichaen fragmentary text points at *farn* in human shape as well: Shenkar 2014, 39, 140. For a possible representation of a pre-Kushan Chorasmian deity who could be associated to the local personification of the glory (Chorasmian *farn*), see: Shenkar 2019, 13-14. The walled crown as an attribute of a Tyche-like deity seems more convincing than the identification of that same god with Sraosha: Grenet 2018, 73; Minardi 2018, 101-102.

149 Lerner, Sims-Williams 2011, 169.

150 Stuart Piggott proposed to reconstruct the decoration of one unexcavated

stage in the development of the composite creature under examination here could have taken place somewhere between Central Asia and Persia. One could actually think at Khorasan or Sistan that are still less investigated than other Iranian regions.

fragmentary painted pottery from Quetta region (Pakistan) as a pseudo-*simurgh* within a pearl roundel frame: Piggott 1949, fig. 1. However, that scholar considered it to be dated to the Kushano-Sasanian period (third-fourth century). Just because of the presence of such a decorative element, this fragmentary pottery (and other unexcavated pottery shards from central Afghanistan-northern Pakistan embellished with many other motifs) could be actually considered to be early or proto-Islamic: Compareti 2020a, 25-26.

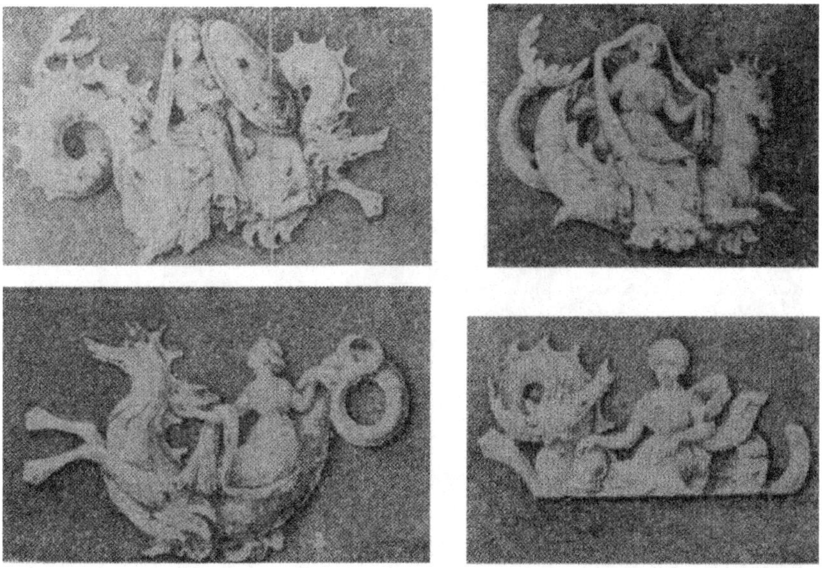

Figure 1a-d. Nereids carrying the weapons of Achilles. Part of the decorative frieze on a wooden sarcophagus from the necropolis of Gorgippa, Russia (third century BCE). The State Hermitage. After: Vaulina, M., Wąsowicz, A. (1974). *Bois grecs et romains de l'Ermitage.* Wrocław-Warszawa-Kraków-Gdańs, fig. 36-37.

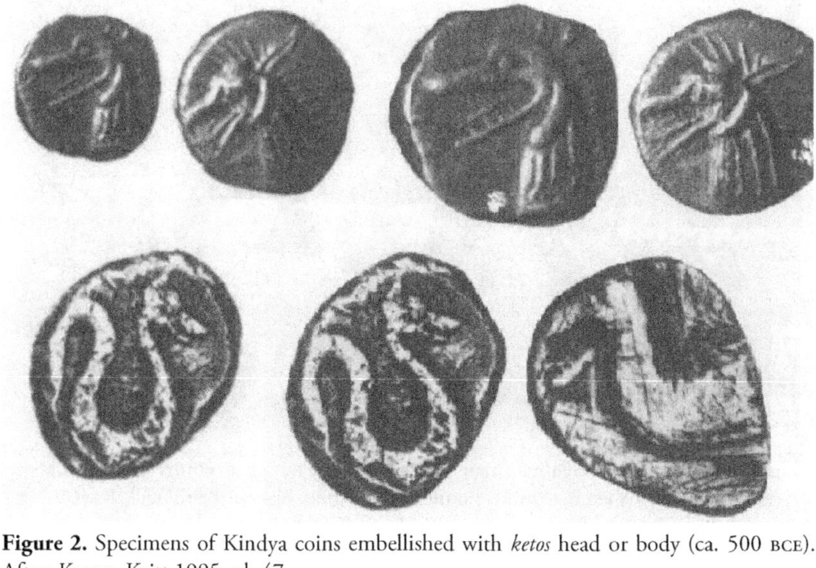

Figure 2. Specimens of Kindya coins embellished with *ketos* head or body (ca. 500 BCE). After: Kagan, Kritt 1995, pl. 47.

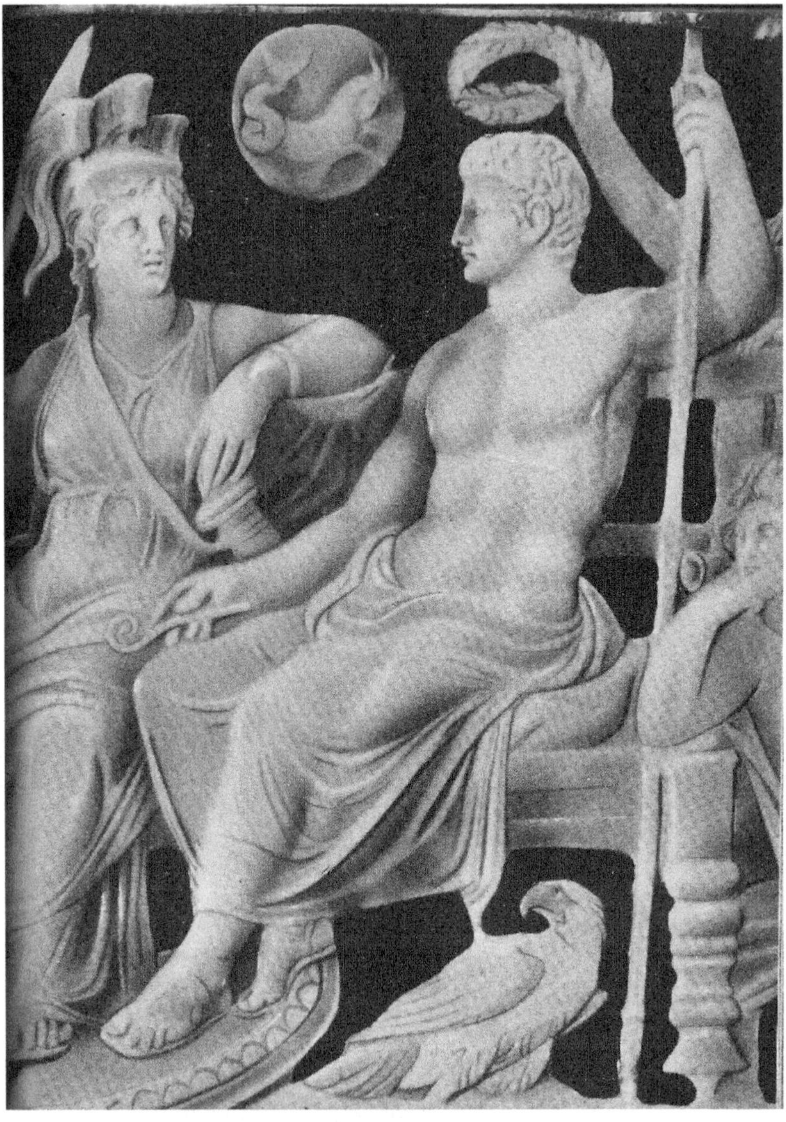

Figure 3. Detail of the Gemma Augustea (first century BCE-first century CE). Kunsthistorisches Museum Vienna, Antikensammlungen. After: Bianchi Bandinelli, R. (1969). *Roma. L'arte romana nel centro del potere*. Milano, fig. 196.

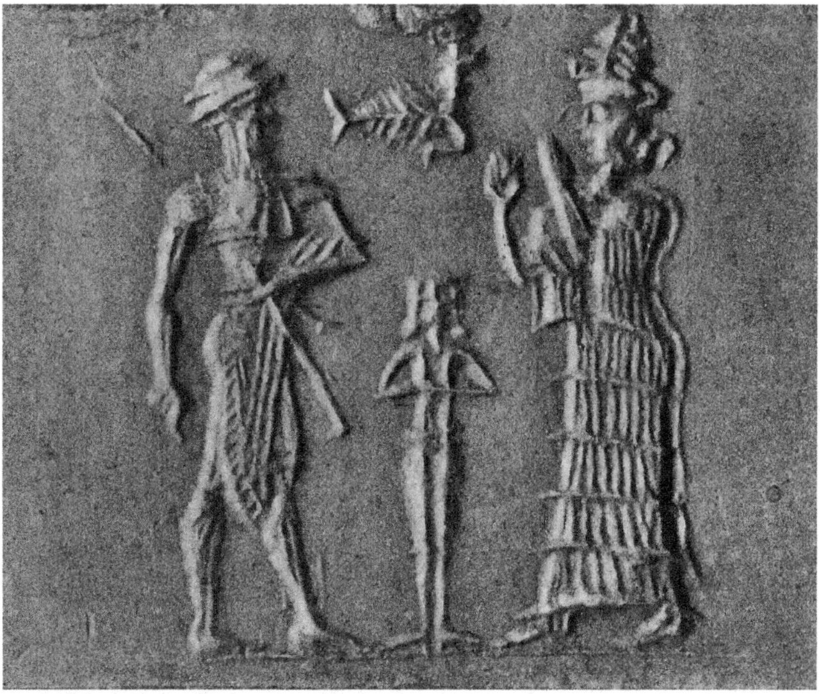

Figure 4. Old Babylonian seal. London, British Museum 102530. After: Wiseman, D.J. (n.d.). *Cylinder Seals of Western Asia*. London, 45.

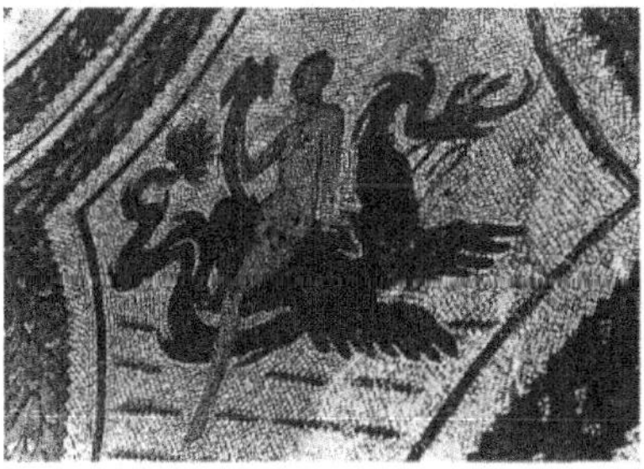

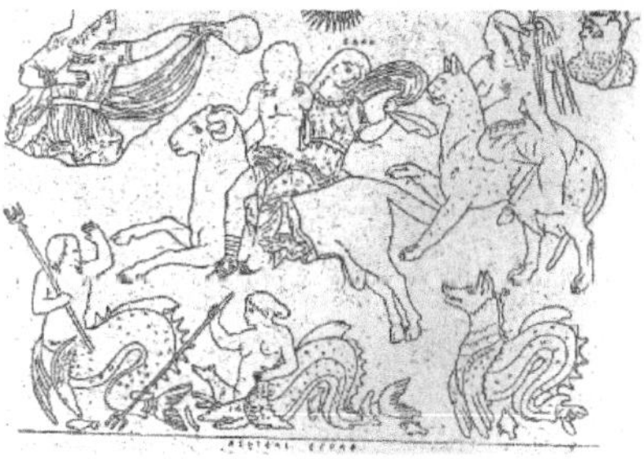

Figure 5a-b. Aquatic creatures in Greco-Roman mosaic from the House of Sorothus, Sousse, Bardo Museum, Tunis (left) and in a Greek painted vase from Santa Maria Capua Vetere (right). After: Boardman 1997, fig. 34; Favaro 2008, fig. 3.

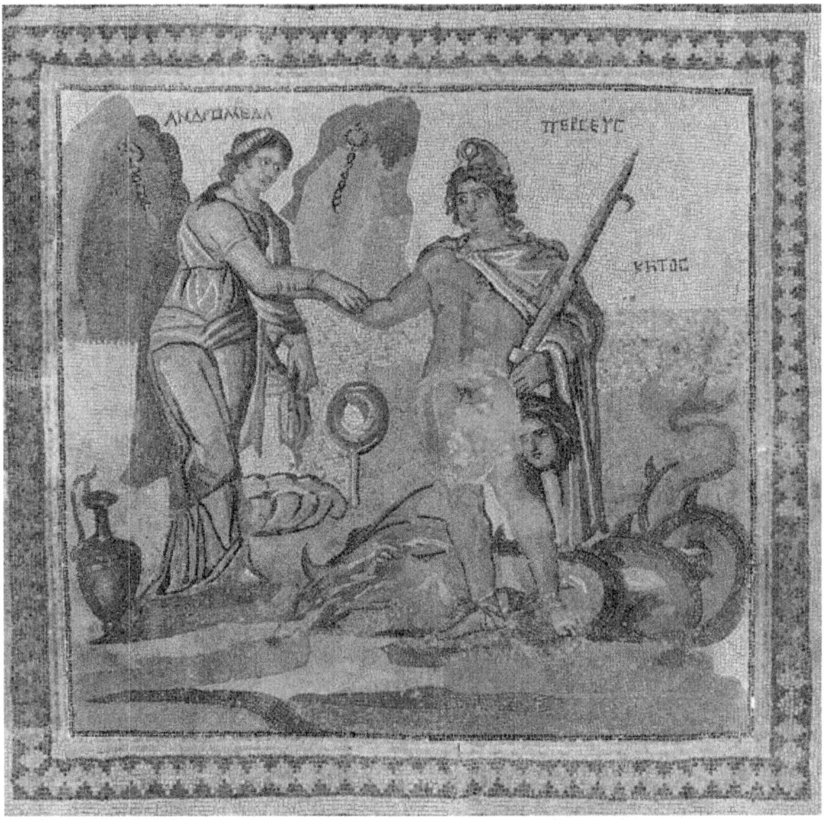

Figure 6. Roman mosaic with representation of Perseus, Andromeda and *ketos*, House of Poseidon, Zeugma (second-third century). Gaziantep Museum, Turkey. After: Görkay, K. (2017). Mosaic Programmes in Domestic Contexts at Zeugma. *Journal of Mosaic Research* 10, fig. 3.

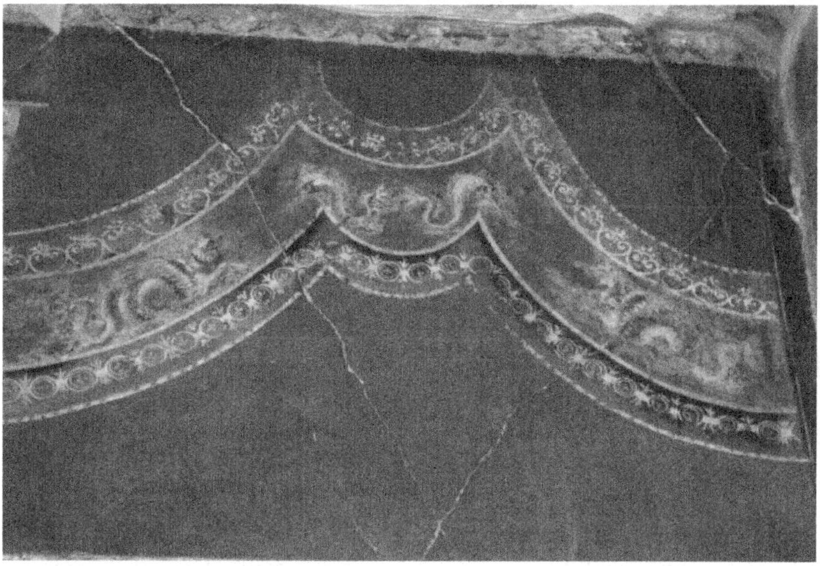

Figure 7. Roman decorative frieze from the "Casa del Tramezzo di Legno", Herculaneum (in situ, first century CE). Photo: author.

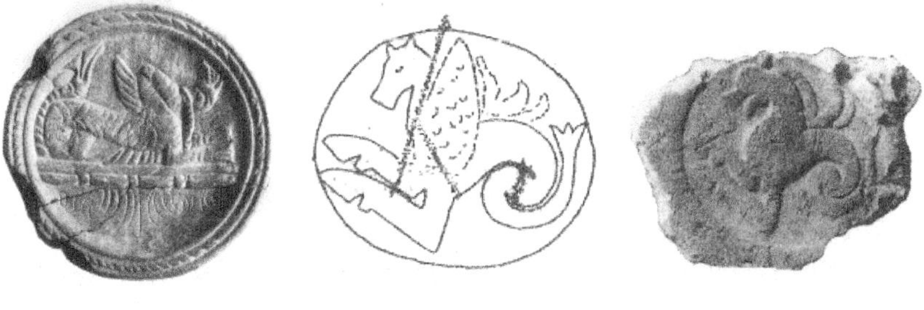

Figure 8a-c. *Ketos* on a Gandharan toilet tray from Sirkap, Pakistan (left) and *ketos/hippocampus* on Bactrian potteries from Kampyr Tepe, Termez (center and right). After: Francfort, H.P. (1979). *Les palettes du Gandhāra*. Paris, pl. XXIII, 45; Huff, D. (2002). A Hippokamp from Kampirtepe. *The History and Material Culture of Uzbekistan* 33: fig. 2; Dvurechenskaja, N.D. (2016). *Terrakotovaja plastika drevnejshih gosudarstv Srednej Azii IV v. do n. e.-IV v. n. e. (arheologicheskij aspect)*. Sankt-Peterburg, fig. 241.3.

2.2 Taq-i Bustan rock reliefs

Taq-i Bustan is probably the controversial monument par excellence of Sasanian art. First of all, its location is very unusual since it is among the very few Sasanian rock reliefs not concentrated in the region of Fars.[151] One rock relief in the open and two rock reliefs inside a larger and a smaller grotto compose the site. The most enigmatic part of Taq-i Bustan can be found inside the bigger grotto that presents two low relief lateral panels and one scene carved almost in the round in the back of the grotto (fig. 9). As already noted by Pierfrancesco Callieri,[152] the lateral panels were probably executed by the same artist while the reliefs in the back of the grotto are not only unusual but stylistically very different. According to some scholars, the scene in the upper part of the back of the larger grotto reproducing a Sasanian king between a god on the right and a goddess on the left would represent a direct borrowing from Byzantine art. In fact, that triad could call to mind similar representations in the apse of a Christian church where Jesus appears sometimes between the Virgin Mary and a saint, usually Saint John, not to mention the clear association with triumphal arches in Roman art with similar winged Victories carrying a garland or a laurel crown.[153]

The rock reliefs at Taq-i Bustan were studied in detail by Japanese teams during the 1960s and 1970s. However, no real archaeological excavations have ever been carried out.[154] Unfortunately, recent restorations have completely changed the aspect of Taq-i Bustan as it appeared until just a few years ago: not only were a pool and a canal created directly in front of the site but also all the figurative column capitals and sculptures that had been collected there were moved to

151 Harper 1999.

152 Callieri 2014, 156-157.

153 Mackintosh 1978; Musche 1994.

154 Fukai, Horiuchi, Tanabe, Domyo 1984.

some office in Kermanshah.[155] The dramatic decision seems to be justified by the new director of the site in order to safeguard the integrity of the reliefs, especially the larger grotto.

The main obstacle in proposing any reliable chronology for Taq-i Bustan is presented by the identification of the king who is depicted in the innermost part of the larger grotto wearing a crown that has no clear parallel in Sasanian numismatics. Attempting to identify that crown has kept scholars of Iranian studies very busy since the beginning of the last century. Despite the absence of a crown on the head of the main person in the hunting panels, all the reliefs of the bigger grotto have been usually attributed to one Sasanian sovereign.[156] This idea is very problematic because, as noticed by Callieri, the hunting panels on the sides are stylistically very different than the reliefs on the back of the grotto.

Some of the most recent studies on Taq-i Bustan point to a later chronology for this site. Markus Mode had proposed that the larger grotto at Taq-i Bustan cannot be earlier than the mid-sixth century because of the shape of the quiver that is hanging on one side of the warrior king's statue. This is not the only idea that Mode has recently expressed regarding Taq-i Bustan. In fact, some other observations inevitably point to a later chronology for this site especially because of the weapons and garments reproduced there. The same scholar also expressed an interesting identification for the equestrian statue that, in his opinion, can only be a king and not a divinity: it would have been extremely inopportune to have a deity under the feet of the statues in high relief in the upper level of that same part of the grotto.[157] Mode also accepted another hypothesis by Heinz Luschey who noticed different stages in the preparation of the innermost reliefs of the larger grotto. In fact, the two hunting panels are carved at a level that is not the same as the equestrian statue. This is carved

155 Compareti 2016a.

156 Movassat 2005.

157 Mode 2006.

much more deeply into the rock although the square frame around the scene remained at the same level of the lateral hunting panels.[158] Therefore, it could be proposed that at least two construction phases can be traced at Taq-i Bustan. Initially the hunting panels were carved. It is possible that three of them were prepared: a boar hunt panel on the left, a deer hunt on the right, and – once again, according to Mode – another hunting panel in the center, possibly a lion hunt. Actually, the presence of the lion hunt panel at Taq-i Bustan will never be confirmed although some similarities with Neo-Assyrian hunt reliefs constitute a very interesting parallel.[159] Boars, deer, and lions are the most common animals on presumed Sasanian gilt-silver dishes embellished with hunting scenes. Later, in a following phase, the central panel at Taq-i Bustan was destroyed and substituted with the equestrian statue that could only be executed much deeper into the innermost wall.

The equestrian and armored warrior should be identified as a king who is the same represented above at the upper level between two deities in the act of giving him beribboned rings. These two deities have been identified as Ahura Mazda on the right and Anahita on the left. They are presenting important symbols to the king in order to legitimize him as a representative of the Sasanian royal house. It is worth observing once more a substantial difference from early Sasanian rock reliefs that presented only Ahura Mazda together with the king. Not only in the back of the bigger grotto there are two deities but in the external rock relief (to be possibly attributed to Shapur II defeating the Roman emperor Julian) Mithra with a rayed nimbus could be identified on the left and Ahura Mazda on the right of the triumphant king.[160]

More evidence in support of the arguments for a later chronology of the bigger grotto reliefs has recently been presented by Gianroberto

158 Luschey 1996, 122-123.

159 Compareti 2019b, 27.

160 Wood 2017, 85-88.

Scarcia. According to written sources and local legends studied by Scarcia, the site could be attributed to Bastam (called also Bistam, Bishtam or Vishtam, etc.), a maternal uncle of Khusraw II Parwiz (590-628) who had Parthian origins and rebelled against the Sasanians.[161] He was able to control a vast territory in western Iran and even mint coins in his name until his final defeat and death around 600 CE most likely in a place not too far from Taq-i Bustan, around Hamadan according to Dinawari (ninth century).[162] Local people such as Kurds, Azeri and Armenians (with all their linguistic variations) and ancient authors (mainly Arab and Persian ones) call that site Taq-i Bastam, "the Arch of Bastam", or simply Bastam and not Taq-i Bustan, "the Arch of the Garden". In his book *Mukhtasar Kitab al-buldan*, al-Faqih al-Hamadani (ninth-tenth century) called Taq-i Bustan simply *Wastan* which is another form for Bastam.[163] In the twelfth century Persian text *Mojmal al-Tawarikh*, the anonymous translator from the original Arabic reported something really interesting about one image of Shabdiz, Khusraw Parwiz favourite horse. It is said that Shabdiz image appeared in "Kermanshahan at the village called Bishtam that is also a name of Kustehan [Bastam], the uncle of Parwiz".[164] In a recent study dedicated to the builder of Taq-i Bustan according to Persian texts, Paola Orsatti considered suspect such an attribution to Bastam. That scholar preferred to identify the "general" of Khusraw responsible for the construction of the site with historical Shahbaraz.[165] As a suitor, this mysterious general was also a rival of Khusraw II's and was confused with Farhad of the story *Khusro and Shirin* by Nizami (twelfth century). In any case, it is worth observing that according to written sources of the Islamic period some

161 Cristoforetti, Scarcia 2013; Scarcia 2017.

162 Scarcia 1980, 100.

163 Massé 1973, 261.

164 Mohl 1842, 126. See appendix 2 of this study for a translation of the passage in French.

165 Orsatti 2019, 30.

other person and not the Sasanian sovereign was considered to be in charge of the construction of (parts of) Taq-i Bustan. Moreover, its late chronology seems to be confirmed.

All these arguments proposed by Mode, Scarcia and Callieri could suggest a different scenario for the construction of Taq-i Bustan. The monument could have been started by Bastam who was inspired by "western" elements or simply wanted to present himself as the continuator of traditions possibly even rooted in ancient Mesopotamian civilization.[166] He promoted the representation of hunting scenes including his own portrait as a sovereign wearing garments embellished with specific symbols and without a typical Sasanian crown. Some parallels between the hunting panels at Taq-i Bustan and the almost contemporary seventh century Sogdian paintings from Afrasyab (pre-Islamic Samarkand) would point to a very similar source that should be searched for in Central Asia. Non-religious Sogdian paintings such as those at Afrasyab present a realistic touch that is completely unknown in Sasanian art whose aim (in the few specimens that we know) was just the exaltation of the king.[167]

As already mentioned above, Bastam had Parthian origins and he maintained very close relations with eastern Iran. According to Antonio Panaino, the Arsacid Parthians wanted to be represented as archers on their coins and art in an attempt to be associated to the mythical Aresh whose name could have been perceived as a popular

166 Compareti 2019b, 25-33.

167 Compareti 2016a, 76; Compareti 2019b, 20. The great scholar of Iranian studies Ernst Herzfeld had already proposed to associate the hunting panels at Taq-i Bustan to painters and not sculptors because of their dynamic and realistic touch that was completely unknown in typical Sasanian rock reliefs mainly concentrated in Fars region: Herzfeld 1928, 139. As a matter of fact, Herzfeld did not know Afrsyab paintings that were going to be discovered only in 1965 nor many other Central Asian specimens from historical Sogdiana and Bactria. In any case, his intuition suggests his deep knowledge of Sasanian rock reliefs and his activity as an attentive observer.

etymology for Arshak/Arsaces.[168] As an anti-Parthian counter-action, the Sasanian kings possibly did not reproduce images of archers on their coins. Silver vessels attributed to Sasanian Persia present in several cases the king hunting animals with his bow but this kind of scenes is completely absent in rock reliefs with the only exclusion of Taq-i Bustan, Rag-i Bibi[169] (that, in any case, is an eastern Sasanian monument) and, possibly, Bishapur IV.[170] Such observations by Panaino could further suggest Parthian elements in the hunting panels at Taq-i Bustan that point at an initial non-Sasanian sponsor.

Bastam was also appointed governor of Khorasan (and, in another moment, Armenia or Azerbaijan) by Khusraw II Parwiz when he was still on good terms with the Sasanians.[171] Details of his garments at Taq-i Bustan, such as the belt with hanging straps, and some of his weapons (such as the quiver or the bow-case that, to be precise can be better observed in the equestrian statue) were definitely adopted from the steppes, most likely after the second half of the sixth century.[172] It should not be ruled out that textile decorative elements observed at Taq-i Bustan do not represent examples of Sasanian fashion but rather Central Asian importations as well. Prudence Harper was inclined to think in these terms although she did not mention from where "the introduction of a new monstrous image in the late Sasanian period" arrived.[173] Harper's "monstrous image" is our pseudo-*simurgh*. In a personal communication, Nikolaus Schindel rightly observed that the coinage of Bastam restricts his actions to the area of Rayy, in central Iran, where he minted his coins.[174] This is definitely correct but it

168 Panaino 2019.

169 Grenet, Lee, Martinez, Ory 2007.

170 Overlaet 2009.

171 Shahbazi 1989.

172 Mode 2006.

173 Harper 2006b, 22.

174 Göbl 1990, 53. There was another Sasanian rock relief in Rayy that Qajars destroyed in the nineteenth centrury. This is very unusual because, apart from Taq-i

does not rule out another scenario. In fact, Bastam could have started the construction of Taq-i Bustan when he was still on good relations with Khusraw II and did not yet mint any coinage in his own name. According to the *Mojmal al-Tawarikh*, Farhad (who we should identify with Bastam) directed the works at Taq-i Bustan according to the orders of Khusraw II Parwiz. At the end of the construction phase, Khusraw had a great party at the site and donated the entire monumental area to Farhad/Bastam (see appendix 2 of this study).

Some more arguments in support of a late chronology of the larger grotto at Taq-i Bustan could be found just among the textile motifs represented on those rock reliefs. On the garments of the colossal archer reproduced twice in the wild boar hunting scene (fig. 10) and on the fabric that covers the legs of the horse rider at the rear of the grotto itself (fig. 11), a composite creature that has always represented a big problem for scholars appears for the first time in Sasanian art. According to an old theory by K. Trever reported in the previous chapter of this study, that creature with a dog's face, wings and a peacock tail should be identified with the *senmurv/simurgh* of Iranian mythology. This idea has been proved to be problematic since the real *simurgh* has always been described and represented as a colossal bird, especially in Islamic book illustrations since the Mongol period. Parallels offered by Persian Islamic book illustrations constitute an important term of comparison with eighth century Sogdian mural paintings. It seems very probable that a small group of Ilkhanid and Inju'id *simurgh*s could be the last representatives of more ancient local artistic traditions whose only pre-Islamic specimens survived just in Sogdian paintings at Penjikent in the painted program of the so-called Blue Hall (room 41, sector VI) depicting the trials of the great hero Rustam.

Bustan, most of Sasanian rock reliefs were carved in Fars region. According to one scholar, the destroyed relief in Rayy could be attributed to Bahram VI Chubin or even Bastam: Dorudiyan 2016, 60.

Representations of a winged creature with a dog's face and peacock's tail started to appear as countermarks together with the Middle Persian inscription GDE/GDH (*gad*, the arameogram for *xwarrah*) *'pzwt* (*abzud*, increased) "the glory increased" on seventh-century Hunnish coins from Zabulistan and Arachosia, in south-eastern Afghanistan (fig. 12).[175] Slightly later, those same epigraphic countermarks could also be found on some Sogdian coins.[176] In this case, the inscription should be read as *farn* which is *xwarrah/farr* in the Sogdian language (fig. 13).[177] A very clear parallel could be traced between the creatures in Sogdian paintings and those in Sogdian epigraphic countermarks in order to establish their identification exclusively with *farn* and nothing else. The problem is unfortunately much more complicated since, as it will be observed below (see figs. 32-33), the inscription *farn* appeared together with other animals and, in at least one case, a person (probably a deity) on Sogdian coins, seals, and seal impressions. In any case, its presence on Hunnish and Sogdian coins strongly suggests some connection between that composite creature and the concept of *xwarrah/farn/farr*.

At this point, one could wonder if the composite creature symbolizing *xwarrah* itself is really a Sasanian creation and not another importation from Central Asia. As already observed above, the first

---

175 The famous numismatic Robert Göbl (1967, 156-157) was the first to suggest that the winged composite creature with the rear part of a dog could be actually a symbol of *xwarrah/farr* along with the bird or the bird carrying a necklace on Hunnish coins. See also: Nikitin 1984, 234; Gyselen 2009, 154-156; Vondrovec 2014, 642, 894.

176 Nikitin, Roth 1995. Some seventh-eighth century Sogdian bronze coins present the inscription *prn* (glory) next to the royal bust or together with other inscriptions on the reverse: Smirnova 1981, nos. 1356, 1359, 1472. The winged dog with a peacock tail countermark without inscriptions started to appear on Arabo-Sasanian silver coins mint in Persia during the early Omayyad period. Touraj Daryaee thinks that, in this case, the image should be a substitute for the Middle Persian legend *xwarrah* that occurred exactly in that point on some specimens: Daryaee 2015, 46; Daryaee 2016, 78.

177 Provasi 2003.

construction phase at Taq-i Bustan should be attributed to Bastam who had strong connections with Central Asia. It should not be ruled out that he also imported some symbols to be used on his garment in the panel of the wild boar hunt to accentuate his importance. According to the *Mojmal al-Tawarikh*, Khusraw was initially in good terms with Bastam and even donated to his general and uncle the entire site of Taq-i Bustan. Later the situation changed and Bastam openly rebelled to Khusraw. Having eliminated Bastam, Khusraw II could have appropriated his enemy's monument and also that composite creature as a symbol of glory to be shown on his own garments as a trophy. This reconstruction does not rule out the hypothesis that the pseudo-*simurgh* had apotropaic properties that Khusraw wanted to have actually reproduced on his royal garments. Prudence Harper traced a very interesting parallel between the pseudo-*simurgh* and the cross among Christians that had the power to repel demons and curses.[178]

As can be observed on seventh-century Hunnish and Sogdian coins, the composite winged creature with a dog's head was quite explicitly associated with the Iranian concept of glory that began to be imported from Central Asia into Persia at the end of the Sasanian period. Slightly later, that creature started to be represented also in Byzantine and Islamic art and soon spread to the Near East, the Caucasus, western and eastern Europe at least until the beginning of the thirteenth century. There is now some archaeological evidence in support of the popularity of this composite creature even among early Tibetans. Its exact meaning among Muslims and Christians is still a matter of debate, although it was definitely considered a very appropriate decoration for religious and secular purposes.

One of Bastam's attendants in the boar hunting panel is wearing a garment embellished with several birds with ears and long tails standing on a pedestal decorated with successive circles. Despite the description given by Mihoko Domyo, the birds do not look like cocks

178 Harper 2006b, 22-23.

nor peacocks (the latters actually appear on the garments of some other servant).[179] The textile decoration of another attendant of Khusraw in the same scene has been carefully re-designed. That garment was actually embellished with quatrefoil-frames containing one eared bird spreading its wings (fig. 14).[180] The elements on the head of the bird on the pearl pedestal are quite precisely depicted. They look like ears of a mammal and not horns nor feathers. Birds like this can be observed in the eastern Iranian (probably Bactrian) Cherdyne plate (fig. 73) and, some centuries later, in Islamic arts (fig. 70). Also on the clothes of one attendant riding an elephant there are birds with ears or feathers above their head.[181] Every hint seems to point at an identification of this strange bird at Taq-i Bustan with a typology of phoenix/*simurgh* that was introduced into late Sasanian Persia from Central Asia via precious textiles trade routes. It is worth observing that, in his *Mukhtasar Kitab al-buldan*, al-Faqih al-Hamadani mentioned the *'anqa* among the birds represented at Taq-i Bustan, a place that, as already observed above, he called Wastan.[182]

Before concluding this part on Taq-i Bustan and pre-Islamic Persian art, it would be interesting to say something about the representation of magic birds and composite creatures in pre-Sasanian times. As already mentioned above, Achaemenid artists accepted and adapted many Mesopotamian decorative elements. Images of a human bearded bust holding a round object in one hand coming out from a winged ring can be observed very often in Achaemenid art. That motif appears in the Bisutun reliefs, at Persepolis, the royal

179 Domyo 1984, 104, fig. 60.56, table 1; Domyo 1997, 21; Otavsky 1998a, 135-137.

180 Domyo 1984, fig. 46a, 60.61; Otavsky 1998a, 138-139. The second attendant is wearing a garment embellished also with winged rams in the lower part. It is not easy to identify every creature on Taq-i Bustan textiles nor proposing a precise correspondence with pre-Islamic Persian deities. The presence of the wings seems to be an allusion to a supernatural fantastic animal: Compareti 2014a, 155.

181 Herzfeld 1920, pl. LXIII.

182 Massé 1973, 261.

tombs at Naqsh-i Rustam and a large number of Achaemenid seals and seal-impressions. Scholars proposed different names for this motif such as "winged disk" "winged genius", etc.[183] Unfortunately, many specimens of un-epigraphic Achaemenid seals and seal-impressions do not represent scientifically attested discoveries being very often part of private collections donated to museums or acquisitions from the antiquarian market.[184]

The "original" winged disk is probably an Egyptian creation that was later adopted and transformed through the Hittites, Urarteans and many other Near Eastern peoples who maintained in many cases (but not exclusively) some associations with solar deities.[185] Despite many points not completely understood, it seems that the motif of the winged disk was very popular in all these regions and could have been adapted extremely easily in different cultural spheres from Egypt to Anatolia, from Syro-Palestinian coast to Mesopotamia. It should not be ruled out that it also pointed to the divine presence and protection in more general terms.[186] Some scholars have associated this motif in Achaemenid art to the representation of the idea of *xwarrah*/*farr* that occurred in Old Persian inscriptions as *farnah* mainly in theophoric names.[187] According to Dietrich Huff, the wings of the symbol under discussion should be considered as an allusion to *farnah* while the human bust depicts Ahura Mazda.[188] The typical Iranian concept of *farnah* was definitely well known by the Achaemenids but it is only in a precise moment of the Sasanian period (in the fifth century) that the idea of "glory" (specifically the "glory of the Kayanids") became the main argument of legitimization of Persian propaganda.[189] The

183 Shenkar 2014: 47-51.

184 Garrison 2017.

185 Cornelius 2014, 155.

186 Ornan 2005b.

187 Shahbazi 1980.

188 Huff 2008: 39.

189 Gnoli 1999.

concept of *xwarrah* started to become an important component of Sasanian ideology only after the reign of Narseh (293-302) as his inscription at Paikuli confirmed.[190] Not only the term *xwarrah* started to appear quite regularly on Sasanian coins in the fifth century but others such as *kay* for "Kayanid".[191] It is worth observing that this term occurred some time earlier on Kushano-Sasanian coins that were mint in eastern Iran.[192] For this reason, the identification of the human bust above the winged ring as the manifestation of glory in Achaemenid arts does not seem to be completely convincing. It seems more reasonable to identify it as a symbolic representation of Ahura Mazda based on Assyrian and Urartean prototypes.[193]

Despite the great number of birds in ancient Persian sfragistics, no clear representations of colossal nor magic birds that could be identified with the *simurgh* appear in Achaemenid art. One scholar realized that the lost standard of Darius III in the famous "Alexander Mosaic" from the so-called "Casa del Fauno" in Pompei (National Archaeological Museum, Naples) was actually decorated with the image of a yellow bird. In that scholar's opinion, such a detail could be considered the reproduction of a real Achaemenid standard and not a Greek invention (fig. 15).[194] Several Classical authors insisted on the "golden eagle" as a special symbol of Achaemenid kingship that embellished clothes and standards of the royal house.[195] Xenophon reported the golden eagle with spread wings on the standard of the Persian king both in the *Anabasis* [I. 10.12] and *Cyropaedia* [VII. 1.4].

---

190 Shenkar 2017, 57. O. Skjærvø had already proposed to restore some fragmentary parts in the Middle Persian text of Paikuli with the insertion of the word GDE (*xwarrah*) that seems to be actually the correct reading: Humbach, Skjærvø 1983, 83.

191 Schindel 2013, 836-837.

192 Rezakhani 2017a, 79; Rezakhani 2017b, 204.

193 Shenkar 2014, 47-51; Compareti 2020b.

194 Nylander 1983.

195 Harmatta 1979, 307; Jamzadeh 1982, 92.

There is no evidence for images of the *simurgh* in early Parthian art either. Ovidius [*Fasti* v 586] reported that Surena took seven golden eagles to the Romans at the battle of Carrhae (53 BCE) and dedicated them to the temple of Anahita in Ctesiphon. Could we assume that the Parthian general identified the Roman golden eagles with some important bird of Iranian mythology? After all, the family of this Parthian general originated in Central Asia and could have considered the golden eagle as a symbol of the *simurgh* or some other important Iranian mythological bird.[196] In the late fourth-early fifth century, Claudian compared the phoenix accompanied by other birds to a Parthian official along with his soldiers in a curious passage of his famous poem [*Phoenix*, 83-88].[197] This was obviously just a poetic image with no historical nor realistic elements.

Traces of birds that could had a role in the exaltation of an Arsacid king or a Parthian object of art are not unusual. The rock relief at Khang-i Nuruzi in ancient Elymais presents also birds holding a ring in front of the most relevant people (probably kings) that were represented according to Hellenistic and Parthian artistic models.[198] An inscribed and unexcavated late third century BCE silver plaque from Iran presents a very interesting decoration that includes two birds of prey beside a central altar (fig. 16). According to Gnoli, the Aramaic dedicatory inscription in the upper part of the plaque presents Parthi-

196 Traina 2010, 95-96. The idea that the eagle hunting a ram represented on a golden buckle from Nehavand (Iran) and at present kept in the British Museum would be the "symbol of the royal power of the Parthians" could have been inspired by Ovidius: Vanzan 2012, 140-141. Classical authors did not conceal their hostility towards the Parthians and therefore any information should be considered with great caution. For example, the Greek *drákon*, Latin *persici dracones* that Classical sources mentioned among the Roman trophies could have been simple standards and not special devices used in battle by the Parthians to frighten their enemies: Trever 1964, 168; Coulston 1991; Kuehn 2011, 40-41. The Armenians who, until the fifth century CE have been ruled by the Arshakuni Dynasty of Parthian origins, adopted this kind of dragon banners as well: Russell 1994-1995, 80-84.

197 Zambon 2004, 25-26.

198 Vanden Berghe, Schippman 1984, fig. 1.

an borrowings and could be translated as "the hunt that Xwanbndank did and left to the god (or goddess) Gaddi for his own life and for the lives of his brothers and uncles (or friends)".[199] Since the plaque does not reproduce any hunting scene, the birds of prey could be identified as referring to the Iranian concept of *xwarrah/farn* whose echo can be definitely recognized in the name of the Semitic god Gaddi. Theophoric Parthian names proved that the idea of *xwarrah* was very important (but probably not central) for this ancient Iranian dynasty too.[200]

Birds identified as eagles with a crescent above their head represent a common subject on seal impressions from Parthian Merv. This symbol could be connected to the idea of kingship.[201] Other birds with a diadem in the beak used to exalt the image of a king recurred in Parthian coins (fig. 17). Their origin could be traced back to Greek art and had a strong impact on the Persian coinage of the Fratarakas, Kings of Persis and early Sasanians as well.[202] Some coins of Fratarakas and Kings of Persis present on the obverse a person in the act of worshiping a tower-building with a "winged genius" above flying in the air while, on the other side of the building, there is sometimes a standard surmounted by a big bird.[203] According to the most recent numismatic study on Frataraka coinage, the winged genius would be a representation of *xwarrah* while the bird on the

199 Gnoli 1995. Personifications or protective deities of Syrian and Mesopotamian cities were quite common in the Hellenistic period. They were mainly female and usually worn the walled crown of the Greek Tyche. One colossal image of a male deity wearing such a crown was found among the paintings of the Akchakhan Kala Chorasmian site (ca. first century CE). Shenkar has proposed to identify him with the Gad of the Amu Darya River or a local version of the god of glory, *farn* in Chorasmian language: Shenkar 2019, 13-14.

200 Weber 2003.

201 Bader, Gaibov, Koshelenko 1998, 30.

202 Vardanyan 2001, figs. 3.11-12, 11.2, 4, 6, 14.9; Sinisi 2008; Sarkhosh Curtis 2012, 71-72.

203 Panaino 2003.

standard would be the *vareghna* falcon.[204] Unfortunately, the author of that publication did not support his ideas with any precise information nor bibliographical reference. Vesta Sarkhosh Curtis too took for granted that the "winged genius" was a representation of *xwarrah* that the Fratarakas would have inherited from the Achaemenids.[205] Associations with the Iranian idea of glory should not be ruled out although these motifs could just represent symbols adopted from Greco-Roman art where they expressed the corresponding manifestation of *tyche* or *fortuna* particularly important for kings and rulers.[206]

At the Parthian site of Kal'a-ye Zahak in Eastern Azerbaijan, Iranian archaeologists found some stucco decorations that include also a giant bird attacking an animal looking like a bull. The remains which are all preserved in the archaeological museum in Tabriz should be dated to the first century BCE-first century CE on the basis of some inscribed potteries excavated at the same site. One Iranian scholar proposed to associate the bull of the stucco relief with Mithraic religion that, however, did not leave many traces in Persia.[207] Unfortunately, it is not possible to say much about the giant bird attacking the bull because the portion of the decoration at Kal'a-ye Zahak is very fragmentary and no clear parallels can be traced in other artistic milieu. The position of the bull could call to mind the sacrificial animal killed by Mithra in Roman art although in Kal'a-ye Zahak there is nobody approaching the animal, just the big bird on its back. There are simply not enough elements to propose any connection with Mithraism either.

In consideration of all these premises, one should admit that birds were considered very appropriate animals to express kingship, glory and divine benevolence in pre-Islamic Persia. Some connections with a local phoenix could have existed in Parthian or Sasanian culture but very little traces can be detected in visual arts.

---

204 van't Haaff 2020, 11-12, 27.

205 Sarkhosh Curtis 2010, 379-380.

206 Calmeyer 1979; Sinisi 2017, 870-876.

207 Zare 2008.

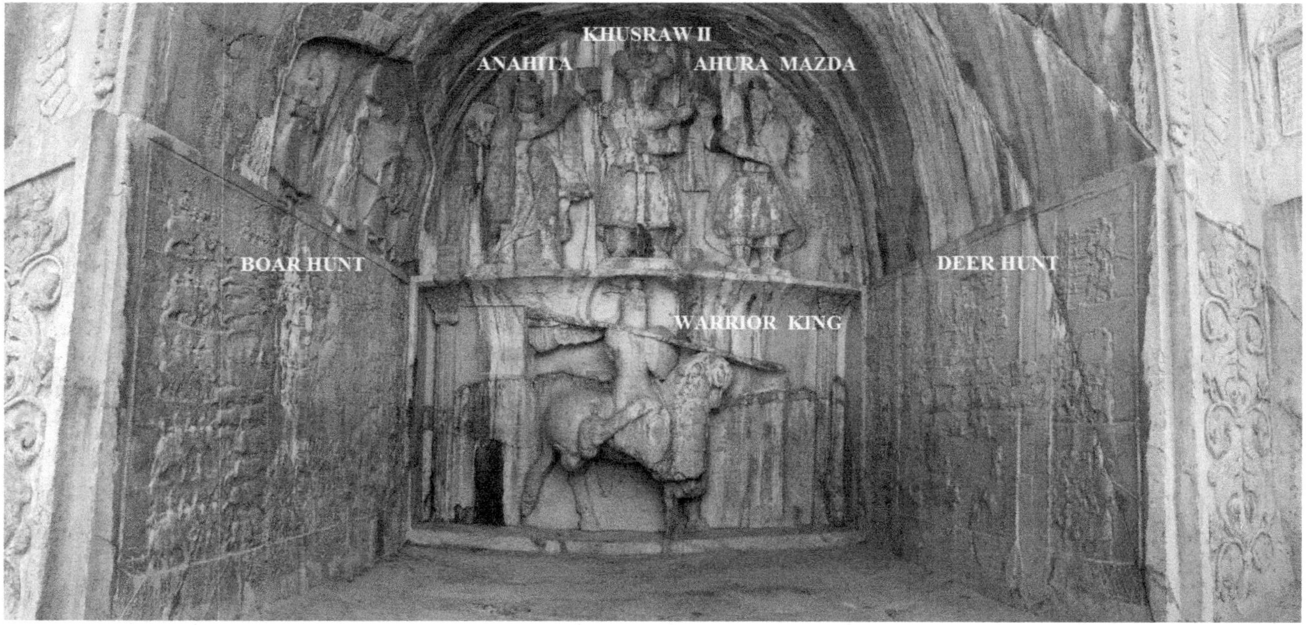

Figure 9. The large grotto at Taq-i Bustan, Kermanshah (end of the sixth-beginning of the seventh century). Photo: Li Sifei.

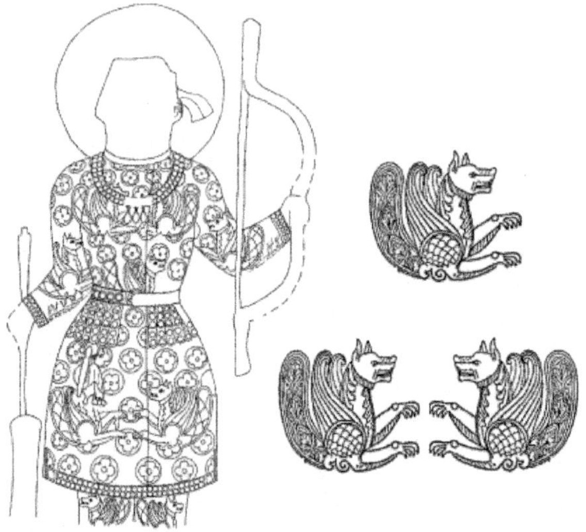

Figure 10a-b. Detail of the main archer on a boat in the wild boar hunting panel, Taq-i Bustan. After: Domyo 1984, figs. 44, 60.65.

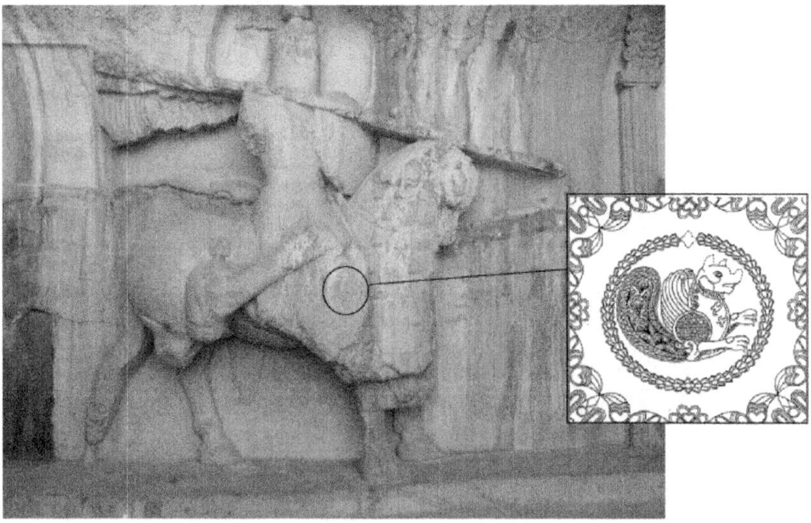

Figure 11. The warrior king (Khusraw II) in the back of the big grotto at Taq-i Bustan. Photo: M. Compareti. Sketch after: Domyo 1984, fig. 62.

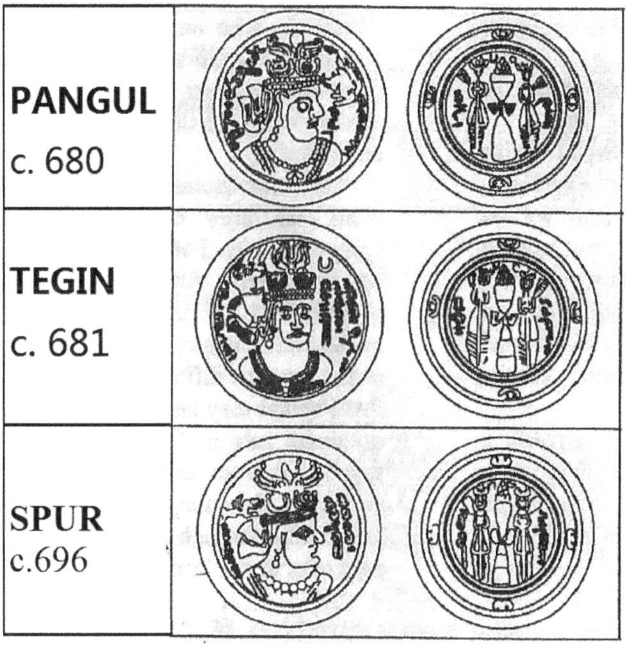

Figure 12a-c. Hunnish and Turkish copper coins from Zabulistan (end of the seventh century). After: Gyselen 2009, fig. 7.

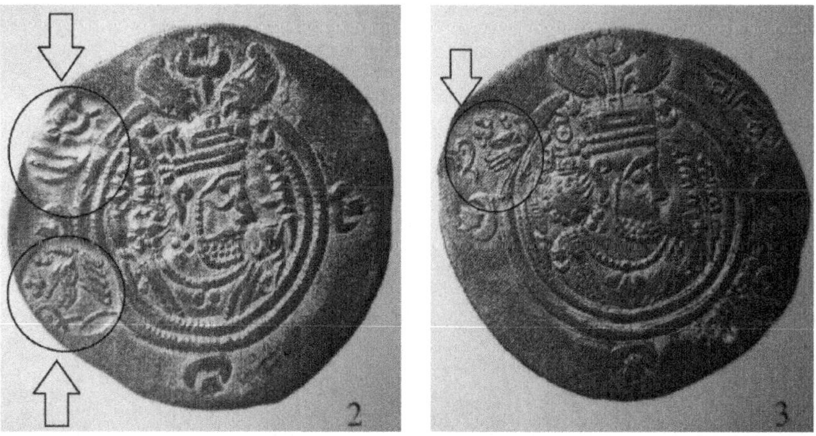

Figure 13a-b. Silver Sasanian drachms or Sogdian imitations of Sasanian drachms with epigraphic countermarks (seventh century). After: Nikitin, Roth 1995, figs. 2-3; Compareti 2019a, fig. 6.

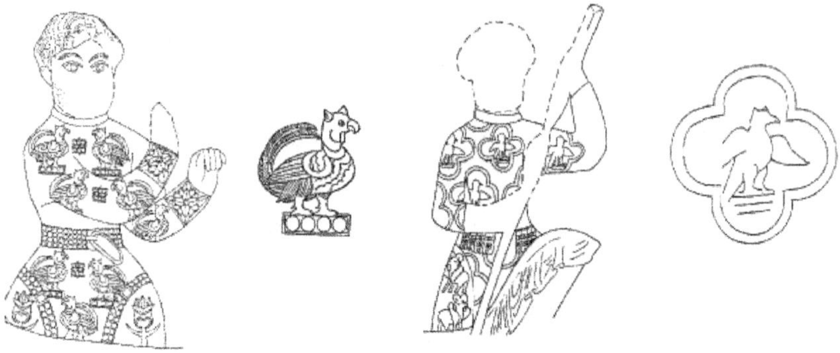

Figure 14a-b. Attendants of the king standing on boats in the wild boar hunting panel, Taq-i Bustan. After: Domyo 1984, fig. 40, 46a, 61b; Otavsky 1998a, fig. 69.

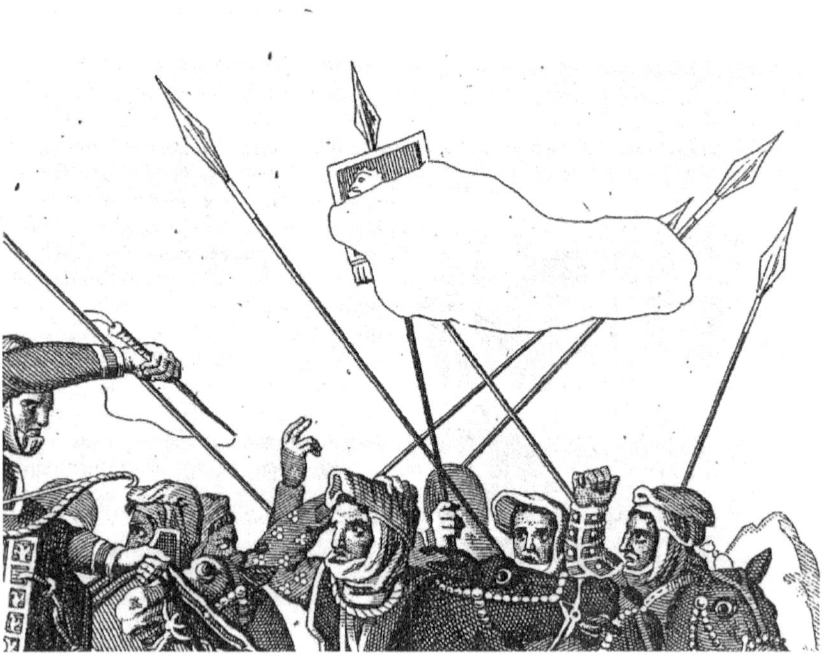

Figure 15. Detail of the Persian standard in the "Alexander Mosaic" from Casa del Fauno, Pompei (first century CE). Museo Archeologico Nazionale, Napoli. After: Nylander 1983, fig. 12.

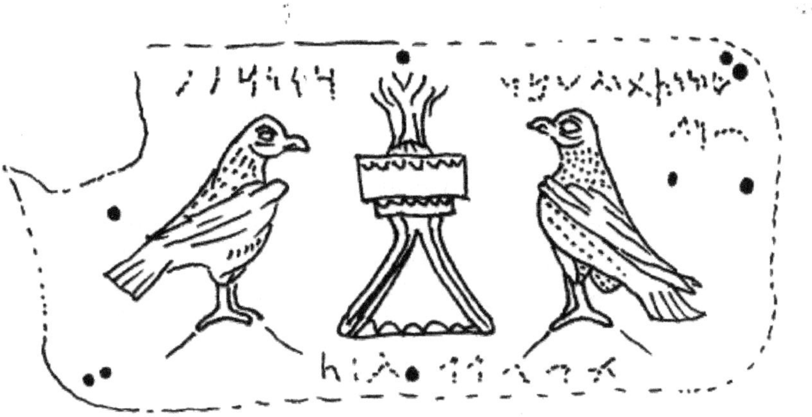

Figure 16. Parthian inscribed silver plaque, Foroughi Collection (third century BCE). After: Gnoli 1995, 89.

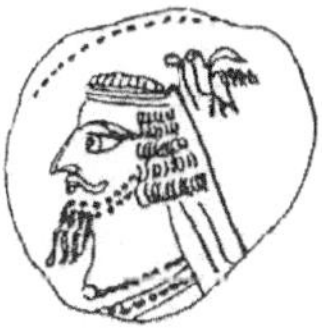

Fraate IV, Ar dr. (Sel. 52.10-ss.)

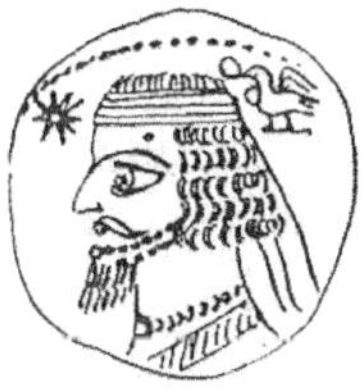

Fraate IV, Ar dr. (Sel. 53-3-ss.)

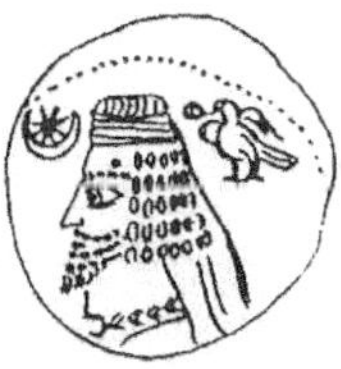

Fraate IV, Ar dr. (Sel. 54.7-ss.)

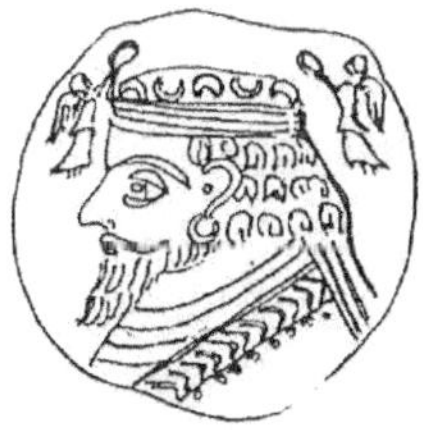

Fraatace, Ar tetr. (Sel. 57.3)

Figure 17a-d. Parthian drachms of Fraates (38-3/2 BCE) and Fraataces (2 BCE-2 CE) with birds, astronomical symbols, and winged victories. After: Vardanyan, R. (2001). Tendenze culturali e ideologiche nell'impero partico riflesse dalla monetazione. *Parthica* 3, figs. 11.2, 4, 6.

2.3 The Caucasus

Few regions of the world presents a complex anthropological situation such as in the Caucasus. The Sasanians controlled most of this region where Zoroastrianism was the main religion until the conversion to Christianity in the early fourth century. Not many traces of Zoroastrian religion have left remains that could be archaeologically attested. Among the most interesting pre-Christian art objects one should mention carved steles and terracotta statuettes.[208]

The pseudo-*simurgh* was very popular among Armenians, Iberians, and other people of the Caucasian region. In fact, it appeared quite often as an architectonic decorative element of churches. In this uncontestable religious context, that composite creature can be found as an isolated motif or a substitute for monstrous creatures described in the Bible. The operation was not started by the Christians since the *Septuagint* already presented the *ketos* in the place of *leviathan* [LXX Job 40: 25]. One scholar argued that in this case, *ketos* did not mean sea dragon but whale.[209] Representations of the *ketos* as a decorative element for luxury objects appeared in ancient Armenian art, as it is possible to observe in a silver component of a vase and seal impressions from the second-first century BCE Hellenistic capital Artashat.[210]

The composite creature that we proposed to call pseudo-*simurgh* already appeared among the decorations of the Ejmiacin Cathedral, precisely on column capitals whose construction should be attributed to 620 CE (fig. 18). Since the chronology of that part of the Armenian cathedral has been established quite precisely, this should be considered one of the most ancient representations of the pseudo-*simurgh* being practically contemporary with the one in the wild boar hunting panel at Taq-i Bustan.[211] On the western façade of the Ateni Sion

208 Compareti 2017a.

209 Uehlinger 1999, 515.

210 Au pied du Mont Ararat. Splendeurs de l'Arménie antique 2007, cat. 124; Khachatryan, Neverov 2008, pls. 843-861.

211 Hakobyan, Mikaelyan 2018, 41.

church (Georgia, not far from the ancient Iberian capital Mc'xeta) there is a pseudo-*simurgh* that could be dated to the seventh century as well (fig. 19). It is carved in a white material that is different than the rest of the stone used to build the church and the possibility cannot be ruled out that it could even be more ancient that the building itself.[212] The reproduction of this creature on churches could point at its use as an auspicious symbol with apotropaic functions.

These Armenian and Iberian specimens are extremely important in order to trace a probable provenance and chronology of the pseudo-*simurgh* from the Iranian world. There are no further early examples that can be precisely dated in Anatolia, Syria, or other regions under Byzantine rule but very opened to Persian culture. At least two eighth-century Cappadocian churches at Al Oda (fig. 20) and Ağaç (fig. 21) present rich painted programs that include single pseudo-*simurgh* inside vegetal medallions.[213] They are probably among the most ancient dated Byzantine composite creatures of this kind and it is worth observing that they appear, once more, in a religious context. The most ancient representation of a pseudo-*simugh*, however, can be found among the decorations of the Blachernae Palace in Constantinople that was erected in the early ninth century. It is not clear if, in this specific case, the context could be considered religious or civil. In fact, according to N. Asutay-Effenberger, the meaning of this "Persian" creature was used as a "sign of protection or victory".[214]

Some centuries later, the *leviathan* of the story of Jonah on the southern façade of the Armenian Cathedral of the Holy Cross on the island of Aght'amar (Van Lake, ancient Vaspurakan region, today in eastern Turkey) presented clear analogies with the pseudo-*simurgh* (fig. 22). It is worth observing that among the paintings embellishing

212 Compareti 2014b, 33; Iamanidze 2019, 97.

213 Thierry 1976. At least two sculptures from ninth century Croatian churches seem to be, most likely, just inaccurate representations of peacocks: Jurković 2015.

214 Asutay-Effenberger 2019.

the interior of the cathedral of Aght'amar, there is also a representation of the snake tempting Adam and Eve with head, paws, and even wings resembling the Iranian composite creature under examination (fig. 23). For some reason, the Armenians adopted the iconography of the pseudo-*simurgh* to enrich different Biblical episodes that embellished their churches.[215] In this way, the religious sphere is definitely clear, although that composite creature does not seem to present completely positive characteristics since it was a substitute for the *leviathan* or the tempting snake. The representation of the tempting snake at Aght'amar is very interesting since, in the sculptural decoration on the exterior of that church, there is another illustration of Adam and Eve together with the snake depicted as a kind of dragon with legs but no traits resembling a pseudo-*simurgh* (fig. 24).[216] Christian artists definitely searched for their models in different cultural contexts. Armenian sculptors and painters looked at the *ketos* that already underwent some transformations in a "Mediterranean" Christian milieu and, as it is obvious to expect, at the pseudo-*simurgh* from the Iranian world. As already observed, the latter too developed from the Greek *ketos* although, possibly, in a more ancient period.

It seems that the Christians were particularly receptive to composite creatures and monsters in general not only in the Caucasus. In proto-Christian art, in fact, Classical iconographies were recycled quite easily, for example in the case of the Greco-Roman *ketos* in place of the *leviathan*. Students of the Bible remarked that there were similarities between the *leviathan* in the story of Jonah and the *ketos* in the myth of Perseus.[217] Exactly like the *ketos* that could be a positive and

---

215 Compareti 2014b, 17-30; La Porta 2019.

216 De' Maffei 1980; Curatola 1989, 63. The "Eden serpent" had characteristics such as legs, arms, and even human voice in Jewish and Christian traditions both in literature and visual arts: Kelly 1971.

217 Day 1985, 111. In the Armenian version of the Book of Jonah, the swallowing monster is called *ket* (clearly from Greek *ketos*) while its name in the following phase of the story, when it vomited Jonah, is rendered as *vishap jkann*, literally "dragon fish": Russell 1990-1991, 142. Scholars observed long ago that the same creature

a negative creature in Greek myths, its iconography among "eastern Christians" could be used for the "good" *leviathan* and the evil tempting snake. Once more, the versatile iconography of the *ketos* resulted particularly attractive for Christian artists who adopted and adapted it to their figurative necessities. Its first attestation in Christian art was in the representation of the Biblical sea-monster that swallowed Jonah, which can be found in the third century paintings of the Chapel of the Holy Martyrs in Cimitile (not far from Naples, Italy). Those paintings in Cimitile could be contemporary or slightly older than Rome catacombs and Roman Christian sarcophagi (fig. 25).[218]

Precious garments embellished with pseudo-*simurgh*s within pearl roundel frames (another typical Iranian element) were found during controlled excavations at the eighth/ninth-century cemetery of Moshevaja Balka, in Caucasian Russia, and are at present kept in the State Hermitage Museum. The main garment is a green caftan that was probably made from silk imported from the Byzantine Empire, specifically Constantinople or Syria (fig. 26). A child's hat in "Byzantine silk" represents a smaller but extremely interesting finding (fig. 27). Both present a pseudo-*simurgh* within pearl roundel frames.[219] The people of that part of the Caucasus controlled the passage of goods and they possibly received precious textiles as toll payments in exchange.[220]

The most popular motif among composite creatures in the Caucasus was definitely the pseudo-*simurgh*. It is significant that the very last occurrence of this motif appeared among the paintings of an Armenian church, specifically the one built by the tradesman Tigran

---

at Aght'amar is represented according to two different iconographies in the same scene. In fact, it has no wings when it is swallowing Jonah and it is complete when it is vomiting him (fig. 22). According to James Russell (1990-1991), the fish under the monster that is vomiting Jonah at Aght'amar could be referred to the textual description and should be identified with the *jkann* of the name *vishap jkann*.

218 Mazzoleni 1992; Ebanista, Fusaro 2010, 36.

219 Ierusalimskaja 2012, 86, 179-184, 235-241.

220 Riboud 1976.

Honenc' in Ani (today in eastern Turkey) that is precisely dated to 1218 (fig. 28).[221] Even though it is a painted decoration, it clearly reproduces a precious textile just like the so-called *velaria* of medieval European churches. These were paintings that reproduced extremely expensive textiles usually embellished with highly fashionable motifs.

After the thirteenth century, the pseudo-*simurgh* motif lost its popularity and disappeared completely on the whole Eurasian continent. It was no longer a motif favored by the Christians while, among the Muslims, it was abandoned long before. It is not clear the reason of its fate among the Muslims although it should be noted that the pseudo-*simurgh* did not appear in one single instance in the Islamic religious milieu and, to tell the truth, neither in book illustrations.[222] On the contrary, it always had some religious associations in Christian art. This was probably due to the facility of adopting the iconography of the pseudo-*simurgh* to represent creatures such as the tempting snake and the *leviathan*. However, the reason for its reproduction as an isolated motif even exalted by the pearl roundel pattern is not clear. In fact, if that composite creature was used as a substitute for negative monsters related to Biblical stories, how is it possible to find it as if it were an important element to be observed so often in churches and other objects of luxury arts? Should we suppose that Christians were very familiar with that composite creature as a symbol of Iranian glory and then adopted it without major changes into

221 Compareti 2015, 33-35. Some experts of Islamic studies considered the pseudo-*simurgh* in Ani paintings as an important elitist symbol that could have reached the Caucasus region from the East travelling along the Silk Road network: Guidetti 2017; Blessing 2019, 233-235. This observation is definitely correct although, in the early thirteenth century (when the church of Tigran Honenc' was built), the pseudo-*simurgh* had already entered the repertoire of fantastic creatures of Armenian, Iberian and, most likely, Albanian artists at least six hundred years before.

222 As it will be discussed below, just some representations of the *qitus*/whale constellation in Arabic and Persian astrological manuscripts presented similarities with the pseudo-*simurgh*: Bausani 1978b.

their own cultural milieu as an auspicious apotropaic sign? On the whole, the idea of glory (Armenian *p'ark* or *baxt*, Georgian *didebay*, Greek *doxa*) represented (and represents) a very important concept in Christian religion.[223] Its use as an apotropaic symbol could represent another possibility. Armenian legends mentioned magical creatures called *arlez* (or *aralez*, *yaralez*, literally "blood lickers") described as dogs (possibly winged) that could resurrect the dead.[224] Should we consider this hypothesis valid for the other people of the Caucasus as well?

It is not easy to find an answer to these questions. However, it could be considered that the iconography of the pseudo-*simurgh* arrived in the Caucasus region from eastern Iran due to the important position occupied by Bastam in the last part of the sixth century according to Muslim authors. In fact, when his brother Binduya was arrested and executed by the Sasanians, he was trying to reach Bastam in Azerbaijan where the latter was appointed governor when he was still on good terms with his nephew Khusrow II Parwiz.[225] It should not be ruled out the hypothesis that the importance of this composite creature among the "Zoroastrian" Sasanians determined its fortune also among the Christians of the Persian Empire exactly as happened to other motifs such as the spread wings motif that became very popular in the Caucasian region such as in Byzantine and Omayyad arts.[226] If Armenian legends already included magic dogs (*arlez*), rooted in pre-Christian (and, possibly, even Mesopotamian) traditions, it is then possible to imagine that the adoption of the canine pseudo-*simurgh* was furthermore facilitated.

Boris Marshak traced a very similar phenomenon in Sogdian art. In fact, when Sogdian artists had started to adopt the iconography of

---

223 Garsoïan 1976, 228; Gnoli 1984, 217-218.

224 Ajello 1978; Russell 1986; Russell 1987: 344, 416-418; Borghini 1999; Mahé 2008, 221-222.

225 Shahbazi 1989.

226 Compareti 2010.

the Indian god Shiva at least since the sixth century CE, they not only adapted it to represent the local deity Weshparkar (the Avestan god of the wind Vayu) but, for some reason, they did the same with the king of demons in some eighth century paintings at Penjikent. Curiously enough, wild boars appeared attached to the chariot of the king of demons because, in Sogdian art and culture, that animal was the *vahana* of Weshparkar.[227] Sogdian artists (and, most likely, "magi" too) superimposed some non-Indian attributes of their own god to the characteristics of the king of demons who, on the other hand, appeared like Shiva. If Indian iconographic formulae were going to be faithfully respected and reproduced, one would have expected the chariot of the king of demons to be drawned by a bull (*Nandi*) that was the *vahana* of Shiva. Such a mixture of iconographies could have generated some confusion for observers who entered a private Sogdian house embellished with religious and, possibly, epic scenes too. It is not completely clear if the positive or negative aspect of the human figure whose iconography presented the same traits of Shiva in Sogdian art was completely clear for local observers even in the case that they were aware of foreign borrowings, especially Indian ones. This could explain the presence of a Sogdian inscription on the leg of Weshparkar depicted as Shiva (with three heads and a trident in one hand) on an eighth century painting from Penjikent (room 1, sector XXII).[228] Inscriptions in Sogdian and other languages do exist on paintings in Afrasyab and Penjikent and art objects in general but they are quite rare. Moreover, in very few cases those inscriptions helped to identify some of the people represented in Sogdian paintings. However, only Weshparkar was labeled with his own name while the other deity in front of him in the same scene in room 1, sector XXII (possibly Apam Napat) does not present any identificative inscription. As a matter of fact, this is just a hypothesis but it strongly suggests that something similar could have probably happened among the Christians of the

227 Marshak 2002b, 37-38, 110. On Weshparkar see now: Taasob 2020.

228 Shenkar 2014, 154-157.

Caucasus for a versatile symbolic creature imported from the (eastern) Iranian world such as our pseudo-*simurgh*. Local artistis could have used it in different scenes attributing to it opposed characteristics exactly like for the *ketos* in Classical art and Shiva in Sogdiana. This was probably a very common phenomenon in the Late Antique world.

In a first stage, the pseudo-*simurgh* and some other Iranian symbols entered different parts of the Persian Empire from eastern Iran because of the prestige that they possibly held at the Sasanian court. Later, such symbols began to be used for other reasons even in a religious context to represent ominous monsters or good composite creatures. For sure, the pseudo-*simurgh* did not constitute a substitute for the phoenix of the Greco-Romans nor *'anqa* of the Arabs.

What about possible representations of the "real" *simurgh* in the Caucasus? The fifth century Armenian author Eznik Koghbaci reported that, according to the "ancient religion" here intended to be the Caucasian form(s) of Zoroastrianism in vogue before Christianization, Ahriman created the peacock in order to prove that he was "not unable but rather unwilling to do good".[229] It is not clear if Christians favored the peacock as a reaction against other religions such as Zoroastrianism or Islam. Curiously enough, the Yazidi Kurds who lived in close contact with Armenians in medieval and modern times as well, always considered *Melek Ta'us* "the Peacock Angel" as a central figure of their religion and even associated it with the phoenix.[230]

Images of birds looking like peacocks appear frequently in Armenian seals and seal impressions from the Hellenistic city of Artashat[231] and the Sasanian period "capital" Dvin.[232] During the recent excavations at Aghcʿ (not far from Yerevan), the archaeologists found fragmentary tiles and potteries embellished with a beribboned peacock

229 Asatryan 2005, 164.

230 Asatryan, Arakelova 2014.

231 Khachatryan, Neverov 2008, pls. 692-730.

232 Kalantaryan 1982, pls. I-XI.

in front of a tree realized in typical pre-Islamic Iranian style.[233] Although it is not possible to identify with absolute certainty this kind of decorated bird with a local version of the phoenix (or *senmurv*), its appearance reminds one of the Albanian stone pedestal for a cross with confronted beribboned peacocks beside a tree from Mingechevir (or Mingechaur), at present kept in the National Museum of History of Azerbaijan (Baku) that scholars had already associated to Sasanian art long ago.[234] The territory of ancient Azerbaijan – known as Caucasian Albania – was part of the Sasanian Empire and adopted Christianity in the fourth century like the neighboring countries such as Iberia (eastern Georgia) and Armenia. Other less decorated but more fragmentary peacocks can be observed in early Armenian churches at Dvin, Ptghni, etc.[235] It is not possible to be more precise about the figure of the peacock in the pre-Christian culture of the Caucasus. Some connection between the phoenix and the peacock existed in Greco-Roman art, for example in the Pompeian paintings of Euxinus Inn (fig. 67), and it is just obvious to expect the same association in the Christian milieu.

The Christian milieu of the Iranized artistic production in the Caucasus allows tracing a precise parallel with similar decorations in European churches where, possibly, the peacock itself (sometimes even embellished with ribbons)[236] could be just a substitute of the

233 Kalantaryan, Karakhanyan et al., 2009: 74-85.

234 Trever, 1959: 299-300.

235 Arakelyan 1949, pls. 68, 71. The eagles above the columns of the Armenian church of Zvart'noc' (seventh century) could be just a symbol of kingship and do not seem to be connected to any specific fantastic bird: Arakelyan 1949, pls. 77-80. Birds of prey beside a central eight-rayed star or rosette have been used as symbols of kingship in Armenian art since the time of king Tigran II (95-55 BCE) as it is possible to observe on his coins: Harmatta 1979, 311; Invernizzi 2007.

236 Bagnera 1994. Birds with ribbons attached to their neck in Byzantine mosaics have always called the attention of scholars searching for Sasanian decorative elements: Ocadiah, Ovadiah 1987, pl. XXVII.2; Farioli Campanati 1992, 291-292.

phoenix as suggested in some classical and medieval poetical texts.[237] In fact, they both represented immortality. Pliny reported in his *Naturalis Historia* [x, 43-44] that the peacock was considered to loose the feathers of its tail during the cold season to get them regenerated again in spring. Such a legendary "rebirth" of the feathers of the peacock called immediately the attention of Christian authors who developed a slightly different story. According to Saint Augustine [*De Civitate Dei*, xxi.4, 1], the meat of the peacock would never get rotten and, for this reason, its incorruptibility rendered it a very appropriate symbol of the resurrection of Christ.[238] Its early representations can be already observed in third-fourth century Roman catacombs.[239] Some time later, peacocks beside a central *kantharos* started to be quite common in Egypt, for example, in the fifth century church at Sohag.[240] The peacock seemed to have different symbolic meanings as a decorative element in Christian churches. According to medieval bestiaries, it was mainly a symbol of vanity although its representation in arts usually beside a central tree or *kantharos* seems to remind immortality. Combinations of the phoenix with confronted peacocks can be found in sixth century church mosaics such as in Umm Gerar (Palestine) and Sabratha (Lybia).[241] Other interesting mosaics with peacocks can bc found in the territory of Jordan where, curiously enough, the phoenix was not a popular motif. It can be observed in one unique floor mosaic in the sixth century church of the Bishop Sergius in Um er-Rass, not far from Madaba.[242]

237 The Greek author Achilles Tatius wrote between the second-third centuries that the phoenix was an "Ethiopian" bird similar to a peacock in size and color: *Leucippe and Clitophon* [iii, 25]: Zambon 2004, 25. On medieval poems that compared the phoenix to the peacock, see: Carrega, Navone 1983, 470-471.

238 Semi, Rota 1987, 48; Carile 2016, 76.

239 Grabar 1966a, figs. 115, 228.

240 McKenzie 2007, fig. 460.

241 Van den Broek 1972, pls. xxxii-xxxiii; Amad 1988, figs. 7, 9a-9b.

242 Piccirillo 1989, 279.

Confronted peacocks beside a central basket filled with fruits constituted the main decorative frieze in the Sogdian paintings of room 9 at Afrasyab (pre-Islamic Samarkand) that should be dated around 660 CE.[243] This basket could be actually a local version of the Greco-Roman *kantharos* and, in fact, its decoration calls to mind the one of Iranian silver vessels in general. Russian archaeologists excavated one slightly later wooden panel embellished with confronted beribboned peacocks beside a central plant at the Bactrian site of Kal'a-ye Kafirnigan (Esanbaj, Tajikistan).[244]

Confronted peacocks beside a central *kantharos* embellished sometimes the mosaics in the synagogues of North Africa and Palestine.[245] The peacock had no relevant part in the Bible. It appeared just in a list of treasures of King Solomon [*Kings* 10, 22]. However, birds in general represented very popular motifs in ancient Jewish literature such as for the hoopoe of Solomon. Frantz Grenet considered one painted ossuary from a necropolis in Merv to be a specimen of Central Asian Jewish art. According to Grenet, the bird with a thread in its beak reproduced on that Merv ossuary should be identified with the dove sent by Noah from the ark.[246]

The peacock was an important decorative element in Islamic arts as well.[247] Two peacocks occur beside the canopy above a court scene on the southern wall of the west aisle in the Omayyad paintings at

---

243 Al'baum 1975, pl. I. Single peacocks within pearl roundel frames were quite popular in Sogdian textiles: Otavsky 1998a, fig. 96. Single and confronted peacocks within pearl roundels on textiles excavated at the early Tang period graves at Astana (Turfan, Xinjiang) represent one of the most popular motif along with winged horses and the wild boar head within roundels: Zhao 2012, 215. These textiles were probably produced in Turfan or other parts of Sui-Tang China by Sogdian immigrants: Compareti 2004.

244 Litvinskij, Solov'ev 1985, fig. 14.

245 Ovadiah, Ovadiah 1987, pls. CXVI.2, CXVII.2; Fine 2010, 126-127.

246 Grenet 1986a.

247 Al-Khamis 1998, 12-14; Asatryan 2005.

Qusayr 'Amra.[248] Many elements of Qusayr 'Amra paintings remind one of Greco-Roman art such as the Greek inscriptions above the tail of the two birds. The peacock tail in the representation of the pseudo-*simurgh* could have contributed to generate some confusion between this creature and the real *simurgh* (that was the phoenix) and was possibly perceived as a kind of peacock. It is worth observing that the tail of the peacock was part of the standard iconography of the *buraq* in Islamic book illustrations. This composite flying creature usually represented with human head, equine body and peacock tail transported Muhammad and other prophets during his Ascension (*mi'raj*) to the sky.[249]

Peacocks occurred in Sasanian seals and sealings.[250] As it happens often for this kind of objects, their decorations are quite small and inscriptions are not always present so it is not possible to be completely sure about their identification and attribution. Two fragmentary silk textiles non-scientifically excavated at Antinoe (Egypt) in 1896-1897 considered to be Sasanian and at present part of the Musée Historique des Tissus (Lyon) and the Louvre (Paris) present peacocks and "griffins".[251] Despite some decoratives elements that could be rooted in Iranian art, those textiles could just point at local products. The body of the eared birds described as griffins is not visible. For this reason it should not be ruled out the possibility that they were intended to be just eared birds or even two-headed eared birds. Moreover, the birds identified as peacocks have ears as well, necklaces and a very stylized body. Behind them, a circular and jagged element that M. Martiniani-Reber identified as the tail of a male peacock could be

248 Fontana 2019, fig. 2.

249 Piemontese 1974.

250 Bivar 1969, pl. 21. Peacocks appear also on some of the few excavated Sasanian seals and sealings specifically from the site of Qasr-i Abu Nasr (Shiraz): Harper 2006b, fig. 41.

251 Martiniani-Reber 1986, cat. 8; Martiniani-Reber, Bénazeth 1997, cat. 16.

just be a decorative motif in the background and not a tail that both bird shared.

Some scholars considered the images of single peacocks within roundels on stucco decorations from Ctesiphon and Barz Qawaleh (Luristan, Iran) as typical Sasanian specimens. However, on iconographical basis, these stuccoes could be actually dated to the early Islamic period as the three pendants necklace in the beak of the peacock suggests.[252] It seems that the peacock became a popular subject only in Persian art of the Islamic period. According to Islamic legends, the peacock was a beautiful bird but with a ugly voice or, in some variants of the story, horrible feet.[253] It was therefore not a completely positive animal. One thirteenth century Persian manuscript on talismans and magic known as *Daqa'iq al-haqa'iq* in the Bibliothèque National de France [Ms. sup. persan 174, fol. 112r] includes a curious image of the "*jinn* of the appearance of the passage of the Sun from Virgo to Libra" that is a double-headed peacock with arms.[254]

It should not be ruled out that something similar had occurred also among eastern Christian groups such as Syriac, Armenians, Albanians, and others. In Coptic Egypt and even in Christian Nobadia (or Nubia, corresponding to northern Sudan) Byzantine culture and art had always played a very important role. Images of confronted peacocks beside a central tree, a cross, and, sometimes, an *ankh* (or *crux ansata*) appeared quite often in Coptic textiles.[255] One scholar regarded the bird with a long tail resembling a peacock or an eagle with a necklace or ribbon around its neck and a cross above its head as a

252 Ghirshman 1962, fig. 274; Karamian, Farrokh 2017, fig. 12. The image of a woman represented frontally under an arch from that same site is wearing a necklace like the one in the beak of the peacock: Karamian, Farrokh 2017, figs. 9-10. Three pendants necklaces like this appeared in Sasanian numismatic only during the early seventh century and helped to propose better chronologies for Taq-i Bustan: Gyselen 1990; Tanabe 2006.

253 Asatryan 2005.

254 Barrucand 1990-1991, fig. 8.

255 Cortopassi 1998.

typical representation of the phoenix in Nubian art.[256] Even though it is not possible to propose a precise identification for these birds, they clearly had some important role in the decoration of churches on a wide territory that, most probably, included northeastern Africa too.

Other composite birds with human face or a ram face appeared among the numerous fantastic decorations at Aght'amar. There are not enough elements to identify these creatures with the phoenix. The first one, in fact, is possibly a representation of a Classical siren according to the "Islamic style" that was in fashion in tenth century Vaspurakan; the second one could have some astrological/astronomical connections that look like symbolic representations of lunar mansions in sixteenth century Islamic Persian book illustrations and more ancient (and rare) seal impressions from Sasanian Iran.[257] Despite the presence of many Armenian inscriptions on the Aght'amar church that identify most of the Biblical scenes reproduced there, no inscriptions accompain any fantastic creature whose identification remains highly hypothetical and controversial.

256 Belluccio 1987-1988.

257 Compareti 2014b, 21-25.

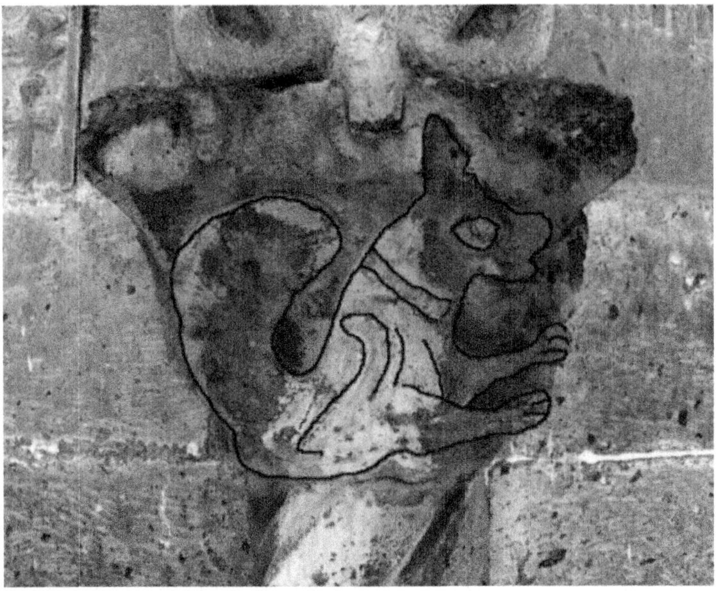

Figure 18. Decorative architectonic element, Ejmiacin Cathedral, Armenia (ca. 620). After: Hakobyan, Mikaelyan 2018, fig. 3 (modified).

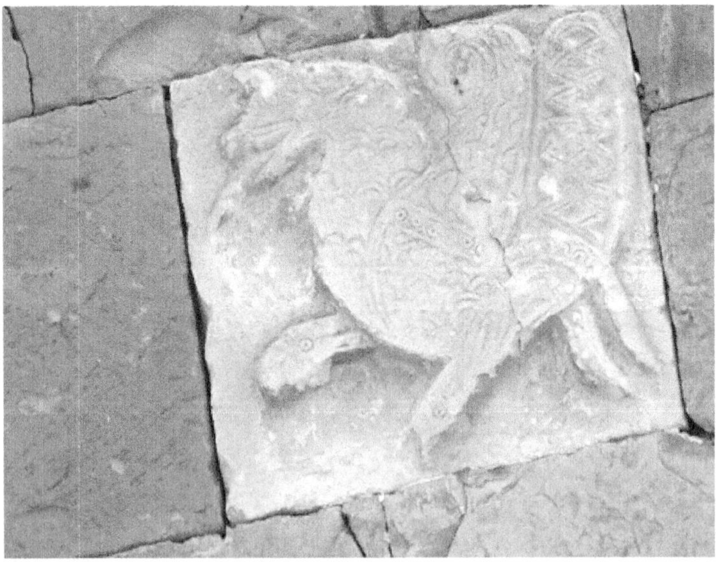

Figure 19. Decorative architectonic element, Ateni Sion, Georgia (seventh century). Photo: author.

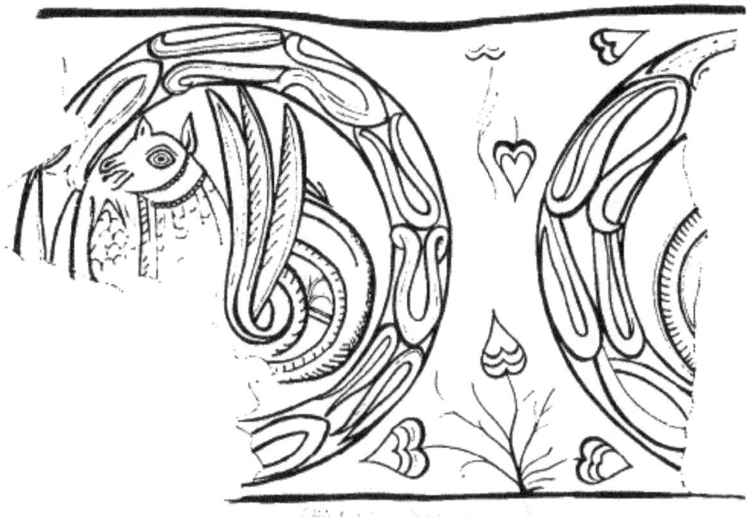

Figure 20. Detail of the decoration of the Cappadocian church of Al Oda, Turkey (eighth century). After: Thierry 1976, fig. 10.

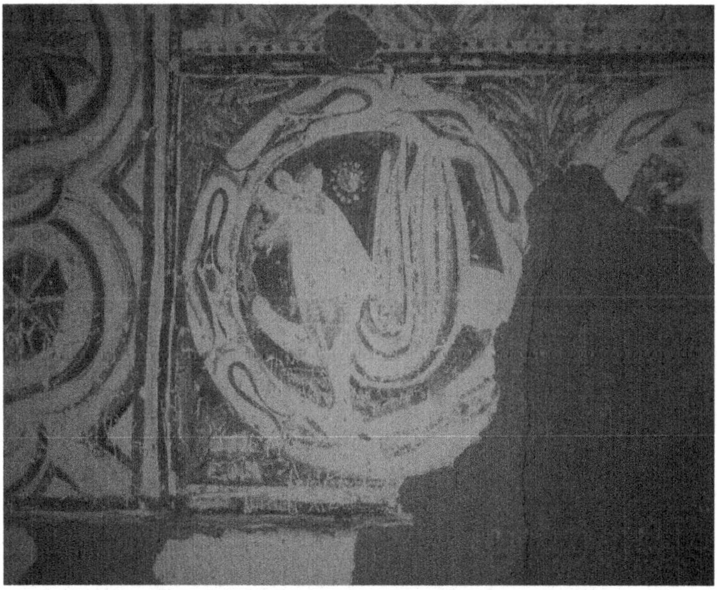

Figure 21. Detail of the decoration of the Cappadocian church of Ağaç, Turkey (eighth century). Photo: Rudy Favaro.

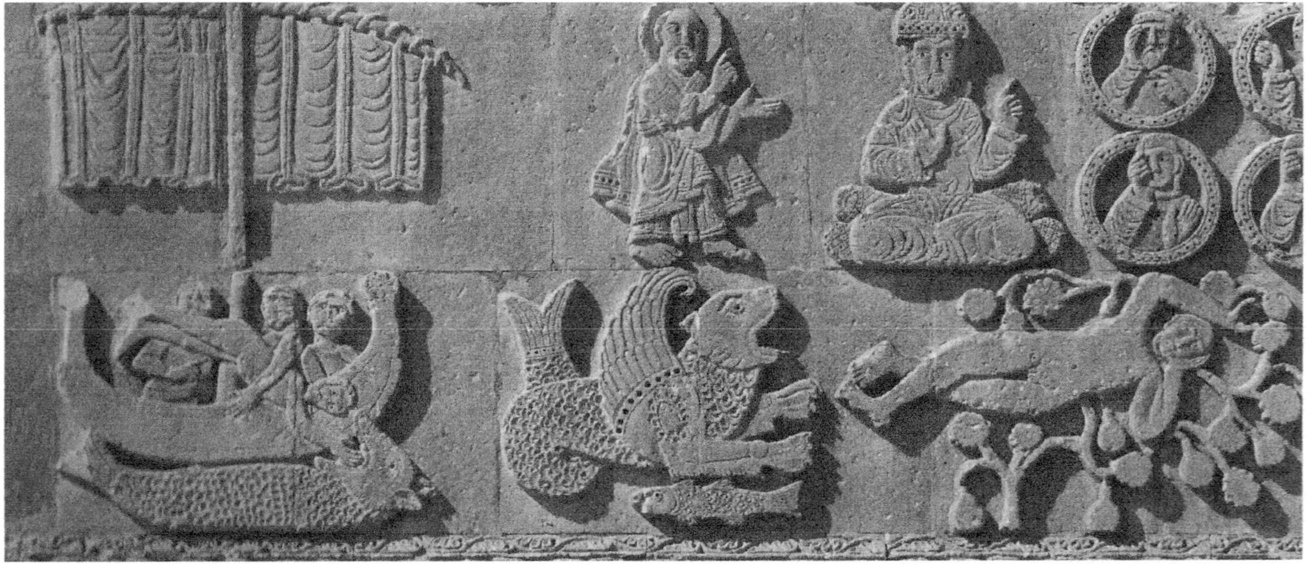

Figure 22. The story of Jonah on the south façade of the Church of the Holy Cross, island of Aght'amar in the Van Lake, Turkey (915-920), ancient Vaspurakan. After: Mnatsakanian, S. (2010). *Aghtamar. A Jewel of Medieval Armenian Architecture*. London-Istanbul, fig. 27.

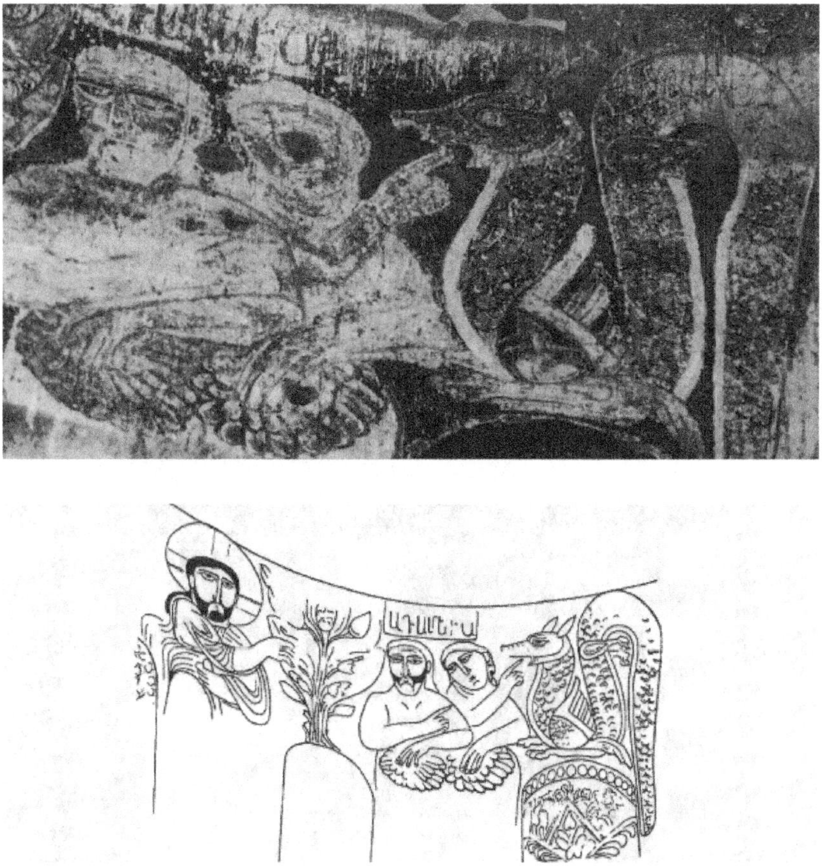

Figure 23a-b. Detail of the inner painted decoration of the Church of the Holy Cross at Aght'amar, Vaspurakan (915-921). After: Donabédian, P., Thierry, J.M. (1989). *Armenian Art*. New York, fig. 266; Thierry, N. (1983). Le cycle de la creation ed la faute d'Adam à Ałt'amar. *Revue des Études Arméniennes* XVII, fig. 5.

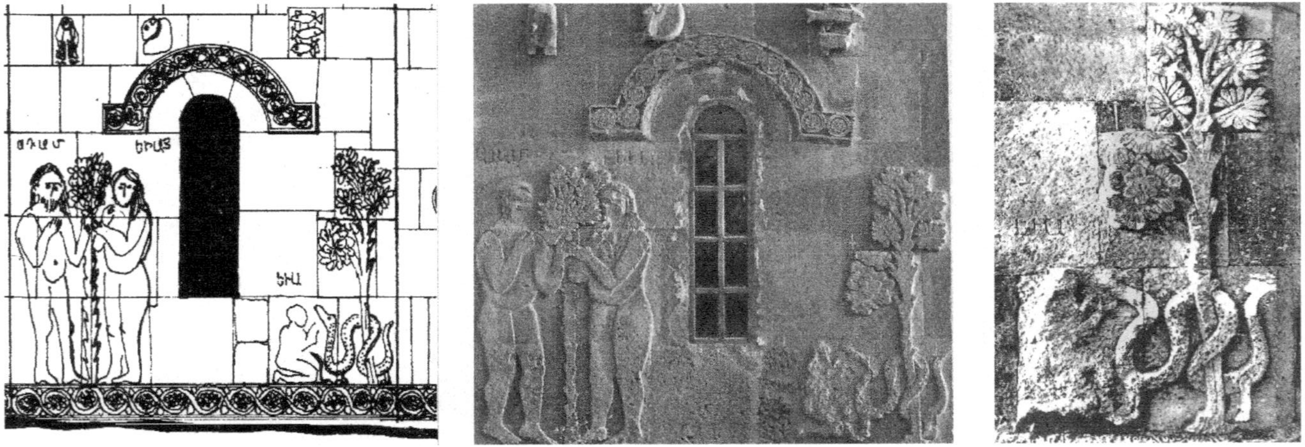

Figure 24a-c. Adam and Eve eating the apple in Eden and the tempting snake talking to Eve on the north façade of the Church of the Holy Cross, island of Aght'amar in the Van Lake, Turkey (915-920). After: Mnatsakanian, S. (2010). *Aghtamar. A Jewel of Medieval Armenian Architecture*. London-Istanbul, 109, fig. 43; de' Maffei 1980, fig. 7.

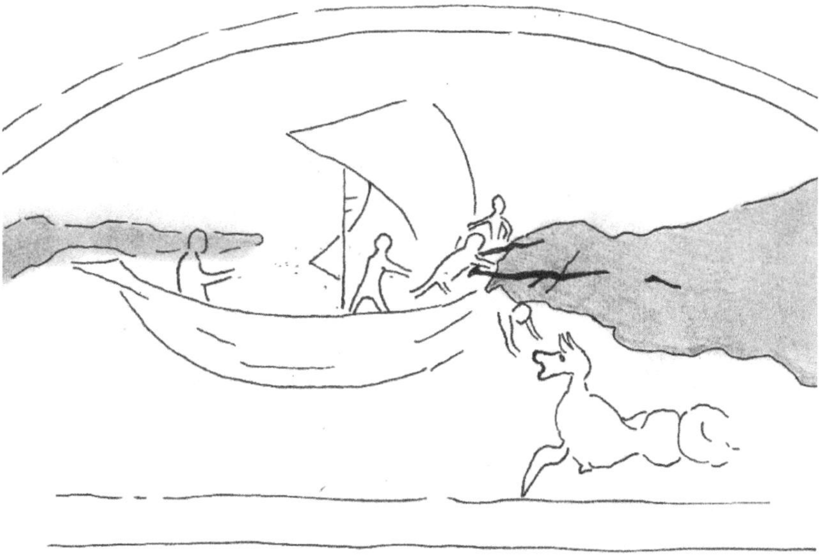

Figure 25. Jonah swollen by the *leviathan*, Chapel of the Holy Martyrs, Cimitile, Naples (third century). After: Ebanista, Fusaro 2010, 36.

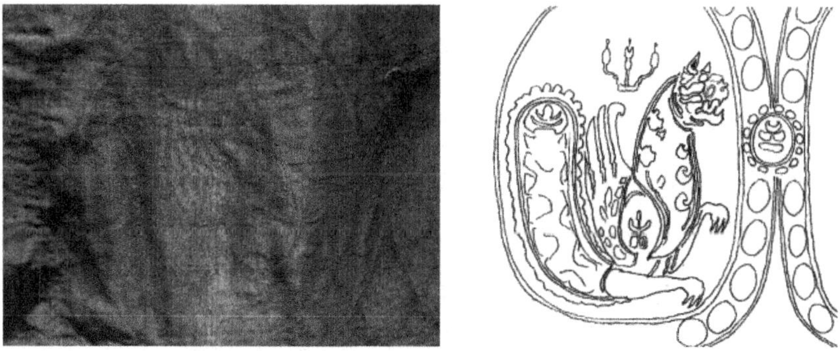

Figure 26a-b. Detail of a silk garment excavated at Moshevaja Balka, Russia (ca. ninth century). The State Hermitage Museum, St Petersburg. Photo and sketch: author.

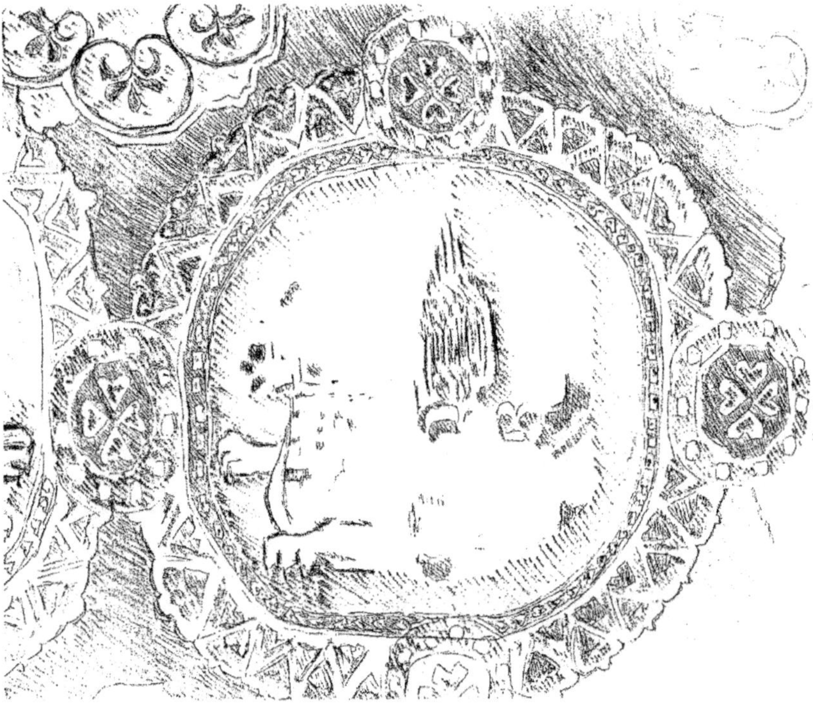

Figure 27. Headgear of a child from Moshevaja Balka, Russia (ca. eighth-ninth century). The State Hermitage Museum, St Petersburg. After: Ierusalimskaja 2012, fig. 110.

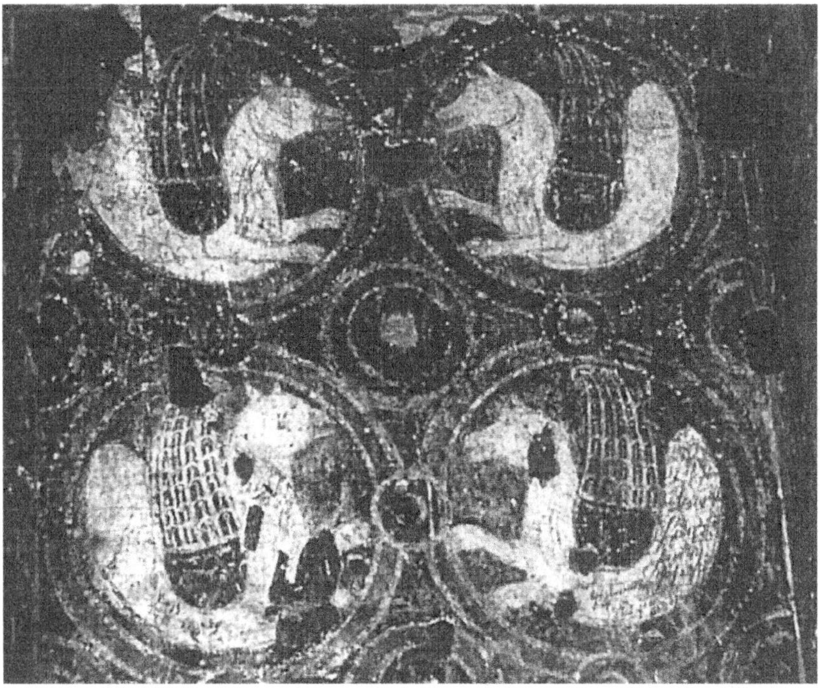

Figure 28. Mural painting in the church of Tigran Honenc' in Ani, eastern Turkey (1218). After: Donabédian, P., Thierry, J.M. (1989). *Armenian Art.* New York, fig. 384.

2.4 Sogdian paintings

The ancient Sogdian site of Penjikent is at present located in western Tajikistan, approximately 60 km east of Samarkand, not far from the border with Uzbekistan. Among the most interesting findings at Penjikent there are the famous wall paintings which have been excavated in the two temples, the citadel and the residential houses that belonged to the wealthy people. Those paintings are particularly important to try to reconstruct the religion of the Sogdians before the conversion to Islam after 750 CE. Every hint to be found in Sogdian art points at a religious system very close to Persian Zoroastrianism although many of the divinities represented at Penjikent do not have a parallel in Sasanian art. According to Chinese sources, Sogdians and Persians had very similar religious systems.[258]

Not only religious scenes embellished the rooms of the dwelling sectors at Penjikent: also hunts, festivities and banquets were possibly celebrated in those same houses and represented in their mural paintings. Room 41 of sector VI was excavated by Boris Staviskij in 1956-1957 and immediately became one of the most important discoveries at Penjikent because of its evident epic contents. In fact, it was quite clear that room 41 (also called the "Blue Hall") displayed a painted program, which was, in all probability, identified with the trials of the Iranian hero Rustam. Once confirmed, his identification among the Sogdian paintings at Penjikent could be considered his first representation in visual arts.[259]

On the basis of archaeological evidence, the painted Rustam program should be dated around 740 CE. There are some Sogdian inscriptions on the paintings but, despite their epigraphical importance, they do not say anything about the scene represented there.[260] Epic heroes and other figures of the legend of Rustam have been found

258 Riboud 2005.

259 Marshak 2002b.

260 Lur'e 2014.

in ninth century Sogdian texts from Dunhuang, China. The longer episode, which survives in a fragment from the British Library [Stein Ch. 00349, Or. 8212/81] and the Bibliothèque Nationale de Paris [Pelliot Sogdien 13], does not appear in the story that was included in the *Shahnameh* by Firdousi.[261] Further evidence was studied by Yutaka Yoshida who also found in a Sogdian fragmentary text the mention of Rustam and, even more interesting, the *synmry* (*simurgh*) whose characteristic was to be wise. This bird was previously attested in one unpublished Sogdian Buddhist text in place of *Garuda*.[262] This is an extremely interesting evidence since it could support the hypothesis that also in the Sogdian sphere, the *simurgh* was represented as a bird or, better, as a fantastic bird.

It soon appeared in the paintings of the Blue Hall that a main person was represented sequentially several times, always wrapped in a leopard skin and in profile. Since all the other human figures of that painted program are represented in three-quarter view, a parallel has been proposed with Hunnic coins where the unusual traits of king Mihirakula seem to be very close to the one of the supposed Rustam of Penjikent. Rustam features calling to mind those of Mihirakula are: big forehead, wide eyebrows, small mustache, a pointed chin and, possibly, the cranial deformation which has been practiced by the people of Central Asia since ancient times. One can consider at this point that the Alchons (who belonged to the so-called group of the "Iranian Huns") controlled those parts of Iranian lands that originally were under the Saka people and, as it is well-known, Rustam was an offspring of the Sakas.[263] Rustam's name could be translated as "strong as a river" and seems to have been transmitted in Sogdi-

261 Sims-Williams 1976. The Armenian author Grigor Magistros (990-1058) knew the *Shahnameh* and its epic heroes but reported summaries that did not correspond to the story by Firdousi: Tchukasizian 1964.

262 Lurje 2010, 360; Yoshida 2013, 206, 208, 211.

263 Marshak 2002b, 37-38.

an texts through the Persian language.[264] The most convincing element contributing to the identification of that painted program with Rustam's trials is the presence of the leopard skin. If the main character of room 41 paintings is actually Rustam, it is obvious to expect represented somewhere in his vicinity the *simurgh*.

A creature very similar to Trever's pseudo-*simurgh* is represented for the first time in Sogdian paintings at Penjikent, on the eastern wall of the northern chapel of Temple II, dated to the end of the fifth century CE.[265] In this fragmentary painting, it is still possible to observe the creature on one side of the throne supporting a deity usually called the "white goddess" (fig. 29). Thrones in the shape of animals that are also to be considered the vehicle or an attribute of the divinity sitting on it are very common in Sogdian art. Animal-protomes coming out from both sides of a divine throne can be observed in many other Sogdian paintings at Penjikent, Varakhsha and Kal'a-ye Kahkakha. However, in some cases, the divinities are sitting directly on the animal according to a style that shares many points of contact with Indian art, exactly as other Indian traits have started to have been adopted in the representation of Sogdian divinities since the sixth century.[266] For this reason the animal-shaped throne of Sogdian deities is usually called by its Sanskrit name, *vahana*. Despite some problems still to be solved in order to propose a precise identification of Sogdian deities, the study of those Indian elements can facilitate this entire process. Some Buddhist Sogdian texts where descriptions of the divinities can be found exist but they are not always completely clear.[267] According to Guitty Azarpay, the "white goddess" should

264 Sims-Williams, Sims-Williams 2015, 251-252.

265 Belenitskii, Marshak 1981, 70-71.

266 This is the case of another deity usually called the "red goddess" represented in the paintings of the niche of chapel 4-6, room 5 in Temple II at Penjikent (sixth century). The "red goddess" is sitting on a dragon shaped as an Indian *makara* and has four hands: Minardi 2016, 176-177; Mode 2019.

267 Compareti 2009a; Grenet 2010.

be a personification of the Zoroastrian Den who was described in Middle Persian texts as a woman with a dog.[268] On the other hand, for M. Shenkar and F. Grenet she is Anahita while the winged dog covered with scales (that, however, look like feathers) is a "water-dog" (*sag i abig*) of Middle Persian texts.[269]

Only the upper part of the animal in the northern chapel of Temple II survives. Its face is very similar to a dog although the fur is absent and, in its place, there are feathers like those on the visible wing. Such feathers could actually be scales. The other wing is partially covered by the body and only the longer final feathers can be observed. Behind the pointed ears, there is a little horn and on the cheek, a flower is represented in a stylized way. The little horn calls to mind a similar creature of Mesopotamian origins that can be observed quite often in the representations of the so-called "snake-dragon" or *mushhushshu* accompanying Marduk or Nabu (fig. 30).[270] Ancient Mesopotamian elements occurred quite often in late antique Iranian arts (Persian, Sogdian, Bactrian and Chorasmian) despite the long gap between the two periods. For example, Nana was the most venerated goddess in ancient Sogdiana and she had Mesopotamian origins.[271]

Mesopotamian and, specifically, Assyrian elements appear quite often in Achaemenid official art. A fragmentary Achaemenid gate ex-

268 Azarpay 2011.

269 Shenkar 2014, 78; Grenet 2020, 23.

270 Black and Green 1992, figs. 7, 31, 53, 76, 105, 110, 137, 159. Prudence Harper recognized Mesopotamian elements for the creation of the pseudo-*simurgh*: Harper 2006b, 73. A goddess sitting on a dragon appeared sometimes on Iranian metalwork such as on an eighth century Persian plate kept in the Metropolitan Museum (Harper 1972), the early Islamic northern Persian plate in the State Hermitage (Marschak 1986, fig. 184), and on the so-called Soltikoff Bactrian silver plate of the Bibliothèque Nationale (Grenet 2016). The horns of the dragon on the northern Persian and Bactrian plates and the little horn behind the pointed ears of the winged creature in the northern chapel of Temple II at Penjikent strongly suggest ancient Mesopotamian models.

271 Shenkar 2014, 116-128; Compareti 2017b.

cavated at Tul-i Ajori (approximately 3 km south of Persepolis) represents the main discovery of the Italo-Iranian expedition in the Marv Dasht. Images of a bull, a lion and *mushhushshu* in relief embellished that gate, which should have been very similar to the decorations on the famous Ishtar Gate from Babylon at present kept in Berlin.[272] It is obvious to consider this kind of fantastic creatures (and animals) as guardians of the gate with apotropaic functions.[273] It is not uncommon to observe in Mesopotamian religion and art the use of demons and fantastic creatures as helpers of the hero or deity who defeated them and, evidently, "domesticated" them against any future (supernatural) enemies. Such an use seems to be especially true in the case of the demon *Pazuzu* and the *mushhushshu*.[274]

It should not be ruled out that the composite creature under the throne of the deity in the northern chapel of Temple II at Penjikent is actually a *mushhushshu*-like dragon with horn and scales and not a winged dog. The similarities with our pseudo-*simurgh* could just be apparent. The lower part of the body of the winged (and horned) creature was not preserved so it is not possible to say whether this was exactly the pseudo-*simurgh* of Taq-i Bustan. In any case, Marshak identified the two creatures as the same being and, in his opinion, on the other side of the throne too another similar fantastic animal should have been represented.[275] Marshak hypothesis is corroborated by other depictions of deities sitting on thrones like this in Sogdian art although the identification of the winged composite creature under the throne of the "white goddess" at Penjikent Temple II (and the goddess herself) is quite obscure. In ancient Mesopotamian religion, the patron of scribes Nabu formed a divine couple with Nana and continued to be represented with his wife in Central Asian arts. The possibility that the "white goddess" in chapel 2/4-6, room 5 (period III) is not a female deity but

272 Callieri 2017.

273 Westenholz 2004, 68-69.

274 Heeßel 2011; Angelini 2018, 52-53.

275 Belenitskii, Marshak 1981, 70-71.

Nabu with his symbolic dragon should not be ruled out. Sogdian artists superimposed the image of local Tish (the Avestan rain god Tishtrya) to Nabu and transformed his stylus (a symbol of the scribes) into an arrow while the *mushhushshu* became similar to a dog that was another symbol of Tish. Also, the so-called "red goddess" should be identified as an image of Nabu whose aspect (and attributes) became more Indian in sixth century Penjikent (period IV). Both deities hold in the left hand a stick embellished with square decorations that could actually be the same attribute: an arrow? The same identification could be considered true for the deity in a feminine attire with a stick (arrow?) in one hand and sitting on a dragon on an eighth century Chorasmian bowl in the State Hermitage (acquisition number not indicated, see: Marshak 2000a). For some unclear reason, Tishtrya/Tish has been depicted as Greek Artemis on second century Kushan coins and, possibly, his feminine attire continued to persist in Sogdian and Chorasmian art until the Islamization of Central Asia. Feminine Tish and Nana appeared also in a ninth-tenth century paper icon from Dunhuang at present in the Bibliothèque Nationale de France (Pelliot Chinois 4518.24) where, however, the canine *mushhushshu* was omitted.[276]

A complete representation of that flying creature (our pseudo-*Simurgh*) in Sogdian paintings has been found at Afrasyab (fig. 31). It occurs among the textile decorations of one of the foreigners who is presenting gifts to the local king, possibly on the occasion of the *Nawruz* festivity. In this case, the creature is the same as at Taq-i Bustan.[277] Since the Afrasyab paintings appears to be dated around 660 CE, then

276 Compareti 2017b. For this reason, I think that the "twin temples" (I and II) at Penjikent were probably dedicated to Nana and Tish: Compareti forthcoming.

277 Compareti 2019a, 65-66. Markus Mode proposed to reconstruct an animal with open mouth and big fangs in a fighting scene at Afrasyab with a representation of the pseudo-*simurgh*: Compareti 2016c, 189. Unfortunately, it is not completely clear from which portion of the mural paintings at Afrasyab that fragment came from. It is however worth remembering that very few elements in Afrasyab paintings show fantastic creatures (such as the dragon under one boat in the aquatic scene on the northern wall): Compareti 2016c, 184-185.

the flying creature with a dog face completely represented there is the most ancient one in Sogdian paintings and almost contemporary with the Taq-i Bustan reliefs.

Other images of the pseudo-*simurgh* exist in Sogdian art such as on silver vessels (sometimes inscribed)[278] and possibly textiles.[279] However, in no case are those artifacts the result of controlled excavations and, so, every attribution should be considered highly hypothetical. The most interesting among these representations are those of some seventh century CE countermarks on Sasanian coins or Sasanian imitation coins used in Sogdiana. The counter-marks present a creature not completely clear but apparently very similar to the pseudo-*simurgh* (fig. 13). There is also a Sogdian inscription together with those images and it can be read as *prn* (*farn*).[280] Despite the similarities of the creatures in the countermarks and the pseudo-*simurgh*, Etsuko Kageyama observed that those countermarks are very small (less than 1 cm) and, for this reason, she expressed some doubts about very precise identifications.[281] Non-excavated pottery shards from Varakhsha (Bukhara) and Samarkand prove that stylized pseudo-*simurgh* countermarks continued to be used at least until the eleventh-twelfth century.[282]

Some further evidence could be found in Sogdian sfragistic. A large number of archaeologically excavated seal and seal-impressions from

278 According to Marshak, some of the silver vessels embellished with the figure of a pseudo-*simurgh* could be considered eastern Iranian and not necessarily Sogdian: Marschak 1986, figs. 22-23. All Sogdian or eastern Iranian metal objects embellished with the image of (or shaped as) a pseudo-*simurgh* were dated by Marshak to the seventh-eighth century. It is worth observing that, in his book on eastern metalwork (recently published in Russian), every metal object decorated with the image of a pseudo-*simurgh* was considered by Marshak to be a product of pre-Islamic or, sometimes, Islamic eastern Iran (Central Asia or Khorasan).

279 Compareti 2015; Compareti 2019a, 64.

280 Nikitin and Roth 1995.

281 Kageyama 2006, 321.

282 Shishkin 1963, fig. 10.4; Rempel' 1978, pl. 119.

the site of Kafir Kal'a (not far from Samarkand) present many decorations and inscriptions in Sogdian language. One seal-impression was embellished with the Sogdian inscription *prn* (*farn*) while in another one there is clearly a wild boar in front of a small tree. Just under the neck of the wild boar, scholars were able to read once more *farn*. For this reason, they assumed that the wild boar of that seal-impression could be a symbol of glory (fig. 32).[283] Other Sogdian seals and seal impressions present different kind of animals together with the inscription *farn*. One unique and highly enigmatic unexcavated golden seal kept in the State Hermitage Museum embellished with a person sitting on an elephant presents also the Sogdian inscription *prn βγγ* that could be translated as "god *farn*".[284] According to Pavel Lurje, this inscription does not seem to be referred to a personal name.[285] The male(?) figure sitting on the elephant is very big and has a dotted halo around his head. These characteristics would be very appropriate for a local deity (fig. 33).

There can be then little doubt that the Sogdians (and, in all probability, other ancient Iranian peoples as well) identified different kind of animals and composite creatures with representations of the glory or charisma that was necessary for a king to rule. This is not only because of a certain number of specimens in visual arts but as already mentioned above, because of the information that can be deduced in Middle Persian and Islamic texts. However, it should not be com-

283 Begmatov, Berdimurodov, Bogomolov, Murakami, Teramura, Uno, Usami 2020, 12. However, the Sogdian god Weshparkar who corresponded to the Avestan wind god Vayu (Bactrian Wesho) is represented on a chariot drawn by wild boars in a sixth century CE painting from the western portico of Temple I at Penjikent: Belenitskii, Marshak 1981: 43-44; Shenkar 2014, 154-155.

284 Belenitsky 1975, pl. 75.

285 Lurje 2010, 300. I wish to thank Pavel Lurje who informed me about another unpublished Sogdian seal with the image of a lion and the inscription *prn*. Pavel Lurje proposed the idea that those Sogdian seal impressions do not represent a personification of *farn* and, moreover, the inscriptions should not be considered as referred to the images accompanying them.

pletely ruled out the possibility that the inscription *farn* could be just a generic auspicious formula to be accompanied to animals, deities, or fantastic subjects that owners wanted to be represented on their seals or amulets without any associations with those images. As already observed above, the inscription *farn* can be found sometimes on Sogdian coins next to the bust of the king.[286] In this case, its association with kingship, legitimation, and divine protection is very clear.

In his study of epic images in Sogdian paintings, Marshak proposed some reconstructions of the extant parts of the painted program of the so-called Blue Hall at Penjikent whose entrance was originally located on the western wall. On the eastern wall, just in front of an observer who was entering the room, there was a colossal image of the goddess Nana sitting on a lion. Unfortunately, only small fragments of this divine image have been preserved.[287]

According to the reading of the painted program given by Marshak, the starting point should be located on the western wall, on the right of the entrance while the very final part should be on the left of the same entrance. Neither the beginning nor the final parts are preserved as well as some other sections and, for this reason, a complete reading of the entire program is impossible. The figure of Rustam can be identified at least six times along the entire painted program. He is wearing the leopard skin and his massive reddish horse can be identified with Rakhsh in the literary text. Several other people appear in the program but they are all in three quarter view while, as already observed, Rustam is always in profile and he has very peculiar facial traits. He should be considered the focus of all the scenes also because, sometimes, a composite creature is flying in front of him. As it has been already considered above, this is a way to exalt the main character of a scene in Sogdian paintings and, in few words, to facilitate the reading to an observer who could easily make a distinction between the hero and the villain of the story.

286 Smirnova 1981, nos. 1354, 1359.

287 Marshak 2002b, 28.

Typical Iranian ribbons attached to the flying composite creature can be observed as well in its inferior part. Ribbons pointed at the importance of the person or animal that they embellished and, in fact, they can be seen very often in Sogdian paintings and in Sino-Sogdian art as decorative elements of deities and their emanations: the composite creatures under exam. There is an obvious connection between the ribbons of Sogdian paintings and those in Sasanian rock reliefs although, some centuries earlier, these decorative elements already appeared on Kushan coins.[288]

Rock formations have been used by the artist (or the group of artists) who embellished the Blue Hall in order to separate one scene from another. On the corner between the northern and eastern walls there is a complex battle scene between humans and demons. Only the portion of the northern wall including the battle has survived but it is interesting to observe the half-human and half-animal demons fighting on foot or from a winged chariot. A bird is flying behind the demonic chariot and it is probable that it is a vulture attracted by the dead bodies. The beribboned flying creature was not preserved in this point but, in all probability, it was represented also here in front of the main hero.

At the very beginning of the eastern wall, Rustam is fighting with his bow against an adversary armed with a spear dangerously close to the hero's chest (fig. 34).[289] In front of Rustam there is the usual beribboned winged creature while behind him a bird stands on a small rock (fig. 35). Its attitude recalls those images of the *simurgh* in Islamic book illustrations that are not based on the iconography of the Chinese phoenix and will be considered below. We shall again consider this bird since, it is highly probable that this is just the *simurgh* that has appeared in this scene because that battle was a very dangerous one for Rustam.

288 Sinisi 2017, 850-851; Shenkar 2017, 63; Shenkar 2018.

289 Kulakova 2016.

The very end of the register is fragmentary and only partial scenes with one standing and kneeling person by a (metal?) container can be observed in the part close to the entrance on the western wall. It is very probable that the final scene of the hero's trials was going to take place in the presence of a giant yellow bird as some recent restorations by the personnel of the State Hermitage Museum have revealed (fig. 104).

Before proposing some parallels for those possible images of the *simurgh* in Sogdian art, an introduction to Omayyad art and Islamic book illustrations is necessary.

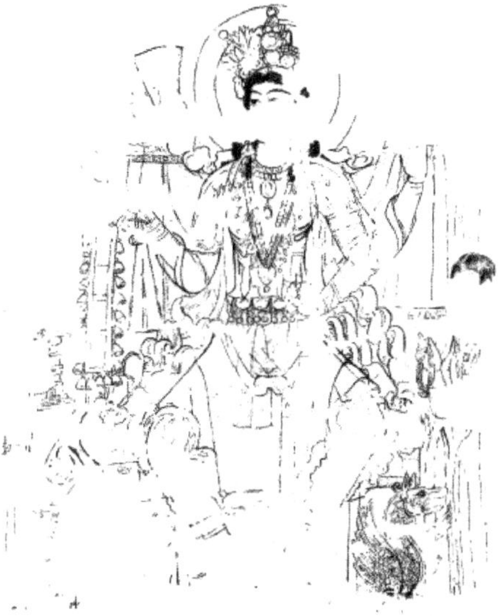

Figure 29. Tish on a throne supported by a canine *mushhushshu* in a Sogdian painting on the eastern wall of the northern chapel 4-6, room 5 of Temple II, Penjikent (end of the fifth century). The State Hermitage Museum, St Petersburg. Sketch after: Belenitskii, Marshak 1981, fig. 34.

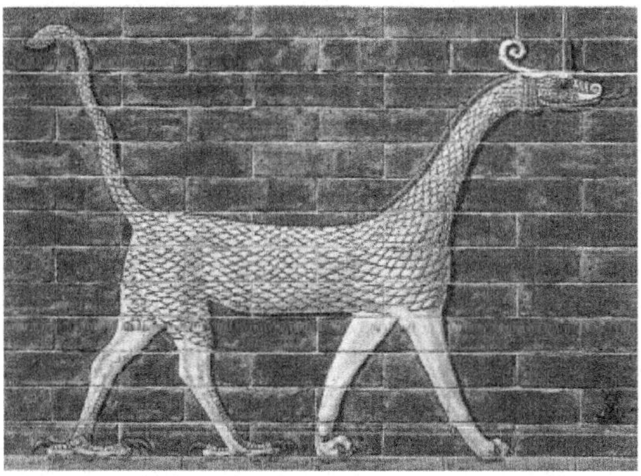

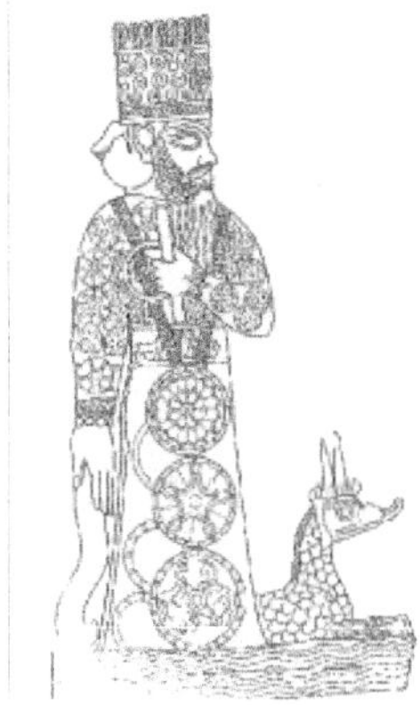

Figure 30a-b. Images of the snake-dragon in Mesopotamian art. Left: *mushhushshu* on the Ishtar Gate, Babylon (sixth century BCE). After: Harper 1961, fig. 6. Right: Marduk and the *mushhushshu* on a seal of the Babylonian king Marduk-zakir-shumi I (ca. 854-819 BCE). After: Black, Green 1992, fig. 105.

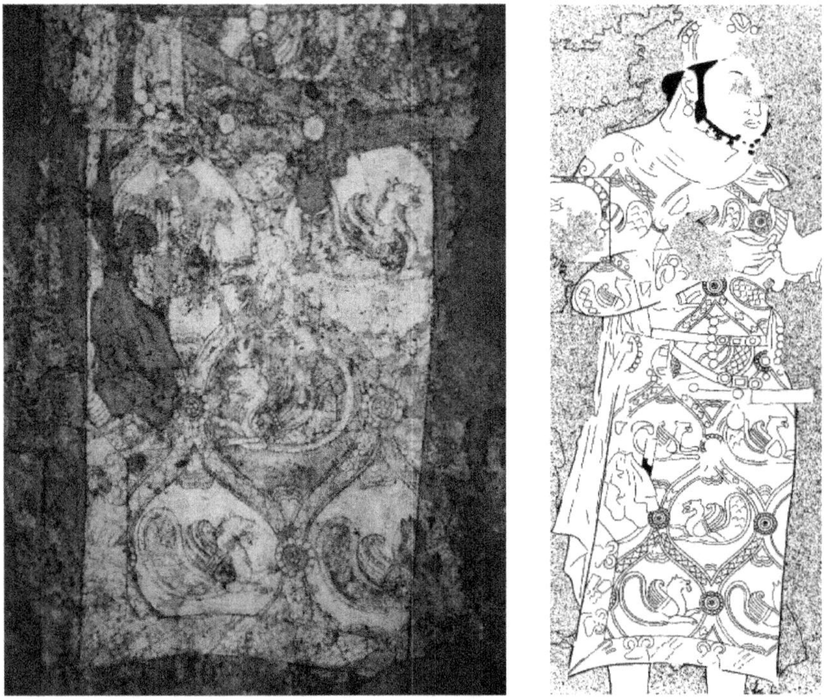

Figure 31a-b. Detail of the garment of a foreign envoy on a Sogdian painting on the western wall of the Hall of the Ambassadors, Samarkand (ca. 660). Photo: author. Sketch after: Belenizki, A. (1980). *Kunst der Sogden*. Leipzig, 14.

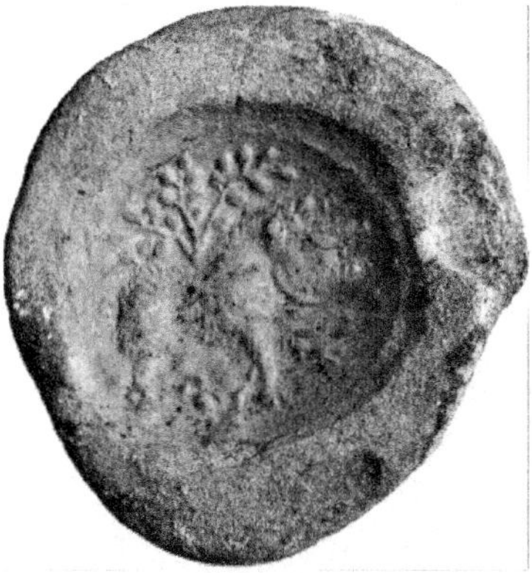 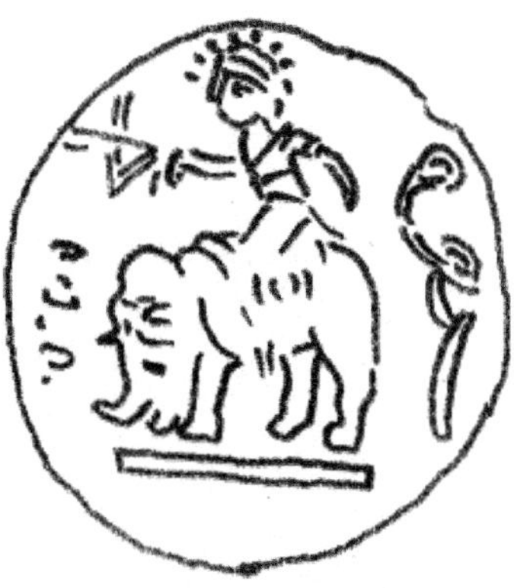

Figure 32. Seal-impression from Kafir Kal'a (Samarkand) with wild boar and Sogdian inscription *farn* "glory" (ca. seventh century). After: Begmatov, Berdimurodov, Bogomolov, Murakami, Teramura, Uno, Usami 2020, fig. 9b.

Figure 33. Unexcavated golden seal embellished with a haloed deity (?) on an elephant and the Sogdian inscription *prn βγy*. After: Belenitsky 1975, pl. 75.

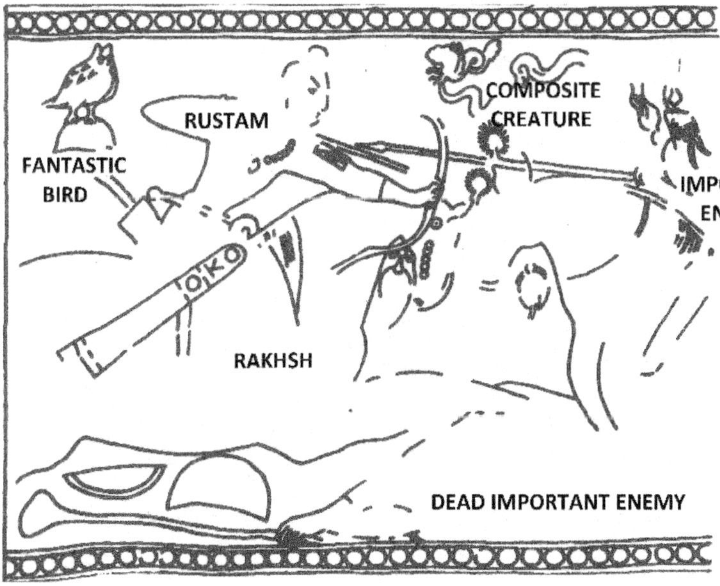

Figure 34. Rustam (left) fighting a powerful opponent, possibly Isfandyar (right) on the beginning of the eastern wall of room 41, sector VI "Blue Hall", Penjikent (ca. 740). The State Hermitage Museum, St Petersburg. After: Marshak 2002b, fig. 16 (modified).

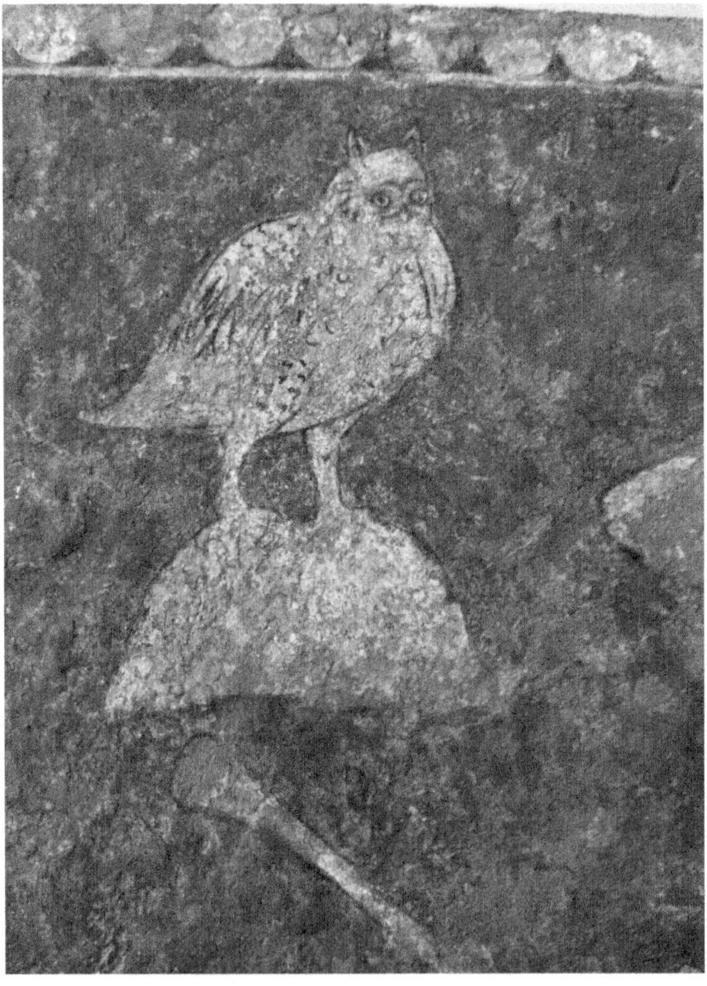

Figure 35. Detail of the "fantastic bird" in fig. 34. Photo: author.

2.5 The Omayyad Caliphate

It is not easy to identify precisely the phoenix (or, in Arabic, *'anqa*) in early Islamic art because birds represented one of the most popular subjects in the decoration of Omayyad and Abbasid palaces and buildings. Eared birds occur in stucco decorations in the Omayyad palace at Qasr al-Hayr al-Gharbi. One specimen at present kept in the National Museum of Damascus in a good state of preservation still presents a necklace and pearls of the visible wing which could suggest some kind of important symbolic animal.[290] Unfortunately, no inscriptions can reveal exactly if this was just a common bird or a fantastic bird. Only Islamic book illustrations in Arabic, Persian and, some time later, Turkish allowed scholars (or just general readers) to identify more easily animals, humans or entire scenes thanks to the written part that usually accompanied the images. Unfortunately, no illustrated manuscripts from the Omayyad and early Abbasid periods survived. Even in the case of inscriptions on early Islamic art objects such as silver vessels, textiles, seals (fig. 80) or coins (fig. 81), there is no clear correspondence between text and image.

Our pseudo-*simurgh* was definitely very popular in Omayyad art and played an important role for the new Islamic ruling class as a symbol of glory with possible apotropaic functions. Omayyad rulers wanted this (eastern) Iranian composite creature to be included in decorative friezes that embellished their buildings together with other fantastic animals such as griffins, tritons, centaurs, and others rooted in Greco-Roman traditions. It never appeared in mosques that, in any cases, did not preserve very complex decorations usually limited to geometrical and vegetal elements. It is worth observing, however, that pseudo-*simurgh*s were never part of the decorations of Zoroastrian religious buildings in Persia nor in Central Asia and the Caucasus. As already observed above, it was very popular among Christians who used it to embellish churches and precious ritual objects or reliquar-

290 Paribeni 2004, fig. 2.

ies. Scholars of Islamic studies have individuated architectonic elements that Omayyads borrowed from Sasanian Persia and not from Roman-Byzantine buildings of the Syrian-Palestinian region.[291] Most of these Persian elements find a precise parallel in Sasanian Mesopotamia that was much closer to Taq-i Bustan than other regions with important buildings such as Fars or Khorasan.

The pseudo-*simurgh* was an extremely popular motif that had already called the attention of the late Sasanians at Taq-i Bustan (fig. 11) and continued to be represented in Persian art of the early Islamic period. Stucco decorations of the region around modern Rayy included also one pseudo-*simurgh* from Nizamabad (fig. 36) and less fragmentary pseudo-*simurgh*s within pearl roundel frames from Chal Tarkhan-Eshqabad (fig. 37). While the fist specimen is at present kept in the Museum für Islamische Kunst (Berlin), stuccos from Chal Tarkhan are part of many museum collections around the world: National Museum of Iran, Philadelphia Museum of Art, Museum für Islamische Kunst, British Museum, Fine Art Institute, Chicago, and others. Investigations at both sites strongly suggest that these stucco decorations should be dated to the seventh-eighth century.[292] Should we assume that they were private mansions or religious constructions? Scholars do not agree on the use of the buildings at Nizamabad and Chal Tarkhan whose excavation did not continue for many seasons. This is particularly true for Chal Tarkhan as one scholar lamented.[293] If the absence of pseudo-*simurgh* could be considered as valid for mosques as for Zoroastrians temples, there could be then some little but extremely precious evidence to suggest a civil use for Nizamabad and Chal Tarkhan buildings. However, this is just a hypothesis that could be confirmed (or discarded) only when excavations will start again.

291 Ritter 2019.

292 Thompson 1976; Kröger 1982, 148-186.

293 Kröger 1990.

The pseudo-*simurgh* motif was as popular in Persia as it was in the rest of the Omayyad Caliphate. Even though it is not possible to propose very precise chronologies for most of Omayyad buildings, those embellished with pseudo-*simurgh* motifs were most probably erected in the first half of the eighth century in the core of the Caliphate that was the Syrian-Palestinian region. The palace of Khirbat al-Mafjar, not far from Jericho (Palestine) whose construction is attributed to the Caliph Hisham (724-743) was excavated during the years 1934-1948 and most of its remains are now kept in the Rockefeller Museum, Jerusalem.[294] Archaeologists found two kinds of pseudo-*simurgh*s in stucco and painted continuous friezes within interlacing medallions that call to mind typical frames of Greco-Roman art (fig. 38). Reconstructions of the paintings and researches in the archives of the Rockefeller Museum gave very interesting results.[295]

Other painted pseudo-*simurgh*s within pearl roundel frames appeared during the excavations of the palaces of Qasr al-Hayr al-Gharbi, Siria (fig. 39)[296] and Qasr al-Hallabat, Jordan (fig. 40).[297] It is worth observing that these two typical (eastern) Iranian motifs occurred combined together in Omayyad art. Many scholars kept for granted that both pseudo-*simurgh* and pearl roundel patterns represent Sasanian inventions while, as repeated many times in this study, such an assumption is probably incorrect. Not only their origin should be searched in Central Asia but their meaning too has been misunderstood for a long time.

Two more pseudo-*simurgh*s come from the territory of Jordan. Among the decorations of the façade of the Mshatta Palace there is also one pseudo-*simurgh* confronting a griffin beside a *kantharos* from which an intricate vegetal decoration sprouts without leaving any empty space. Some more plants come out from the mouth of

294 Hamilton 1959.

295 Da'adli 2019.

296 Schlumberger 1986, pl. 34-38, 40.b.

297 Bisheh 1993, fig. 7.

the composite creature (fig. 41). Associations between griffins and pseudo-*simurgh* was not unknown in medieval Europe.[298] The decoration of the Mshatta façade has entered the collection of the Museum für Islamische Kunst (Berlin) in 1903 after some works in the area of the international airport of Amman (30 km to the south of the Jordanian capital).[299]

The last specimen is also the most recently discovered one at the water basin of Azraq, 100 km to the east of Amman. Some blocks of basalt from this site discovered in the '80ies of the last century revealed several composite creatures in relief such as winged horses and one pseudo-*simurgh*. Most of them are kept in the Museum of Jordanian Heritage of the Yarmouk University in Irbid, in northern Jordan (fig. 42). The specimen from Azraq seems to be very stylized and it should not be ruled out that some parts were completed with paint or even stucco. On the chest of the creature, there is one unusual decoration that includes also a crescent.[300]

It is quite obvious that the Omayyads attached great importance to this motif as evidenced by its popularity in monumental art, coins and seals. During the Abbasid period, the pseudo-*simurgh* continued to enjoy widespread approval despite being found mainly on objects of luxury arts. These objects were found only in rare cases in archaeological contexts and, therefore, do not have the same relevance for this study. After an initial period of great popularity, for some enigmatic reason, this motif started to disappear in Islamic monumental arts. Despite the great number of fragmentary paintings reproducing humans, animals and, above all, birds, pseudo-*simurgh*s did not occur in one single instance in the paintings of Samarra (Iraq).[301] It is not clear if the decision to avoid it could be connected to the original meaning of the pseudo-*simurgh* that is, in our opinion, an expression

298 Eichert 2018, 117-118.

299 Enderlein, Meinecke 1992.

300 Bisheh 1986, pl. 14C.

301 Fontana 2002, 37-39; Hoffman 2008; Dahmani 2020.

of glory, charisma or even divine protection. It could have apotropaic functions too and, in fact, as it can be seen in the next part of this study, our composite creature had some role in the iconography of constellations and astrology/astronomy.

It should be admitted that this auspicious composite creature was very popular during the Omayyad period in the core of the Caliphate and Persia. Reproductions on Arabo-Sasanian coins from Fars attest its fortune and popularity. As remarked by R. Gyselen, Fars in the Omayyad period was "a cultural and religious melting pot" whose minting variety presented a completely different situation than during the Sasanian period.[302] Based on the few traces left in Sasanian art, the pseudo-*simurgh* must not have been a particularly favored motif in pre-Islamic Persia being attested only at the problematic site of Taq-i Bustan. That composite creature embellished the textile covering the legs of Khusraw II Parwiz represented as a mounted warrior on the back of the grotto. Since Khusraw II died in 628, it seems obvious to imagine that the pseudo-*simurgh* arrived in Persia before that date and, some time later, Omayyads represented it on their coins and palaces. The important late Sasanian site even embellished with precise decorative elements that possibly inspired Arab artists could be individuated just with Taq-i Bustan.

302 Gyselen 2009, 170.

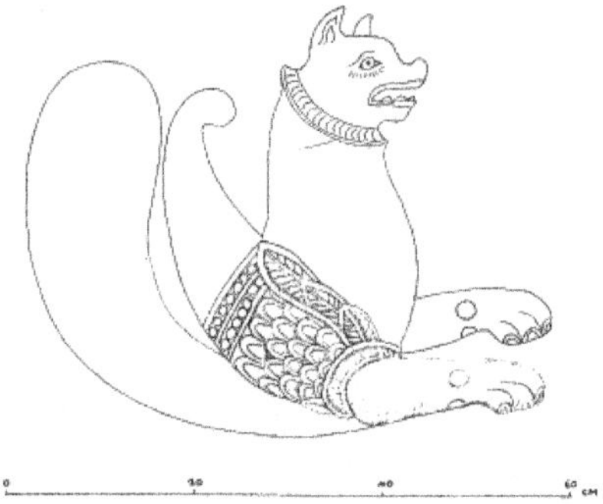

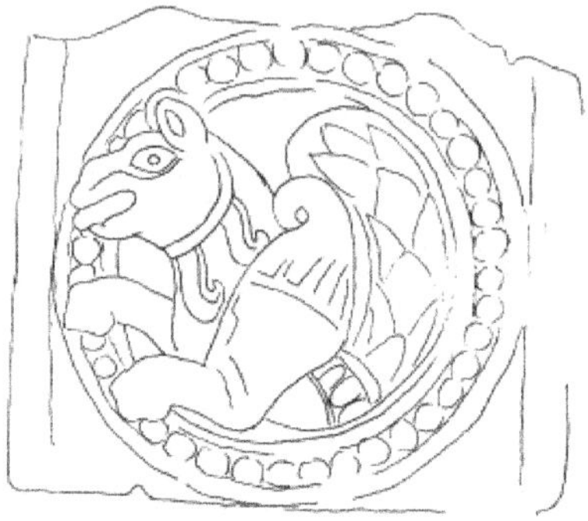

Figure 36. Fragmentary pseudo-*simurgh* in the stucco decoration from Nizamabad, Rayy (early Islamic period). Museum für Islamische Kunst, Berlin. After: Kröger 1982, fig. 114.

Figure 37. Pseudo-*simurgh* in a stucco frieze from Chal Tarkhan, Rayy (early Islamic period). The British Museum. Sketch: author.

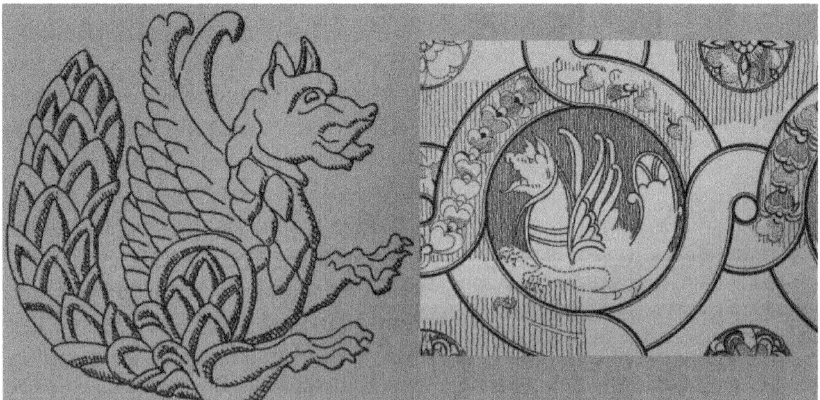

Figure 38a-b. Pseudo-*simurgh*s from Khirbat al-Mafjar, Palestine (first half of the eighth century). Stucco frieze on the left, reconstruction of a fragmentary painting on the right. The Rockefeller Museum, Jerusalem (Israel). After: Hamilton 1959, fig. 118, 253.

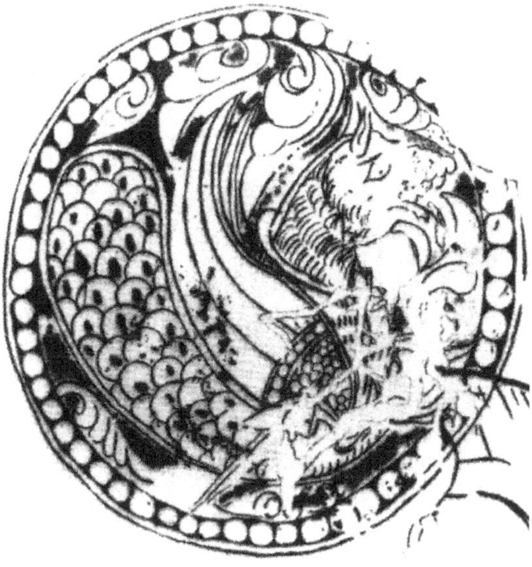

Figure 39. Painted pseudo-*simurgh* from the Omayyad palace of Qasr al-Hayr al-Gharbi, Syria (first half of the eighth century). National Museum of Damascus. After: Fontana 2002, fig. 9c.

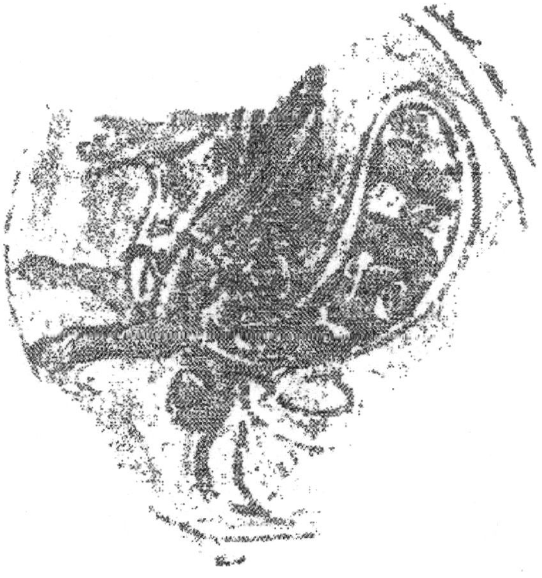

Figure 40. Painted pseudo-*simurgh* from the Omayyad palace of Qasr al-Hallabat, Jordan (first half of the eighth century). After: Fontana 2002, pl. 4.

Figure 41. Detail of the stone façade of the Mshatta Omayyad palace, Jordan (first half of the eighth century). Reconstruction panel at the Museum für Islamische Kunst, Berlin. Photo: author.

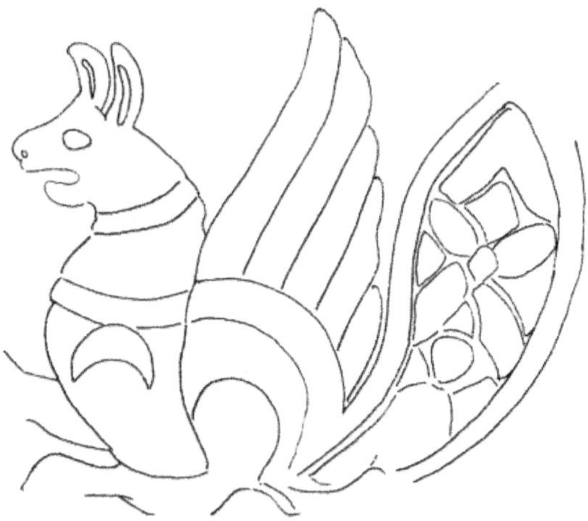

Figure 42. Fragmentary stone relief from the water basin of Azraq, Jordan (first half of the eighth century). Museum of Jordanian Heritage of the Yarmuk University, Irbid. Sketch after: Bisheh 1986, pl. 14C.

2.6 Islamic book illustrations

Most manuscripts of the *Shahnameh* also had some illustrated parts and, as it is well-known, the *simurgh* is usually represented as a Chinese *fenghuang* (usually translated as phoenix). It is very likely that this adaption process was defined during the Ilkhanid period (1256-1353) when many other Chinese elements entered into Persian art and especially in the field of book illustrations. Chinese art of the Song period (960-1279) had a great impact on Islamic Persian book illustrations. Decorative elements include parts of the landscape (trees, clouds, flowers, and mountains) but also fantastic animals such as the phoenix (*fenghuang*) and dragon (*long*).[303] Another imported element might be the way of representing some Islamic angels that looks as if their wings were attached directly onto their arms.[304] This might be another detail adopted from Chinese art and, more precisely, from the iconography of the immortals who sometimes had wings attached to their arms and in other cases on their back.[305]

The first image of a *simurgh* in a Persian book illustration is in a manuscript *Manafi'-i hayawan* "The Benefits of Animals", at present preserved in the Pierpont Morgan Library in New York [M.500] which is dated 1297-1300.[306] One note in Arabic on the margin of

303 Rawson 1984, 146-200; Sims 2002, 41-50; Grube 2006, 71-79; Kuehn 2011, 215-228. Images of dragons and phoenixes reproduced according to Chinese models (*long* and *fenghuang*) did not appear only in Mongol illustrated manuscripts but also in tile revetments of the summer royal palace of the Ilkhanid sovereign Abaqa (1265-1282) at Takht-i Sulayman (Western Azerbaijan, Iran): Gierlichs 1993, figs. 11, 37-38; Masuya 2002, 84-103; Gierlichs 2005; Kadoi 2017, 641-642. Fantastic birds represented according to Chinese models were also very popular motifs on painted ceramics from the Islamic world in general such as in the case of a fourteenth century fragmentary painted bowl from Egypt in the Benaki Museum (Athens): Philon 1980, cat. 209.

304 Blair 2002, fig. 133.

305 Elisseeff 2011, 77.

306 Schmitz 1997, fig. 26; Hillenbrand 2002, 141-143. According to L. Rempel', a twelfth century Persian bronze casket at present kept in the Samarkand Museum

the page identifies the bird as *'anqa*, that is phoenix in Arabic. The *simurgh* of the Pierpont Morgan Library manuscript is not flying but, in any case, its iconography is definitely rooted in Chinese art since it has the aspect of the Chinese phoenix/*fenghuang* (fig. 43). From around the same period (ca. 1300), is the image of a standing *simurgh* from the British Library [Or. 14140, fol. 122v] in the so-called "London Qazwini" manuscript, whose only Chinese-style element is the tail (fig. 44).[307] That *simurgh* looks more like a rooster and in fact, the illustrations of the two birds in that same manuscript are very similar with regard to the tail and comb.[308] Some other specimens in Ilkhanid *Shahnamehs* present very similar peculiarities.[309] Another manuscript of *'Aja'ib al-mahluqat wa ghara'ib al-maujudat* "The Wonders of Creation and the Oddities of Existence" by Zakarya ibn-Muhammad ibn-Mahmud al-Qazwini, copied in Farsi in 1322 and kept at present in Istanbul Süleymaniye Library [MSS Yeni cami 813, fol. 166a], presents a similar image of the *'anqa* as an owl (fig. 45).[310] This iconography was a constant in the art of Persian book illustrations, but for a small number of specimens that share all the same provenance (Fars, Isfahan or, possibly, Mesopotamia), and all should be dated between the 1430s and the 1450s. Chronologically and geographically, these illustrated manuscripts can be attributed to the Inju'id court.

The Inju'id Dynasty (ca. 1325-1353) was created in Fars by Iranized Muslim Mongols when the Ilkhanids started to lose control

---

at the site of Afrasyab includes among its decorations also the image of a bird of prey transporting a person that could be actually the earliest representation of Zal and the *simurgh*: Rempel' 1987, 140-141. No inscription on the casket can confirm the identification of Rempel'.

307 Schmitz 1997, 21, figs. 26-27.

308 Carboni 2015, figs. 5.29, col. 74. Another fourteenth century copy of the *Manafi'-i hayawan* at present kept in the El Escorial, Madrid [893] presents very similar characteristics for the image of the pheasant (folio 79 R): Ruiz Bravo-Villasante 1980, fig. 17.

309 Simpson 1979, figs. 1-3.

310 Berlekamp 2011, fig. 29.

of their wide territory. Maria Swietochowski and Stefano Carboni have collected a good number of Inju'id book illustrations including non-Chinese *simurghs*. They found such a typology of *simurgh* both in *Shahnamehs* and in other Persian literary works such as the *Mu'nis al-ahrar* or "The Free Men's Companion to the Subtleties of Poems". The two authors realized that the iconography of those fantastic birds (undoubtedly identifiable as *simurghs* because of the text that accompanied the images) should have been rooted in another tradition whose result was something quite different than the Chinese *fenghuang,* more similar to a rooster, a parrot or an owl.[311] Swietochowski and Carboni's idea concerning the image of the *simurgh* in this group of illustrated manuscripts is definitely correct and it would be extremely interesting to find some more evidence in pre-Islamic arts in order to support their theory.

The first two specimens studied by Swietochowski and Carboni are part of a poetical book in Persian (*Mu'nis al-ahrar*) whose pages are preserved in different museums: two pages with the *simurgh* respectively in the Cleveland Museum of Art [45.385] (fig. 46) and the Freer Gallery of Art [46.14 B] (fig. 47). It mentions several animals and also the *simurgh* that is represented as a mixture of different birds such as a rooster and a parrot. A bird more similar to a rooster appears in an illustration from a *Shahnameh* in the Berlin Staatsbibliothek [Diez Album, Fol. 71, S. 7], representing the birth of Rustam (fig. 48). Zal is shown while sitting next to an incense burner that he just used to evoke the *simurgh*, and Rudabeh, his wife, is going to give birth behind a curtain attended by four women. The *simurgh* is represented on the left and is not completely shown, although Zal is speaking to it in order to receive instructions on how to perform a caesarean for Rudabeh. This illustration is almost unique in early Islamic book illustrations since, usually, the *simurgh* is represented in the scenes of the rescue of Zal by his father Sam. Swietochowski and Carboni collected a couple of interesting book illustrations con-

311 Swietochowski, Carboni 1994.

cerning this precise episode: the first is preserved in the St Petersburg State Public Library [ex Dorn 329] (fig. 49) and the second one is in the Metropolitan Museum of Art from an illustrated *Shahnameh*, known as the "Gutman Manuscript" (fig. 50). An illustration from the so-called "Stephens *Shahnameh*" in the Nasser D. Khalili Collection of Islamic Art [MSS 920r] precisely dated 1352-1353 presents the scene of the birth of Rustam.[312] Despite the short interval between the execution of the illustrations in the Berlin Staatbibliothek and the "Stephens *Shahnameh*" (less than twenty years), the style of the latter manuscript is completely different and no *simurgh* appears at all.

Two additional illustrations from *Shahnameh* pages executed in early fourteenth-century Shiraz, and not published by Swietochowski and Carboni, should be mentioned. One is in the Kuwait National Museum, the al-Sabah Collection [LNS 36 MS] (fig. 51);[313] the other is part of the "Stephens *Shahnameh*" [folio 24r] (fig. 52).[314] The latter illustration is particularly interesting because the *simurgh* has two feathers or horns on the top of its head like in the one in the St Petersburg State Public Library manuscript. In all these illustrations, the *simurgh* does not present Chinese characteristics such as the articulation of the wing and tail feathers and it is never represented as flying in the air. In fact, in Islamic book illustrations, the *simurgh* is usually flying, although, in some early cases, there is another kind of bird that is not flying whose iconography was rooted in Chinese art, as can be observed in the one preserved in the Pierpont Morgan Library. As will be shown below, the non-flying position is of great importance in correctly identifying the *simurgh* in the painted program of Rustam at Penjikent.

Another aspect of the iconographical complexity related to the *simurgh/'anqa* in Islamic traditions deserves further discussion. In the Islamic period, the phoenix was also translated with a specific

312 Stewart, Mistree 2013, cat. 114.

313 Berlekamp 2007, figs. B, E.

314 Sims 2013.

term in Arabic and Persian: *samandar*, clearly from "salamander."[315] As is well known, this animal was commonly associated in alchemy with the element fire and the igneous symbol of the phoenix. Also in Medieval Europe, the salamander was considered to be the only animal that could survive fire and not suffer any harm.[316] Already in the first century CE Pliny the Elder mentioned the salamander several times, yet it seems that he did not believe in the association of this animal with the element of fire. In one passage of his *Naturalis Historia* [XXIX, 23], Pliny explicitly says that the "magi" (Oriental priests) transmitted the information about the salamander and its capacity to extinguish fire.[317] Jewish legends mentioned the salamander together with a mysterious *shamir* and both had connections with fire.[318] In Persian legends, preserved only in Islamic texts, the powerful Sasanian king Khusraw II Parwiz had a kind of garment "called *adersheb* that was woven with hairs of salamanders".[319] No doubt the equation of *samandar*/ *'anqa* became popular during the Islamic period because of the association of both creatures with fire and the use of Arabic language.

At least one scholar of Classical art has associated Medusa with the salamander since a small animal looking like a lizard appears quite often in Greek art when the myth of Perseus or the *gorgoneion* alone

315 Other variants of this term were *samand* and *samandal*: Dozy 1877-1881, 687; Laufer 1915, 318-323. This myserious animal was considered to live on the very enigmatic Islands of Waqwaq: Laufer 1915, 321.

316 Scarcia, Vercellin 1970; Cristoforetti 2003, 321.

317 Laufer 1915, 317, 339.

318 Ginzberg 1995, 49-50.

319 Mohl 1842, 128. This story probably referred to the asbestos. One century after the anonymous author of the *Mojmal*, Marco Polo [XLVIII] wrote that the "salamander" was not an animal but a kind of stone that Central Asian people excavated like lapis lazuli and woven like wool: Laufer 1915, 325-327. Some Chinese sources of the Tang period use the term "fire hair" to mean asbestos that was considered to be obtained from salamander wool. It was usually a gift from Persia and this could explain the use of the name "fire hair": Schafer 1963, 199.

was represented (fig. 53). He expressly stated that "the salamander over Medusa is a solar allusion".[320] It is not possible to decide if this was an arbitrary deduction. In fact, that paper does not shed any light on the "solar" aspect of the salamander or Medusa. The only possible "solar allusion" in the case of the salamander would be its association with the phoenix which is, however, not specified by that author. Possibly Frothingham had some knowledge of previous studies about the salamander and its association with the phoenix in Europe during the Middle Ages whose origin, in a first instance, is from Islamic lands. Mentions of wonderful lands beyond the "sea of England and Ireland" can be found in medieval legends describing also birds that were born from a ray of light and are called salamanders.[321] In more recent times, another scholar preferred to identify this animal with a common lizard (although sometimes called also gecko or newt, the latter being a kind of aquatic salamander) which was possibly represented together with Perseus killing Medusa, or in other scenes just as an allusion "to the realm of the weird, the eerie, the supernatural".[322] It is however evident that two animals resembling lizards were represented sometimes symmetrically alongside the *gorgoneion* like a fixed iconographic subject or in mythological scenes where nothing supernatural appeared. In other images, that little animal seems to be eating a fly or other insect and, in so doing, it seems to give a completely natural touch to the scene and represents nothing supernatural at all.

Some confusion persists about the reason for its representation in medieval Europe. For example, the grave of a Byzantine princess married to a French nobleman precisely dated to 1286 found in Greece also presents salamanders combined with peacocks and the cross. The scholar who studied it was not able to give a convincing explanation for the salamander and preferred to insist on its presumed resistance

320 Frothingham 1911, 374.

321 Laufer 1915, 323-327; Carboni 1988, 87.

322 Hurwit 2006, 132. See also: Krauskopf 1988, fig. 272.

to fire, in this case to infernal fire.[323] However, the combination of this animal with the peacock could be more precisely considered an allusion to immortality because of the association of the salamander with the phoenix. The peacock itself could be just another way to represent the phoenix and, in fact – as already observed above – they both represent a symbol of immortality, incorruptibility, and resurrection. Other examples could be observed in Islamic sources and art, possibly to explain this problematic point.

In Persian, *samand* means "horse" or, more accurately, "steed". This is another element that contributed to the confusion over the representation of the phoenix, which began to be described as a horse or, better, a Pegasus. According to one Islamic legend, the Prophet Muhammad himself saw a pillow belonging to his wife that was decorated with winged horses and hysterically began to laugh to the point that he was going to die.[324] This could clarify the genesis of both the wings of the horse and the Islamic *topos* of a terror causing such an irrepressible laughter as might result in death: the re-reading of the both tragic and "vaginal" myth of the Gorgon Medusa/Baubo who gave birth to Pegasus from her beheaded neck.[325] Even if it is not expressly stated in any written source, it is highly probable that Medusa did not only petrify people but she could also provoke such strong laughter in whoever looked at her monstrous face (vagina) to cause his death. Hence, the Islamic Pegasus is renamed as *samandar*, that is phoenix, but it also superimposes its own image onto the functions

---

323 Vanderheyde 2012.

324 Noja 1983.

325 Vernant 2014, 40-41. According to some ancient traditions, which became quite common in the Middle Ages and the Renaissance period, the Pegasus became the transport of Perseus who started to be confused with Bellerophon. There could have been a parallel not only between these two heroes but also the monstrous creatures that they defeated, the chimera and *ketos* that was connected to Medusa: Pugliara 1998. Among the big number of Central Asian statuettes in different materials that have been found during archaeological excavations, one could mention one single glass pendant in the typical shape of Baubo from Merv: Simpson 2004.

of the *simurgh* in Turco-Iranian legends. In the Middle Persian text *Ayadgar i Zareran* "Memorial of Zareran" [ch. 84], the protagonist's horse is called *sen*, that is Avestan *saena*, undoubtedly our *simurgh*.[326] As observed by G. Scarcia fifty years ago, the identification between the salamander and a flying horse is extremely clear in the definition of *semenda* (*samandar*), pertaining to the "extreme borders of India" as reported by Niccolò De' Conti (1395-1469): that Far East where the phoenix/*semenda* is inextricably connected with both the winged horse and music. The form normally read in Persian *samand-i aslar* points at the monster that kills itself after looking at its own image. According to Scarcia, the name should be corrected to *samanda* (horse) *salar* (bird) which is not graphically distinguished in Arabic letters.[327]

No image of the Pegasus/*samandar* survives in Islamic book illustrations although one page of the early fifteenth century *Kitab al-bulhan* "Book of wonders" [Bodleian Library, Oxford, MS. Bodl. Or. 133] also presents the *Al qawl 'ala jabal al-nar wa tayr samandar* "Discussion on the mountain of fire and the salamander-birds".[328] The birds mentioned in the text do not present fantastic peculiarities but it is clear that they can survive on the mountain of fire exactly like the phoenix and, for this reason, they could have been confused with the salamander (*samandar*), the animal commonly associated with the igneous element in the ancient world (fig. 54). Pegasus-like animals and demons appear quite often in Islamic illustrated manuscripts. For example, the *faras al-ma'* (hippopotamus) in the London Qazwini of the British Library [Or. 14140] is not depicted as an "aquatic steed" but as a galloping spotted Pegasus.[329] Greek astronomical treatises in-

326 Pagliaro 1927, 15.

327 Scarcia, Vercellin 1970, 45; Scarcia 1979, 92-106.

328 Carboni 1988, fol. 42v.

329 Carboni 2015, fig. 5.13. There is a very clear connection between the Pegasus and water because, according to the myth, the winged horse could cause fountains to flow wherever it stomped the earth with its hoof.

cluded also a constellation dedicated to Pegasus which later appeared in the illustrated Arabic and Persian texts as well.[330]

In some Turco-Iranian legends, there is also the story of a hero who is transported by the *simurgh* (or *kuknos*)[331] to the land of the "mountains of fire." In order to pass them without burning, he has to cover his body with the fat of the *samandar*, described as a winged horse.[332] According to Scarcia, this odd creature that killed people or other animals just by looking at them, could even kill itself with laughter just by looking at its image in a mirror.[333] This is another echo of the Greek myth of Medusa. Something similar occurred in the history of the construction of the lighthouse of Alexandria that was constantly boycotted by aquatic monsters and demons. Alexander the Great was able to get rid of them by submerging a portrait of those demons into the water, thus causing their flight.[334] Mas'udi spoke of their images in iron, leather, and stone on some pillars by the shore, to be used to frighten those monsters that could not bear the sight of their own images.[335]

There are at least two Turkish book illustrations reproducing a hybrid human-headed snake looking in the mirror that a man is holding in front of it. One of them is dated ca. 1582 [suppl. turque 242, fol. 90v] and it is at present kept in the Pierpont Morgan Library, New York (fig. 55).[336] The second illustration [M.788, fol. 89v] is dated to

330 Wellesz 1959, figs. 30, 50, 60.

331 This is obviously the Greek *kúknos* that was rendered in Latin as *cycnus* or *cygnus*, English "swan". 'Attar described it as an Indian bird with a beautiful voice that died and resurrected in the same way of the phoenix: Contadini 2005, 97. Aeschylus described the Graeae to be swans [*Prometheus bound*, 790]. As it is well-known, the Graeae were sisters of the Gorgons.

332 Melikoff 1962, 37-39, 42. According to Jewish legends, the blood of the salamander protects from fire: Ginzberg 1995, 49-50.

333 Scarcia 2003, 20.

334 Miquel 1988, 99-101.

335 Di Branco 2011, 84.

336 Schmitz 1997, 83.

the same period and is kept in the Bibliothèque Nationale de France, Paris (fig. 56).[337] In both miniatures, Medusa has been substituted by a giant snake whose head could be one of a woman, as is suggested by her long hair. In the upper part of both illustrations there is also a label identifying them as *Shekl-i mar-i qahqaha va ayne* "the laughing snake and the mirror". Although textual descriptions are completely absent, the "laughing snake" could be associated with Zahak, another (male) serpentine heckler or mocker of Iranian legends that was rooted in more ancient Indo-Iranian myths[338]. The female creature in the book illustrations preserves all her negative nature and, in fact, she is threatening humans as symbolized by a walled city in the background. For this reason, a man, part of a group of people, approaches her holding the mirror to prevent her assault. It seems obvious to expect that the human-headed snake would die or run away after looking at her image in the mirror since her aspect could cause her (to laugh herself to) death. Also the idea of killing others with one's gaze presents some connections with serpentine monsters such as Medusa or the basilisk[339] but it emerges later in recent Slavic legends, possibly also rooted in more ancient Indo-Iranian myths.[340]

337 Stchoukine 1966, pl. 46.

338 Schwartz 2012. On Iranian legends connecting Medusa to Zahak and the description of Zahak as including two snakes or/and horns, see: Vercellin 1973. Part of Zahak's haloed head with a snake on the right shoulder is represented in one sixth century Sogdian mural painting from the northwestern corner of the portico of the principal hall of Temple I, at Penjikent: Belenitskii, Marshak 1981, 67-69. If confirmed, this painting would be the most ancient representation of Zahak.

339 Carboni 1988, 109. According to Lucanus [*Pharsalia* IX, 724-726], the basilisk was born from a drop of blood that fell from the bag (*kibisis, kibisos*, etc.) where Perseus kept Medusa's head while flying over the Lybian desert. Its connection with kings (Greek *basileus*) is preserved in Pliny's *Naturalis Historia* [VIII, 33], where it is described as the white spot in the shape of a crown on its head. The basilisk acquired many characteristics that are more "gorgonic" during the medieval period. According to medieval legends, Alexander the Great himself would have defeated a basilisk using a mirror since that creature had a deadly gaze like Medusa: Borniotto 2004-2010.

340 Pistoso 1974; Scarcia 2018, 45.

Creatures with deadly gazes are well-known in Islamic literature too and are not necessarily connected with snakes. Birds present in some cases the peculiarity that, in any case, could be considered another reflection of Medusa's (offspring) myth. Islamic bestiaries (*Manafi'-i hayawan* and *'Aja'ib al-mahluqat*) reported interesting stories about a magic animal called *suryanas* (siren) or *arghun*, that was sometimes described as a sea bird with a long beak in which there are holes from which to produce a wonderful music. This melody was so pleasant that it rendered those who listen unable to move. However, that same sound had healing properties. It is worth noticing that in his Arab text almost completely devoted to strange creatures, *'Aja'ib al-mahluqat*, Qazwini expressely reported that the *suryanas* lived in the region of Kabul and Zabulistan.[341] Such characteristics call to mind both the deadly gaze of Medusa, the magic songs of the half-bird half-woman Greek sirens, and the feathers of the Iranian *simurgh*. Curiously enough, Islamic authors still considered the sirens as magic birds although, as pointed out by other scholars, seventh-eighth century medieval European texts already described them as women with a fish body.[342]

In the same text, Qazwini introduces the *'anqa* (phoenix) as a peculiar and exclusive animal that shares some characteristics with other fantastic creatures. In the part dedicated to the *'anqa*, he also refers to the animal called *sannaja*, which is even more fantastic than the giant bird, having been classified under the chapter on *Insects and Creeping Animals*, while at the same time being "the largest animal on earth".[343] The *sannaja* is a beast that no one has ever seen, living

341 Contadini 2005, 94-95. As already observed above, the *simurgh* too has a special relation with music: During 1988-89; Scarcia 2003, 7-10. When Zal died, the *simurgh* sadly shouted from the top of a mountain in eastern Iran: Scarcia 2003, 17. Curiously enough, when Saint Jerome translated the word *tannin* in the Bible, he used the term *sirenas* [*Isaiah* 13, 22] and, on another occasion, *dracones* [*Isaiah* 43, 20]: Vercellin 1973, 110, n. 9.

342 Faral 1953; Zambon 2018, XXII.

343 Berlekamp 2011, 106-115.

in the mountains of Tibet and reminiscent of both the Abominable Snowman and Greek Medusa.[344] Its colossal size could call to mind also the description of the *behemoth* in Jewish legends. In fact, the *behemoth* was the largest animal on earth, while the *ziz* was the largest bird, and the *leviathan* the largest aquatic creature.[345] Strangely enough, the *sannaja* can be represented as a kind of bear or something like a turtle with obvious vaginal traits, but also as an animal resembling a (winged?) horse.[346]

In the mystical treatise *'Aql-i sorkh* "The Red Intellect" by Shihab al-Din Sohravardi (twelfth century), there is an interesting description of the famous battle between the eastern Iranian hero defender of old tradition Rustam and the champion of Zoroastrianism, Isfandyar. According to this story, Zal knew that anyone who looked at the reflection of the *simurgh* in a mirror would be dazed and, for this reason, he had the armour and helmet of his son Rustam thoroughly polished. Later, Zal had the *simurgh* passing before these weapons. During the battle, Isfandyar was dazed by Rustam's armour. He thought he was wounded in the eyes and, as a result, he died.[347] This episode does not appear in Islamic book illustration nor in the earlier representation of Rustam's trials in Sogdian paintings from Penjikent. However, if the *simurgh* is identified with the phoenix that in the Islamic world can be confused with the salamander and Pegasus, then it seems quite obvious that all these legends deal with Medusa's deadly gaze that was eventually transmitted to her equine son.

In the Rustam painted program at Penjikent (room 41, sector VI) there is another representation of a battle, although this time the hero

344 Carboni 2015, 81.

345 Ginzberg 1995, 44-46; Batto 1999; Kulik 2009. In one thirteenth century illustrated Jewish manuscript kept in the Biblioteca Ambrosiana in Milan [MS B 32 inf., fol. 136r], the three animals appear in the upper part of the page, the most interesting iconography being the one of the *ziz* that is reproduced as a griffin: Angelini 2018, 75-76.

346 Berlekamp 2011, figs. 52, 56.

347 Yarshater 1998, 588.

is fighting a half-human monster with snake body and tail (fig. 57). In the sequence there is a missing frame since Rustam is going to be swallowed by the monster on the left and, on the right, he is moving forward while the human snake is lying on the ground already dead. Pavel Lurje has suggested that the missing frame should have been the killing of the monster from inside of its belly that the hero cut with the weapon he holds in his right hand behind his back in the first part of the sequence.[348] This hypothesis seems to be corroborated by the numerous wounds on the body of the monster from where fire, and not blood, is erupting. Monsters and specifically snake-like giant creatures and dragons with poison instead of blood were created by the demoness Tiamat and the abyss Apsu in order to form a demonic army to fight Marduk in the Babylonian epic poem *Enuma Elish* "When on high" [1, 136]. Three names of dragons in the army of Tiamat appear in the poem: *ushumgallu*, *bashmu*, and *mushhushshu*.[349] It is not possible to demonstrate that the snake ogress in Penjikent paintings was connected to Tiamat's offspring although, in the light of other Mesopotamian elements in Sogdian culture and art, the association does not seem completely out of place.

The story of the hero swallowed by a monster (usually a giant sea creature or a dragon) represents a very well-known *topos* in world mythology: it can be found in ancient Greece (in the story of Heracles or Perseus) as well as in the Bible and the Christian world.[350] Curiously enough, under further examination, the third trial of Isfandyar, as described in the *Shahnameh*, represents a possible parallel with the scene depicted at Penjikent. In that story, Isfandyar is swallowed by a drag-

348 Lur'e 2014.

349 Bottéro, Kramer 1989.

350 Propp 1949, 343-446. On Greek demigods who killed monsters aftr being swallowed, see: Angelini 2018, 134-136. Saint Margaret was able to open the belly of the dragon that swallowed her with a cross used as a knife as reported by Jacobus de Varagine [*Legenda Aurea* XII, XCIII]. A very similar story can be found in one (Manichaen?) fable in Sogdian language where the name of the giant fish, Kar, refers to the Avestan *kara- masya-*: Provasi 2008, 129-130.

on, but is able to defeat the monster by cutting its belly open from inside. Rempel' has already noted this curious similarity between the two Iranian dragon slayers, and Azarpay considered that dragon fighter as not connected to any specific hero.[351] In the painting of the Blue Hall at Penjikent, however, the hero wears panther skin garments typical of Rustam – not of Isfandyar, his fiercest enemy.

From an iconographical point of view, the snake demon at Penjikent does not present any clear parallel with illustrations of the trials of Rustam or Isfandyar, as are sometimes included in *Shahnameh* manuscripts. In fact, when those heroes are represented as fighting with snake dragons in Islamic book illustrations, the iconography of the monster is usually the Chinese *long*, a serpent-like creature imprecisely rendered as "dragon" in Western literature. Few dragons in Islamic book illustrations present non-Chinese traits. One example is represented by the illustrations of the *Shahnameh* dated 1333 in the State Public Library at St Petersburg [ex Dorn 329].[352] In some cases, the iconography of dragons in that manuscript appears as an unusual mixture of Chinese and non-Chinese elements which shows a possible attempt to change from more ancient stylistic formulae into more "fashionable" imported elements from the Far East.[353] Such surviving specimens of non-Chinese dragons in Islamic paintings are extremely interesting and would deserve a study apart. They are probably among the very few examples of traditions that were going to be abandoned soon to favour Chinese taste and fashion. Even for fantastic animals that were not usually described in translations of the Bible as dragons, such as in the case of the biblical episode of Moses transforming the stick of Aaron into a snake in front of the Pharaoh [*Exodus* 7, 9-12], Muslim artists opted sometimes for a composite creature resembling the Chinese *long*. This is what one can observe in a fourteenth century illustrated Bal'ami's *Tarjama-ye Tarikh-i Tabari* "Translation of the

351 Rempel' 1987, 136; Azarpay 1981, 96-97.

352 Adamova, Giuzalyan 1985, figs. 39, 41.

353 Adamova, Giuzalyan 1985, fig. 9.

History of Tabari" in the Freer Gallery of Art, Washington [F59.16, 47.19 and 30.21].[354] Most likely, the preference accorded to a dragon by the artist who illustrated this manuscript was due to a precise lecture of the Bible where the creature is actually called *tannin*. In the same episode, when the Pharaoh called his "magicians" in order to transform their own sticks into "snakes" that could contrast the one of Aaron and Moses, the Bible use the plural form *tanninim*.[355]

The Sogdian paintings of the Blue Hall at Penjikent raise many questions about Iranian traditions, which we might regard as the literary foundation of the *Shahnameh* itself (with or without illustrations). It seems plausible to conclude that it was in Sogdiana (or eastern Iran) rather than in Persia that many pre-Islamic Iranian traditions were preserved. Images such as those depicted in the Sogdian paintings at Penjikent did not appear in pre-Islamic Persian art because the Sasanians identified more with Isfandyar, the champion of Zoroastrianism, than they did with Rustam, who was treated as a heretic.[356] Only several centuries later was Rustam accepted in Islamic Persia as a proper Iranian hero; or, in his case, as an "Iranized prophet," just as another antagonist of Zoroastrian literature – Alexander the Great – was treated before him.[357]

As was mentioned some time ago by Marshak, the monster of the Sogdian painting is a female one.[358] This can be proved by her long hair (intermingled with human skulls) and pointed breast. Pavel Lurje has drawn upon Tajik folklore to propose a different reading of the story of Rustam fighting a female snake demon, as depicted in

354 Fitzherbert 2001, pl. 7 a-b.

355 Angelini 2018, 26.

356 Davis 2007, 56-61.

357 Di Branco 2011, 49-50; Compareti 2018a, 97. It is worth remarking that, according to Firdousi, Alexander had on his forehead "the sign of the Kayanid Dynasty" that rendered him the legitimate successor of the Achaemenids: Kampouri-Vamvoukou 2014, 292.

358 Marshak 2002b, 40.

the Penjikent paintings. He showed that there is in fact at least one Tajik fable about a snake demon who was the mother of monstrous offspring.[359] In this fable, all of the offspring would eventually devour people. In other words, the reason why the Sogdian paintings seem to be independent from the Persian text is probably because they were following eastern Iranian traditions, of which Firdousi was either unaware or chose to ignore.

Despite the lack of human arms in the giant snake of Turkish book illustrations already observed, the image under examination represents the only parallel in Sogdian paintings that could demonstrate the presence of female snake-demons in the Iranian milieu at the dawn of the Arab invasion. It is not completely clear if this section of those Sogdian paintings at Penjikent could be associated precisely to the story of Medusa, and it is worth observing that Rustam does not hold a mirror in his hands. However, at least from an iconographic point of view, the Sogdian monsters and the human snake in those rare Islamic book illustrations could be considered female and very similar.

Something more could be suggested for the Islamic illustration embellished with "salamander-birds" although not every element is easy to identify. Possible connections between the salamander, phoenix, and Medusa through her son Pegasus, point to an elaboration of Medusa's myth in the Islamic milieu. Many aspects of the process of acceptance and adaptation of Greek myths in the Islamic world

359 Lur'e 2014. Vladimir Propp had already individuated his typology of female snake-dragons in Russian folklore: Propp 1949, 349-350. Both Marshak and Lurje knew very well the studies by Propp (and other scholars) on fables and mythology. There could be some parallels with two versions of the very ancient Hittite "Myth of *illuyanka*" that was a voracious giant snake with monstrous offspring: Laroche 1966, 321. Armenian fables mentioned a she-dragon called *shahmaran* that could be a corruption of Persian *shah-i maran*, literally "king of snakes". According to James Russell, this name could be a folk etymology for the Biblical Queen Semiramis (Armenian Shamiram) whose main characteristic was lust: Russell 1987, 422. Modern Turkish and Kurdish fables usually insist on her healing properties with a possible allusion to the snake of Asclepius.

remain doubtful because of the lack of written sources and numerous still unanswered questions. One quite neglected aspect of the story of the deadly monster's gaze in Greek art is that it could actually be traced back to Mesopotamia.[360] Elements simply not observed or not completely clarified previously could possibly be reconstructed because of what has been preserved in Sogdian paintings or Islamic book illustrations. The important role played by Persians and Central Asians in the transmission of the myth of Medusa to the Islamized Turks and possibly the Arabs could be better understood by recognizing those Iranian elements that enriched this story. In some instances, the Greek myth could be completely or better understood because of the Islamic component or, in other instances, the story has been further elaborated, such as in the case of the mirror. In fact, according to the Greek story, the reflection of Medusa's face did not cause any problem to Perseus while, in the Islamic version, the monster itself could be killed or frightened just by looking at its own image.

Despite the transformation of some iconographic traits, these elements could be just considered external importations or, as seems very likely, they represent the emergence of Greek parts of the original myth not completely preserved in Classical written sources or arts. In both cases, Iranian cultural traits should have been very important in this process.[361]

One last important aspect of Islamic art preserved very strong connections with Classical traditions. Early Muslim artists and astrologers were familiar with the image of the *ketos*. This composite creature, in fact, appears in the eighth century Omayyad paintings at

---

360 Sonik 2013.

361 Compareti 2018b. Iranian elements can be found in Armenian legends as well such as regarding "the snake *bebch'ogh* whom the eye of man sees not for one hundred years. He becomes a dragon and ascends". The name *bebch'ogh* resembles *bebghosh* that could have been a bird. According to James Russell, this kind of snake-bird could be associated to Armenian dragons (*vishap*) that were invisible but caused storms and sudden winds. In order to avoid *Vishaps* to grow too big, God takes them into the sky and burn them in the sun: Russell 1994-1995, 89.

Qusayr 'Amra in an aquatic scene on the southern wall of the central aisle that was identified as a representation of the story of Jonah.[362] The *ketos* was very well known in astronomical Islamic manuscripts because the constellation of the whale (Arabic *qitus* or *qaitus*) was represented exactly like that Greek composite creature and with the same function (and name). Astronomy-astrology may have played a very important role, not only in the transmission but also in the creation of fantastic creatures. It is no coincidence that the most ancient Islamic illustrated manuscript is an astronomical treatise. This is an early eleventh century copy of the Arabic *Suwar al-Kawakib al-Thabitah* "Book of the Fixed Stars" by 'Abd al-Rahman ibn 'Umar al-Sufi (tenth century) and at present it is kept in the Bodleian Library, Oxford [Marsh 144]. The constellation of *qitus/qaitus/ketos* is depicted as a dog with the tail of a fish but no wings. This *qitus* presents many similarities with the first image of the same constellations in Islamic art, which has been preserved in a very fragmentary way in the Omayyad palace at Qusayr 'Amra (fig. 58).[363] One fourteenth and one fifteenth century copy of the aforementioned *'Aja'ib al-mahluqat wa ghara'ib al-maujudat* of al-Qazwini presents much more elaborate winged dog-fishes to point at the *qitus* constellation that could call to mind both the pseudo-*simurgh* of pre-Islamic late Sasanian and Sogdian art and the *ketos/leviathan* of the story of Jonah as represented at

362 Fontana 2012. On the northern wall of the western aisle at Qusayr 'Amra there is another aquatic scene which includes also a horse with a fish tail: Fontana 2012, fig. 4b.

363 Wellesz 1959, fig. 34; Fontana 2012, 291-292. According to Anna Caiozzo, the *qitus* constellation in a fifteenth century copy of the *Suwar al-Kawakib al-Thabitah* at present kept in the Bibliothèque Nationale de France [Ms. B. N. ar. 5036, fol. 188r] would be similar to the Chinese *qilin* (sometimes rendered as "unicorn"): Caiozzo1999, 17. However, the *kardunn* "unicorn" appears as a winged horned animal in the thirteenth century *Kitab na'at al-hayawan* of the British Library [Or. 2784, fol. 197v]: Contadini 2003, fig. 4. Other "typical" dragons in Islamic astronomical texts were constituted by the head and the tail of the monster that Muslim (including Persian and Indian) astrologers considered to be responsible for eclipses. They do not represent any iconographic anomaly: Kuehn 2011, 133-

Aght'amar (fig. 59).[364] The pseudo-*simurgh* of Omayyad palaces and the *qitus* of Islamic astrological texts presented a very similar iconography. This was most likely due to the fact that both of them shared the same model that was the Greek *ketos*. It is not given to know if the painters who depicted the *qitus* in those Islamic manuscripts had a memory of the pseudo-*simurgh* in Omayyad art. In case they knew something, it could be imagined that they considered that composite creature as an auspicious symbol that granted protection and fortune.

Despite its very ancient Mesopotamian origins, this iconography presents very strong connections with Greek astronomy-astrology. A winged composite creature that was very similar to the symbol of *farr* (our pseudo-*simurgh*) continued therefore to be reproduced in Islamic astrological texts to represent the *qitus* constellation and not the real *simurgh* in the *Shahnameh* that was a bird.[365]

364 Bausani 1978b, 279; Rempel' 1987, 67-68.

365 This study does not include any observations on the minor southern celestial hemispheric constellation called Phoenix which was first depicted as a bird in Dutch star atlases only in the late sixteenth-early seventeenth century.

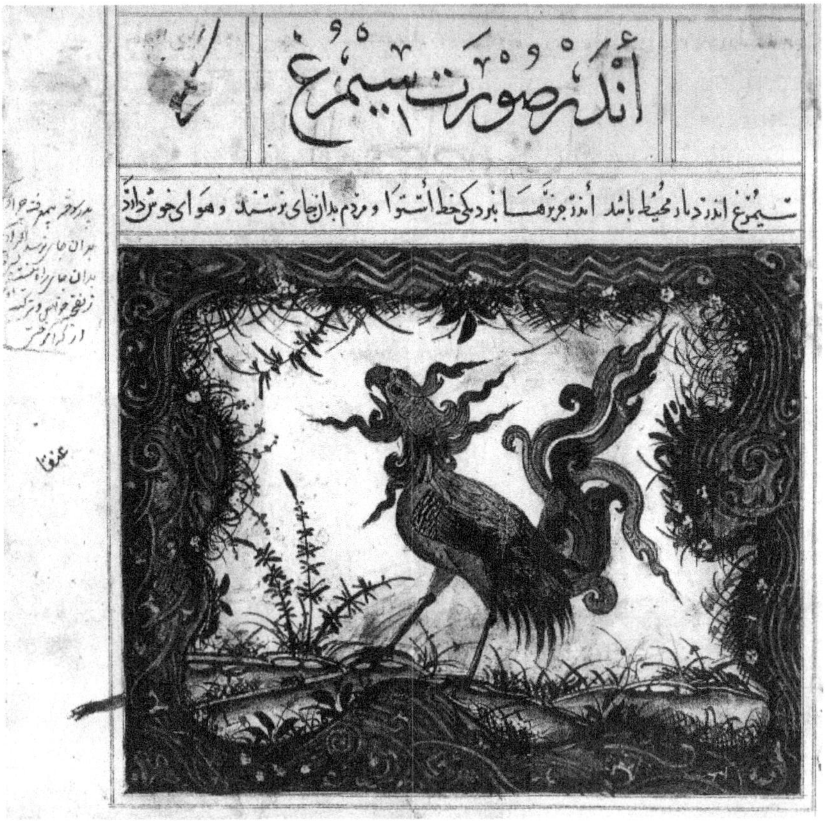

Figure 43. *Simurgh* in the Persian *Manafi'-i hayawan* "The Benefits of Animals", Pierpont Morgan Library, New York [M.500] (Iran, ca. 1297-1300). After: Schmitz 1997, fig. 26.

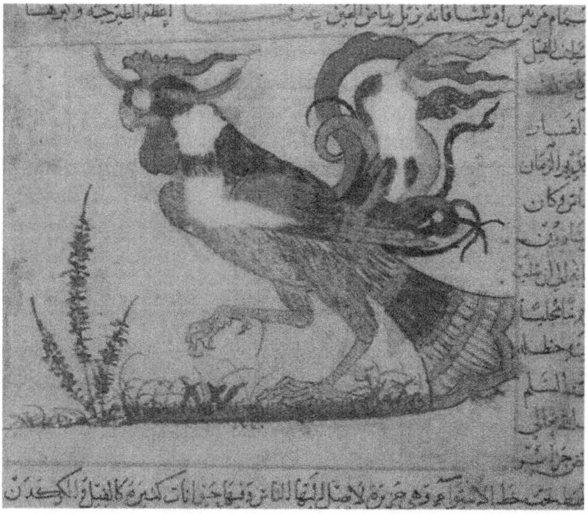

Figure 44. *Simurgh* in the *'Aja'ib al-mahluqat wa ghara'ib al-maujudat* "The Wonders of Creation and the Oddities of Existence" of Zakarya ibn-Muhammad ibn-Mahmud al-Qazwini, the so-called "London Qazwini" [Or. 14140, fol. 122v], British Library (Iran, early fourteenth century). After: Schmitz 1997, 21, figs. 26-27.

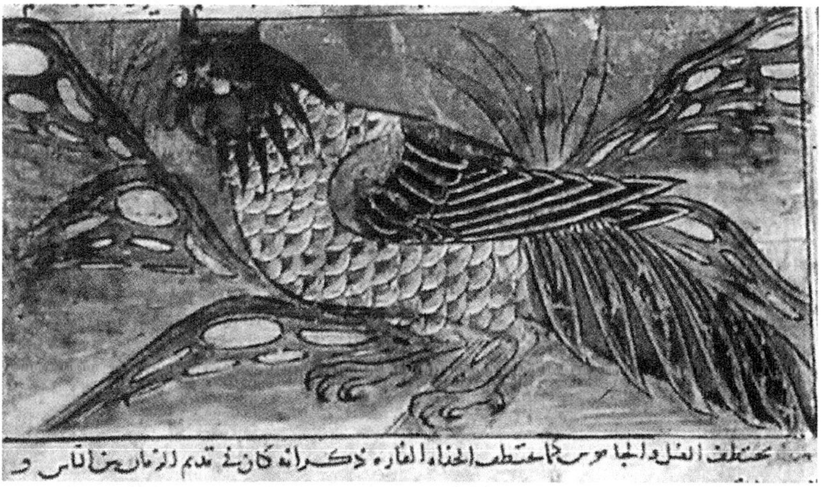

Figure 45. *'Anqa* in the *'Aja'ib al-mahluqat wa ghara'ib al-maujudat* "The Wonders of Creation and the Oddities of Existence" of Zakarya ibn-Muhammad ibn-Mahmud al-Qazwini, Istanbul Süleymaniye Library [MSS Yeni cami 813, fol. 166a] (Iran, 1322). After: Berlekamp 2011, fig. 29.

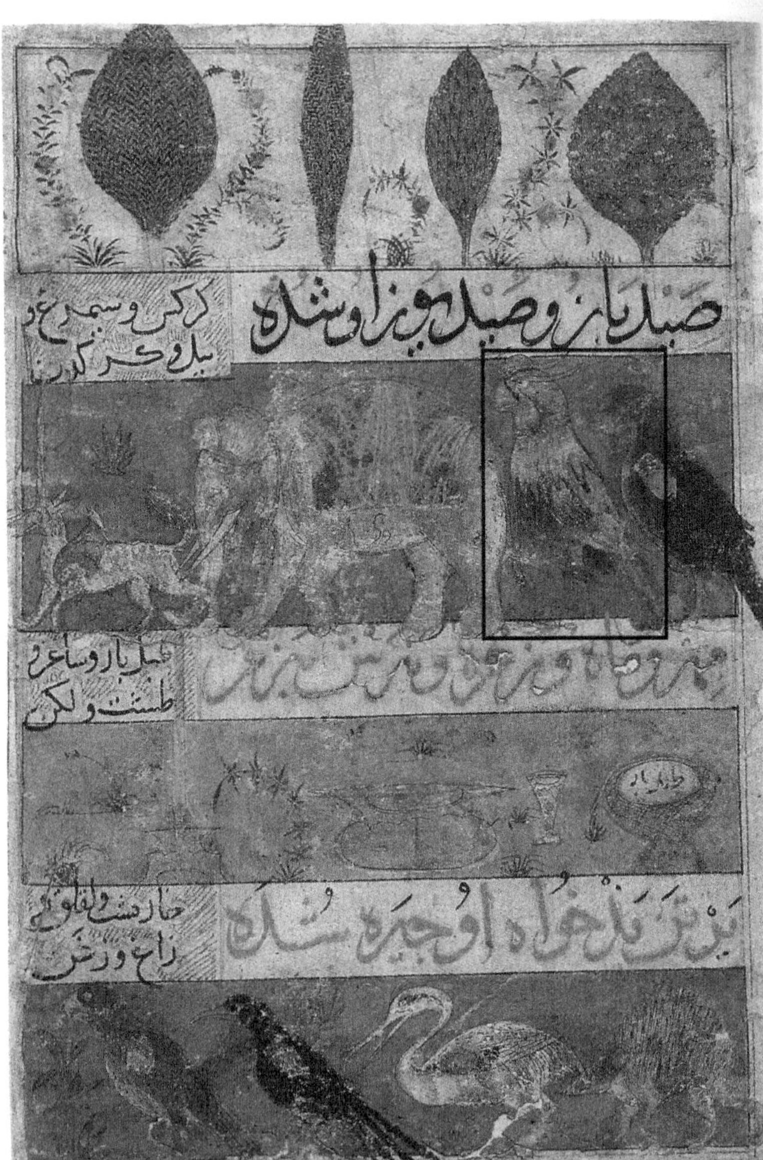

Figure 46. *Simurgh* in the Persian *Mu'nis al-ahrar* "The Free Men's Companion to the Subtetlies of Poems", Cleveland Museum of Art [45.385] (Iran, early fourteenth century). After: Swietochowski, Carboni 1994, fig. 3 e-h.

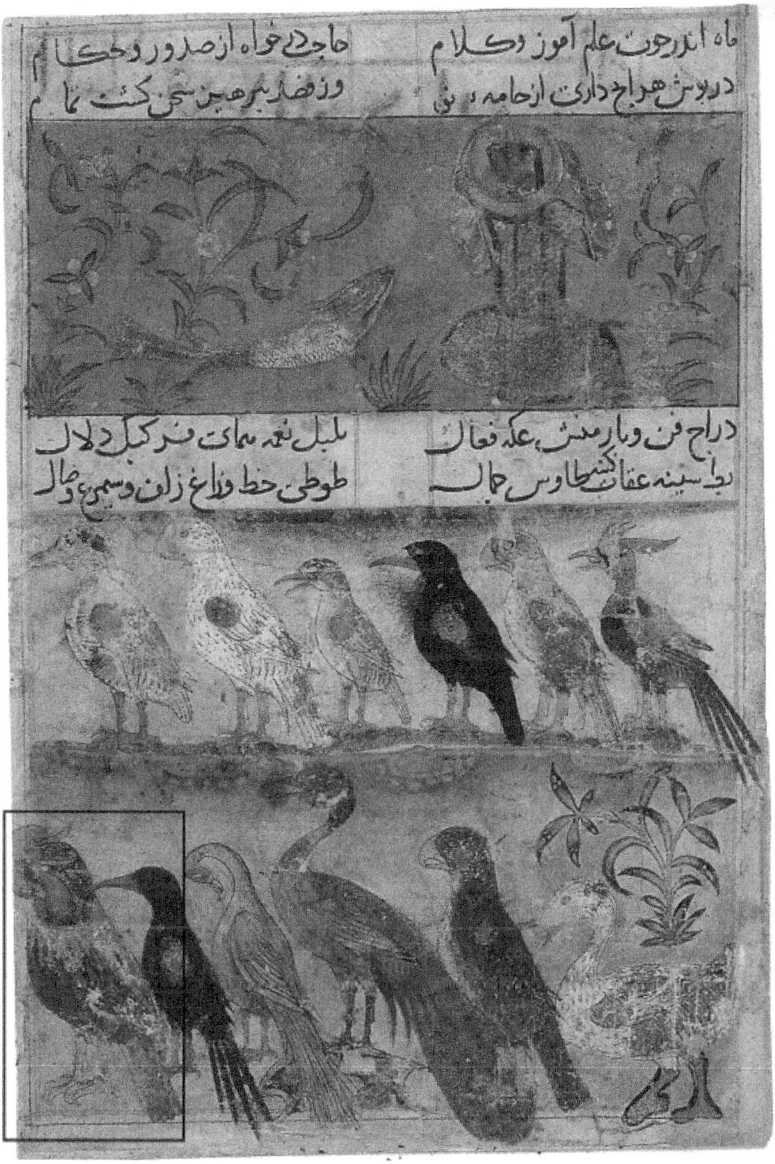

Figure 47. *Simurgh* (first one on the left, bottom row) in the Persian *Muʿnis al-ahrar* "The Free Men's Companion to the Subtleties of Poems", Freer Gallery of Art [46.14 B] (Iran, early fourteenth century). The *homa* is the second white bird on the left, upper row. After: Swietochowski, Carboni 1994, fig. 7 a-b.

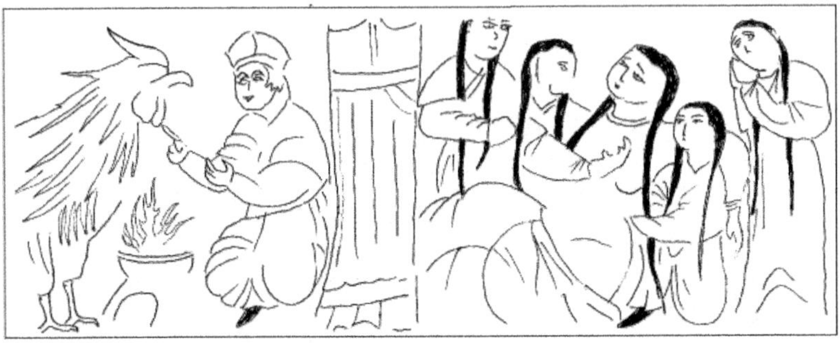

Figure 48. The birth of Rustam, *Shahnameh* in the Berlin Staatsbibliothek, Berlin [Diez Album, Fol. 71, S. 7] (Isfahan ca. 1335). After: Swietochowski, Carboni 1994, fig. 17.

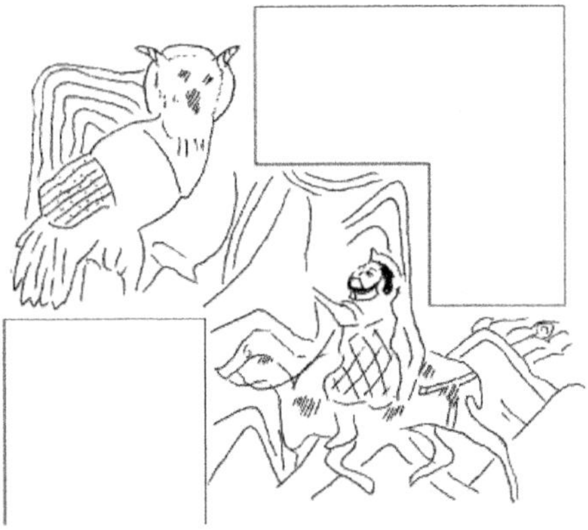

Figure 49. *Simurgh*, Zal and Sam in the St Petersburg State Public Library *Shahnameh* [ex Dorn 329] (Shiraz 1333). After: Swietochowski, Carboni 1994, fig. 25.

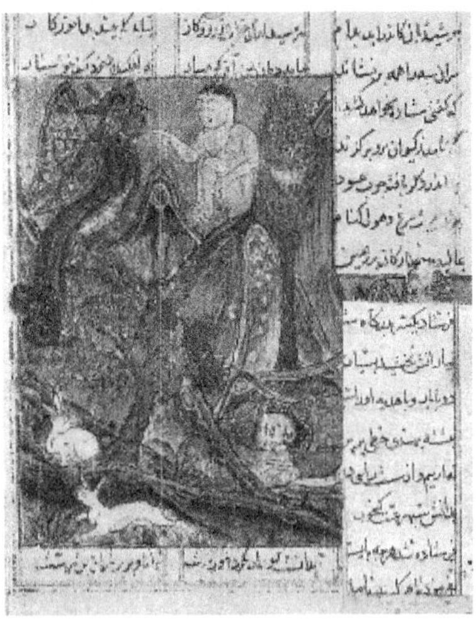

Figure 50. *Simurgh*, Zal and Sam in the Metropolitan Museum of Art, the so-called "Gutman Manuscript" [1974.290.2 v] (Iran, early fourteenth century). After: Swietochowski, Carboni 1994, cat. 8.

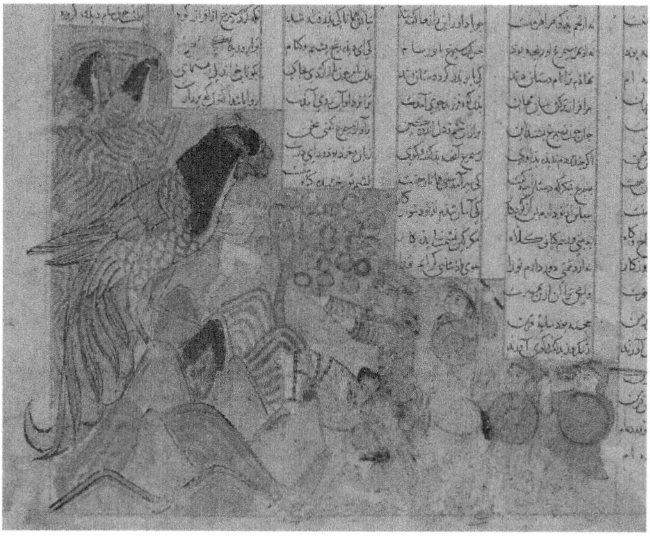

Figure 51. *Simurgh*, Zal and Sam in the Kuwait National Museum *Shahnameh*, the al-Sabah Collection [LNS 36 MS] (Shiraz, first half of the fourteenth century). After: Jenkins, M. (1983). *The al-Sabah Collection. Islamic Art in the Kuwait National Museum*. London, 98.

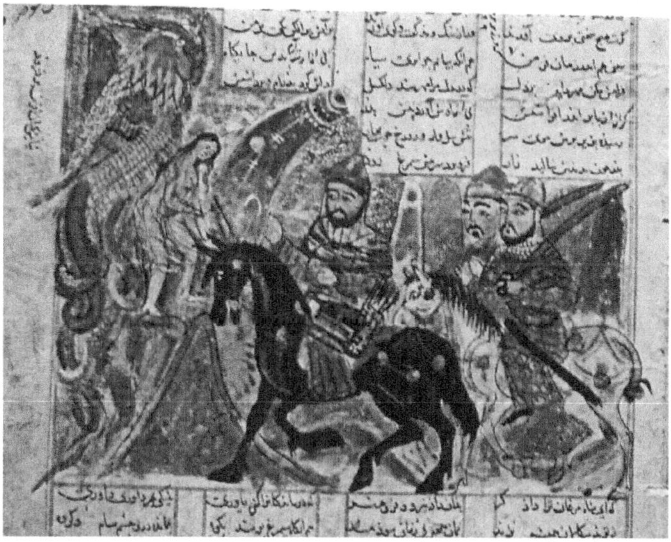

Figure 52. *Simurgh*, Zal and Sam in the "Stephens *Shahnameh*" [folio 24r] (Shiraz, 1352-3). After: Sims 2013, pl. xxvi, fig. 2.

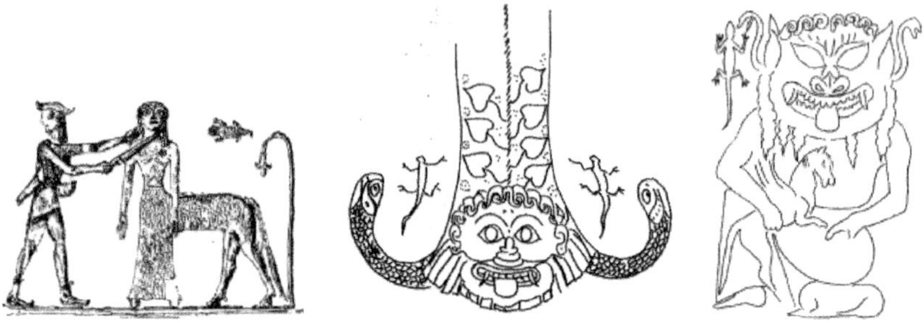

Figure 53a-c. Medusa and the "salamander". Left: Cycladic relief *pithos* embellished with Perseus killing Medusa as a centaur and a salamander or lizard behind her (ca. 675-650 BCE). Louvre Museum, Paris [CA 795]. After: Frothingham 1911, fig. 12. Center: bearded Medusa and "salamanders", detail of an Attic black-figure amphora (ca. 540-530). Louvre Museum, Paris [F 99]. After: Hurwit 2006, fig. 10. Right: Medusa, Pegasus and the "salamander" on a metal part of a shield from Olympia (ca. 600 BCE). Olympia Museum. After: Krauskopf 1988, fig. 272.

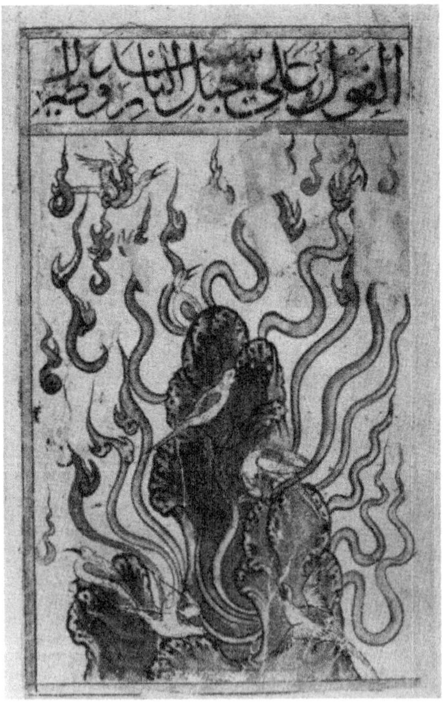

Figure 54. *Al qawl 'ala jabal al-nar wa tayr samandar* "Discussion on the mountain of fire and the salamander-birds" in the *Kitab al-bulhan* "Book of wonders" [Bodleian Library, Oxford, MS. Bodl. Or. 133] (early fifteenth century). After: Carboni 1988, fog. 42.v.

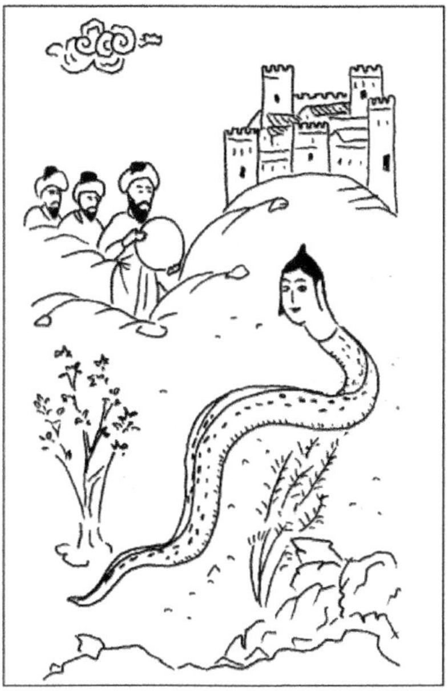

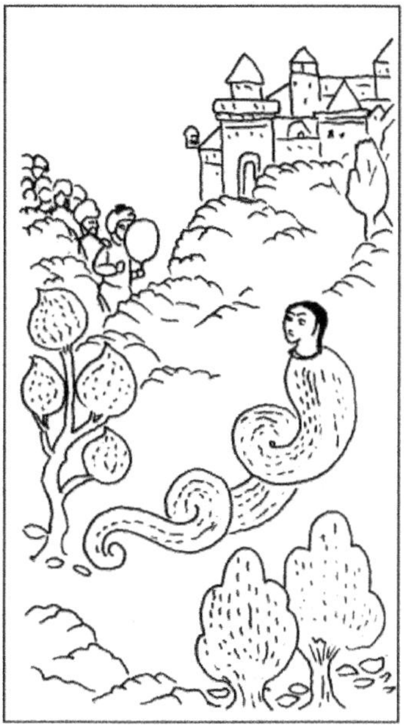

Figure 55. Turkish book illustration with a snake she-demon. The Pierpont Morgan Library, New York [suppl. turque 242, fol. 90v] (ca. 1582). After: Compareti 2018a, fig. 4.

Figure 56. Turkish book illustration with a snake she-demon. Bibliothèque National de France, Paris [M.788, fol. 89v] (ca. 1582). After: Compareti 2018a, fig. 5.

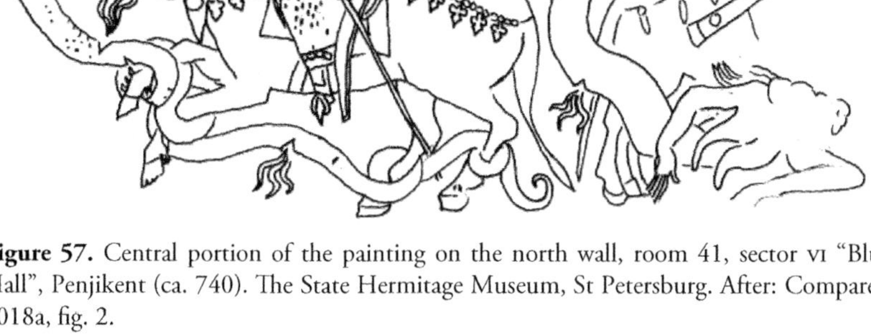

Figure 57. Central portion of the painting on the north wall, room 41, sector VI "Blue Hall", Penjikent (ca. 740). The State Hermitage Museum, St Petersburg. After: Compareti 2018a, fig. 2.

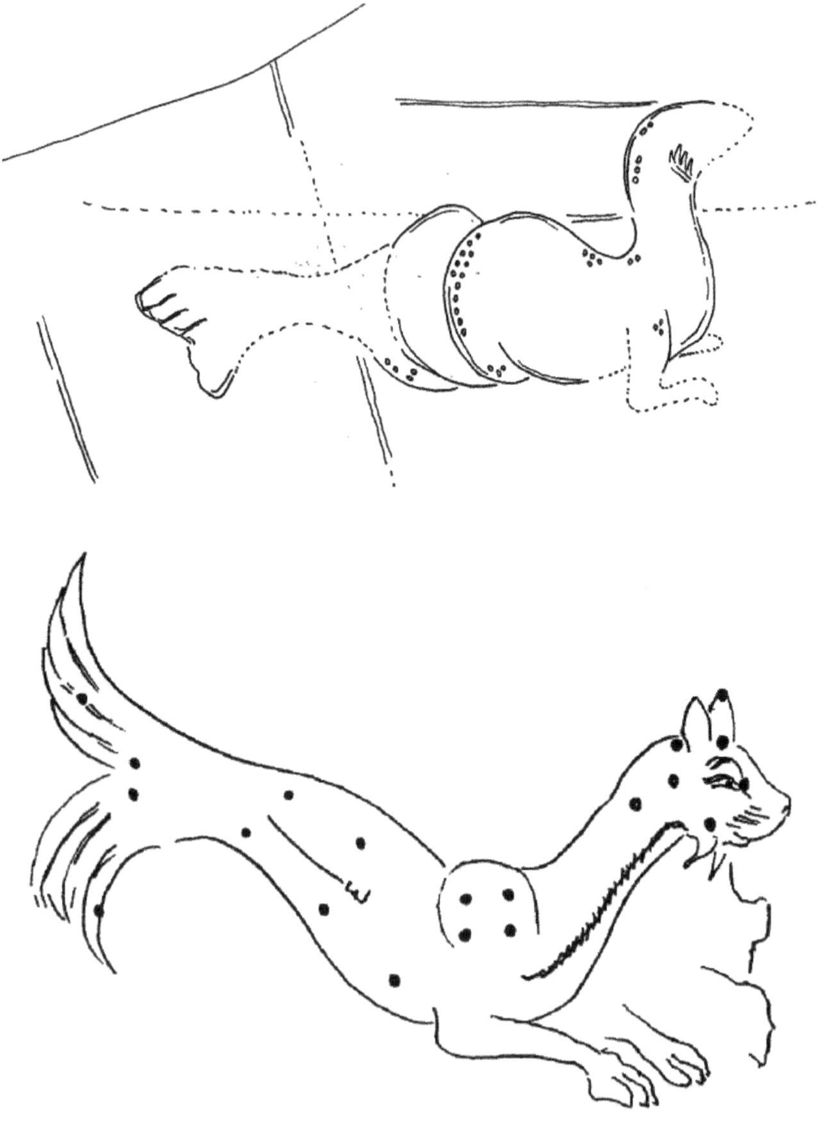

Figure 58a-b. Above: *qitus* from Qusayr 'Amra, Jordan (c. 743). Below: *qitus* in the *Suwar al-Kawakib al-Thabitah* "Book of the Fixed Stars" by 'Abd al-Rahman ibn 'Umar al-Sufi, Bodleian Library, Oxford (1009-1010) [Marsh 144]. Sketch: author.

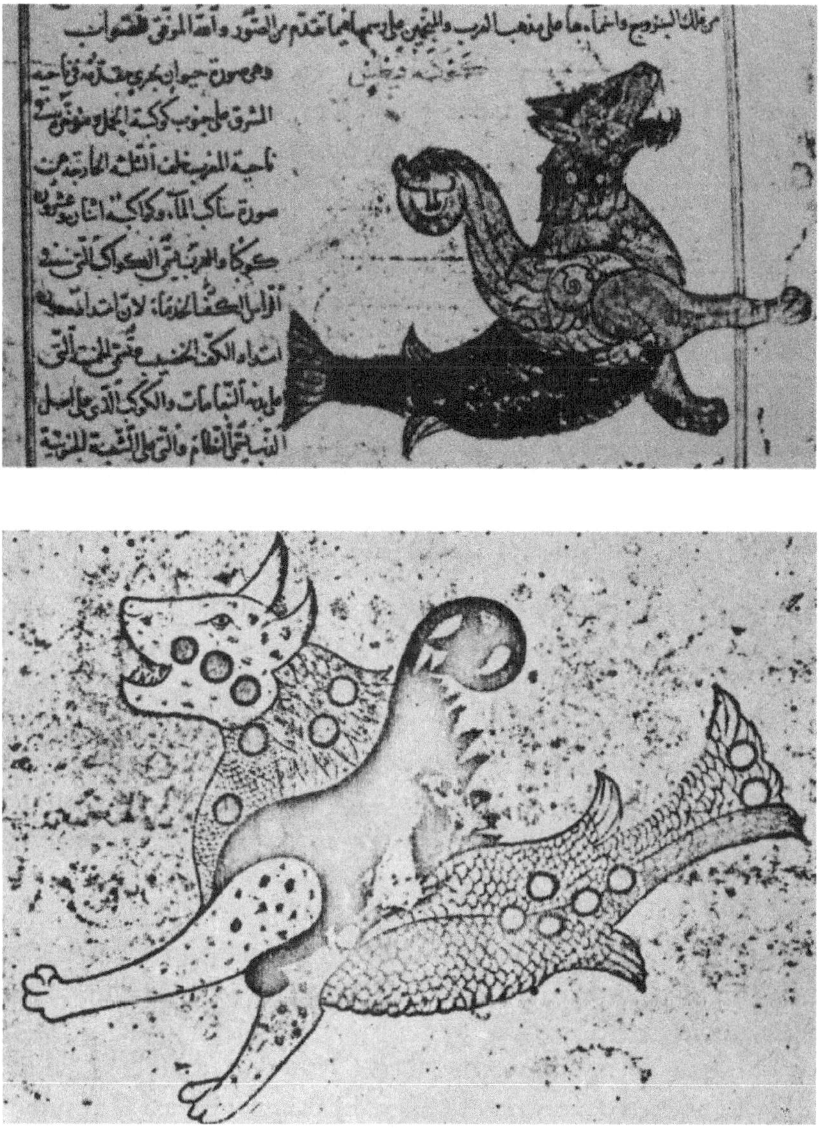

Figure 59a-b. Above: *qitus* in the *'Aja'ib al-mahluqat wa ghara'ib al-maujudat* of al-Qazwini, Österreich Nationalbibliothek, Vienna (Jalayarid, fourteenth century). Below: *qitus* in the *'Aja'ib al-mahluqat wa ghara'ib al-maujudat* of al-Qazwini, Freer Gallery of Art, Smithsonian Institution (fifteenth century) [54.46r]. After: Bausani 1978b, pls. IV a-b.

2.7 The Himalayan region

Symbolic composite creatures that were very popular among Zoroastrians, Christians, and even Muslims did not encounter the same fate among Central Asian Buddhists. In fact, images of the so-called pseudo-*simurgh* was never found in Buddhist Bactria, neither in Bamyan, nor in the Tarim Basin nor Dunhuang. It is not easy to explain the reason for this absence. How is it possible that other typical Iranian symbols such as the wild boar head within pearl roundels were so popular in Buddhist Central Asia while the pseudo-*simurgh* did not appear in one single instance? Creatures like the pseudo-*simurgh* cannot be found among the Buddhists of the Himalayan region in spite of very tight relationships between Tibet and Kashmir with Sasanian Persia and above all Sogdiana.[366]

In eastern Tibet, the region commonly known as Amdo or also "greater Tsaidam Basin," at present under the administration of the Chinese province of Qinghai, is the place where one finds many graves that belonged to Tuyuhun and Tubo royal clans. The Tuyuhuns (Tibetan '*A-zha*) were probably Altaic language-speaking groups who formed a powerful kingdom around Qinghai Lake (or Koko Nor) between the fourth and seventh centuries. Tubo is the name that the Chinese had given to the Tibetans at least since the sixth century when they began to become more and more powerful in the Himalayan region after defeating the Tuyuhun and unifying the entire Tibetan plateau under the Pugyel (or Yarlung) Dynasty (634-842). As a matter of fact, the Tuyuhuns did not disappear after their defeat and continued to live in that territory together with the Tibetans at least until the tenth century.[367]

Those significant graves are located at Reshui in Dulan County, a few kilometers southwest of Qinghai Lake. Controlled excavations were carried at Reshui of only a few graves while many others suffered

366 Flood 2005; Compareti 2009c.

367 Molè 1970.

incessant looting.[368] In 2018, local police officers arrested a group of twenty-six criminals and confiscated a large number of metalwork objects. Other objects such as textiles and painted wooden coffins had already entered the collections of the Xining Museum of Tibetan Culture, Dulan County Museum, and others in China and abroad. Most of the objects that were excavated and confiscated display very clear Iranian elements such as animals within pearl roundels or vegetal frames. An embroidered inscription in Middle Persian on the back of a textile fragment, at present kept in the Dulan Museum, was found in the 1990s.[369] Another entire, well-preserved although unexcavated textile that was recently on display in Dunhuang presents one Middle Persian inscription repeated twice. It is at present part of the Abegg Stiftung Museum (Switzerland) and was published in a booklet that accompanied the exhibition in Dunhuang.[370] It is not easy to establish a precise chronology for those graves and scholars do not agree about their attribution or identification. Experts in Tibetan studies prefer to date those graves to the eighth or ninth centuries.[371]

The Museum of Tibetan Culture in Xining (Qinghai Province) also preserves among its collections a large number of fragmentary textiles probably imported from Central Asia, and even three entire tunics embellished with silk inserts perfectly preserved because of the favorable climatic conditions of the burial sites. Many of these textiles could be included in the so-called "*zandaniji*" group that has been considered for a long time to have been produced in the village of Zandane not far from Bukhara, in historical western Sogdiana. Such an identification proved to be wrong since *zandaniji* were woven in

368 Heller, 1998; Heller 2006; Tao, Wertmann 2009; Tao 2013.

369 Weber 2010, 352-354.

370 Cultural Exchange along the Silk Road, 2019: 10. The Abegg Stiftung Museum collected and restored many textiles coming from the antiquarian market that were possibly found in Dulan. From a stylistic and technical point of view, they belong to the so-called *zandaniji* group: Otavsky 1998b.

371 Heller, 1998; Heller 2006.

cotton and one inscription identified on the well-known fragment preserved in the Huy Cathedral (Belgium) has been established to be actually in Arabic and not the Sogdian language.[372] Even if it is completely wrong, the name *zandaniji* appears very frequently in scientific literature to designate a specific group of silks, most likely dated to the Islamic period (precisely the Samanid Dynasty period), that are enriched with colorful patterns, probably rooted in Sogdian art. Several textiles belonging to the so-called *zandaniji* group are part of the collections of the Museum of Tibetan Culture in Xining and the Dulan Museum. It is not completely certain if the unexcavated textiles in the Xining museum had been looted in Reshui, since they could have been found at other sites in the Tsaidam Basin. Every attribution should be considered highly hypothetical.

One unique, well-preserved textile fragment at present kept in Xining museum displays pseudo-*simurgh*s within rhomboid frames embellished with a double row of pearls (fig. 60).[373] Every characteristic of this textile, such as colors, decorative elements around the pseudo-*simurgh*s and on the same body of those composite creatures, point to the so-called *zandaniji* typology. Above the head of every pseudo-*simurgh* there is an element that might be intended to be grapes. This is the only specimen that could help to identify the place of provenance (Tsaidam?) of many similar textiles, since other fragments belonging to the same typology appeared on the antiquarian market some years ago.[374] One specimen belongs to the Silk Museum of China in Hangzhou (fig. 61),[375] while art dealer Carlo Cristi has two more textiles embellished with this composite creature in his collection (fig. 62). According to experts, weaving techniques and C14 tests conducted on one of the fragments in the hands of Carlo Cristi suggest that they also belong to the so-called *zandaniji* typology, pro-

372 Marshak 2006b; Sims-Williams, Khan 2008; Dode 2016.

373 Compareti 2020c, fig. 8.

374 Gasparini 2020, 83-86.

375 Gasparini 2016: 90-91.

duced somewhere (possibly Samanid Central Asia) around the eighth or ninth centuries.[376] One of the textiles in the collection of Carlo Cristi looks very similar to another fragment in the al-Sabah collection in Kuwait (fig. 63).[377]

Even though none of the textiles under examination comes from controlled excavations, the specimen in the Xining Museum suggests that looters could have found precious silks of the so-called *zandaniji* typology embellished in many ways (possibly also with pseudo-*simurghs*) in the greater Tsaidam region. Many textiles of this kind that entered museum and private collections still present very bright colors and clear decorations because, in all probability, they were found at sites whose climatic conditions allowed them to be preserved exceptionally well. It is highly probable that the place where they were found could be identified as the cemetery at Reshui in Dulan County, even though other archaeological sites in the same region that were disturbed in the past by looters should not be ruled out. Not only the pseudo-*simurgh* but also other typically Iranian decorative subjects, such as winged horses, ducks with a vegetal element in the beak, rams, etc. appear very frequently among the textiles confiscated at Dulan and those in the Xining museum. Stylistically, too, the motifs embellishing these textiles should be considered Iranian, since they occur quite often, even if they are not identical, in seventh-eighth century Sogdian paintings from Afrasyab, Varaksha, and Penjikent.[378] Those Sogdian paintings preserved decorative motifs that were to be developed into something extremely accurate and refined, such as so-called *zandaniji* textiles.

However, the wild boar head within pearl roundels that appears very often on the garments reproduced in Sogdian paintings is completely absent from the textiles of the so-called *zandaniji* typology from greater Tsaidam and other sites. Its absence could be explained

376 Compareti 2015, 36-37.

377 Spuhler 2014, 120-121.

378 Azarpay 1981.

on chronological bases: most probably, those textiles were produced in Central Asia during the Islamic period when the depiction of wild boars became problematic in the same way as that of other "impure" animals, such as pigs. Exceptions existed, as in the case of an unexcavated textile in the Abegg Stiftung Museum recently published in a booklet that accompanied an exhibition in Dunhuang.[379] It is an exceptional textile because Middle Persian inscriptions can be observed in two points. Several animals embellish the textile in the Abegg Stiftung Museum as well as two entire wild boars. All the animals on that textile could be considered ideal prey for a noble hunter, possibly the important person who bought or even ordered such a textile. Some other unexcavated fragmentary textiles in private and public collections present wild boar heads within pearl roundels but they do not look sufficiently elaborate to be considered *zandaniji* specimens.[380]

The pseudo-*simurgh* on those textiles from Qinghai definitely points at the Islamic periods since, as already observed above, the only clear representation of this composite creature appeared in Sogdiana in the seventh century paintings at Afrasyab. Sogdian weavers could have started to produce textiles embellished with pseudo-*simurgh*s only after this period, most likely, when most of Central Asian territory was under Abbasid or Samanid rule. The chronology proposed by Tibetologists for the Qinghai textiles (eighth-ninth century) seems to be confirmed.

As already observed above, Buddhists did not favor the pseudo-*simurgh*, and the Qinghai textile embellished with that composite creature does not seem to be an exception. In fact, nothing among the finds from Reshui presents clear connections with Buddhism, simply because that religion had not yet spread among Tuyuhun or Tubo at the time of the creation of those tombs. The textile in the Xining Museum embellished with pseudo-*simurgh*s constitutes a very good

379 Cultural Exchange along the Silk Road, 2019: 10.

380 Spuhler 2014, 116-117.

argument for the proposal of better chronologies for the tombs at Reshui and, more generally, for the greater Tsaidam region.

Among the excavated silk fragments from the Reshui tombs there are also two specimens embellished with magic birds. One of them presents the image of a typical standing Tang *fenghuang* within a vegetal roundel. According to the scholars of the Qinghai Institute of Archaeology who found it, this silk samite should be dated to the eighth-ninth century.[381] The other silk fragment – much more interesting, in our opinion – is embellished with a giant haloed bird carrying a person within vegetal roundels [QK 001857].[382] It is worth observing that the bird even has two pointed ears that could call to mind horns or the feathers of an owl (fig. 64). As it will be discussed below, the two elements above the head of the bird are probably just ears like those of a mammal. This excavated textile from Reshui kept in the Qinghai Cultural Relics and Archaeology Institute (Xining), represents another example of imported goods from Central Asia that should be included in the group of *zandaniji* silks from the Tsaidam region. Its iconography is probably rooted in the Greek myth of Ganymede or Aegina abduced by the eagle of Zeus that was later adopted in Gandharan Buddhist art. For some reason not completely clear, it enjoyed great popularity at least until the twelfth-thirteenth century in the whole of Eurasia. Painted samples can be observed in the Palatine Chapel in Palermo and the Cefalù Cathedral (Sicily).[383] In light of the ideas expressed about the presence of pseudo-*simurgh*s in this group of precious textiles, it could be argued that Tuyuhun-Tubo elites probably did not appreciate such an iconography for its Buddhist content.

Local pre-Buddhist (Bon) legends linked magic birds with horns on their head (*khyung*) to the royal house of Zhangzhung in western Tibet, whose capital was eloquently called Khyunglung (Khyung Valley).[384]

381 Zhao 2004, 75.

382 Xu 2006, fig. 231; Zhao 2012, 217; Tao 2013, 107-111.

383 Kapitaikin 2016.

384 Vitali 2008.

Following the rise of Buddhism in Tibet, *khyung* birds were inevitably assimilated to *Garuda* although they maintained some of their original characteristics, such as the horns. Several unexcavated ninth-eleventh century Tibetan metal amulets (*togcha*) and statuettes present this unusual iconography.[385] Amy Heller proposed to identify the composite winged creatures that embellish an eighth-ninth century silver jug in the Pritzker Collection (Chicago) with representations of *khyung* birds featuring also strong Sogdian elements. According to Heller, typical Sogdian decorative motifs would have entered Tibet through precious textiles embellished with confronted birds and other animals inside vegetal or pearl medallions.[386] This observation could be particularly true for the excavated *zandaniji*-like textile from Dulan with an eared (or, in this case, horned) bird carrying a person. In fact, even though Sogdian tradesmen could have been completely unaware of Tibetan legends about the *khyung*, locals would have definitely appreciated eared birds that carried people exactly like the more familiar (although horned) *Garuda*. As it will be discussed in the next chapter of this study, Sogdians adopted the Indian iconography of *Garuda* abducting a woman as it can be observed in the higher part of an unpublished early eigth century painting from room 1/sector XXII at Penjikent. This kind of iconography was well-known in Central Asia and probably continued to be reproduced in precious textiles in Islamic times. Vegetal or geometric roundels that started to substitute pearl medallions in eighth century Sogdian paintings also displayed confronted animals. This formula is typical of Islamic time *zandaniji* textiles while pearl roundels in seventh-early eighth century Sogdian paintings at Penjikent, Afrasyab and Varakhsha mainly framed single animals. The same could be considered true for Sasanian customs since confronted animals have never represented a constant rule in pre-Islamic Persian art.[387]

385 Heller 1999, 64, fig. 41; Heller 2015, 14-21.

386 Heller 2003, 63-64.

387 Compareti 2004; Compareti 2009b.

One should however observe that composite birds with feline or deer heads such as those on the Pritzker silver jug could be associated with special Chinese monsters called *feilian* that will be discussed in appendix 1 (fig. 94). Tibetans definitely adopted typical Chinese commodities and decorative motifs, and even reproduced wooden painted coffins decorated with directional animals rooted in Chinese culture.[388] These included also the "red bird of the south" (*zhuniao* or *zhuque* or *chiniao*), whose iconography was the same of the phoenix/*fenghuang* (figs. 85, 87). As Heller remarked, such painted coffins "have so far only been excavated in Dulan" and, in my opinion, the analysis of their decorations could help to propose better chronologies even for those tombs that were unfortunately disturbed by looters. Parts of an unexcavated wooden coffin possibly from Delingha (not far from Dulan) present some of the twelve animals of the traditional Chinese calendar inside pearl medallions.[389] Pearl roundel frames were typically represented on Sogdian luxury clothes and constituted the stage before the development into vegetal, geometric or, in any case, very elaborated medallions in *zandaniji* textiles that have been found in great quantity in Dulan Tuyuhun-Tubo royal tombs.

Central Asian and probably Chinese and Indian merchants had found very interesting commercial nodes in the Tsaidam Basin and other regions of the ancient Tibetan Plateu during the period of military and cultural expansion of the Pugyel Dynasty. Imported luxury goods from Samanid Central Asia were kept in extremely high esteem by the Tibetan ruling class that used them for everyday life and funerary outfits in the pre-Buddhist period. It is very unlike that the pseudo-*simurgh* and other motifs on so-called *zandaniji* textiles had a religious meaning. In any case, those ornaments did not yet disturb Tuyuhun-Tubo royal clans who adopted many typical Iranian decorative elements and considered them particularly indicated for the funerary sphere.

---

388 Heller 2013, 120-121.

389 Tao 2013, 137-138.

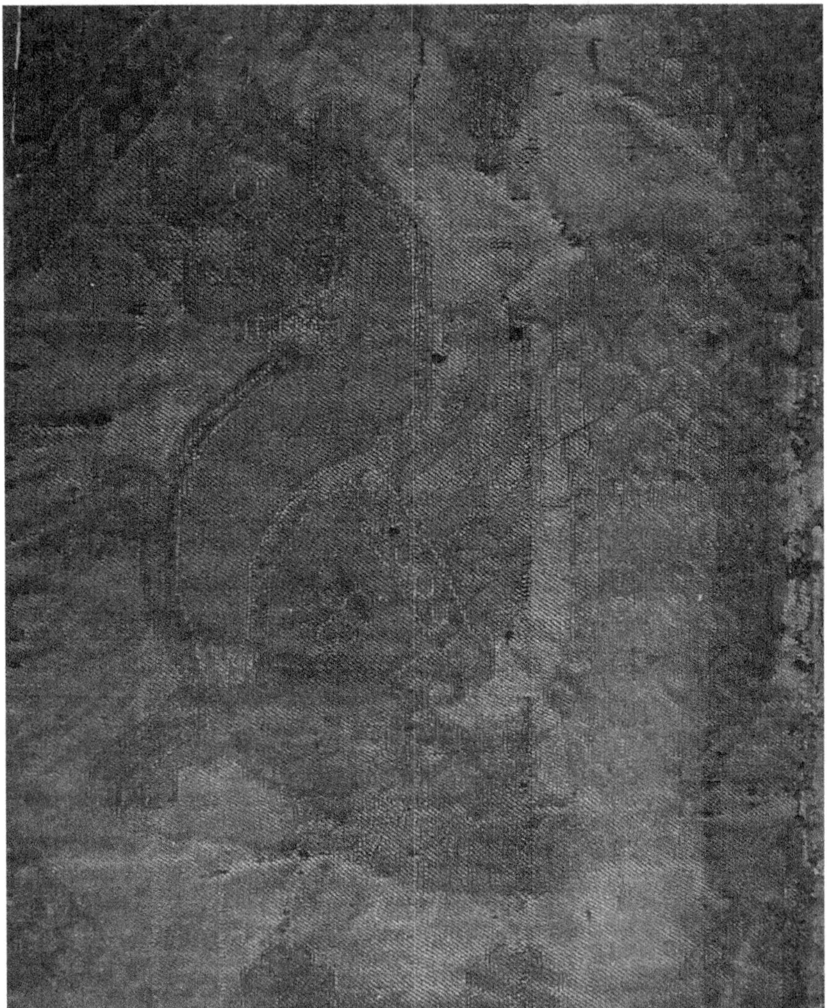

Figure 60. Pseudo-*simurgh* on a silk possibly from Reshui, Dulan (eighth-ninth century). The Museum of Tibetan Culture, Xining, Qinghai Province, China. Photo: author.

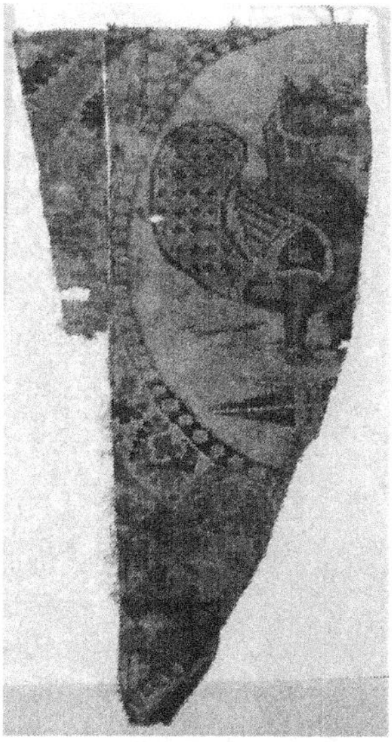

Figure 61. Pseudo-*simurgh* on a silk possibly from Reshui, Dulan (eighth-ninth century). China National Silk Museum, Hangzhou. After: Gasparini 2016, fig. 19.

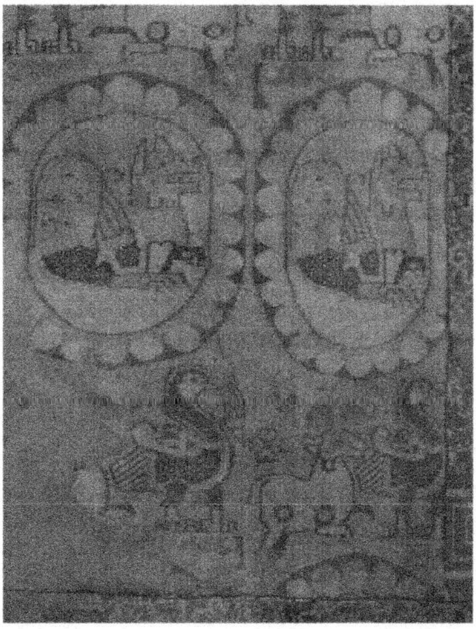

Figure 62. Pseudo-*simurgh* possibly from Reshui, Dulan (eighth-ninth century). Carlo Cristi Collection. After: Compareti 2015, fig. 1.

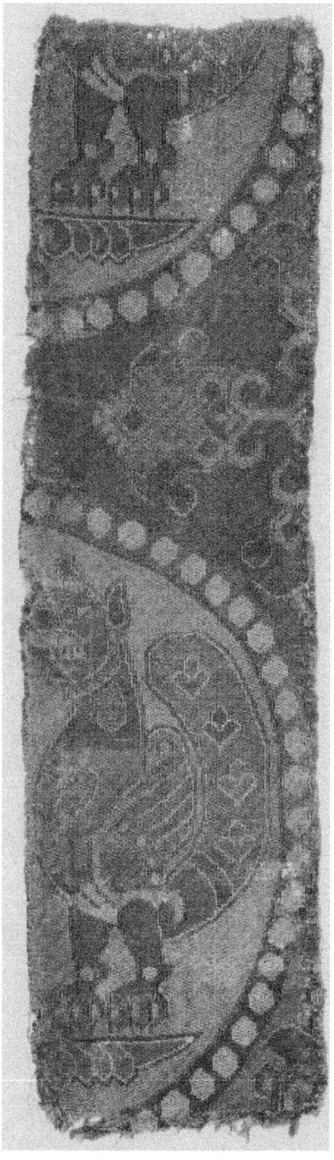

Figure 63. Pseudo-*simurgh* possibly from Reshui, Dulan (eighth-ninth century). The Kuwait National Museum, al-Sabah Collection. After: Spuhler 2014, cat. 2.8.

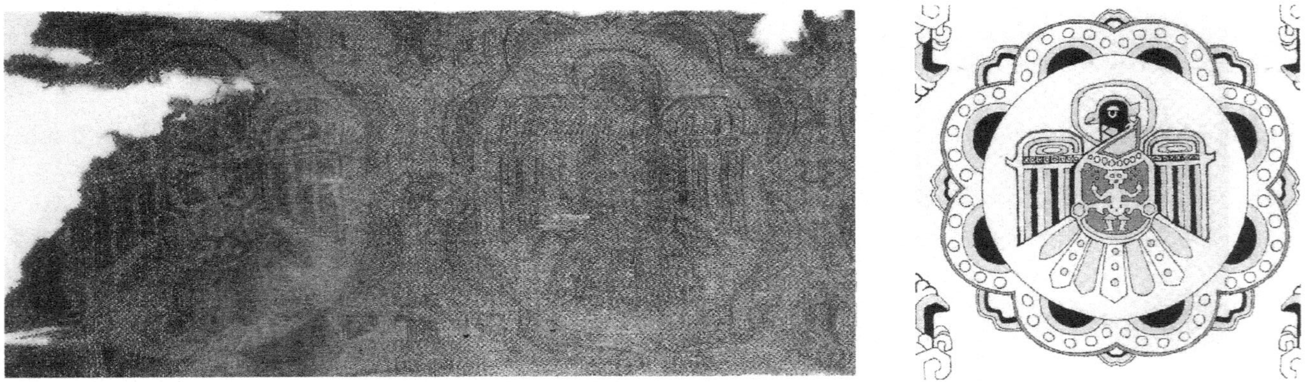

Figure 64a-b. Giant eared bird carrying a person, excavated at Reshui, Dulan (eighth-ninth century). Qinghai Cultural Relics and Archaeology Institute, Xining [QK 001857]. After: Zhao, F. (2004). *China Dawn of a Golden Age*. New York, cat. 246.

Chapter 3
Simurgh and *farr(eh)*

The bird behind Rustam on the very beginning of the eastern wall in the Blue Hall at Penjikent definitely shares many characteristics with the *simurgh* already observed in Inju'id Islamic book illustrations. Its presence is discrete, and it is not flying in the sky. The feathers on the head and the open wide eyes are very similar to those of an owl in the illustrated manuscript of the Hermitage *Shahnameh* (fig. 35).

I had the opportunity to observe this bird on the occasion of a special temporary exhibition (Fall 2015) in the State Hermitage Museum, since this part of the painting from the Blue Hall has been under restoration for a very long time and was not on display.[390] Thanks to the kindness of Larisa Kulakova and Pavel Lurje, I was able to study this part of the painted program. Several details of that bird call to mind the *simurgh* that is reproduced in Islamic book illustrations representing Sam rescuing his son Zal. In all these illustrations, the *simurgh* seems to have something above its head resembling feathers, such as an owl or, in some cases, little horns. It is important to note that the bird represented on the famous painted vase from Merv (ca. sixth century CE) belongs to this artistic tradition deeply rooted in Iranian culture (fig. 65). In fact, as I have attempted to demonstrate in another study, despite its position in front of a hunter on horse, that bird is not the target, which is the gazelle represented behind the rider. The presence of that bird with elements on its head resembling feathers or horns seems to belong to another scene, probably a wedding or a funeral, also depicted on this Merv painted vase. Something very similar can be observed in some panels of the so-

390 Kulakova 2016.

called Sino-Sogdian funerary monuments.[391] Scholars have recently suggested that the presence of the owl could refer to a very long battle that lasted throughout the night as well.[392] This is a very interesting observation although it does not take into account that *simurgh*s appear sometimes in Inju'id book illustrations as an owl. As it will be argued below, there were probably some connections between the owl and *simurgh* in Zoroastrian texts.

Moreover, on the occasion of the International Conference "Technical Art History of Serindia: Zerafshan River-Turfan Basin Project" held at the School of Art of Renmin University of China, Beijing (31 October 2016), Larisa Kulakova (State Hermitage Museum) presented some recently restored portions of the Blue Hall, where a yellow giant bird also appears on the western wall (fig. 104). Just behind the giant bird, there are two undistinguished persons, one is kneeling in front of an object that could be a (metal?) basin and the other standing figure seems to be in the act of throwing something in it. Even though this portion of the scene is not well preserved, there could be some similarities with the *Shahnameh* illustration in Berlin [Diez Album, Fol. 71, S. 7] representing Zal while interrogating the *simurgh* after evoking it (fig. 48). The position of Zal calls to mind the kneeling man behind the giant bird in the mural painting from the Blue Hall, while the basin could be identified as an incense burner for the feather of the *simurgh*. In fact, the standing person has one hand almost inside it. This does not change significantly the general scheme and identification of the main subjects of the Blue Hall since the *simurgh* should always be identified as a bird, possibly reproduced more than once in the same painted program even though not always in colossal form, while the composite winged creature flying in front of Rustam is probably the manifestation of his *farn*. In the study of Islamic book illustrations, it is worth considering Penjikent paintings because this specific aspect of Sogdian art has already inspired many

391 Compareti 2011, 26-41.

392 Grenet 2015, 427.

scholars in the past to better investigate Islamic paintings. These constitute the best parallel with the Sogdian paintings in the Blue Hall since, in both cases, the *simurgh* could appear as a giant bird in the presence of Zal (or Sam or even Isfandyar) or a more discrete owl-like bird that apparently does not seem to take part to the main scene. Unfortunately, there are no Mongol nor Inju'id book illustrations representing the battle of Rustam and Isfandyar in the presence of the *simurgh* as we can see (in my opinion) at the beginning of the eastern wall in the Blue Hall at Penjikent.

Another almost complete Sogdian painted cycle was excavated at the site of Kal'a-ye Kakhkaha (Tajikistan). On the east wall of room 4 of the palace, there is a procession of fantastic creatures including also two giant birds. Unfortunately, their heads were not preserved but it is clear that they are magic animals since there is also a horned creature and a dragon behind these two large birds.[393] It is impossible to determine whether one of those birds was a *simurgh*, although it is worth observing that the feathers and other elements could call to mind the possible *'anqa* represented in the Qarakhanids wall paintings at Samarkand.[394] Etsuko Kageyama noticed a fragmentary painting from the palace at Kal'a-ye Kakhkaha embellished with pearl roundels containing pseudo-*simurghs* (fig. 66).[395] It is not possible to identify precisely those fragments since they were found scattered on the ground completely out of context. The paintings at Kal'a-ye Kakhkaha date back to the ninth century and are later than those in Penjikent. In this way, the paintings of Kal'a-ye Kakhkaha could be considered a kind of missing link between pre-Islamic Sogdian arts at Penjikent, Afrasyab, Varakhsha, etc. and Islamic book illustrations.

393 Institute of History, Archaeology and Ethnography, Academy of Sciences, Tajikistan, National Research Institute for Cultural Properties, Tokyo 2010, 142.

394 Karev 2003, 1724-1726.

395 Institute of History, Archaeology and Ethnography, Academy of Sciences, Tajikistan, National Research Institute for Cultural Properties, Tokyo 2010, 287.

For this reason and because of some literary evidence that, in my opinion, could correctly identify the symbolic representation of the glory/charisma of Iranian kings and heroes as a flying chimera, I think that the beribboned creature that is flying in front of Rustam in the Blue Hall is the *farr* (or *farn*) of the hero. The *simurgh* should be identified with the bird resembling an owl in the portion of painting on the eastern wall. One hypothesis is that the *farr* was represented according to different iconographical traits, while the *simurgh* was always a colossal or, in any case, a fantastic bird sometimes resembling a rooster, or a parrot, or an owl. In every case, the *simurgh* has two elements above its head looking like horns or feathers.

As Herodotus recorded [II, 73], the phoenix (*benu*) was originally the bird of the city of Heliopolis, in Lower Egypt, and in Greco-Roman art looks more like a heron, with a decorative element resembling a feather on the top of its head, long legs and, usually, a rayed halo. As obviously can be expected, many of these iconographic traits have been borrowed from Egyptian art where the *benu* is usually represented with a feather or other elements above its head.[396] At least two frescoes from Pompei, even accompanied by Latin inscriptions, present exactly the Egyptian phoenix (*benu*) or the Roman perception of the *benu* in the frame of the cult of Isis that was very popular in first century CE Rome (fig. 67).[397] It is not to be excluded that the phoenix could have been confused in Greco-Roman religion with a series of divine hypostases in the form of birds. Although there are several pagan gods who were accompanied by or symbolized by a fantastic bird (such as Aion or Helios), it is the eagle of Zeus that appears to be the most interesting.[398] Zeus could manifest himself as

396 The *benu* (possible ancient pronunciation **boin* or **boine* but see: Guilleux 2001) is mentioned in many parts of the Egyptian *Book of the Dead*: Van den Broek 1972, 14-32.

397 Van den Broek 1972, pls. IV-V; Zambon 2004, 19.

398 Sbordone 1935, 2-3; Albrile 2000, 82. Pliny already compared the phoenix to an eagle: *Naturalis Historia* [X, 2-3]. The goddess Venus was sometimes associated to the phoenix in Greek and Latin poetical texts possibly rooted in

an eagle or could send his giant bird as a messenger, or as a raptor like in the myth of Ganymede and Aegina.[399] Judeo-Persian translations of the Bible and even medieval Jewish Persian authors of non-Biblical texts used the term *simurgh* in the place of the eagle which was not intended to be a phoenix or other magical bird. This curious substitution is particularly evident in descriptions of the feet of the throne of Solomon or the four creatures of Ezekiel's vision that included an eagle too.[400]

It is worth observing that the phoenix in the frescoes at Pompei, mentioned above, has some kind of feathers or protuberance on its head. This detail occurred quite often in the reproduction of fantastic birds in Pompeian paintings although it slightly changed in fourth century Roman art. In fact, in the famous mosaics of the Villa

---

more ancient Egyptian traditions: Van den Broek 1972, 269-270; Gasti 2018, 6. Chinese astronomical texts of the Tang period that explicitly mentioned Iranian components, reported the iconography of the planet Venus as a woman wearing a bird hat although she could be also represented sitting on a large bird looking like a rooster or a phoenix (see fig. 98 of this study): Kotyk 2017, 54-55; Kotyk 2018, 64-67. Funerary wooden statuettes from early Tang period Astana graves in Turfan (Xinjiang) sometimes present women with a bird on their head: Qi, Wang 2016, 293, fig. 8. This was definitely part of high class Chinese women's headgear until the post-Tang period as it can be confirmed by archaeological investigations: Filip, Hilgner 2014. One second-third century gilt silver plate with a central image of Dionysus on the back of a panther surrounded by the busts of the twelve Olympian gods (*dodekatheon*) with their animal symbols from Gansu Province attests the importation of these luxury objects into China already in the pre-Christian period. It is worth observing that most of the Olympian deities have a bird as a symbolic animal such as the eagle of Zeus, the peacock of Hera, the owl of Athena and dove or swan of Venus: Marshak 2004.

399 Zeus could use the eagle to transport demigods, heroes and even special objects in the sky to become new constellations. On some possible connections between the eagle of Zeus, the thunderbolt and the lyre from an astronomical-astrological perspective and for some possible iconographic borrowings from the Greco-Roman world and India to model the image of Adbagh/Ahura Mazda in Sogdian art, see: Compareti 2016b, 229-230.

400 Asmussen 1990, 5.

del Casale at Piazza Armerina, the personification of India appears together with the symbolic animals of that distant land such as the elephant, tiger, and phoenix. The latter is easily recognizable because of the rayed halo around its head and the burning nest. There are no feathers nor other elements on its head.[401]

Representations of fantastic birds in Byzantine art included elements on the head that resemble well-defined pointed ears like a mammal, and not feathers like an owl. It is however evident that the owl of Athena could be represented with pointed ears and not feathers such as in a sixth century BCE un-epigraphic Greek seal kept in the State Hermitage Museum. The owl in the seal is definitely the symbolic animal of Athena because the head of the goddess wearing her typical helmet appears next to the animal.[402] Those ears seem to confer to the owl some further supernatural touch. This characteristic calls to mind the aspect of the Mesopotamian *anzu* that was described as a magic bird with a beak like a saw and lion ears. Moreover, it appeared as a dark cloud.[403] Eared birds attacking another animal occurred in Scythians golden objects but it is not clear, if they point at supernatural birds or griffins or if such a detail is just a stereotyped way to represent owls or other real birds of prey.[404]

Other characteristics of this kind of phoenix in Pompei and Greco-Roman art in general is the splendid tail that resembles that of a pheasant or peacock. One of these birds is reproduced on the ivory seat of bishop Maximianus in Ravenna (546) on the right of the scene of the baptism of Jesus (fig. 68).[405] It is represented among the vine trees together with other animals and birds, although its characteristic

401 Dorigo 1971, pl. 8.

402 Neverov 1976, cat. 8.

403 Dalley 2016, 255.

404 Ghirshman 1962, fig. 112a; Bunker, Chatwin, Farkas 1970, figs. 19a, 21; Harmatta 1979, 313; Schiltz 1994, figs. 172, 175-176. See also: Vanzan 2012, 140-141.

405 Gardini, Novara 2011, 83.

ears and long tail seem to allude to its divine nature. Another sample in stone embellished the ancient Sorrento Cathedral (ninth-eleventh century) and is kept at present in the Museum Correale di Terranova.[406] Two-eared birds with long tails and a vegetal element in their beak stand beside a central tree within a medallion. Reproductions of confronted animals were typical of Byzantine and Islamic arts. No inscriptions, nor other elements that could shed light on the identification of those birds, appear in any object of art, although the presence of the ears and their inclusion in the round frame point to supernatural creatures. Some tenth- and eleventh-century Byzantine objects of art present typical Tang *fenghuang*s that were probably introduced and appreciated in Constantinople because of their identification with the phoenix (fig. 69).[407] It is curious that scholars focused on clear representations of Byzantine exotic phoenixes that were definitely imported from China, but mainly neglected "discrete" local versions despite their innatural peculiarities such as the ears or feathers above the head. A very similar problem affected the correct identification of the *simurgh* according to non-Chinese iconographical characteristics in Sogdian paintings and Islamic book illustrations.

Colossal eared birds were also a popular subject in Islamic art. They can be observed in precious textiles and lusterwares from Fatimid Egypt to Seljuk Iran or Central Asia.[408] Other fantastic characteristics, such as two heads, haloes, and necklaces occur quite often and, in many cases, these birds are attacking an animal or transporting a person into the air. Some paintings in the Palatine Chapel in Palermo (ca. 1140) reproduce exactly such a motif (fig. 70), that

406 Bromberg 1983, fig. 5; Lucidi 1994, cat. 100.

407 Walker 2008; Walker 2012, 53-56, 71-77.

408 One Fatimid luster bowl depicting an eared bird in almost perfect condition is kept in the Metropolitian Museum of Art, New York: Jenkins 1983, 12. This kind of fantastic birds continued to be used in the Islamic world for a long period. One fourteenth century glass medallion from Ak Tobe (western Kazakhstan) proved that motifs possibly roote in Buddhist Central Asia were still quite popular in Islamic times: Galkin 1976.

could be connected with the ascension in the sky of Alexander the Great or Kay Kavus in Fatimid, Seljuk and even Buyid art (fig. 71).[409] Double-headed birds with pointed ears or feathers are certainly identifiable with the *'anqa* in some sixteenth century Qazwini's *'Aja'ib al-mahluqat* copied in India. In this case, however, they do not carry any person (fig. 72).[410] Very popular apotheosis images in Classical art probably inspired Muslim artists and occurred in some earlier Islamic texts. Even the most ancient Persian comment on the Koran *Tafsir al-Qur'an* by Abu'l-Futuh Husayn Razi (twelfth century) mentioned the *simurgh* as a kidnapper of animals and people.[411] The same story reported by Mas'udi also included a curious description of the *'anqa/simurgh* that had a human face and was therefore iconographically confused with a Classical harpy or siren.[412] As already argued above, the fantastic bird called by Qazwini and other authors *suryanas* or *arghun* could paralyze other animals and people with its songs but, at the same time, cured human diseases. Birds like these were very often represented in Islamic illustrated texts. On the contrary, the contribution of Sasanian artists for this kind of subjects is not easily detectable.[413]

---

409 Kapitaikin 2016. See also: Abdullaeva 2009-2010. Eared birds appear also in the contemporary and stylistically related richly painted ceilings in the Cefalù Cathedral (Sicily): Gelfer-Jørgensen 1986, pl. 6b; Aurigemma 2004, fig. 224. One eleventh century lusterware from western Iran in the al-Sabah collection presents an eagle abducing a person, probably a woman. In this specimen, the eagle has no ears nor feathers on its head: Curatola 2006, 66.

410 Carboni 1995, 87-89.

411 Amoretti Scarcia 1968, 34.

412 Christensen 1941, 68; Bivar 2009, 3-5. One scholar thought that Chinese birds with a human face or body were adopted from Greek and, possibly, even Egyptian art: Bradford 2013. This hypothesis seems to be arbitrary. Birds with a human (possibly female) face are depicted in eighth century Sogdian paintings: Rempel' 1987, 54-60. They are different from so-called bird-priests that should be considered male: Riboud 2007; Rose 2018.

413 Lerner 1975.

Prototypes were already found in Central Asia or even Buddhist India whose connections with the Greek story of Ganymede's kidnap by Zeus' eagle, or even the Mesopotamian myth of *anzu*, seem quite evident. Guitty Azarpay argued that an unexcavated silver gilt dish in the State Hermitage Museum from Cherdyne (Perm Region, Russia) could be a late Sasanian object embellished with a scene rooted in Buddhist art.[414] Its decoration includes an eared bird holding a naked woman who is feeding the raptor, while two children in the lower part of the dish hold a bow and an axe (fig. 73). The latter detail was interpreted by V. Lukonin as a symbol of day and night because of the precise comparison with a post-Sasanian dish from Klimova (Perm) embellished with the chariot of the moon god whose attribute was an axe. Among the attributes of the sun god, such as Apollo in the Classical world, Mithra in Iran, Surya in India, etc. the bow is always mentioned or represented. The whole scene, in Lukonin's identification, would be the representation of the equinox with the giant raptor as the sun.[415]

Most likely, the Cherdyne dish is not Sasanian but Bactrian or, in any case, eastern Iranian. Moreover, in the light of the similarities between *Garuda*, the *simurgh*, the eagle of Zeus/phoenix and the Mesopotamian *anzu* bird, the giant eared bird in the Hermitage dish could be considered more precisely as a representation of time.[416] However,

414 L'Orange 1953, 69-71; Azarpay 1995. The scene has been identified as *Garuda*'s abduction of the queen of Varanasi as told in the *Kakati Jataka*: Guy 2007, fig. 16. *Garuda*'s Indian iconography changed during the centuries. One of its first depictions can be found on the east gateway (*torana*) of stupa 1 at Sanchi (first century CE). The fantastic bird looks like a giant parrot with human ears: Trainor 1996, fig. 7. During the Gupta period (fourth-sixth century), *Garuda* was mainly represented as a bird with a human head: Raven 1994, 3-8, 17-25, 142-160. Some Gupta seals presented the image of a giant bird carrying a woman who is feeding it: Raven 1994, pl. 19.

415 Lukonin 1977, 195. See also: Harmatta 1979, 316. The axe was probably a royal attribute in Central Asia as observed in second century Kushan coinage (Sinisi 2017, 828-829) and in seventh-eighth century Sogdian art (Shenkar 2017, 66).

416 Compareti, Scarcia 2012, 245-246.

such an identification (and the one by Lukonin) does not explain the woman and the reason why she is naked and friendly toward her giant bird. Nudity could suggest a Greco-Roman model and, in fact, this hypothesis will be discussed below.

Pre-Islamic Central Asian paintings sometimes presented the scene of the giant bird carrying a naked woman. In one case, at Termez in northern Bactria, the context was definitely Buddhist (fig. 74)[417] while in Penjikent was Zoroastrian, although strongly indianized. In the higher part of an unpublished early eigth century painting from room 1/sector XXII at Penjikent, Marshak recognized the figure of a giant bird transporting a woman in its claws and holding a snake in its mouth. Marshak realized that the image had a clear parallel in Indian art but he was also aware that the sphere at Penjikent was Iranian, so an identification with the *chamrush* bird that is mentioned in the Avesta in association with Apam Napat (possibly represented in the same Sogdian painting) seemed more appropriate.[418] Around the scene of the giant bird carrying a woman in Termez paintings (ca. fourth-fifth century) there are flowers and, curiously enough, fishes too. Frames of aquatic creatures for the representation of Ganymede abduction to the sky are well known in Greco-Roman art[419]. Associations between wings and water are not exclusive of Classical art. For example, it is not uncommon to see winged creatures in the water in Neo-Assyrian reliefs from eighth century BCE Khorsabad.[420]

Silver vessels produced in the sphere of Sasanian art, such as the Cherdyne plate, should actually be considered the product of Central Asian artists. Birds of prey or beribboned birds with a necklace or a

417 Compareti, Scarcia 2012, 245. Birds like this with ears or feathers above the head can be found sometimes in (possibly non-Buddhist) Bactrian seals: Lerner, Sims-Williams 2011, 171.

418 Marshak 1990, 308-309.

419 Compareti, Scarcia 2012, 242.

420 Favaro 2008. In this case too, a possible astronomical-astrological approach could possibly offer a solution to this curious association: Bausani 1978b.

jewel in their beak that were represented very often on silver vessels could actually be considered non-Sasanian.[421] Very few metal objects come from controlled excavations at pre-Islamic archaeological sites in Iran.[422] As already argued above, the same problem affects non-excavated precious textiles that are at present kept in many public and private collections around the world. In fact, they could be Islamic Persian or Sogdian or, in more general terms, Central Asian.[423]

Penjikent paintings very often reproduce precious garments that usually present pearl roundel patterns containing different subjects. Beribboned birds with a necklace in their beak and sometimes even standing on a pearled pedestal were a very popular decorative element.[424] These are however just auspicious motifs without any clear connection with the *senmurv/simurgh* of Iranian mythology. Moreover, they do not usually have any feather, nor ears above their head. Precious textiles in mural paintings from Afrasyab, Penjikent, and Varaksha obviously reflected the most fashionable motifs of seventh-eighth century Sogdiana and the rest of Central Asia. Textile decorations at Taq-i Bustan are not only (at least) fifty-sixty years earlier but – as I have argued above – were probably imported from Central Asia by Bastam who had Parthian origins and was appointed governor of Khorasan by the Sasanians.[425] Moreover, the motifs at Taq-i Bustan are not exactly the same of Sogdian paintings because

421 Harper 2006a; Marshak 2006a.

422 There are six specimens, to be precise: two from Susa, one from Qasr-i Abu Nasr, another one from Tell-i Malyan and, lastly, two more from eastern Georgia (ancient Iberia). Only one silver bowl from Susa presents a decoration which includes a bird within a central medallion: Harper 2000, 47-48.

423 Compareti 2009b. The bird with a necklace in its beak was a quite popular motif in Gupta art too and, according to some scholars, it was directly imported into China during the Tang period directly from India: Li 2014. See also a sixth century *mithuna* couple from Bihar, Chhatrapati Shivaji Maharaj Vastu Sangrahalaya, Mumbai: Joshi 2007.

424 Marshak 2006b; Raspopova 2006.

425 Compareti 2019b.

those Persian specimens represented an early stage of Central Asian fashion that was going to reach maturity some time later. As I have tried to demonstrate in other papers of mine, other textile motifs that scholars considered typically Sasanian such as the pearl roundel pattern actually point at Central Asia as its place of origin.[426] Hypotheses about Sasanian Persia as the propagator of "typical" Iranian patterns and artistic formulae that were exported everywhere in the ancient world is actually based on fifty (or more) years old arbitrary deductions by Roman Ghirshman and André Grabar.[427] Such deductions and theories deserve, in my opinion, revision and critical approaches.

Objects like the Cherdyne plate probably had a great impact on the metalwork production of nomadic people as well. In the seventh-eighth century Sânnicolau Mare Avar treasure there are also two golden objects embellished with an imagine of the eared giant bird kidnapping a naked woman who is feeding the animal (fig. 75). As correctly observed by Bruno Overlaet, from an iconographic point of view these objects do not present any direct connection with Sasanian Persia. They could have reached "barbaric" Europe via very mobile nomads, such as the Avars who had some connections with Constantinople. Overlaet suggested also that the image of a bird of prey carrying a person should be studied in the context of the new cultural milieu where such an iconography was adopted.[428] A reading relating to Ganymede, Alexander's ascension, or the myth of *anzu* is not convincing since it is obvious that the person transported by the bird is a naked woman. The same objection could be made for the Cherdyne plate, since the woman feeding the bird does not match with the image of Zal nor Kay Kavus in an Iranian milieu. Therefore, from a mere iconographic point of view, the image of the giant eared bird carrying a woman seems to be rooted in Buddhist India that had already adopted many Greek elements. David Bivar has already

426 Compareti 2004; Compareti 2009b.

427 Ghirshman 1962, 282-342; Grabar 1971.

428 Overlaet 2015.

argued that the model for the image of *Garuda* abducting a woman (*nagini*) could be found in the Greek myth of the nymph Aegina who was kidnapped by the eagle of Zeus.[429] It is not possible to say if the Indians superimposed their own version to this story or they just adopted it from Greece without any great change. In any case, the image on the Cherdyne plate seems to have already undergone some iconographical changes and it displayed an Indianized touch. If the adoption of Indian iconographies by Eastern Iranian people or the Avars responded to precise intentions to be adapted to local mythology or legends is not known and would suggest another definition. Indian themes imported into Central Asia did exist, they were aesthetically very attractive and responded to the search for beautiful objects that were characteristic of many royal courts during Late Antiquity.

Very little evidence about the Ganymede/Aegina-like myth could be found in western Iran. A pair of second century CE silver bowls with an identical Parthian inscription, at present kept in the al-Sabah collection (Kuwait), also presents a related internal decoration. In fact, one bowl is embellished with Leda and the swan while the other has Ganymede and the eagle.[430] Despite the presence of the inscription and some other "eastern peripheral" elements, the scene with Ganymede does not reproduce the kidnapping but a more convivial moment that calls to mind Classical prototypes. A scene of a giant bird abducting a woman, who could be Aegina, is reproduced on a seal-impression that Ph. Gignoux and R. Gyselen included in one of the most complete publications on Sasanian seals.[431] P. Harper argued that a Sasanian or eastern Iranian seal mounted in a golden ring decorated with a beribboned, eared bird carrying a woman could have some astrological implications because of other symbols appearing around the central scene of abduction. Harper focused precisely on

429 Bivar 2005, 15-19; Bivar 2009, 5.

430 Carter 2015, 276-281.

431 Gignoux, Gyselen 1987, 112.

the snake that swallowed a globe and a fish.[432] This hypothesis is very interesting and could actually call to mind similar representations in Greco-Roman and Bactrian art, already observed above, where a fish or dolphin curiously occurred quite often in aerial scenes. Another study on Sasanian sphragistic caught the attention of scholars on one interesting un-epigraphic seal-impression in the Metropolitan Museum of Art in New York, adorned with an eared bird whose body is shaped like a human face [99.22.59]. It is very similar to Classical models that could refer to the kidnapping of Ganymede (fig. 76)[433] or, one could argue, the myth of Aegina. In this case too, there is not enough evidence to propose definitive identifications, although it seems that Sasanian artists favoured representations of birds (for example, on seals and sealings) and attached great importance to them. Decorative ribbons, necklaces and objects in the beak that very often decorated birds in Sasanian seals and luxury arts could refer to the Zoroastrian paradise or royal hunting parks. In any case, they were considered auspicious animals exactly as in Sogdian art. Attendants of the sovereign are represented in the deer hunting panel relief at Taq-i Bustan, while embellishing an animal with ribbons. Most likely, the royal hunter could better recognize this beribboned deer (probably female) in order to avoid shooting her.[434] Some scholars however, identified decorative ribbons and many other elements as symbols of *farr* in pre-Islamic Persian art.[435]

It is very probable that, in early Sasanian art, the idea of *farr* (that presented strong connections with kingship) was shown as an angel (or *putto*) or Eros holding a beribboned diadem, such as in two rock reliefs depicting Shapur I (Bishapur II and III), triumphant over three Roman emperors (fig. 77).[436] However, in the most recently found

432 Harper 2015.

433 Gyselen 2006, 99.

434 Compareti 2016a, 75.

435 Soudavar 2010.

436 Vanden Berghe pl. 23. Just a *putto* and not a winged victory is depicted in

Sasanian rock relief at Rag-i Bibi (Afghanistan), the Sasanian king represented in the act of hunting rhinoceroses, and probably identifiable with Shapur I, is wearing a belt embellished with a *ketos*-like creature.[437] It is very similar to the fantastic animal flying in front of Rustam in the Blue Hall at Penjikent, because this kind of fantastic creatures was quite frequent in eastern Iranian arts. It is very probable that they had just the same (apotropaic) meaning that is a symbolic representation of glory or charisma.

In Sogdian paintings the symbolic representation of *farr* had a very wide range of iconographic variants because, possibly, every divinity had a different symbolic creature or, more simply, the person who ordered the paintings was choosing his favorite composite animal or subject. Among the symbols of *farr* or divine protection in the paintings at Penjikent, one can observe a winged horse (room 12, sector XXV) or camel (room 1, sector XXIV) with a fish tail (a clear borrowing from Classical art), a bird with a necklace in the beak (room 28, sector XXV) or with a ring in the beak (room 7, sector XXVI), a human bust holding a necklace (room 41, sector VI) and, in at least two cases (room 1, sector XXIV and room 12, sector XXV), even a flying hand holding a garland with ribbons attached to it (fig. 78).[438] The position of those symbols of *farr* in Penjikent paintings looks very similar to the one of composite creatures in epigraphic Sogdian and Hunnish

---

a late second century CE Kushan painting on textile kept in a private collection in Bangkok (Marshak 2006c) and on some rare Kushan seals and sealings (Sinisi 2019, fig. 1-2). The presence of this kind of child-angel in Kushan art suggests that the early Sasanians could have borrowed Greek elements directly from the Roman Empire or the Parthians without excluding possible connections with the Kushans in Central Asia.

437 Grenet, Lee, Martinez, Ory 2007, 260-261.

438 Azarpay 1975; Naymark 2001, 360. Despite the fact that in Sogdian paintings it is a left hand, this symbol could be rooted in representations of the *dextera dei* (the right hand of God) that appeared already among the third century decorations of the Dura synagogue and more frequently in Christian art: Goodenough 1964, 107, 128-131, 182-184, 191. See also: L'Orange 1953, 159-162.

coins already observed above. On at least one coin from the Pangul mint in Zabulistan, dated to around 680, the composite creature on the right of the king's bust has a flower or vegetal element in its mouth, probably offered as a homage (fig. 12).

The beribboned winged camel was probably considered a very important symbol in Sogdian art and culture. In Chinese literature referring to the seventh to eighth century, it is said that the kings of different city-states that formed Sogdiana used to sit on thrones shaped as symbolic animals. The king of Bukhara (*An* in Chinese) was sitting on a golden throne in the shape of camels.[439] A male divinity holding a fire altar can be observed sitting on a camel on some fragmentary terracotta statuettes from different Sogdian archaeological sites and, much more interesting, on an altar painted in the "Eastern Hall" at Varakhsha, the site that has been identified as the residence of the king of Bukhara in the eighth century.[440] As already observed above, flying beribboned camels were represented in eighth century Penjikent paintings and on a seventh century silver ewer found in the village of Malcevo (Perm region) in 1878 that is considered by experts the masterpiece of Sogdian toreutics.[441] Despite the problems concerning its identification, this fantastic creature is definitely identical to the one in Penjikent paintings in room 1/sector XXIV. Not only the position of the legs and the open mouth is the same but the shape of the wings and tail and, above all, the ribbon attached to the legs is identical. B. Marshak had already noticed these similarities and proposed to identify the winged camel as a representation of divine protection or a specific symbol of the Avestan god of war and victory

439 Compareti 2016c, 252.

440 Silvi Antonini 2006. The figure of a camel appears sometimes among the decorations of crowns on ancient Chorasmian coins: Vajnberg 1977, 23-24, pls. X, XIII.

441 Marschak 1986, figs. 55-56. The ewer presents also an inscription in Sogdian language that, unfortunately, does not mention the subject embellishing it.

Verethraghna who was called Washaghn in Sogdiana.[442] Grenet proposed to identify the camel as the symbolic animal of the Sogdian god of glory (a personification of *farn*)[443] although, according to some Zoroastian texts, another deity, Dahman Afrin could manifest himself as a camel.[444] Marshak was perfectly aware that this kind of composite creatures appeared quite often is Sogdian art and any precise correspondence with local deities was very problematic. Despite their clear connection with local culture and religion, there is no undisputable evidence (ideally, even supported by captions on the very paintings or other written sources) to propose any precise correspondence between Zoroastrian deities and the representation of composite creatures flying in front of relevant people in Sogdian paintings. Such composite creatures were used by Sogdian artists to exalt deities, kings, heroes, hunters and, possibly, rich merchants as well.

The composite animal configured from the rear part of a winged dog with a peacock tail (what has been identified by Trever as the *simurgh*, our pseudo-*simurgh*) was just a variation of these creatures. It is not clear when it first appeared in Iranian arts, although in Persia it can be only observed at Taq-i Bustan. It is precisely this fantastic creature which had great vitality in the western part of the Iranian world between the late Sasanian-early Islamic period and, possibly, from there it entered (maybe not at the same time) the Caucasus, Byzantium, Arabic lands, and "barbaric" Europe where it continued to be represented (although, probably, with a different meaning) at least until the early thirteenth century. Eastern European graves that have been excavated as far as modern Tatarstan (Russian Federation) produced a lot of interesting metal objects very often embellished with typical Iranian motifs. Some decorative elements for belts from the late eighth-early ninth century cemetery of Bol'she Tigani present composite creatures that could remind a dragon-*ketos* and the

442 Marshak 2000b.

443 Grenet 1993b, 156-159.

444 Shenkar 2014, 162.

pseudo-*simurgh*.[445] It should not be ruled out that the tomb occupants actually made a distinction between the two creatures that they copied from different sources. Many chance findings from this part of Russia have revealed since the Zarist period special attention of local populations for Iranian silver vessels (Sasanian or Central Asian).[446] It is worth observing that most of these unexcavated metal objects were found in graves and definitely had some connections with funerals of local relevant people.

Despite Prudence Harper's and Rika Gyselen's claim, a creature that presents the same characteristics as the pseudo-*simurgh* symbolizing the *farr*, appears in Sasanian sphragistic.[447] A single Sasanian seal in the British Museum [120341, EG 20] presents the image of a composite creature very similar to the pseudo-*simurgh*. It has not been excavated and, so, any chronological hypothesis is highly speculative (fig. 79).[448] Metalwork and textiles within the context of Sasanian art are very difficult to date and even to be considered a genuine core Persian production. In addition, an inscription in Pahlavi appears in the lower part of the seal. It is to be read *'pzwt* (*abzud*) which is part of a formula usually written *xwarrah abzud*, "the glory increased," pretty common on Sasanian coins minted after the fifth century.[449] The formula *xwarrah abzud* can be found on an unusual and rare series of gold coins of Khusraw II Parwiz accompanying the bust of a deity

445 Halikova 1976, fig. 11.

446 Marshak 2006a.

447 Harper 1961, 95; Gyselen 2000a, 66. A group of seal-impressions in the Metropolitan Museum of Art considered to be embellished with "the *sen* bird" – our pseudo-*senmurv* – actually presents in every specimen the image of a griffin: Brunner 1978, 85-86. For some reason, students of pre-Islamic Persian art confused very often the griffin with the pseudo-*senmurv* even though the two creatures presented completely different heads and, in the case of the griffin, a very clear beak: Keall 2002, 69.

448 Bivar 1969, pl. 13. I am grateful to Judith Lerner for pointing this seal out to me.

449 Daryaee 2013, 18.

encircled with flames, whose identity has not been clearly established. According to one scholar, the deity could be Adur or the personification of *xwarrah* or, less probably, Anahita.[450] Why in the British Museum seal does the word *abzud* only appear? Could we assume that, possibly, the word *xwarrah* of the usual formula has been substituted by a figurative representation of that concept? This is just a hypothesis and it is not supported by other similar findings. The seal is in fact extremely rare and it corresponds quite precisely to the special seal of Khusraw II described by Mas'udi as embellished with a *Khurasan khurra* image that Biruni associated to a "flying fox". Its chronology has been established by Bivar as late Sasanian on epigraphic bases[451] although it could even be proto-Islamic since Middle Persian was still used in Persia and Central Asia until at least the tenth century.

It is worth noting that in Islamic art also our pseudo-*senmurv* started to appear quite early and specifically on seals. The National Library of Austria also includes in its collection the so-called "Archduke Rainer Papyrus" [Inv. Ar. Pap. Nr. 17] that presents an epigraphic image of a pseudo-*senmurv* in ink from an original clay seal considered to be Omayyad (fig. 80). Unfortunately, the Arabic inscription on the seal is not useful to identify the composite creature on it, being just an Islamic religious formula "God gives long life to one who follows Him".[452] The same may also be considered valid for the image of pseudo-*simurgh*s and Arabic or Middle Persian inscriptions on early Omayyad coins commonly called "Arab-Sasanian".[453] Therefore, the use of Middle Persian on the seal in the British Museum studied by Bivar strongly suggests that it is an object which should be dated to the (late) Sasanian period.

The Middle Persian formula *xwarrah abzud* appeared not only on Khusraw II drachms but also on late seventh century Hunnish

450 Gyselen 2000b.

451 Bivar 1969, 81.

452 Creswell 1940, fig. 686; Santi 2020.

453 Treadwell 2008; Daryaee 2015.

coins from Arachosia and Zabulistan, already observed in this study (fig. 12). Several emissions from Arachosia and Zabulstan present the flaming deity on the reverse that appeared first on Khusraw II rare coins. Copper coins of a Hunnish or Turkish king called Spur (late seventh century) presents also his bust with a pair of pseudo-*simurgh* on the obverse and the deity with a flaming nimbus on the reverse (fig. 81). It is not possible to be sure about the identity of this god or goddess although the flaming nimbus could be considered an allusion to the glory that is mentioned very often in the Middle Persian formula *xwarrah abzud*. The presence of that deity on Hunnish/Turkish coins, where it appears together with the pseudo-*senmurv* in front of the king, could corroborate such a hypothesis. We could therefore assume that both symbols could be an allusion to *xwarrah*: the deity with a flaming nimbus was probably Sasanian while the pseud-*simurgh* was Central Asian. Rika Gyselen has already cautiously proposed that the flaming nimbus, or even the same deity with that nimbus, was a symbol of GDE (*xwarrah*).[454] Persians appreciated the flaming nimbus more, while the pseudo-*senmurv* became very common in eastern Iran. Such a geographical distribution probably reflects the place of origin of those motifs.

Starting from the problematic identification of Kamila Trever, Rika Gyselen wrote in one of her studies on Arabo-Sasanian coins that "it is astonishing that no Sasanian seal seems to depict the Sēnmurw [our pseudo-*senmurv*/*simurgh*]. In the East Iranian borderlands the Sēnmurw was frequently depicted, particularly on the coins issued by the 'Iranian Huns'. From this evidence it looks like if the Sēnmurw has a specific meaning in relation to investiture, but no such relation is explicitly stated in Sasanian Iran".[455] Some time later, in another paper on the Sasanian monetary heritage, on copper coins of early Islamic Arachosia and Zabulistan, R. Gyselen identified again the pseudo-*senmurv*/*simurgh* as a "Sasanian royal symbol" although she

454 Gyselen 2010, 237.

455 Gyselen 2000a, 66.

admitted that "the term *sēnmurv*, literally meaning dog-bird [sic], is used for convenience here; in fact, this creature more closely resembles a lion than a dog".[456] The situation appears much less complicated nor astonishing at all if we admit that the pseudo-*simurgh* did not belong to the Sasanian artistic repertoire but to the Central Asian one that the Huns and Turks knew very well.

When the Persians began to adopt this symbol and to represent it at Taq-i Bustan, the Arab invasion took place which would have changed the entire scenario. In the specific situation under exam, the arrival of the Arabs probably accelerated the adoption of the pseudo-*simurgh* as a much requested auspicious symbol as it is possible to deduce by the study of most popular decorative motifs in Omayyad art. Arab artists in service of the first caliphs inherited such symbolic composite creature from eastern Iran like everybody else in the seventh century or slightly earlier.

Pseudo-*simurgh*s were reproduced on Persian coins only in the early Omayyad period but not in front of the king. In fact, the pseudo-*simurgh* usually occupied the entire space on the reverse of copper coins. This makes the situation even more complicated since it is extremely hard to decide who invented a symbol such as the flaming nimbus and who borrowed it. In the case of the pseudo-*simurgh*, one could imagine that it was introduced into Sasanian Persia from eastern Iran where it has been quite popular, at least since the late fifth century. This is what we could deduce from the incomplete throne of the Sogdian deity in Penjikent Temple II painting (fig. 29). Some time later, the pseudo-*simurgh* started to be used as a special symbol of *xwarrah*/*farn* in front of a king, as seen on seventh century eastern Iranian Hunnish and Turkish coins or seventh century Sogdian countermarks. In the West, it started to undergo several changes before being completely accepted in Persian art, where it never appeared in front of a king. However, its presence on the clothes of sovereigns at Taq-i Bustan strongly suggests some kind of connections with for-

456 Gyselen 2010, 228.

tune, glory, charisma, kingship, etc. Arabo-Sasanian coins continued to present the human bust with flaming nimbus which was based on the coins of Khusraw II type and, for some time, this motif and the pseudo-*simurgh* appeared along with other unusual ones that scholars would have expected to find on pre-Islamic coinage.[457] It is not given to know the precise meaning of these motifs that do not look Islamic at all. Unfortunately, the inscriptions in Arabic or Middle Persian on Arabo-Sasanian coins just repeat formulae without any description of the motifs accompaining them.

The unique epigraphic seal in the British Museum only presents the pseudo-*simurgh* and no other images. This may provide another hint towards a (late) Sasanian Persia attribution. No other Iranian art objects with a representation of a pseudo-*senmurv*/*simurgh* has been found during controlled excavations. The same objection could be considered valid for so-called Sasanian textiles that, in many cases and, mainly, from an iconographic point of view, have been thought to be the result of Sogdian, Byzantine or early Islamic productions.[458] For this reason, there is no real evidence to consider that composite creature as a genuine Sasanian creation. It could have been introduced very easily from eastern Iranian lands, possibly Khorasan-Sistan or Zabulistan, that is to say, the homeland of Rustam. Moreover, the standard of Rustam is described in the *Shahnameh* as embellished with a dragon [Khalegi Motlagh II, 530; III, 1183; VII, 512-513][459] and, as already mentioned above, a pseudo-*simurgh* (or a similar creature) appears on coins from Zabulistan.[460]

Could this be another allusion to an association between this epic Iranian hero and the creature symbolizing *farr*? The real *simurgh* could therefore be considered to be a bird and the protector of Zal and Rustam while the glory or charisma of these heroes appeared in

457 Gyselen 2009.

458 Compareti 2009b.

459 Kuehn 2011, 42.

460 Nikitin 1984, 234; Gyselen 2009, 154-156; Rezakhani 2017a, 174-175.

the shape of a chimera that local dynasties (even "barbaric" ones) adopted on their coins in order to legitimize themselves. On the other hand, the *farr* of Rustam took the shape of a creature similar to the pseudo-*simurgh* in Sogdian paintings and, maybe, it could also have been reproduced on the banner of that hero. Both *simurgh* and a pseudo-*simurgh*-like creature appeared together with Rustam in literary texts and (as argued in this study) in the visual arts. This co-presence of fantastic creatures could have just contributed to some confusion. It was not rare to notice in Timurid book illustrations that the standard of Rustam was sometimes embellished with a typical Chinese phoenix (*fenghuang*) definitely alluding at the *simurgh*. The most famous of these illustrations can be found in the so-called *Baysunghur Shahnameh*, at present kept in the Golestan Palace in Tehran that is precisely dated to 1429-1430.[461] The choice to represent the *simurgh* and not a dragon as described in the *Shahnameh* could have generated some more confusion among ancient readers and contemporary scholars.

These observations do not explain the complete disappearance of the pseudo-*simurgh* in Islamic arts around the eleventh century. As observed above, composite creatures (and especially the pseudo-*simurgh*) became extremely popular in Persia during the very end of the Sasanian and early Islamic period. Numismatic studies demonstrated that pseudo-*simurgh*s were not anymore reproduced as countermarks or marginal elements beside the portrait of Hunnish rulers but took all the space on one side of coins. This composite creature definitely had a central role and, most likely, was introduced from Central Asia into Persia and the rest of Eurasia. The pseudo-*simurgh* was very popular in Omayyad arts. If the so-called *zandaniji* textiles could be actually considered a production of the Samanid Emirate (819-999),[462] there could be then some evidence to think at the pseudo-*simurgh* as a symbol of glory or charisma that Arab and Islamized Iranian dynas-

461 Binyon, Wilkinson, Gray 1971, pl. XLVIII.A.

462 Compareti 2015, 36-37.

ties appreciated despite its pre-Islamic roots. It is quite improbable that the pseudo-*simurgh* had religious connotations for the Muslims while it could have very strong associations with kingship and royal glory. If considered from this point of view, the representation of the pseudo-*simurgh* could have then encountered no big problems to be accepted at Islamic courts.

The end of the Samanid Emirate and all other Islamic Iranian dynasties coincided with the rise of the Seljuk Turks in Central Asia, Persia, the Caucasus, Mesopotamia, and Anatolia. During this period, in the huge territory under Seljuk suzerainty not only the leadership changed but artistic formulae and general artistic taste mutated as well. For some reason, the pseudo-*simurgh* disappeared or its (modified) representations were just limited to the astrological-astronomical sphere, while other composite creatures such as the dragon started to appear more and more frequently in official arts, book illustrations, etc.[463] Among the very few representations of pseudo-*simurgh* in Seljuk art, one could mention a twelfth century silver dish found in Surgut (western Siberia), at present kept in the State Hermitage.[464] The medallion in the center of the dish presents a winged horned creature with the back part composed of feathers. It is probably an unusual and highly modified representation of the pseudo-*simurgh* discussed in this study that does not display anymore canine features.

It seems that the period of Seljuk rule paved the path for the consecration of the "Chinese fashion" as the most requested way of depicting fabulous creatures and many other decorative elements in Persian art. The peak of this "fashion" was going to be reached during the Mongol period about one century later, when the *simurgh* started to be assimilated to the Chinese *fenghuang* and the dragon to the *long*. As already observed in other chapters of this study, Persian book illustrations of the Mongol Ilkhanid period demonstrated special attachment to Chinese elements developed under the Song Dynasty

463 Kuehn 2011, 215-228.

464 Marschak 1986, fig. 163.

(960-1279). If this hypothesis mainly based on chronological observations could be considered convincing, there could have been some symbolic element in the representation of the pseudo-*simurgh* that the Seljuk Turks did not appreciate. This sounds quite strange since it is a very well-known fact that Persian language and culture played an important role at the Seljuk court. Could we assume that the Seljuks did not like the pseudo-*simurgh* because it was a Central Asian and not specifically Persian element? Such an attitude of the Seljuk court could be just another hint to the origin of the pseudo-*simurgh* but it does not completely explain why it disappeared in the whole Islamic world.

Much has been written on Rustam as a Saka hero.[465] His figure was probably accepted more easily in Central Asia than in Persia. As already observed, there are passages of the Rustam saga in the Sogdian language that do not appear in the "standard" edition of the *Shahnameh*. Some other parts of the *Shahnameh* were rooted in pre-Islamic (eastern) Iranian traditions.[466] Marshak tried to identify some of the scenes in the Blue Hall with precise episodes in the *Shahnameh*.[467] In all probability, Firdousi knew these eastern Iranian epic tales very well and he chose to introduce only some of them in his work. However, Firdousi was living in a much later period, when Islam had rendered some literary characters hated by the Zoroastrians more acceptable for Iranian culture. Something very similar had happened to Alexander the Great, who was considered a demon in Zoroastrian literature and only later became an important figure in the (Persian) Islamic tradition.[468] As Scarcia pointed out, Rustam was described in some literature (such as in the *Tarikh-i Sistan*) as the heretic *par excellence*. This tradition is not preserved in the *Shahnameh*,

465 Gazerani 2015.

466 Macuch 2012.

467 Marshak 2002b.

468 Wiesehöfer 2011, 113-132; Compareti 2018a, 97.

but it was known by Muslim authors such as Dinawari.[469] Rustam and his family did not accept the conversion to Zoroastrianism and preferred to maintain their old "pagan" traditions, that is to say, a religious system possibly very similar to the one professed in medieval Sogdiana. If it is true that the Sasanians, at a certain point of their rule, started to consider themselves as the heirs of the "Zoroastrian" Kayanids, then it seems very perplexing that they could have appreciated Rustam and his protector, the *simurgh*. The Sasanians had even included the word *kay* that is Kayanid, in their coins since the fifth century, according to a process that Touraj Daryaee called "Zoroastrianisation of memory".[470]

Something more could be added about the representation of the pseudo-*simurgh*/*farr* on the garments of the king at Taq-i Bustan. As already observed above, Cristoforetti has called attention to a passage by Biruni describing a kind of "flying fox" as *Khurasan khurra*, the same expression translated by Herzfeld as "*gloria Orientis*". This description of the *khurra*/*farr* is very similar to the image of the *ghurm*/*farr* following Ardashir in the *Karnamag*, and the flying dog with a peacock tail among the textile decorations at Taq-i Bustan that is almost contemporary with the same painted motif at Afrasyab (ca. 660), and the coins from Zabulistan with a flying creature in front of the king (ca. 680). If that composite creature had to be associated with a characteristic of the Kayanids (who, in Marshak's opinion, should be the late Sasanians), why it is described as *Khurasan khurra*/*gloria Orientis*? Could this "Orient" be intended as something connected to the Sakas or Parthians who lived in eastern Iranian lands?

According to Scarcia, the name of Taq-i Bustan could be reconstructed as the "arch of Bastam" and can be found in some literary traditions. For this reason, Scarcia advanced the unproven but highly fascinating hypothesis that Bastam could be identified with one of the famous uncles of Khusrau II who had some Parthian connections

469 Davis 2007, 58-59.

470 Daryaee 2006.

and, for some time, was governor of Khorasan. Moreover, the figure of Bastam had been superimposed on the semimythical Farhad that is Phraates, a name that several Parthian sovereigns had in addition to the dynastic Arshak.[471] This could explain the unprecedented flying creatures (and many other motifs) on the garments of the king at Taq-i Bustan: they are attested to in Central Asian art but not much in Persia because they are, in all probability, an eastern Iranian creation. As already observed above, it is very likely that the origins of the iconography of this specific flying creature (our pseudo-*simurgh*) is rooted in Hellenistic art. The *ketos* seems to be the most probable candidate although it was adapted in the Iranian lands to mean something else, not necessarily associated with the passage into the underworld and funerary art in general.

In summary, both the symbolic representation of *farr* as a composite creature and the "real" *simurgh* should be considered importations into Persia from the east and not vice-versa. Some ambiguity persists because the connections between the *simurgh* and *farr* are constant. For example, in the *Shahnameh*, it is reported that the feathers of the *simurgh* contain the *farr*. This ambiguity would have caused several problems and not only in the Iranian cultural sphere *stricto sensu*. In the Georgian translation of the *Shahnameh*, the *simurgh* is rendered as a creature called *paskuj* that is a Middle Persian borrowing for a she-dragon.[472] This is just one case, but it could explain how *simurgh* and *farr* started to be confused both in visual arts and literature.

As pointed out by Ursula and Nicholas Sims-Williams, Rustam should be considered an Eastern Iranian hero whose name appeared very late in Sasanian Persia, practically at the dawn of the Arab invasion when epic traditions originally from Sistan or Central Asia started to be popular also in western Iran. The name Rustam (literally

471 Cristoforetti, Scarcia 2013, 344.

472 Marr 1918, 2081; Buyaner 2003.

"strong as a river") seems to have been transmitted in Sogdian texts through the Persian language.[473]

In any case, it is very unlikely that images of Rustam trials will be ever found in the frame of Sasanian arts because Rustam and the *simurgh* would have been perceived by Zoroastrians as representatives of an inimical branch of the Kayanids. As Rahim Shayegan argued, the identification of the Sasanians with the mythical Kayanids was probably operated for propagandistic reasons at the time of Yazdigard II (438-457), who aimed to make a parallel between the Central Asian Huns and the ahrimanic Turanians of very ancient Iranian legends.[474] Some centuries later, at the time of Firdousi, the eastern Iranian Rustamids were integrated into "official" Persian epic literature that is represented by the *Shahnameh*. This happened only in the Islamic period according to modalities which could remind us of another enemy of the Zoroastrian faith who was later accepted by Muslim authors: Alexander the Great. One could argue that the very problematic Sasanian *Khodhay Namak* ("Book of Lords") that could have constituted the basis for several parts of the *Shahnameh* did not include yet the Sistani cycle or, in case it had dedicated some space to Rustam, this hero would have perceived in a negative way. Unfortunately, there are just sparse and fragmentary information on the *Khadhay Namak* which suggests cautiousness in proposing too precise hypotheses.[475]

The only pre-Islamic context where some traces might be found is Central Asia, such as in the artistic traditions that stretched from Merv to Sogdiana, although it is not possible to exclude that similar traditions could also have existed among other Iranian people of Saka extraction, such as the Khotanese. Before the conversion of most of its population to Buddhism (around the first century CE) the history of Khotan is incompletely understood. The Khotanese documents

473 Sims-Williams, Sims-Williams 2015, 251-252.

474 Shayegan 2013, 807.

475 Hämeen-Anttila 2018.

that have been found in great number in the oases of the southern Tarim Basin (modern Xinjiang) contain only few non-Buddhist traits. Some recently excavated textile fragments from Shanpula (not far from Khotan) display a curious iconography where there is also a hunter on horse who is shooting at a composite monster, and he is accompanied by a bird of prey flying behind him that could suggest ancient roots, even pre-Buddhist ones (fig. 82). The chronology, based on C14 dating, ranges from the third century BCE to the third century CE.[476] It is very difficult to propose any identification for the hunter with a bird, although it is clear that there are no obvious Buddhist elements, and some details of the main character on horseback (such as the geometric traits of his face in profile) offer a parallel with the image of Rustam in the Blue Hall at Penjikent. The hunter is definitely shooting at the monster in front of him and not at the bird flying behind him. Moreover, the bird is too small to be used as a falcon trained for hunting. The animal prey in falconry are, in fact, hares, other birds, or small animals. That bird is just accompanying the hunter and its position behind him calls to mind, once more, the painting of Rustam at Penjikent that is several centuries later. Samanid polychrome underglaze-painted ceramic vessels are represented by the specimens from Nishapur that are commonly dated to ninth-tenth century. A very interesting bowl decorated with a horseman and Kufic inscriptions around the rim kept in the Museum für Islamische Kunst (Berlin) presents also a bird with a flower in the beak on the back of the horse while two more birds are flying in front and below the rider.[477] In this case too, the bird on the back of the horse seems to homage the noble horseman and does not look like a falcon trained for hunting.

Despite the fact that falconry was appreciated and possibly practiced in the Near East from ancient times,[478] there are no works of art

476 Bunker 2001.

477 Heroic Times. A Thousand Years of the Persian Book of Kings 2012, cat. 90.

478 Islamic sources attributed the introduction of falconry into Persia to Jamshid

decorated with motifs undoubtedly associated to this kind of hunting in pre-Islamic Persian arts.[479] Among silver vessels produced in the sphere of Sasanian art, there is one specimen that might recall the hunting scene in the Shanpula textile. The so-called Strelka plate (from Perm region, now in the State Hermitage Museum) presents a court and a hunting scene on two levels (fig. 83).[480] In the hunting scene there is something unusual as two rams escape from the king but only one is lying on the ground, while in the upper left corner there is a flying bird. Such a bird should not be considered a falcon used in ancient times for hunting because the rams represent prey that is too large. Very likely this bird could be a companion of the king such as the *simurgh* of Iranian mythology, or even a representation of the glory (*farr*) of the king exactly as in Sogdian paintings. These observations could help to identify the Strelka plate as an eastern Iranian product which displays very strong Sasanian elements. The Merv vase too could be just another specimen of Iranian objects of art embellished with scenes that included a hunter accompanied by a protecting bird (fig. 65). Therefore, the bird with ears in the Merv vase could actually be part of the hunting scene and not to the wedding or funeral scenes, which are reproduced next to the riding archer.

Although this parallel could be considered to have been emphatically proposed by this author, the only available evidence that one can present lies in the many common details between the Shanpula textiles and the Penjikent paintings in the Blue Hall. If the read-

---

himself who would have written even a treatise on this subject: Pedone 2001, 93. Falconry was much appreciated in pre-Islamic Arabia too: Carusi 2007, 156.

479 Vieira Pinto 2020. Possible representations of falconry on horse can be observed on seventh-eighth century Central Asian seals from Bactria and Chorasmia: Litvinskij, Solov'ev 1985, figs. 12-13. However, such objects are very small and the scenes that embellish them are quite confused. The first clear representation of this hunting practice was found in Nishapur ninth century paintings at present kept in the National Museum of Iran, Tehran: Fontana 2002, 77.

480 Harper, Meyers 1981, 114, pl. 19.

ing that I have proposed in the present study could be considered convincing, then there would be some decisive elements to support the identification of the scenes depicted in the Blue Hall only with Rustam and his trials, as already proposed by Russian scholars based on other evidence.

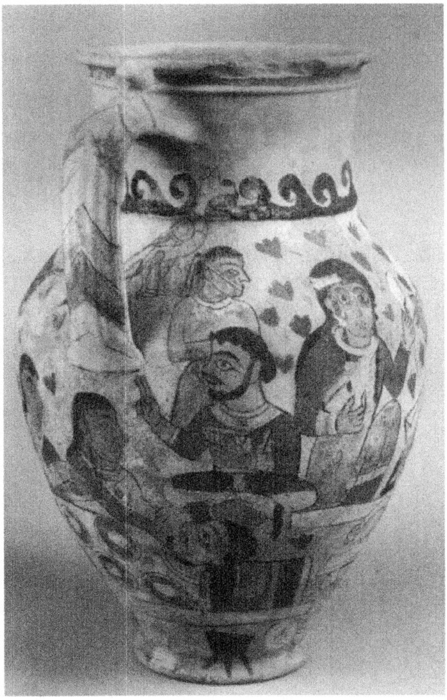

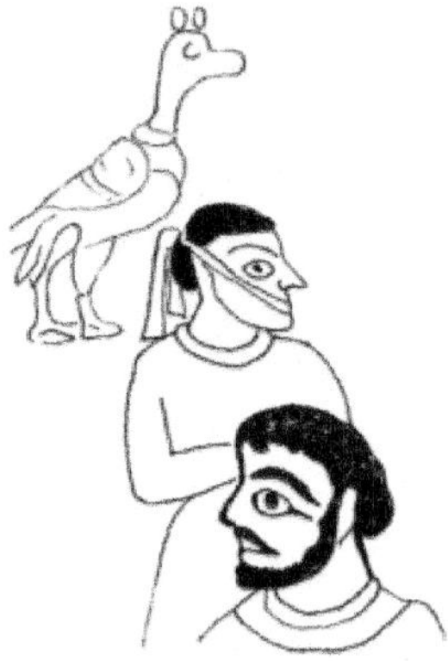

Figure 65a-b. Painted vase from Merv, Ashkhabad Museum (ca. sixth century). After: Manassero, N. (2003). Il vaso dipinto di Merv. *Parthica* 5: pl. v.

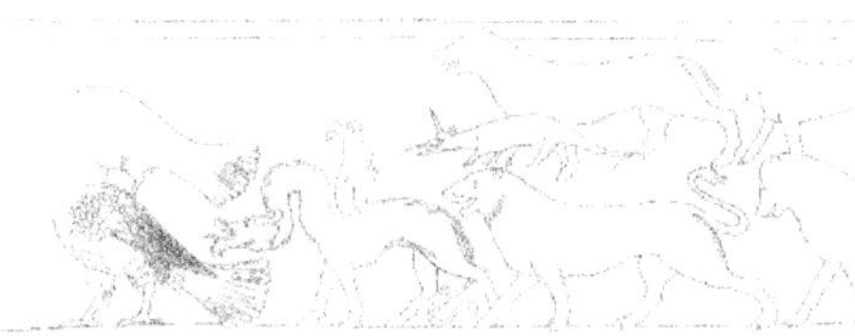

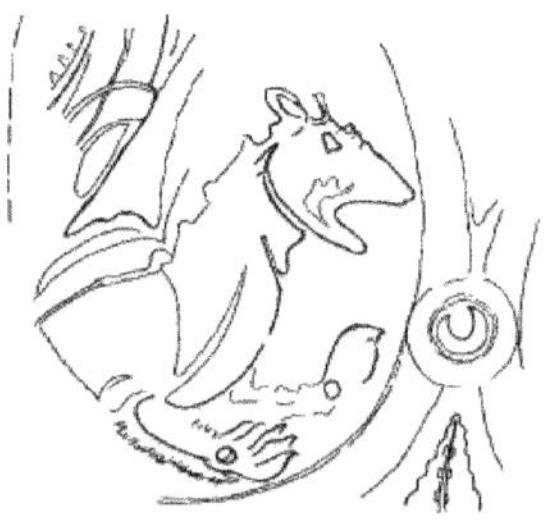

Figure 66a-b. Paintings from Kal'a-ye Kakhkaha palace, Archaeological Museum, Dushanbe (ca. ninth century). After: Institute of History, Archaeology and Ethnography, Academy of Sciences, Tajikistan, National Research Institute for Cultural Properties, Tokyo 2010, 142, 287.

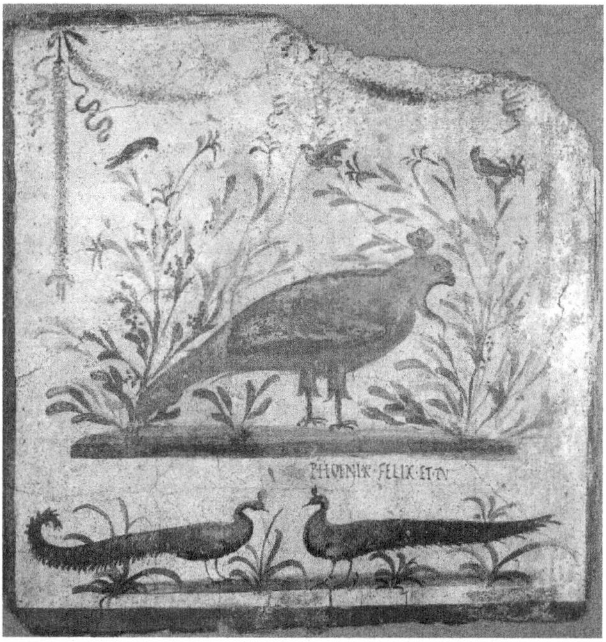

Figure 67. Phoenix with Latin inscription in a fresco from the Euxinus Inn, Pompei [Depositi archeologici, inv. 41761] (first century CE). After: Zambon 2004, 19.

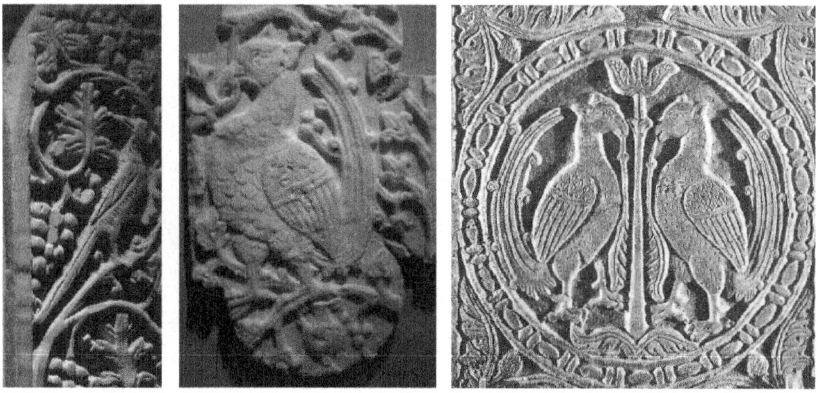

Figure 68a-c. Byzantine eared birds. Left: Seat of Bishop Maximianus (546). Museo Arcivescovile, Ravenna. After: Gardini, Novara 2011, 83. Center: marble relief from South Italy, vicinity of Salerno (ca. 1000). The Metropolitan Museum of Art [2013.268]. Photo: author. Right: marble relief from Sorrento Cathedral (ca. 1000). Museum Correale di Terranova. After: Lucidi 1994, cat. 100.

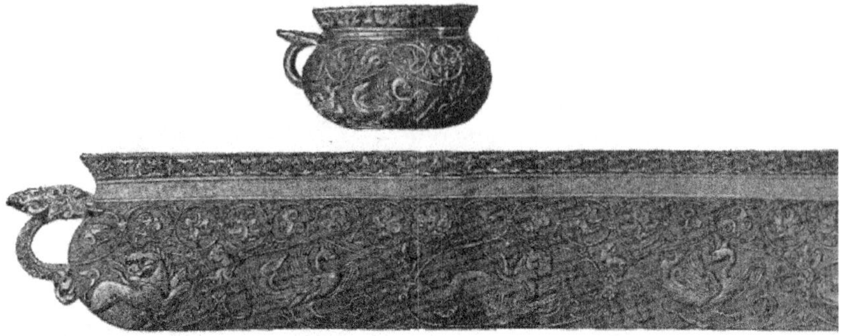

Figure 69a-b. Byzantine bowl embellished with Tang *fenghuangs* and winged lions found in the Kama region, Russia (tenth or eleventh century). Current location unknown. After: Walker 2008, figs. 10A-10B.

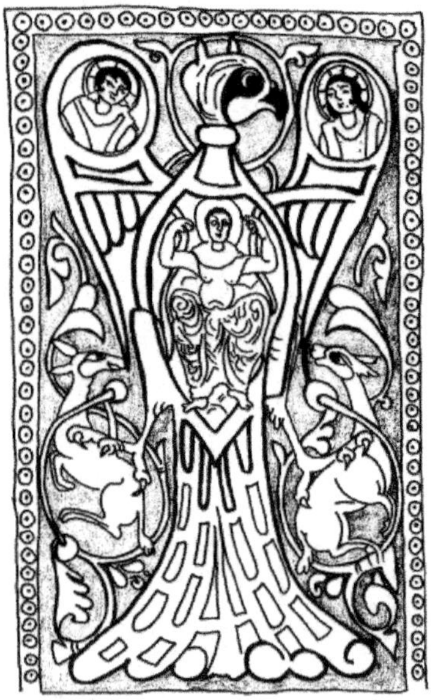

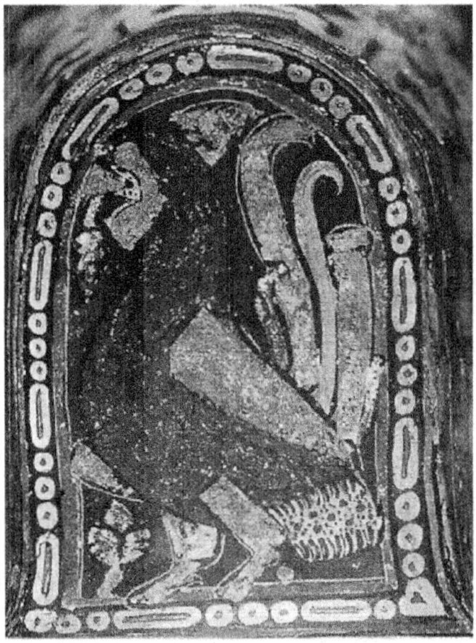

Figure 70a-b. Painted ceiling, Palatine Chapel, Palermo (ca. 1140). Left: giant eared bird carrying a person. After: Compareti, M. (2010). A Short Note on a So-Called Iskandar Dhu'l-Qarnayn in a Bactrian Painting. *Parthica* 12 fig. 11. Right: eared rooster. After: Grube, E.J., Johns, J. (2005). *The Painted Ceilings of the Cappella Palatina*. Genova-New York, pl. XXXI.

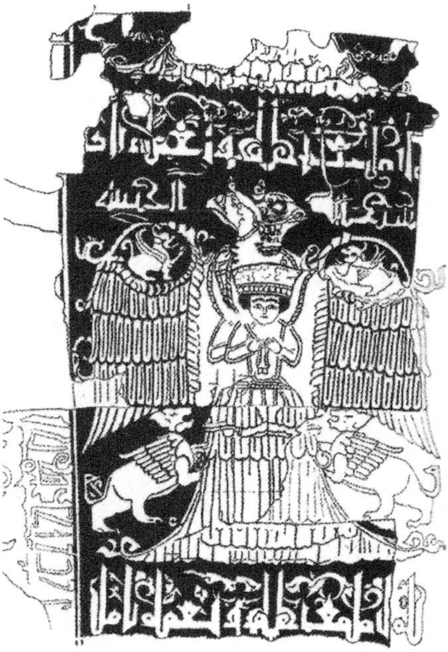

Figure 71. Giant eared bird carrying a person on a Seljuk silk from Rayy (twelfth century). Musée du Moyen Âge, Thermes et Hôtel de Cluny [inv. CL 218-72]. After: Overlaet 2015, fig. 8.4.

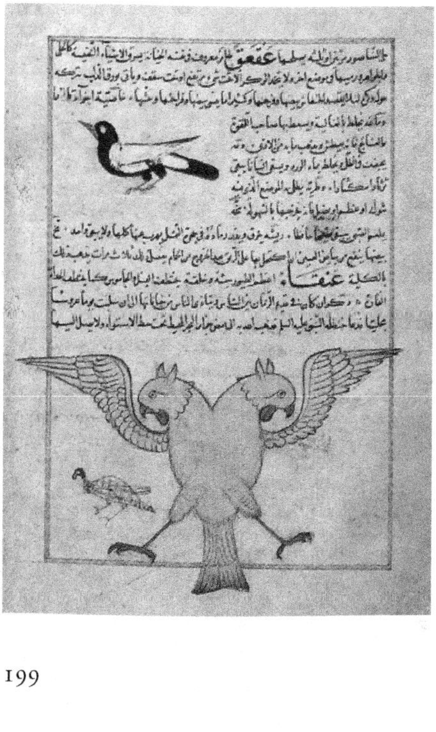

Figure 72. Double-headed *'anqa* from a *'Ajab al-maqhulat* manuscript, probably Deccan (1570-1600). Freer Gallery of Art, Smithsonian Institution, Washington DC [folio 54.104v]. After: Carboni 1995, fig. 13.

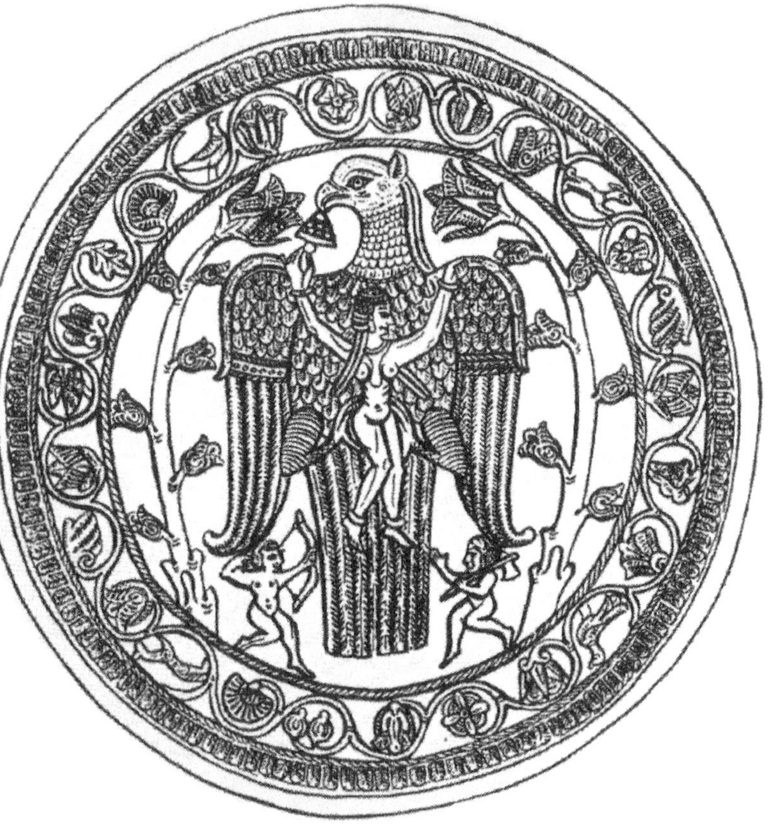

Figure 73. Eastern Iranian (Bactrian?) silver gilt plate from Cherdyne, Perm (sixth-seventh century). The State Hermitage Museum, St Petersburg. After: Egami, N. (1974). On the Figure of the Iranian Goddess Anāhitā as an Example of the Continuity of the Iranian Culture, in: *Commemoration Cyrus. Hommage Universel. Acta Iranica, 1.* Leiden-Tehran-Liège, pl. xxv, fig. 17.

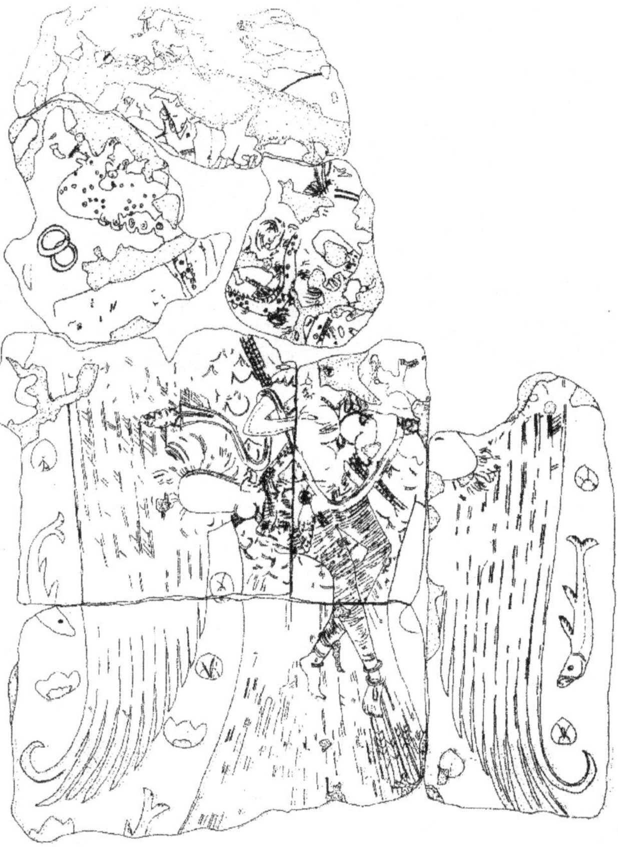

Figure 74. Fragmentary *Garuda* and *nagini* on a Bactrian mural painting from Zar Tepe Buddhist site, Termez, Uzbekistan (fourth-fifth century). After: Pidaev, Sh. R., Reutova, M.A. (2008). Zhivopis' Zartepa. *Istorija Material'noj Kul'tury Uzbekistana* 36 fig. 2.

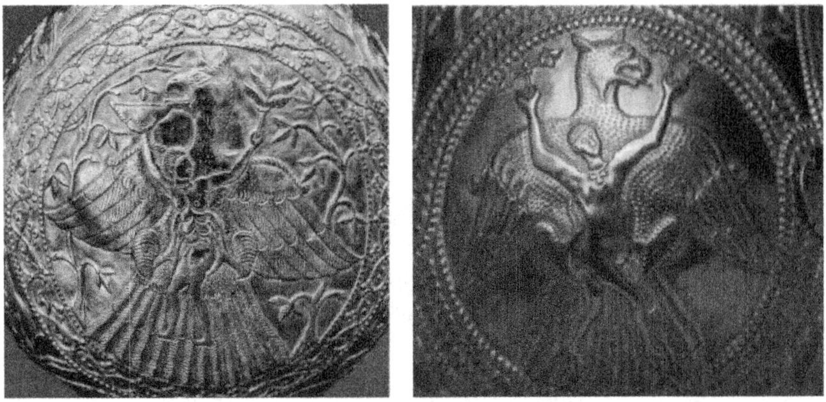

Figure 75a-b. An eared giant bird carrying a naked woman on two golden objects in the Sânnicolau Mare Avar treasure (seventh-eighth century). Kunsthistorisces Museum Vienna. After: Overlaet 2015, fig. 5.

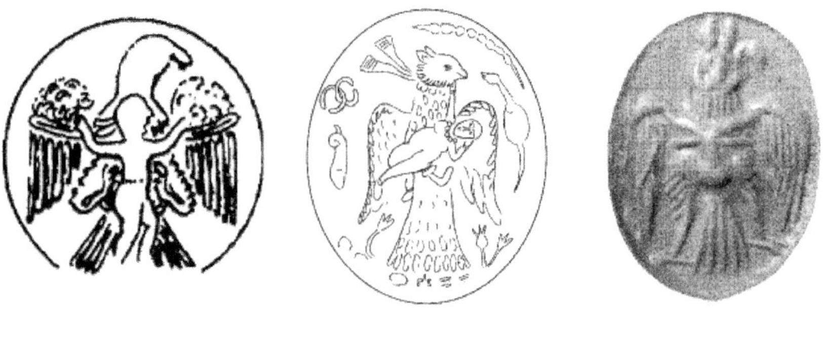

Figure 76a-c. Un-epigraphic seal-impressions. Left: in the Bibliothèque Nationale, Paris. Center: in the al-Sabah Collection, Kuwait. Right: seal-impression embellished with an eared bird whose body is shaped like a human face (late Sasanian). Metropolitan Museum of Art, New York [99.22.59]. After: Harper 2006b, fig. 97; Carter 2015, cat. 91; Gyselen 2006, fig. 20.

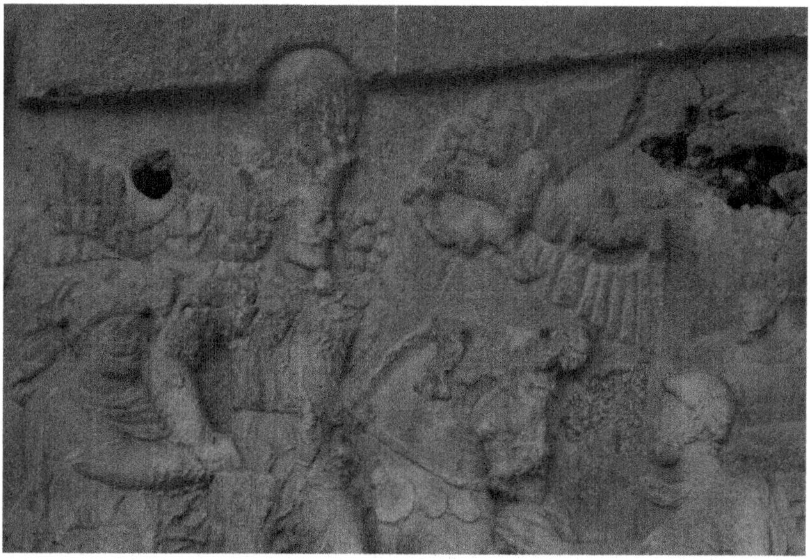

Figure 77. Detail of Bishapur II triumphal Sasanian rock relief, Fars Province, Iran. Shapur I (242-260) receiving a diadem from an angel (*putto*) or Eros. Photo: Li Sifei.

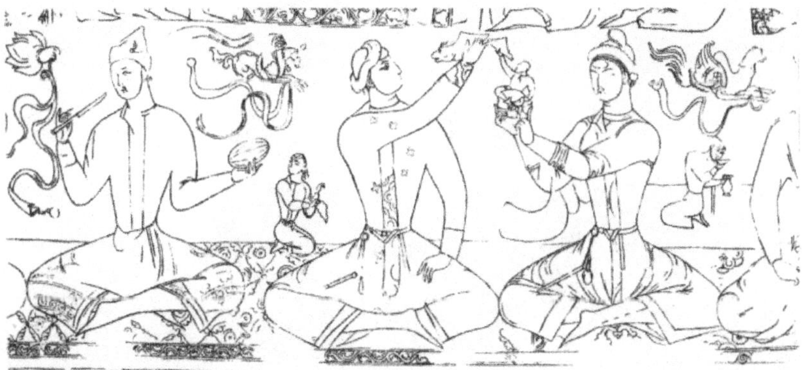

Figure 78. Sogdian banquet on a mural painting from room 12, sector XXV, Penjikent (ca. 740). The State Hermitage. After: Baulo, A.V., Marshak, B.I. (2001). Silver Rhyton from the Khantian Sanctuary. *Archaeology, Ethnology and Anthropology of Eurasia* 3, 7, fig. 4.

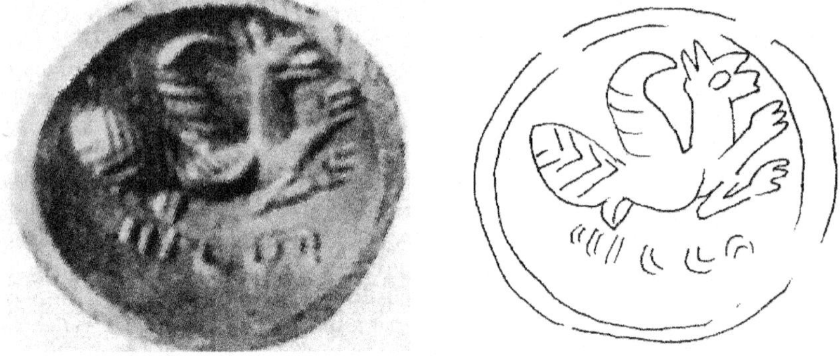

Figure 79a-b. Late Sasanian epigraphic seal, the British Museum [120341, EG 20]. After: Bivar, 1969, pl. 13.

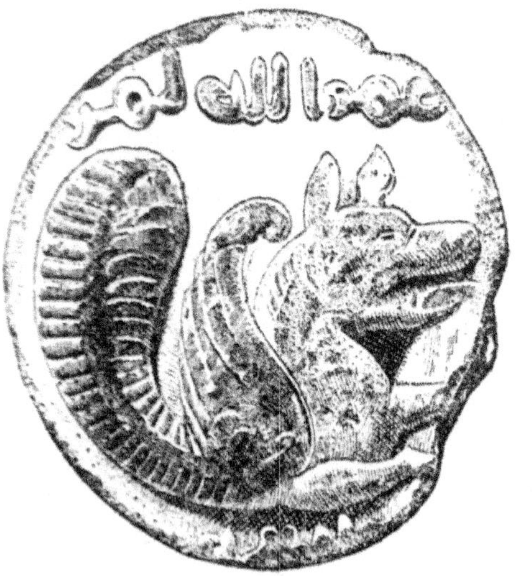

Figure 80. Pseudo-*senmurv* in ink from an original clay seal (Omayyad). "Archduke Rainer Papyrus" National Library of Austria [Inv. Ar. Pap. Nr. 17]. After: Creswell 1940, fig. 686.

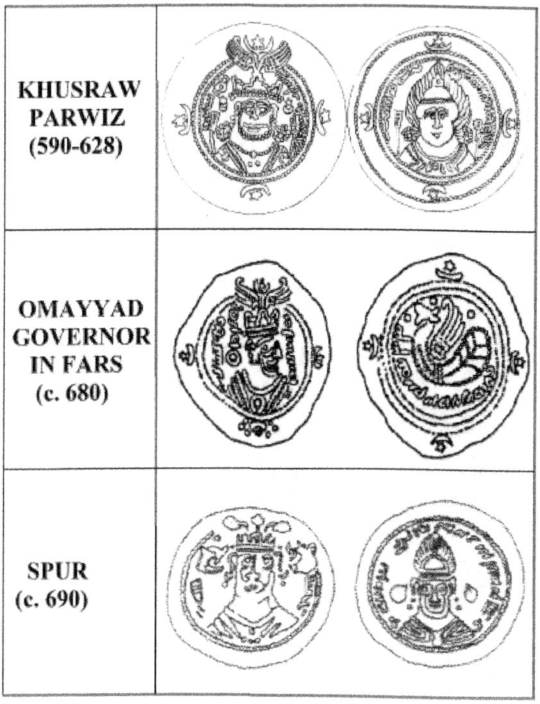

Figure 81a-c. Silver drachm of Khusraw II, copper coin of an Omayyad governor of Fars and copper coin of Spur from Arachosia/Zabulistan. After: Gyselen 2000b, fig. 1; Gyselen 2009, fig. 17; Gyselen 2010, fig. 1.

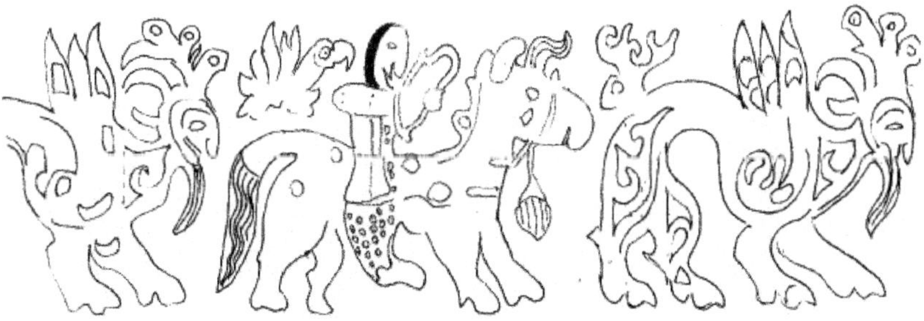

Figure 82. Fragmentary textile from Shanpula Cemetery, Khotan, Xinjiang Uighur Autonomous Province (ca. first-third century). After: Bunker 2001, fig. 8.

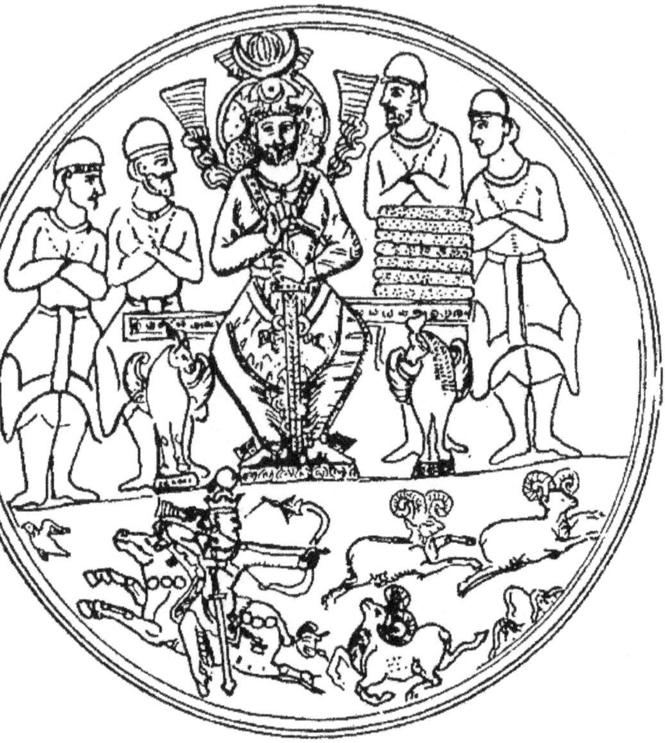

Figure 83. Court and hunting scene, Strelka plate, Perm region. The State Hermitage Museum, St Petersburg (eastern Iran, sixth-seventh century). After: Haskins, J.F. (1952). Northern Origins of "Sasanian" Metalwork. *Artibus Asiae* 15, pl. VII, fig. 3.

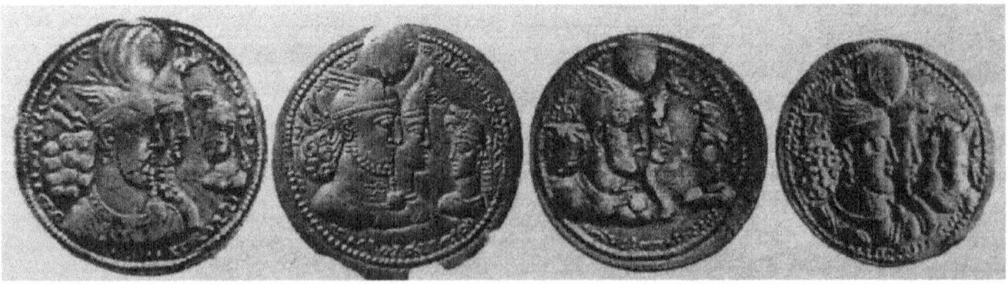

Figure 84. Sasanian drachms of Bahram II (276-293) with king, queen and possibly prince. After: Choksy 1989, figs. 21-24.

Concluding remarks

At this stage of our investigation, two main points should be maintained as firmly established. Firstly, there is no reason to consider the winged composite creature with a dog head and peacock tail as a representation of the mythical bird *saena marega*/*senmurv*/*simurgh*, since every hint points to its identification as a symbol of *xwarenah*/*xwarrah*/*farr(eh)* both in pre-Islamic and Islamic arts. Secondly, it appeared in Persian art very late, only at Taq-i Bustan which is a monument almost contemporary with the Central Asian Hunnish/Turkish and Sogdian coins accompanied by quite explicit epigraphic countermarks (figs. 12-13, 81). In all probability, its introduction into official Sasanian art should be attributed to Khusraw II Parwiz, as Muslim authors appear to confirm.

Every piece of evidence collected in this study strongly suggests that the composite creature symbolizing *xwarrah* was adopted from Central Asia in the very late Sasanian period and was not a genuine Persian invention. The same representation of the *senmurv* as something connected with the family of Rustam in Sasanian art (such as at Rag-i Bibi)[481] seems to be very unlikely. In fact, the Sasanians wanted to be associated with the mythical Kayanids, as the term *kay* that started to appear on their coins at least since the fifth century strongly suggests.[482] Since the Kayanids and their main representative (and Zoroastrian hero) Isfandyar were enemies of the "pagan" house of Rustam, it would be highly unlikely to find any reference to the *senmurv* in the Sasanian milieu. According to Dinawari and other Muslim authors as well (but not Firdousi), Rustam was the heretic par excellence who refused to convert to Zoroastrianism and wanted

481 Grenet, Lee, Martinez, Ory 2007, 260.

482 Schindel 2013, 836-837.

to remain faithful to his original and ancestral religion. The passage of Iranshahri quoted by Biruni in his table on the festivals of the Persians that described the *Khurasan khurra/gloria Orientis* as "flying foxes" representing the wellness of the Kayanids was very probably referred to the Sasanians. Boris Marshak proposed this identification that seems to be the most realistic one.[483]

As the name transmitted by Biruni points out (along with the evidence produced in this study), the so-called pseudo-*simurgh* probably originated in eastern Iran starting from the Hellenistic *ketos* but, after being introduced into Persia, it became an important auspicious symbol even related to the Sasanian royal family and much appreciated by the Omayyads. As already said above, numismatic studies suggest that the Sasanians wanted to be associated with the Zoroastrian Kayanids. Therefore, according to Muslim authors, a symbolic element called *Khurasan khurra* that originally pointed at eastern Iran and possibly the same non-Zoroastrian Rustamids who were enemies of the Kayanids became later (although for a short period) the identificative sign of the Sasanians that is to say, the main admirers of the Kayanids.

If the *Khurasan khurra* corresponded to our pseudo-*simurgh*, it should be then admitted that the Persians had adopted this symbolic creature originally rooted in eastern Iran before the fall of the Sasanian dynasty, possibly during the reign of Khusraw II as it is possible to observe at Taq-i Bustan. Bastam probably built the site according to Khusraw's orders who, in the end, gave Taq-i Bustan as a gift to his uncle on the occasion of the inauguration party. This party took place in the park of Taq-i Bustan as described in the *Mojmal al-tawarikh*. Later on, Khusraw tortured and put to death Bindoe, Bastam's brother, because of his responsibility in the assassination of Khusraw's father Ohrmazd IV (579-590). Bastam was going to be the next victim of Khusraw revenge and, for this reason, he rebelled against the Sasanians. He arrived to control a big territory around

483 Marshak 1998, 85; Marshak 2002a, 140-141; Marshak 2002b, 37.

Rayy and even started to mint his own coins. The rebellion of Bastam finished around 600 when he was defeated and put to death.[484]

Only after Bastam death, Khusraw began some more works at Taq-i Bustan that were probably interrupted because of Herclius invasion of the Sasanian territory and Khusraw execution in 628: this date is the *terminus ante quem* for the final constructing phase of that site that still presents some unfinished parts. Therefore, Khusraw had adopted the pseudo-*simurgh* to embellish his garments on the equestrian statue on the back of the larger grotto at Taq-i Bustan between 600-628. However, the composite creature symbolizing *xwarrah* (our pseudo-*simurgh*) had already arrived in Persia some time earlier between the enthronement of Khusraw in 590 and the defeat of Bastam around 600.[485]

The information recorded by Biruni could have created some more problems for a correct reconstruction of the curious story of this composite creature that did not allude to the fantastic bird of Iranian mythology (*simurgh*). It is worth insisting on the fact that Biruni (and Iranshahri) knew the place of origin of the pseudo-*simurgh* to be individuated in Khorasan as pointed out by the very name that he used. The term Khorasan probably indicated the whole east Iran and not necessarily the historical region still called Khorasan. For this reason, other regions such as Sistan, Zabulistan or even Bactria could also fit into this generic description. For this reason, the name "eastern Iran" seems to be more appropriate.

If the hypothesis expressed in this study about the origin of the pseudo-*simurgh* in visual arts from the Greek *ketos* is considered convincing, there would then be the basis for some further observations. Central Asian (and Gandharan) artists adopted and re-elaborated typical Greek elements but did not change them much. The winged dog under the throne of the deity in Temple II at Penjikent (fig. 29) and, above all, that same creature with a peacock tail at Afrasyab (fig. 31)

484 Scarcia 1980.

485 Compareti 2019b.

constituted something completely new in Sogdian art. Not only the *ketos* started to be used in a non-funerary sphere by local artists but it was re-elaborated and a peacock tail substituted the original fish or snake tail. However, in the Blue Hall and many other Sogdian paintings at Penjikent, flying composite creatures maintained the original aspect that was much closer to Greek prototypes. Sogdian artists just added in many cases floating ribbons and small decorative details. In few words, the Sogdians did not change much the *ketos* and it seems then obvious to think that somebody else added the peacock tail.

It is impossible to precisely establish when and where the peacock tail was added to the iconography of the pseudo-*simurgh*. This process happened probably in eastern Iran before or around the second half of the sixth century CE because of the confrontation with the chronology of Taq-i Bustan.[486] The possibility that this composite creature was not genuinely Sogdian cannot therefore be excluded. Its depiction in Temple II at Penjikent is only partial and it possibly represented the dragon of Tish/Nabu. This creature appeared completely depicted at Afrasyab around the mid-seventh century only on the garments of one foreign envoy (possibly from Chaghanyan, that was part of Bactria in eastern Iran) but it is remarkably absent in other Sogdian paintings. It could therefore be assumed that the pseudo-*simurgh* was created somewhere in eastern Iran in the sixth century (definitely before the enthronement of Khusraw in 590 CE), to be later exported both in Sogdiana and Persia during the sixth-seventh century. Since Bastam was appointed governor of Khorasan (and, at another time, Azerbaijan) in the early part of Khusraw's reign, one could imagine that he imported this motif into Persia (and the Caucasus) from eastern Iran at the very end of the sixth century. This would strengthen the hypothesis that the pseudo-*simurgh* could truly

486 David Stronach proposed to associate the peacock tail of this creature to the shape of the rhyton vases that have been very popular in Persian art since the Achaemenid period: Stronach 2018.

be considered as originating in Khorasan, Sistan, or Rustam's motherland, Zabulistan.[487]

The hypothesis about the eastern Iranian origin of the pseudo-*simurgh* could confirm some of the attributions of unexcavated Iranian silver vessels embellished with this composite creature in the State Hermitage by B. Marshak. In fact, the Russian scholar proposed eastern Iran as the more likely place of origin for most of those silver objects that he dated mainly to the early Islamic period. Among the specimens that Marshak considered genuine Sasanian, there is one unexcavated silver ewer from Pavlovka village (Ukraine) embellished on both sides with a pseudo-*simurgh* within a vegetal roundel in the collection of the State Hermitage.[488] P. Harper, however, proposed to date this object to the early Islamic period because of the vegetal decorations on the body of the creature and the similarities of the plants reproduced in metal with the so-called "tree of life" represented on both sides of the arch of the larger grotto at Taq-i Bustan.[489] Both scholars proposed to date the Pavlovka ewer to the late Sasanian period. On the basis of the chronology of Taq-i Bustan and the introduction of the pseudo-*simurgh* into Persia around 600 CE that have been proposed in this study, it should be admitted that both scholars expressed quite convincing arguments. If the Hermitage ewer could be considered Sasanian, then it should be dated to the reign of Khusraw II or his successors. An attribution to the seventh century seems to be more realistic and even the early Islamic period could be valid.

A specific variety of painted proto-Islamic ceramics unfortunately still archaeologically unattested has started to appear more and more often on antiquities markets and in Afghan museums over the last twenty years. At least one pottery shard was proposed to be reconstructed as a vase embellished with a representation of the pseu-

487 K. Rezakhani had already proposed this idea although he did not develop it: Rezakhani 2017a, 174-175.

488 Marshak 1998, 85; Marshak 2006a, 77.

489 Harper 1991, 73-75.

do-*simurgh*.[490] This very possible reconstruction not only could help to confirm the early Islamic chronology of this group of painted ceramics but also points at the continuation in the local pottery production of decorative subjects that were rooted in eastern Iranian traditions in the territory of ancient Afghanistan.[491]

Several aspects of the transmission of iconographical forms from Central Asia to Persia are not completely clear but they could be used in order to propose a better identification for other fantastic creatures appearing in Sasanian art. Some very problematic Sasanian coins could provide further data. For example, the crown of Bahram II's wife on his coins is, most likely, embellished with a griffin or (less probably) a wild boar head but not a pseudo-*senmurv* (fig. 84).[492] This could be considered correct on chronological bases since the representation of the symbol of *xwarrah* at such an early stage of Sasanian history is very unlikely. On the contrary, its presence on a late Sasanian (probably seventh century) seal in the British Museum (fig. 79) perfectly matches the historical situation of the late Sasanian Empire and the information by Mas'udi on Khusraw Parwiz's seals whose decorations could have been imported.

It is worth observing that on some early third-century Kushano-Sasanian coins, "sub-king (or governor) Ardashir" wears a zoomorphic crown shaped like a bird in profile. This bird has been identified with the (real) *senmurv/simurgh*.[493] Although this is a rather early chronology,[494] such an identification could be accurate since,

490 Piggott 1949, fig. 1.

491 Compareti 2020a.

492 Lukonin 1976, 159, fig. 113; Choksy 1989; Compareti 2019c, 26. Astrological-astronomical connections should not be excluded. In fact, a pre-Mongol treatise by Farid al-Din *Taqwim kavakeb al-sab'a* "Calendar of the Seven Planets" (ca. 1219) at present kept in the al-Sabah Collection (Kuwait) presents the monster responsible for eclipses as an isolated dragon head resembling a wild boar or even an Indian *makara*: Vesel 2008, 169.

493 Loeschner 2010; Vondrovec 2014, 642, 894.

494 Earlier example of crowns surmounted by a bird's head can be observed in

as was discussed in the present study, the *senmurv* was a bird and should be associated with eastern Iranian lands such as Khorasan, Sistan, Zabulistan (Zal's kingdom) or Bactria (Kushano-Sasanians' kingdom) but not Sasanian Persia.

Numismatic seems to further support the hypotheses formulated in this study. Crowns that included a bird and not just wings were typical for one single Sasanain king, Ohrmazd II (303-309).[495] K. Rezakhani recently suggested that he may have been the same person as Ohrmazd II Kushanshah, a Sasanian cadet prince who ruled the Kushano-Sasanian kingdom of Bactria in ca. 300-303.[496] There would be therefore the possibility that he imported his bird-like crown from eastern Iran were he was appointed as a ruler before his enthronement as Sasanian king. Other Sasanian crowns presented different characteristics or spread wings but no entire birds. Ohrmazd predecessor and father was Narseh (293-303) who served as a governor in Sakastan, Turan, Sind and, possibly, Armenia before his enthronement as Sasanian king. Narseh definitely had very strong connections with eastern Iran. Comparisons between the unusual crowns of some

---

Chorasmin paintings from Akchakhan Kala (ca. first century CE) and in pre-Islamic Chorasmian coinage (ca. third-fourth century CE): Kidd, Betts 2010, 660-666; Betts, Yagodin, Grenet, Kidd, Minardi, Bonnat, Khashimov 2012, fig. 7. It is not an easy task to propose any precise identification between the Akchakhan Kala bird-crowns and the *simurgh*. However, the bird on those crowns should definitely have some connections with kingship and, possibly, with the pre-Islamic Chorasmian religion that was a local form of Zoroastrianism. According to the numismatic studies of B. Vajnberg (1977, 19), there could have been some associations between Chorasmian bird-crowns and the Iranian concept of *farreh/xwarrah* (Chorasmian *farn*). Other scholars preferred an association with the Avestan god of war and victory Verethraghna/Bahram: Grenet 1986b, 133; van't Haaff 2020, 12. It is worth observing that, among the fourth-sixth century paintings from the site of Toprak Kala, there is also the fragmentary figure of a bird with feathers on its head usually considered to be a pheasant: Rapoport, Nerazik, Levina 2000, pl. 52. It is unfortunately too fragmentary to propose any definitive identification.

495 Schindel 2013, fig. 43.1, 9.

496 Rezakhani 2017a, 82-83.

comprimaries in Bahram II relief at Naqsh-i Rustam II, early Sasanian coinage and the inscription of Narseh at Paikuli suggested to R. Gyselen that headgears shaped as animals' heads could actually point at Sakastan that, as already observed, was a kingdom in eastern Iran ruled by a cadet branch of the Sasanians.[497]

The Greek *ketos* that, during the centuries, was transformed into the pseudo-*simurgh* in eastern Iran and appeared in Persian art in the end of the sixth century, some time later arrived in the Caucasus and the Byzantine Empire. It started to become very popular among eastern Christians and Muslims in the seventh century. Christians used the pseudo-*simurgh* in religious art while Muslims reproduced it on their coins and in palace decorations. However, early Christians had already adopted the Greek *ketos* to represent the *leviathan* of the story of Jonah long before. We could assume that both Christians of the Mediterranean and Caucasian areas and Central Asian "Zoroastrians" adapted the iconography of the *ketos* to shape a further new iconography. Most likely, when the eastern Iranian "modified *ketos*" came into contact with Christian art, something completely new occurred. In fact, Christian artists started to reshape the *leviathan* of the story of Jonah or the tempting snake of the story of Adam and Eve such as at Aght'amar on the basis of the Greek *ketos* and the pseudo-*simurgh*. These arstists probably identified the Iranian pseudo-*simurgh* as a kind of modified *ketos* that they liked very much and had already started to depict in catacombs and sarcophagi at least since the third century CE.

It is worth observing that, in some cases, Byzantine artists used the pseudo-*simurgh* in the funerary sphere just like early Christians did in the catacombs. The early ninth century floor mosaics of the Particiapazi family chapel in the church of San Ilario (Venice) presented auspicious animals within interlacing medallions among which also one Pegasus and one pseudo-*simurgh*.[498] It is not possible to be too specific on this point although in medieval Byzantine and "barbaric" Euro-

497 Gyselen 2005, 32.

498 Riccioni 2017, 309-312; Riccioni 2019, 180-181.

pean art, the *ketos* shaped more and more similar to a pseudo-*simurgh* had maintained just canine features such as the open mouth with a long tongue. Expert of Byzantine art and culture insisted on the apotropaic properties of this creature that started to be represented in a religious and civil sphere.[499] *Kete* with parts of the body of a ram, panther, bull, etc. that were typical of Greco-Roman or early Christian sarcophagi were completely abandoned and only the dog-fish (mixed with the pseudo-*simurgh*) continued to be represented in medieval European (but also Byzantine and Armenian) art at least until the early thirteenth century. In fourteenth and fifteenth Islamic illustrated astronomical treaties, the *qitus* constellation sometimes appeared with very strong canine features as well (figs. 59a-b). As already observed above, the dog had peculiar funerary characteristics in Classical and Zoroastrian art[500] and it should not be ruled out that this is the reason why also Christians preferred to hold in high esteem this animal or parts of it. In the case of Islamic manuscripts, it seems more reasonable to consider that the contamination took place just at iconographical level. It is however worth observing that these canine features did not disturb much Muslim artists nor astrologers and, in any case, general readers as one scholar had thought.[501]

This is what the evidence collected in the present study can tell us about the pseudo-*simurgh*. What about the "real" *simurgh*? Exactly as occurred with the phoenix in Roman art or the *fenghuang* in China, when the *simurgh* started to be represented in Persian illustrated manuscripts of the Ilkhanid period it was probably confused by ancient authors with other fantastic mythological birds such as the *homa*. Its connection with the ancient Iranian concept of *farr*(*eh*) probably contributed to further confusion from the point of view of textual transmission but representations in visual arts. In fact, in pre-Islamic Central Asia, the *simurgh* was mainly depicted as an eared bird whose

499 Vanderheyde 1994; Asutay-Effenberger 2019.

500 Woodford, Spier 1992; Andrés-Toledo 2013.

501 Khakimov 2012, 20.

iconography was already known in Egyptian and Classical art. It is this kind of *simurgh*-like bird that was depicted on the garments of one (or two) attendant(s) of Bastam in the wild boar hunting panel at Taq-i Bustan (fig. 14). Sasanian artists definitely knew fantastic birds, as demonstrated in the Metropolitan Museum seal depicting an eagle with the body shaped as a human face (fig. 76). However, in no case there are enough clues to propose a definitive identification with the Iranian phoenix/*simurgh* in Sasanian art. The episode in the *Karnamag i Ardashir i Papakan* about the attempt of the queen to poison Ardashir mentioned the miraculous intervention of a bird that symbolized *xwarrah* without any reference to the *simurgh* [ch. x, 7].

This does not mean that fantastic birds similar to the *simurgh* did not exist in Persian traditions before the Islamic period. Information about mythical birds that interacted with important Persian heroes can sometimes be found in ancient written sources. According to Claudius Aelian (second-third centuries), an eagle raised the ancestor of the Persians Achaemenes [*De Natura Animalium* 12, 21]. This was a very common *topos* in every ancient culture of the Near East. Henkelman investigated the similarities between this story and the legendary birth of Gilgamesh.[502] Other Greek authors, such as Pausanias of Damascus (second or fourth century CE), wrote that the ancestor of the Achaemenids was the Greek demigod Perseus who also began the "fire cult" among the Zoroastrians.[503] This kind of non-direct information should be always considered with great cautiousness because ancient Greek authors tended to integrate neighboring peoples into their own cultural sphere that, in this specific case, does not concern historical but mythological aspects.

Nöldeke called attention to the fact that the story reported by Aelian could remind one of the popular Persian legends about the shade of the *homa* bird. In fact, the touch of its shade was considered to be an auspicious sign. 'Attar wrote that the shade of *simurgh* and

502 Henkelman 2006.

503 Boyce, Grenet 1991, 230-231.

homa created kings.[504] Movses K'orenaci (fifth century?) recorded in his *Patmut'iwn Hayoc* "History of Armenia" [II.70] a very similar episode about Ardashir, who was touched by the shade of an eagle and founded the Sasanian Empire.[505] Xenophon reported in his *Cyropedia* that the Persians regarded the observation of an eagle coming from the right side to be a good omen [II.1, 1].[506] In addition, the Bible preserved some interesting information on "Persian" symbolic birds of prey such as in the famous prophecy of Isaiah [46: 11] considered to be referred to Cyrus the Great who was going to take Babylon and set free the Jews: "from the east I summon a bird of prey; from a far-off land, a man to fulfill my purpose. What I have said, that I will bring about; what I have planned, that I will do".

The *simurgh* still plays an important role in modern folklore and tales. János Harmatta collected some Persian and Tajik folktales about the eagle (*simurgh*) eating the fruits of the "tree of life" that grows in one of the gardens of "the king". In one variant of the story, the vegetals falling out from the beak of the magic bird have healing properties and can save the life of the sick father of the hero who is usually a brave and dedicated prince.[507] These are, in any case, fables that had passed through the filter of Islam.

There is then little doubt that ancient Persians considered birds of prey to be very important symbols of power and kingship. These birds had possibly some religious meaning as well although every information comes from non-Persian sources and should be considered highly hypothetical. None of the above-mentioned indirect literary passages presents completely clear associations between magic birds and the

504 Farid ad-Din Attar 1986, 47, 54.

505 Nöldeke 1930, 9. Armenian legends about the rescue of a child by an eagle destined to become king can be found until medieval times. The ancestor of the Arcrunis of Vaspurakan lived a very similar adventure: Russell 1990-91, 8.

506 This story calls to mind the legendary foundation of Rome that included, in a first moment, the observation of birds of prey by Romulus and Remus from a hill to decide who had to be king [Livy, I, 6-7].

507 Harmatta 1979, 318.

Persian royal house despite some representations in visual arts such as the standard of Darius III in the mosaic of the the "Casa del Fauno" in Pompei, Arsacid and Frataraka coins, and very slight evidence in Sasanian art (once more, concentrated in Taq-i Bustan rock reliefs, see fig. 14a-b). A beribboned bird of prey appeared on the crown of Ardashir I (224-242) in his early coins. At least one scholar agreed to identify that bird with a possible representation of *xwarrah*.[508] This is just one possibility although such an early reference to *xwarrah* would be quite unusual on Sasanian coins of the time of Ardashir. Unfortunately, no iscription nor other evidence could allow any clear association between the bird on Ardashir crown and the *simurgh*. That bird seems to have ribbons attached to its neck or a beribboned ring in its beak exactly like in Parthian art and coinage (fig. 17a-d).[509] Early Sasanian art still presented Parthian iconographic peculiarities that were mainly rooted in more ancient Greek traditions. According to R. Schulz (2018), the bird above the figure of Dionysus on a late Sasanian silver plate kept in the State Historical Museum (Moscow) could be the phoenix. It is a very interesting hypothesis although the general scheme of the scene on that plate is definitely rooted in Greco-Roman and not Sasanian art.

As it often happened with every aspect concerning the Sasanian Dynasty, there are very few direct, contemporary written sources. However, it is clear that some kind of mythical birds also had to occur in the Persian legends before the rise of Islam as Greek sources seem to confirm.

---

508 Vieira Pinto 220, 559.

509 Birds of prey with a beribboned ring in their beak embellished also Sasanian seals: Gyselen 2016, 36, 82.

Appendix 1
The *simurgh* between the "Western" phoenix and the Chinese *Fenghuang*

Highly mobile Sogdian tradesmen had begun to settle in different parts of Central Asia and China since at least the early fourth century CE. Epigraphic traces of the Middle Iranian language that they spoke have been found scattered over a wide area, from Sugdaia, in Crimea, to Japan. In fact, this Iranian people travelled everywhere in ancient times without insurmountable difficulties. From the mid-sixth century, Sogdians had become subjects of western Turks, who controlled a wide territory. Sogdians could offer to their Turkish overlords their experience and infrastructures along the "Silk Road" network.[510]

Undoubtedly, some decorative motifs in Sogdian art represent an interesting case of adoption and adaptation of Hellenistic forms that reappeared over a very long time span in Central Asia, also during the fifth/sixth-century "classical revival". The most important phases of this process are well distinguishable, such as the phenomenon of adaptation to typically Iranian concepts and, subsequently, their return from east to west according to dynamics seemingly unsuspected.

Some scholars of mythological studies consider the decorative element I would like to study in this appendix, namely the *fenghuang* (凤凰) of Chinese literature, to be the "Western" Phoenix. However, others had understood long ago that such a superimposition was not to be regarded as automatic but just conventional. In his ground-breaking study on Tang exoticism, Edward Schafer proposed associating the *luan* (鸞), the second most important fantastic bird of Chinese literature after the *fenghuang*, with the *simurgh* of Iranian

510 De la Vaissière 2005.

mythology. Schafer (as many other scholars) was perfectly aware that the *fenghuang* did not correspond precisely with the phoenix, just as the *luan* bird was not the *simurgh*; nevertheless, in his opinion, all these identifications could be maintained because they had become popular among western scholars.[511] Chinese sources mentioned also another bird called *quehuo que* (卻火雀) "fire-rejecting sparrow" that was considered to be a real animal and much requested by emperors as an exotic tribute from distant lands.[512]

A "superimposition" of fantastic creatures belonging to different cultural milieu, such as the one proposed by Schafer, presents a series of problems. First of all, it does not consider the possibility of a direct relation between the phoenix and the *simurgh*. Then it must be kept in mind that the situation was not the same among Iranians (Persians and Sogdians) during the pre-Islamic and the Islamic periods, just as it was different in China during the Sui-Tang and the Song-Yuan dynasties. When Persia, Central Asia, and China were unified under the Mongols between the mid-thirteenth and mid-fourteenth centuries, some cultural traits began to be accepted across the empire. The representations of both the *fenghuang* and the *simurgh* were standardised in the sphere of visual arts only in the Mongol period, and the Chinese model decoded by the post-Tang (most likely Song) artists was also accepted in Persian Islamic book illustrations. Therefore, it is extremely difficult to trace the iconography of the *simurgh* in the Iranian world during the pre-Mongol period, while something useful can be traced in Sogdian art. Moreover, the very iconographic characteristics of single birds in specific contexts are not easily determined and are sometimes confused with those of other similar creatures from the same cultural milieu, such as happened with the *fenghuang* and the *luan*. These are just some of the points that will be considered in this appendix with the support, whenever possible, of written sources.

511 Schafer 1963, 288; Willets 1965, 151-154; Rawson 1984, 99-107; Diény 1989-1990; Hargett 1989; Sterckx 2002, 37.

512 Schafer 1963, 38.

In the first instance, it is important to determine the basic relationship possibly existing between the *fenghuang*, the *simurgh*, and the phoenix. As has already been mentioned above, the *fenghuang* was confused by the Chinese with the *luan* and another bird that was very often represented in funerary art from the Han (206 BCE-220 CE) to the Tang (618-906) dynasties, namely the *zhuniao* (朱鳥) or "red bird of the South", also called by other names such as *zhuque* (朱雀) and *chiniao* (赤鳥).[513] While for the *fenghuang* and the *luan* we have only literary descriptions, the *zhuniao* can be identified without major problems in Chinese funerary paintings especially from the Tang period because it is usually (but not always) represented on the wall facing south in traditionally organized graves.

The *zhuniao* was one of the *siling* (四靈) "four divine creatures" or *sishen* (四神) "four divine spirits" of Chinese culture, together with the *baihu* (白虎) "white tiger" symbolizing the West, the *qinglong* (龍 or *canglong* 蒼龍) "green dragon" of the East, and the *xuanwu* (玄武) "dark warrior" of the North. Substitutes for these four combinations could also have been: the *lin* of the West, the *feng* of the South, the *gui* of the North and the *long* of the East.[514] *Feng* is just another name for *fenghuang* and *gui* (龜) is the turtle. *Lin* is another name for *qilin* (麒麟), a fantastic creature of Chinese mythology usually rendered in English as "unicorn". However, this superimposition presents the same problems as for the *fenghuang* and the phoenix; the same could be said with respect to the *long* (龍), usually translated as "dragon". As is the case with *fenghuang*/phoenix, both *lin*/unicorn and *long*/dragon should be regarded as conventional and not precise translations. At any rate, it is worth observing that in Iranian culture too every direction of the compass is symbolized by the same specific colour, which is to be found in the Chinese tradition.[515] According to some Muslim authors, not only colours but animals too indicate the kings

513 Schmitt 1974; Diény 1989-1990; Salviati 1994.

514 Sterckx 2002, 153-155, 178-179; Wong Pui Yin 2006.

515 Scarcia 1985.

of different parts of the Sasanian Empire. For instance, Khosrow I invested with titles, gifts, and robes embellished with specific images of animals the kings of east Caucasian regions.[516]

These same types of Chinese graves, where each cardinal point was symbolized by a fantastic creature or animal, were later exported to Korea and Japan as well.[517] As already observed in chapter 2.6, Himalayan kingdoms (Tuyuhun and Tubo-Tibetans) that had relations with the Sui-Tang courts adopted many elements of Chinese civilization. In Han engraved and painted tombs, several fantastic and apotropaic creatures are accompanied by their own names, usually written in a cartouche above the head. Among the most ancient representations of the bird that has been commonly identified with the *fenghuang* together with its name in Chinese art, one could mention the Helingol Han tomb in Inner Mongolia that was dated to the late second century CE (fig. 85).[518]

During the second century CE, the Han Empire had relations with Kushan Bactria. This Central Asian region adopted Indian and Greek cultural elements and possibly exported them. Birds resembling the Classical Phoenix can be sometimes observed among the luxury objects excavated in Begram, a site considered by some scholars to be one capital of the Kushans (fig. 86).[519] *Zhuniao* birds present inscrip-

516 Gadjev 2006, 204-205.

517 Berthier 2001; Jeon 2005, 170-171. Seventh-eighth century Japanese wooden "phoenix" figurines have been preserved in the Golden Hall of Horyuji Temple: Hayashi 2000, fig. 31. Several images of typical Tang phoenixes can be observed among the decorations of eighth century luxury objects that have been kept in the Shoso-in imperial repository (Nara) for many centuries: Hayashi 1975, figs. 116, 118, 163.

518 Inner Mongolia Regional Institute of Cultural Relics and Archaeology 2007, 120.

519 Schmidt 1980a, fig. 9; Nehru 2004, fig. fig. 8. Birds with an element above the head resembling the phoenix of Begram appear in other monuments of Gandharan art such as, for example, among the sculptures that decorated the Amluk-dara main stupa in Barikot (Pakistan): Olivieri 2018, fig. 18.

tions sometimes,[520] but their identification is easier to determine because of their funerary functions. One un-epigraphic, low relief image of a *zhuniao* bird from a second-century tomb in Quxian (Sichuan Province) already presents the typical characteristics of the *fenghuang* of the Tang artists.[521] On one clay tile from the fifth-sixth century, well-known site of Dengxian (south-western Henan), at present kept in the National Museum in Beijing, there is also one typical colossal *zhuniao* together with other smaller birds flying around. On other tiles from the same site, there are also the remaining directional creatures and several other subjects. Curiously enough, however, two Chinese characters appears on the right of the bird undoubtedly identifying it as a *fenghuang* (fig. 87).[522] It is then clear that some confusion already existed about the identification of fantastic birds during the Southern Dynasty period. These points also deserve some further investigation.

Among the most interesting Chinese texts where the *fenghuang* is mentioned, the *Shanhai Jing* or "Classic of Mountains and Seas" stands apart. This is a text about every kind of exoticism and fantastic creatures according to Chinese imagery, that has been preserved in its second/first-century BCE Han redaction.[523] Later interpolations can be recognized and only in more recent times, around the beginning of the seventeenth century, illustrated versions began to appear. The description of the *fenghuang* in the *Shanhai Jing* and Chinese literature in general is not detailed. It is described as an auspicious creature associated with music and immortals and, for this reason, it was especially chosen to be represented on graves. The tree where the *fenghuang* lived was located on top of a mountain that, according to Chinese traditions, was the place where immortals lived. The association between mountain and *fenghuang* is not completely clear, although it could constitute another trait in common with the Western

520 Erickson 2011, 10.

521 Pirazzoli-t'Serstevens 1982, 167-170, fig. 109.

522 Juliano 1980, 38-40.

523 Fracasso 1996; Birrell 1999; Sterckx 2002, 36-38, 119-120.

phoenix that lived on Mount Casius, or Qaf for the Muslims. One of the most ancient Chinese silks ever found (second-first century BCE) was excavated in a Xiongnu tomb at Noin Ula (Mongolia, *kurgan* 6). The scene is composed by two birds (possibly *fenghuang*) standing on a mountain beside a central tree (fig. 88).[524] A very interesting seventh/eighth-century CE textile fragment excavated at the cemetery of Astana (Turfan, Xinjiang Province) shows a typical Tang *fenghuang* on top of a mountain with plants, birds, and clouds in Chinese style surrounding it (fig. 89).[525] Some confusion between the *fenghuang* and *zhuniao* could be the source of the association with the colour red and fire. Characteristics of the *fenghuang* do not seem to belong to the original "religious" background of that fantastic bird but, most likely, to the sphere of legends and tales that, as always happens in these cases, started to develop at a popular level. In the *Shanhai Jing* it is specifically reported that auspicious Chinese characters were scattered on its body.[526]

Although it is not always possible to establish how ancient and accurate all these descriptions are, it is at least clear why the *fenghuang* has been associated with the phoenix. The *fenghuang* and the phoenix are not only described both as fantastic birds, but they also share a series of supernatural characteristics (red color, longevity, associations with fire). For all these reasons, the first western literati who began to approach the study of Chinese culture could have chosen a name for the *fenghuang* as evocative as possible, and the phoenix would have appeared as the most appropriate. Not many studies have been devoted to the *fenghuang*-phoenix association, but a very interesting paper on this topic was published by Jean-Pierre Diény some years ago. Diény especially focused on the similarities between these two fantastic birds. He concluded that, even if there are some common

524 Elikhina 2009.

525 Turfan Museum 1992, fig. 182.

526 Fracasso 1996, 14-15.

features, these are only superficial traits and, when considered in detail, they also present discrepancies.[527]

Another aspect should be considered from the iconographic point of view. Diény has already called attention to the representation of the *fenghuang* and the phoenix as legendary and symbolic creatures. Even if they are described in written sources as composed of parts of existing birds, they cannot be expected to have a model in nature despite all the efforts that some scholars made in order to find a convincing real counterpart (peacocks and pheasants were usually indicated). As already observed above, the *fenghuang* and *zhuniao* shared many characteristics and, for this reason, it is impossible to distinguish between them. A bird usually represented with spread wings, an element above its head, and a long tail appears quite often in Han funerary art, such as in Helingol tomb. This bird could be at the basis for the image of the standardised representation of the *zhuniao* in eigth- and ninth-century Tang funerary paintings.[528] Among the stucco decorations of the Buddhist "large temple B" at Toqquz-sarai in Tumshuq (Xinjiang), the French archaeological mission led by Paul Pelliot in 1906-1909 also found pearl roundels containing a typical Chinese *fenghuang*.[529] Experts have dated this architectonic decoration, at present kept in the Guimet Museum, to the sixth-seventh century (fig. 90). Other stuccos with representation of fantastic birds or *Garuda* within pearl roundels from Buddhist Xinjiang were found by Russian archaeologists in the Khotan oasis and are now part of the State Hermitage collection.[530]

A disc with a dark bird inside represented the sun in traditional Chinese culture and art. As it is recorded in written sources (and also in the above mentioned *Shanhai Jing*), this solar bird was a crow (sometimes three-legged) in Han art, the most famous specimen being

527 Diény 1989-1990.

528 Zhang 1995, figs. 190, 194, 209.

529 Feugère 1995, cat. 103.

530 D'jakonova, Sorokin 1960, cat. 1797-1798.

the painted silk banner from *Mawangdui* tomb 1 (Changsha, Hunan Province) precisely dated to 168 BCE.[531] The traditional Chinese solar bird sometimes appears as a typical *fenghuang/zhuniao*, with spread wings and only two legs, in late Tang Buddhist paintings. This is particularly evident in the late ninth- early tenth-century painted book cover from Dunhuang Cave 17, at present preserved in the British Library [OA 1919.1-1.0207].[532] Luxury Chinese goods destined for export and embellished with representations of a bird identified as the *fenghuang* show exactly this iconography. It is this standardised *fenghuang* that can be observed on some tenth- and eleventh-century Byzantine objects of art, possibly produced in Constantinople itself (fig. 69). Byzantines probably accepted this model, deeply rooted in Chinese art of the Tang period, because of their identification of that bird with the phoenix. Moreover, its exotic traits emphasised the prove-

531 Loewe 1979, 50-53, 127-133; Pirazzoli-t'Serstevens 1982, fig. 23.

532 Whitfield, Farrer 1990, fig. 78. A multi-armed goddess holding in her upper hands the sun and the moon represented according to Chinese cultural traits can be observed in some un-excavated paintings on textile or paper from the Tarim Basin (specifically Turfan) or Dunhuang. Despite such strong mixture of Indian and Chinese elements, according to F. Grenet (1995), the cultural milieu of this deity should be Zoroastrian (specifically Sogdian) while, for Bhattacharya-Haesner (2004, 44-46) the cultural milieu is completely Buddhist. In my opinion, the Pelliot Chinois 4518.24 paper fragment studied by Grenet probably depicts the typical Sogdian divine couple Nana-Tish. Four-arm Nana is sitting on a "Chinese lion" while Tish (Avestan Tishtrya) in feminine attire (like in Penjikent chapel 2/4-6 room 5 period III and IV) holds a dish with the image of a dog. Such a realistic dog is probably referred to the canine *mushhushshu* in Penjikent Temple 2 painting (fig. 29). A reflection of Sogdian Tish as the deity corresponding to the planet Mercury started to appear in enigmatic Chinese astronomical illustrations from Dunhuang. In fact, the representation of Mercury as a woman in China has been puzzling scholars for a long time: Kotyk 2017, 51. The Chinese name of Mercury Shui xing literally means "water planet" and could be referred to Tishtrya/Tish as the Iranian rain god. See footnote 276 of this study. A very similar deity (Nana?) can be observed among the seventh century votive painted wooden tablets from Dandan Oilik (Khotan) that were found in a Buddhist cultural milieu in which some pre-Buddhist (Zoroastrian?) local traits could have been preserved: Compareti 2019d.

nance of the phoenix, which was considered to live in distant lands.[533] If the Byzantines imported Tang luxury objects embellished with the *fenghuang*, and if they identified that fantastic Chinese bird with the phoenix, it is obvious to imagine that Central Asians and Persians too knew the iconography and the characteristics of the Tang *fenghuang*. A very similar process happened some centuries later when the Mongols introduced the *fenghuang* of the Song period into Islamic Persia.

One exhaustive study on the Western phoenix exists, also including a description of this creature in art forms.[534] Fortunately, following Classical traditions, inscriptions are added to some representations of this fantastic bird. One early third-century Syriac inscribed mosaic from Edessa (modern Urfa, in southern Turkey) is particularly interesting because the phoenix is clearly identified by an inscription and, at the same time, does not present typical fantastic traits but looks more like a peacock (fig. 91).[535] More ancient inscribed representations of the Phoenix are known in Greco-Roman paintings such as in the first-century CE Euxinus' inn in Pompei [Archaeological Deposits inv. 41761] (fig. 67),[536] although the inscription in the specimen from Edessa much clearly points to the fantastic bird on the altar. Two birds standing on trees beside the altar of the phoenix seem to bow in front of it. The phoenix was equally important during the pagan and the Christian periods. It was represented very often on sarcophagi and apsidal mosaics in churches because of its connection with immortality.[537] Usually, it was standing on an altar or a palm tree: there was an obvious connection between the fantastic bird of immortality and this tree, which in Greek was called *phoinix*, just as the eastern land where the nest of the phoenix was located, Phoenicia. Most likely it is the reddish colour of the date which was the basis

533 Walker 2008; Walker 2012, 53-56, 71-77.

534 Van den Broek 1972.

535 Van den Broek 1972, pl. XIII.

536 Zambon 2004, 19.

537 Bisconti 1979; Amad 1988; Dulaey 2013.

of such an association, and Phoenicia was the place of production of an animal pigment (purple) used in ancient times to dye precious clothes. Curiously enough, the same name *phoinix* can refer in Greek to a horse (or even a bull) whose colour is reddish. It can be found in the Iliad [23, 454] as referring to a reddish horse with a white sign on its forehead, "round as a (full) moon", that was the leader of a group of horses "flying in the plain and moving the dust". Actually, there was some confusion about the place of provenance of the phoenix, because it was said to come from India, Ethiopia, South Arabia and Phoenicia. The mountain where the tree with the phoenix nest was traditionally located has been identified as Mount Casius (or Qaf), on the border between modern Turkey and Syria.[538] The most famous image of a phoenix is possibly the fifth century CE mosaic from the so-called "house of the phoenix" in Antioch (Syria), at present kept in the Louvre Museum.[539] There is no caption in the Antioch mosaic although the iconography of the phoenix in the center of the scene with a nimbus behind its head and standing on a rock definitely refers to the magic bird of immortality described by Herodotus. Curiously enough, the border of the mosaic is composed by beribboned "Sasanian" spread wings supporting two confronted rams. Despite this clear Persian borrowing, the iconography of the phoenix perfectly reflects Roman prototypes on coins, paintings and apsidal mosaics.

In any case, the bird identified with the Phoenix in Greco-Roman art looks more like an ibis, a heron, or a peacock, with a decorative element resembling a feather on the top of its head, long legs and, usually, a halo. As observed above, phoenixes in the frescoes at Pompei referred to Egyptian prototypes although some elements could call to mind a bird of prey. Some similarities between the phoenix and the eagle – specifically, the eagle of Zeus – should not be ruled out.[540] Moreover, the association between the eagle and the lightening of

538 Van den Broek 1972, 63-65.

539 Grabar 1966b, figs. 113, 115; Dorigo 1971, fig. 222.

540 Albrile 2000, 82.

Zeus could be another point in common with the phoenix and fire. There is another epithet that should not be neglected: according to Aeschylus, the eagle that was sent to torment Prometheus was also called the "dog of Zeus" [*Prometheus bound*, 1021-1022]. It is not necessary to discuss all these unusual instances of Classical mythology in detail. It is enough to consider that some connection between the eagle of Zeus and the phoenix probably existed. It is also worth noting that, unlike the phoenix, the *fenghuang* is not connected to an idea of rapacity. On the contrary, rapacity is a peculiarity of the *simurgh*. Even if the connection between the phoenix and rapacity is not completely clear, it is interesting to observe that in Arabic the phoenix and the *simurgh* are both translated as *'anqa,* that was also a raptor.[541] Another fantastic bird of Arab legends that was the raptor par excellence is the *rukh*. This giant bird appeared also in the *Thousand and One Nights*' Second Voyage of Sindbad and it was sometimes illustrated as a parrot with wings and tail similar to the *simurgh*/*'anqa* according to Chinese models.[542] In a quite recent Coptic Egyptian legend, King Solomon had the *rukh* to throw a massive tree trunk over the city of Jerusalem with a trick. The *rukh* found the trunk tree in the Garden of Eden. That same trunk transformed the donkey leg of the Queen of Sheba into a normal human leg when she visited Solomon.[543] There could be an echo of the phoenix/*hol* of Jewish legends that, as already seen, lived in paradise and did not eat the forbidden fruit. As observed above, in the Islamic period, the phoenix was also translated with a specific term in Arabic and Persian: *samandar*, clearly from "salamander", that was commonly associated in alchemy with the element fire and described as many different kinds of animals (bird, lizard, rodent, etc.).[544]

541 Zakharia 2002.

542 Bivar 2009; Sáenz López Pérez 2010; Berlekamp 2011, 60-65.

543 Pennacchietti 2000, 233.

544 Laufer 1915, 318-323.

Superimposition of images belonging to different cultural milieu seems to be a normal phenomenon that could easily supersede borders and inimical neighbours during Late Antiquity. However, the mechanism is much more complicated. Several aspects should be considered despite the lack of written sources and numerous gaps to be filled in. For example, if the Arabs identified the *simurgh* with the *'anqa* that, for its part, was confused with the *samandar* (or winged horse), this does not mean that the *samandar* could be automatically regarded as the *simurgh*.[545] As already observed, the identification of the *simurgh* as a hybrid creature is an error that has caused several problems to art historians. In fact, the *simurgh* should always be considered as a bird.

Representations of the *simurgh* in Persian art appear only in book illustrations accompanied by texts that began to be copied during the Islamic period. There are unfortunately no illustrated *Shahnameh* or other texts that can be dated to the period before the Mongol conquest of Persia and the institution of the Ilkhanid dynasty. It could be stated that the art of book illustration in Persia developed greatly after the coming of the Mongols, and it is precisely because of the unification of China, Central Asia, and Persia that many elements typical of Chinese art were adopted by Ilkhanid artists.

The *simurgh* began to be represented in Persian paintings of the Islamic period according to the standardised representation of the *fenghuang* at the time of the Song dynasty. The most ancient representation of a *simurgh*/ *'anqa* in a Persian book illustration aiming at a Chinese style was copied in Maragheh around 1297-1300 [M.500, fol. 55] (fig. 43). The book is not a copy of the *Shahnameh* but a translation from Arabic, the *Manafi'-i hayawan* "The Benefits of Animals" by Ibn Bakhtishu'. The model for this *simurgh* is definitely not the Tang *fenghuang*/*zhuniao* but something different that followed the development of Chinese art of the post-Tang period. Its tail, wings, and the long legs are all stylistically close to the iconography of

545 Compareti 2018b.

the *fenghuang* under the Song, although the Chinese bird is expected to be represented flying in the air. On the body of this *simurgh*/*'anqa* some flames that could be confused with feathers appear. It is not excluded that this "flaming feathers" are the source of the typical representation of the Persian *simurgh* following Chinese style, that is to say, with such an elaborated tail. It is solely this Chinese iconography that would have become common for the representations of the *simurgh* in Persian painting until very recent times. One other phoenix is reproduced in another illustration in the same manuscript [M.500, fol. 84v] (fig. 92). The fantastic bird is flying in front of Solomon who, according to the legend, was able to speak the language of birds and was especially associated to the hoopoe.[546] However, the phoenix paying homage to Solomon is quite different from the elaborated one appearing in the illustration described above. In fact, several paintings of this manuscript could be attributed to different artists, possibly a master and his disciples.[547]

Just one small group of Persian book illustrations from Fars province or Isfahan, and dated to the Inju'id period, do not follow the Chinese style. The "Inju'id *simurgh*" is portrayed standing and not flying, with a long tail – yet different from the Chinese model – and some elements on its head resembling feathers or little horns. In general terms, that *simurgh* looks more like an owl or, in some cases, a rooster. The figure of the rooster and its association with Persia should not be underestimated. In fact, several Classical authors recorded its importance for the Persians, to the point that the roost-

546 Pennacchietti 2000, 225-241. Islamic book illsutrations include very often King Solomon together with fantastic creatures (angels, demons, *jinns*) and, sometimes, the hoopoe too. See the illustration of the *'Aja'ib al-mahluqat wa ghara'ib al-maujudat* "The Wonders of Creation and the Oddities of Existence" by al-Qazwini from Central Asia (Turkmen period, end of the fifteenth century) in the Bibliothèque Nationale de France [Ms. sup. persan 174, fol. 210v]: Richard 1997, 108.

547 Grube 1978, fig. 1.

er was described as the "Persian bird" par excellence.[548] Jacobus de Varagine reported some more curiosities about the Persian rooster in the *Legenda Aurea* "The Golden Legend" (thirteenth century). According to Jacobus, on the removal of the True Cross from Jerusalem to Shiz in 614, Khusraw Parwiz reproduced a blasphemous parody of the Holy Trinity in one of his wonderful palaces. The Sasanian sovereign was in fact sitting between the True Cross in the place of the Son on the right and a rooster in place of the Holy Spirit on the left [*Legenda Aurea* CXXXVII].[549] No clear parallels between the rooster and the *simurgh* could be found in these sources, although some "oriental" legends say that the song of the phoenix (or griffin) in Heaven causes the call of the roosters on earth.[550] Islamic texts and legends mentioned an angel rooster called Sraosha that Muhammad encountered during his ascension to Heaven. It was illustrated, for instance, in a dispersed Persian *Mi'rajnameh* "Book of the (Miraculous) Journey" dated 1317-1335 [Istanbul, Topkapı Sarayi Muzesi,

548 Cumont 1942; Tuplin 1992; Compareti, Scarcia 2012, 238-239, 243. A German pilgrim who visited Cairo in 1341 reported that the Mamluk king had in his treasure a golden rooster. According to local legends, this object once belonged to Khusraw II Parwiz. However, Heraclius took it into the Byzantine territory after the defeat of Khusraw. The Phophet Muhammad got this trophy when he conquered Tabuk and later his heirs let it arriving somehow in Egypt: Cerulli 1971, 632. The rooster was an important symbolic element in Mesopotamian art too: Ehrenberg 2002.

549 The image of the rooster as the "Persian bird" par excellence was very popular in Europe during the Medieval and Renaissance period. One miniature in the Ghota manuscript of the Saxon world chronicle (thirteenth century) presented Khusraw Parwiz with a stylized cross on his right and a rooster on his left shoulder: L'Orange 1953, 116-117. Piero Della Francesca accepted the story of the *Legenda Aurea* when he painted the History of the True Cross in the apse of the church of Saint Francis, Arezzo (1452-1466). Nothing like this appeared in the representation of the restitution of the Cross on the north portal of the seventh century church at Mren (eastern Turkey): Maranci 2008-2009. Many scholars considered the rooster as an important animal for Zoroastrians (i.e. Sasanians) on this legendary basis: Pfister 1938, 44; Cumont 1942; Jeroussalimskaja 1981, 124; Laporte 1988, 16.

550 Cumont 1942, 299; Kulik 2009, 295, 319.

Hazine 2154, fol. 61v] (fig. 93).[551] Sraosha was in origin a Zoroastrian psychopompic deity whose symbolic animals were the rooster and the dog in Middle Persian texts. The *Videvdad* mentioned the rooster of Sraosha with the name *parodar* [Fargard XVIII, 15, 23] and in the *Avesta* too [*Yt.* XXII.41]. For this reason, Michael Shenkar proposed to identify Sraosha in one single unexcavated Sasanian seal embellished with the image of a human head above two birds (possibly roosters) leaning back to back.[552] Such an identification is possible but it could even be interpreted as another representation of apotheosis. A rooster sometimes appears together with the personification of the planet Mercury in astrological texts and in Qazwini's *'Aja'ib al-mahluqat.*[553] In this case, it is obviously a Classical heritage.

---

551 Subtelny 2011, fig. 3. On Islamic legends about the rooster, see: Tottoli 1999.

552 Shenkar 2014, 145. M. Shenkar was very cautious in proposing a fifth century painting from Dilberjin (Afghanistan) and an eighth century painting from Penjikent room 2, sector XXVI as possible representations of Sraosha riding a peacock: Shenkar 2014, 147. Some scholars proposed to identify a colossal image of a deity in the Chorasmian mural paintings of Akchakhan Kala (first century CE) with Sraosha because of the decorations on his garments that include also the very controversial "bird-priest": Minardi 2018, 101-102; Grenet 2018, 73. Shenkar however proposed another identification on the basis of the Tyche-like mural crown of that god: Shenkar 2019, 13-14. The Avesta [*Yasna* LVII, 27] describes Sraosha as driving a quadriga pulled by four white shining horses with golden hooves but no roosters are mentioned: Cumont 1942, 295. Sraosha was not the only Zoroastrian deity to be described with a chariot like this. Two confronted roosters beside a central monstrous mask on the stone portal of the sixth century Sino-Sogdian funerary monument of Di Caoming (Shaanxi Province), have been identified as the symbolic animal(s) of Sraosha: Luo, Rong 2016, 285-286. According to one of the twelfth century Japanese "scrolls of Hell" (*Jigoku zoshi*), a monstrous giant rooster will torment men who were cruels to animals in Buddhist hell. In that scroll, the giant rooster is represented standing and with spread wings while flames are all around: Terukazu 1977, 86-87.

553 A well-known example can be observed in a manuscript kept in the National Bibliothek, Vienna [ms. arab. Flügel 1438 N. F. 155, fol. 247]: Seznec 1953, fig. 69. The planet Mercury (Arabic 'Utarid) is also represented as sitting on a fabulous bird such as in the Ilkhanid London Qazwini: Carboni 2015, 56-63.

As observed in chapter 3, Grenet identified the standing bird behind Rustam in the Blue Hall at Penjikent as an owl, that could be referred to a long battle that lasted during the night.[554] In my opinion, the parallel with Inju'id book illustrations could represent a better explanation from a stylistic point of view. However, this does not explain the similarity between the *simurgh* in the Blue Hall (or some Islamic book illustrations) and the owl. One detail in the story of Rustam's birth sounds extremely interesting. In fact, Firdousi described the darkness that preceded the apparition of the *simurgh* [Khaleghi-Motlagh I, 1446]. The illustration from the *Shahnameh* in Berlin [Diez Album, Fol. 71, S. 7] seems to confirm that Zal burnt the feather of the magic bird in an enclosed space and, therefore, one could imagine that the *simurgh* had the power to make the room dark. As observed above, the *Bundahishn* [XIII, 23] described the *senmurv/simurgh* together with the bat and in fact, "they both have milk and nourish their young at their breasts". Moreover, one could add, they both fly in the night. There was some connection between *simurgh* and darkness, and that magic bird was considered to be wise, as it is explicitly stated in a Sogdian fragmentary text studied by Yoshida.[555] Such characteristics seem to adapt pretty well to the Classical owl, that was the symbolic animal of Athena and a symbol of wisdom (or a bad omen) for Christians too. No references to this improbable parallel can be found in any Zoroastrians nor Islamic text. Zoroastrians were very ambiguous about the owl, that they considered a bad creature of Ahriman, or benevolent with mankind against demons in some texts of the Islamic period. In the *Videvdad* (literally "Given against the daivas"), the *ashozusta* bird, usually considered to be an owl, was invoked against demons/daivas [Fargard XVII, 9-11]. In the *Bundahishn* [XXIV, 28-29] too, there are references to its singing that can make the demons trembling. Owls had definitely a bad reputation among Muslims.[556]

554 Grenet 2015, 427.

555 Lurje 2010, 360; Yoshida 2013, 206.

556 A'lam 1989.

The only point of comparison for the non-Chinese *simurgh* is found among the mid-eighth century Sogdian paintings from the Blue Room at Penjikent. This specific scene could be a very important moment in the sequence about Rustam's trials, when the hero is in particular need of the protection of the *simurgh.* It is worth observing that only here Rustam is fighting his opponent with a bow. In the legend of Rustam as recorded in the *Shahnameh,* the hero used the bow to fight Isfandyar (and his half brother Shaghad in his very last trial but this episode did include also a hidden pit implanted with spears). It is only because of the intervention of the *simurgh* that Rustam was able to make an efficient arrow to be shot in the eyes of Isfandyar. In this way, two elements of the story of Rustam and Isfandyar could be present in the Sogdian painting: the bow and, most importantly, the *simurgh* that is, on the contrary, absent from the other scenes. Once more, there would be enough evidence to confirm that, in Iranian art, the *simurgh* has always been a bird, while the *farr* has been represented in different ways, including various composite (winged) creatures. Despite their chronological distance, my supposed *simurgh* from Penjikent strictly resembles the undeniable *simurgh* represented in Inju'id book illustrations that does not follow the Chinese style.

These observations could suggest a local Central Asia iconography for at least one kind of fantastic bird that existed independently of the Chinese *fenghuang/zhuniao* before the Islamisation of Iranian lands. Of course, it would be very interesting to find other traces of fantastic birds in Iranian art and consider which relations might exist between them and Chinese fantastic birds.

During the pre-Sui/Tang period, when China fragmented into several dynasties ruling over small territories for short periods, many hybrid creatures were quite often represented in Chinese funerary art. In the Tang period they were to be entirely substituted by the *siling* or *sishen* and, later, only the *fenghuang* and the *long* were given great importance in Chinese art and culture. One of the sixth-century composite flying creatures is a bird with the hooves and head of a deer, although sometimes it looks like a dog, a horned horse, or other animal specimens. According to Chinese scholars, the name of this winged creature is *feilian* and somebody thought that it should be associated from an iconographic point of view with winged Iranian monsters, such as the *farr* or pseudo-*simurgh* (fig. 94).[557] According to other scholars, this fantastic creature is a *qilin*.[558] In my opinion, there is not enough evidence to decide on the matter. However, it is interesting to observe that a very similar flying hybrid animal is portrayed on one panel of the unprovenanced Sino-Sogdian "Vahid Kooros" funerary couch (fig. 95). The catalogue of the exhibition that followed the restoration of this funerary couch described that fantastic animal as an "Iranian *Senmurv*-like hybrid creature".[559] Flying composite creatures, albeit not exactly like the one on the Vahid Kooros couch, can be observed on two more Sino-Sogdian monuments: the Yidu couch (fig. 96) and the Shi Jun stone house (fig. 97).[560]

As already noted above, Sino-Sogdian mortuary couches and stone houses represent a small group of unique funerary monuments executed by local artists for those high-ranking Sogdians who migrated into China in the sixth century. Flying creatures like the *feilian* are very enigmatic and it is extremely difficult to trace their origins. They were popular in a period of intense exchanges with Central Asia, India, and Persia, but it is more probable that they are a Chinese creation since they do not appear anywhere else but inside the borders of modern China. Sasanian seals and seal-impressions present a vast range of hybrid creatures as decorative motifs but they do not exactly resemble the Chinese winged monster under examination. These Sasanian winged animals with horns probably have some astronomical-astrological connection, but it is only during the Islamic period that they had some diffusion in the arts.[561] Astronomical-astrological

557 Sun 1996, 164-175; Compareti 2007; Bradford 2013.

558 Girmond 1993, fig. 4-32, kat. 57.

559 Riboud 2004, 20.

560 Lerner 2013, fig. 7; Yang 2014, figs. 103-105.

561 Compareti 2009-2010, 30-31; Compareti 2014b, 23-25.

connections have been discussed by some authors for Chinese creatures connected with funeral art and directional animals.[562] One tenth-eleventh century painting on silk, copied from an original attributed to Zhang Sengyou (ca. 490-540), and at present kept in the Osaka City Museum of Fine Arts, represent the five planets and, among them, also Venus (*Taibai xing*) as a woman riding a *fenghuang* (fig. 98).[563]

In Sino-Sogdian funerary monuments many kind of birds are often represented. Sometimes they can be considered ordinary birds but, in most cases, they are portrayed with a halo, a necklace, and ribbons attached to their neck, and with something in the beak. These are all characteristics of heavenly creatures in Iranian art; yet these birds could be regarded as animals of the royal park that, in any case, was a real paradise on earth for the king.[564] In three cases, one can observe a bird represented according to the iconography of the *fenghuang/zhuniao* in pre-Song art: on one panel of the Vahid Kooros couch;[565] on a panel in the Shi Jun sarcophagus;[566] on the pedestal of the Kang Ye couch (fig. 99).[567] Among the nine panels that embellish the sarcophagus of Yu Hong, only one does not display beribboned birds. Sometimes these birds hold something in the beak resembling a vegetal element. However, the most interesting bird of the Yu Hong funerary monument is a beribboned peacock with a halo around its head: it is not really flying but, most precisely, floating in the air

562 Juliano 1980, 35-36.

563 Masterpieces of Chinese Paintings 2013, 146; Kotyk 2018, fig. 14.

564 Compareti 2014a. The hypothesis that beribboned or haloed birds in Sasanian art would represent "good fortune" or "imperial power" seems to be completely arbitrary: Qi 2013, 35. Moreover, there is not enough evidence to consider such decorative elements as typically Sasanian since they were common in Parthian, Kushan and Sogdian art as well.

565 Riboud 2004, 26, 31.

566 Yang 2014, figs. 103-105.

567 Xi'an Municipal Institute of Archaeology and Preservation of Cultural Relics 2008, fig. 20.

above a riderless horse (fig. 100). It is worth observing also that in the unprovenanced Anyang panels (today divided between museums in France, Germany and USA), among the beribboned birds represented in several scenes, a sort of peacock too is portrayed at least three times: two with a halo and once without it (fig. 101).[568] Also in the Yidu funerary monument, almost every panel is embellished with a beribboned bird flying in the clouds, although none of them resembles the peacock-type observed in the Yu Hong and Anyang panels.

The peacock-type beribboned bird of those Sino-Sogdian funerary monuments had already called the attention of scholars. Marshak, for example, did not hesitate to identify that bird with the *farr* or "glory-charisma", and at least two more scholars made the same identification independently of Marshak.[569] In this way, a typical Iranian concept would have found its place among this group of monuments executed, in all probability, by Chinese artists. Some other typical Chinese elements had also been accepted by the Sogdians to be represented on their funerary monuments: not just the shape of the couch or sarcophagus but also the underground grave, and some decorative elements (such as the riderless horse and the ox chariot), would point to a borrowing from Chinese traditions.[570] How is it then possible to lay down a precise line of demarcation between what should be considered Iranian, Chinese, or, in some instances, Greco-Roman or Indian?

As it has been observed long ago, in Chinese funerary art fantastic birds appear quite often, especially during the Han period. In some scenes, these birds seem to fly in proximity of people who probably deserved special attention. In ancient Greek art, something very similar can be observed as well: birds holding a beribboned ring or a simple disc in their beak approach people surely in order to exalt them.[571]

568 Scaglia 1958, fig. 4.

569 Marshak 2001, 254; Zheng 2001, 86-90; Qi 2013, 35.

570 Rawson 2001; Riboud 2003.

571 Li forthcoming 2021.

The Nike (Victory) who is usually represented as a small winged woman holding a laurel crown or other symbols of glory in the vicinity of a person should be considered in the same light. Elements like the glorifying bird with a ring in the beak or the winged Nike were borrowed by other peoples in contact with Greek art and culture. Not just the Romans, who were the direct heirs of the Greek experience, but also other Iranian Hellenized people, such as the Parthians, knew these symbols very well and adopted them in their coinage (fig. 17). A poorly preserved Nike can also be observed in a first century BCE Parthian rock relief at Bisutun.[572] A similar phenomenon can also be seen in pre-Islamic Iranian art of Persia and Central Asia. On a couple of Sasanian rock reliefs (Bishapur II and Bishapur III) and on some silver vessels (cautiously) considered to be Sasanian, a flying *putto* offers a diadem to the victorious king (fig. 77).[573] Winged composite animals, and even a flying hand holding a beribboned ring, were represented very often in front of the person that should be exalted in Sogdian art (fig. 78).[574]

In the case of a Sogdian immigrant who commissioned a Chinese artist to create an appropriate tomb for him and his family, the image of a bird like a peacock embellished with ribbons and a halo could have satisfied both audiences, Iranian as well as Chinese. In the tomb of Li Shou, who died in 630, there is also a reproduction of a stone door embellished with a very interesting motif: two typical Tang (or, in any case, pre-Song) *fenghuang/zhuniao* are facing each other above the figures of two birds that could be easily identified as peacocks (fig. 102).[575] Despite the obvious Chinese identity of the tomb occupant, this early Tang grave displays several other elements imported from Iranian lands and the steppes in the funerary paintings, such as the so-called "Parthian shot", the hunting scene, and the foreign attire of

572 Vanden Berghe 1984, 45.

573 Vanden Berghe 1984, 73-74.

574 Azarpay 1975; Naymark 2001, 360.

575 Asim 1993, 183.

some individuals.[576] Some of the friezes show processions of women holding precious metal objects; one of them – a rhyton – is definitely Iranian.[577]

Even more interesting is the *zhuniao/zhuque/chiniao* represented on a Sui sarcophagus excavated in Shuicun, Tongguan County (Shaanxi Province).[578] The colossal bird is standing with spread wings and a very long tail (fig. 103). Flames embellish its neck and there is a pearl in its beak. The wings present the typical division in three parts of Sasanian and Sogdian art. In fact, the part attached to the body is separated from the final feathers by a string of pearls. Two curly elements embellish the lower part of each wing. The same unnatural position of the wings could call to mind similar representations of birds and fantastic creatures in Sasanian and Sogdian art. This *zhuniao* is standing in front of a door beside two guardians and lions. In the upper part of the door, there are some more typical Iranian elements such as a crescent including a star or the sun, and spread wings with curly elements and a central monstrous head represented in frontal view just above the head of the *zhuniao*. Very similar motifs appear in the Shi Jun stone house and they could have been copied by local artists on the basis of Sasanian coins or Sogdian art objects. It is very clear that not only Chinese culture had a strong impact on Sogdian immigrants who lived in northern China during the sixth-seventh century but also Iranian elements were very popular during the Sui and early Tang periods.

So, which identification should be proposed for those fantastic birds on Sino-Sogdian funerary monuments? *Fenghuang/zhuniao* or *simurgh* or *farr*? It is not easy to give a precise answer to this question. As I have tried to prove in another study, the presence of a fantastic bird in a typical Iranian work of art such as the sixth-century Merv painted vase (fig. 65) could offer a very interesting term of compar-

576 Zhang 1995, figs. 1, 5.

577 Asim 1993, fig. 6-28, kat. 73.2.

578 Shaanxi Provincial Institute of Archaeology 2008.

ison for many scenes of Sino-Sogdian monuments.[579] However, it is extremely difficult to decide on a precise identification for that specific bird that could very easily be the *simurgh* or just a manifestation of the *farr*, or even the *homa*, "the bird of royal glory". Since the *simurgh* was represented only as a bird and the *farr* could be *also* a bird (especially in Central Asia), some confusion at an iconographic level could also have affected the most acculturated Iranian observer. From the point of view of a Sogdian high ranking official who wanted to appear as much sinicized as possible, the presence of one or more (Iranian) fantastic birds among the decorations of his funerary monument could also have been easily understood as an auspicious symbol in the sphere of Chinese art and culture of that period (sixth century).[580]

Despite the problem of "western" (that is to say Greco-Roman) iconographic borrowings that can be detected in Sasanian and Sogdian art, it is clear that all these flying (or, sometimes, floating) creatures are just a way to represent auspicious symbols of divine protection or approval that should be considered universal and easy to understand in every cultural milieu. In the case of the fantastic bird, such a mechanism of adoption and adaptation could have moved very easily from one cultural milieu to another, since everywhere there was a cosmic bird associated with good fortune, immortality, and fire. This probably happened also for the pseudo-*simurgh*, another Iranian auspicious symbol that travelled further west but, in this case, from Central Asia to Persia and beyond to become very popular among Christians and Muslims for a very long time span.

It is normal to also expect iconographic exchanges, especially in the period between the sixth and the seventh centuries, when all the

579 Compareti 2011. According to Schulz (2019, 190), the eared bird in the Merv painted vase could be a manifestation of the *farn* like in Sogdian art. However, it should be observed that Sogdian composite creatures of this kind are always flying in the air with something in their beak or mouth. There is moreover to observe that, in my opinion, the Stroganov bowl discussed in Schulz's paper along the Merv vase could be an Iranian version of the Greek myth of Admetus and Alcestis.

580 Compareti 2016d.

regions interested in the caravan trade (from the Mediterranean Sea to China, passing through Persia and Central Asia) were experiencing an exceptionally favourable period of receptivity and search for every kind of exoticism and luxury objects. Many centuries later, the same conditions invested the Mongol Empire. In this case, Chinese models migrated in Central Asia and Persia and started to be adapted to enrich local taste.

When European travellers and scholars noted images of *fenghuang*, *long*, *qilin*, etc. in Chinese arts of the Ming-Qing periods, they identified those creatures as phoenix, dragon, unicorn, etc. of "western" legends because they, probably, had in their mind the exact corresponding fantastic animals of Islamic book illustrations, which had already incorporated many Chinese elements since the Song-Yuan period (or even earlier).[581] Fantastic creatures in Arabic, Persian and Turkish illustrated texts corresponded quite precisely to composite animals of Medieval Europe that were mainly rooted in Greco-Roman or Biblical traditions. However, there is just an illusory correspondence between European and Chinese creatures, which solely includes some iconographies at a very superficial level and during specific periods.

581 Berlekamp 2011, 172-173.

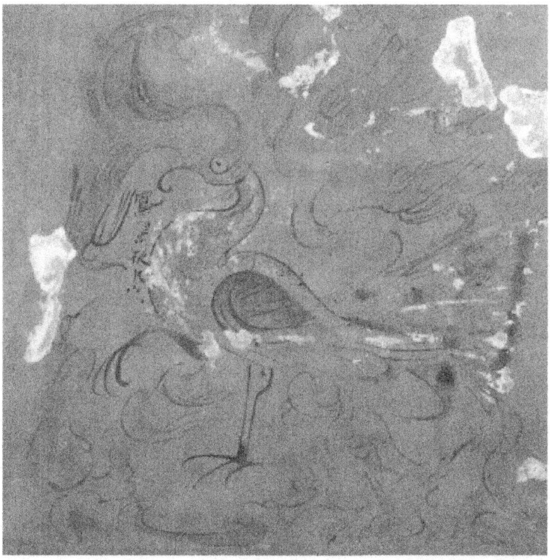

Figure 85. Magic bird labeled as *feng*(*huang*), mural painting from Helingol tomb, Inner Mongolia (Eastern Han, late second century CE). After: Inner Mongolia Regional Institute of Cultural Relics and Archaeology 2007, 120.

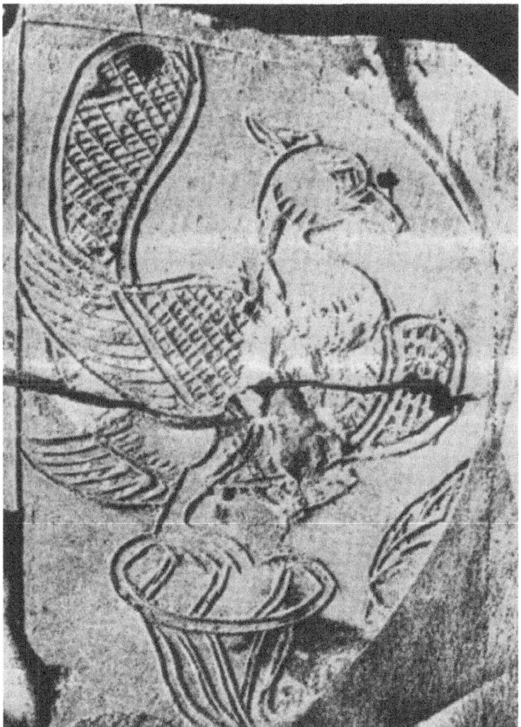

Figure 86. Peacock or phoenix on a lotus. Bone plaque from Begram, Afghanistan (Kushan period) [No. 321/175 e 1]. After: Schmidt 1980a, pl. v, fig. 9.

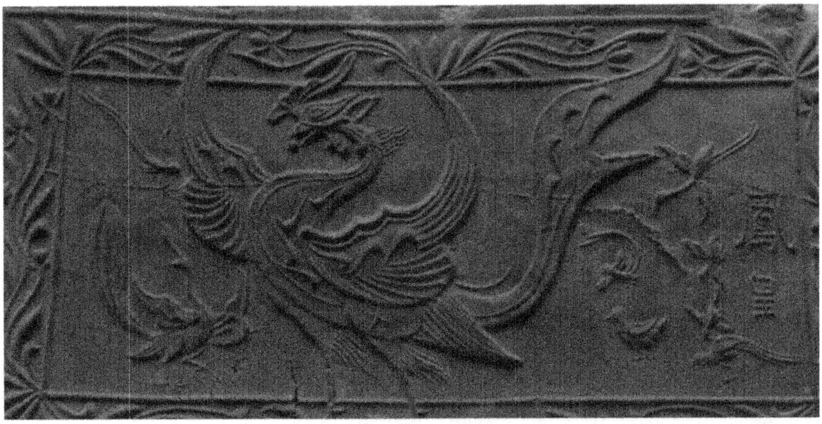

Figure 87. Brick relief with bird labeled as *fenghuang*, Dengxian, Henan (Southern Dynasties period, fifth-sixth century). The National Museum of China, Beijing. Photo: author.

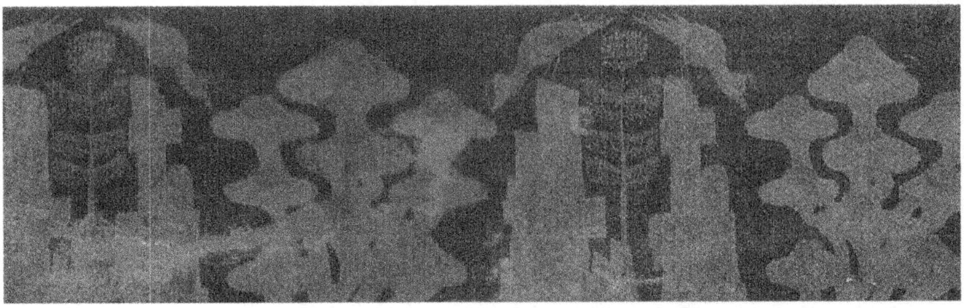

Figure 88. Chinese silk fragment with birds (*fenghuang*?) on a mountain from Noin Ula, Mongolia (first-second century). The State Hermitage Museum. After: Elikhina 2009, cat. 34.

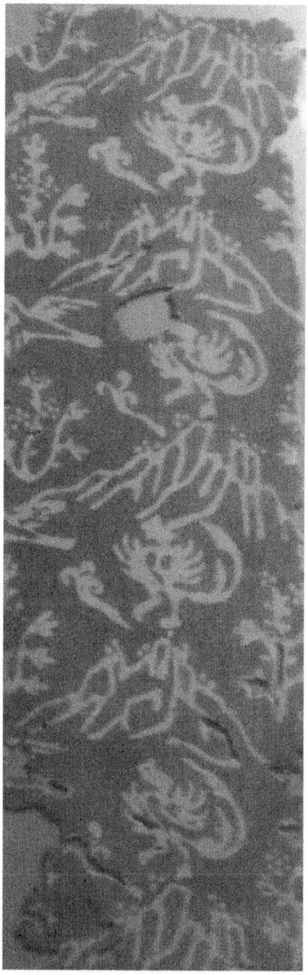

Figure 89. Textile fragment with a Tang *fenghuang* on a mountain from Astana, Turfan (seventh-eighth century). Turfan Museum. Photo: author.

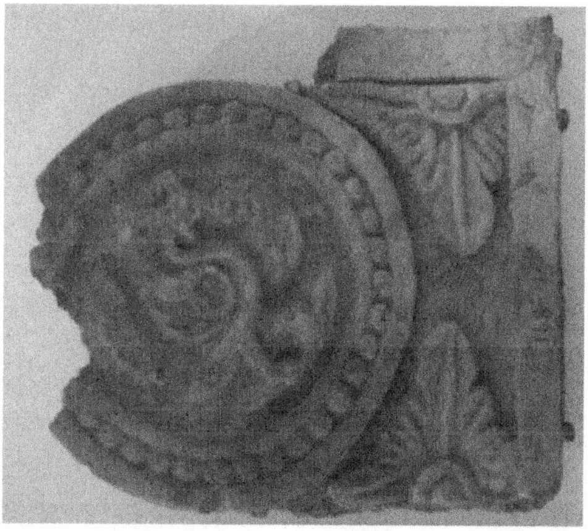

Figure 90. Stucco architectonic decoration from the "large temple B" at Toqquz-sarai, Tumshuq. Guimet Museum, Paris [MG. 17727] (sixth-seventh century). Photo" author.

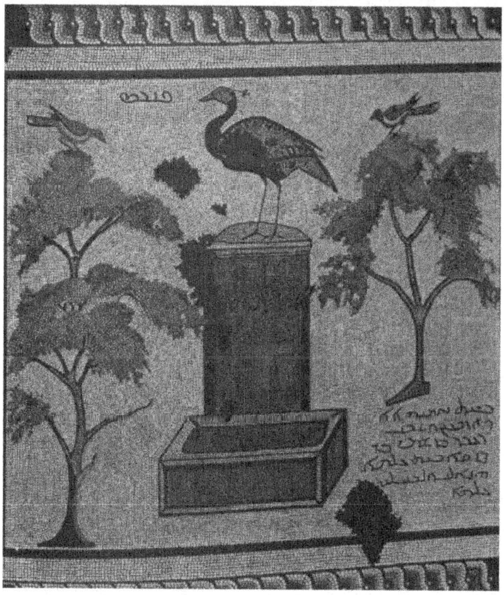

Figure 91. Phoenix labelled in Syriac on a mosaic from Edessa, Turkey (early third century). After: Van den Broek 1972, pl. XIII.

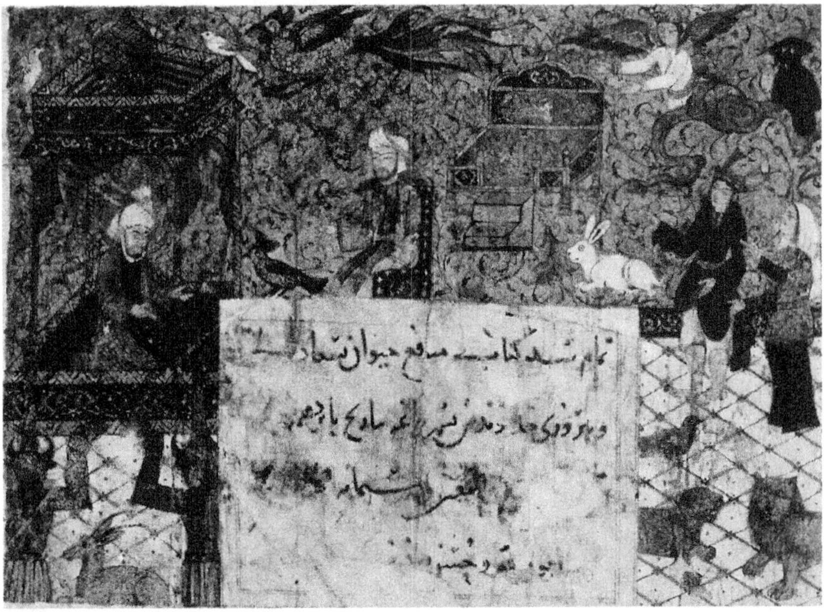

Figure 92. The phoenix and other animals in front of King Solomon, *Manafi'-i hayawan*. The Pierpont Morgan Library, New York [M.500, fol. 84v] (Maragheh, 1297-1300). After: Grube 1978, fig. 1.

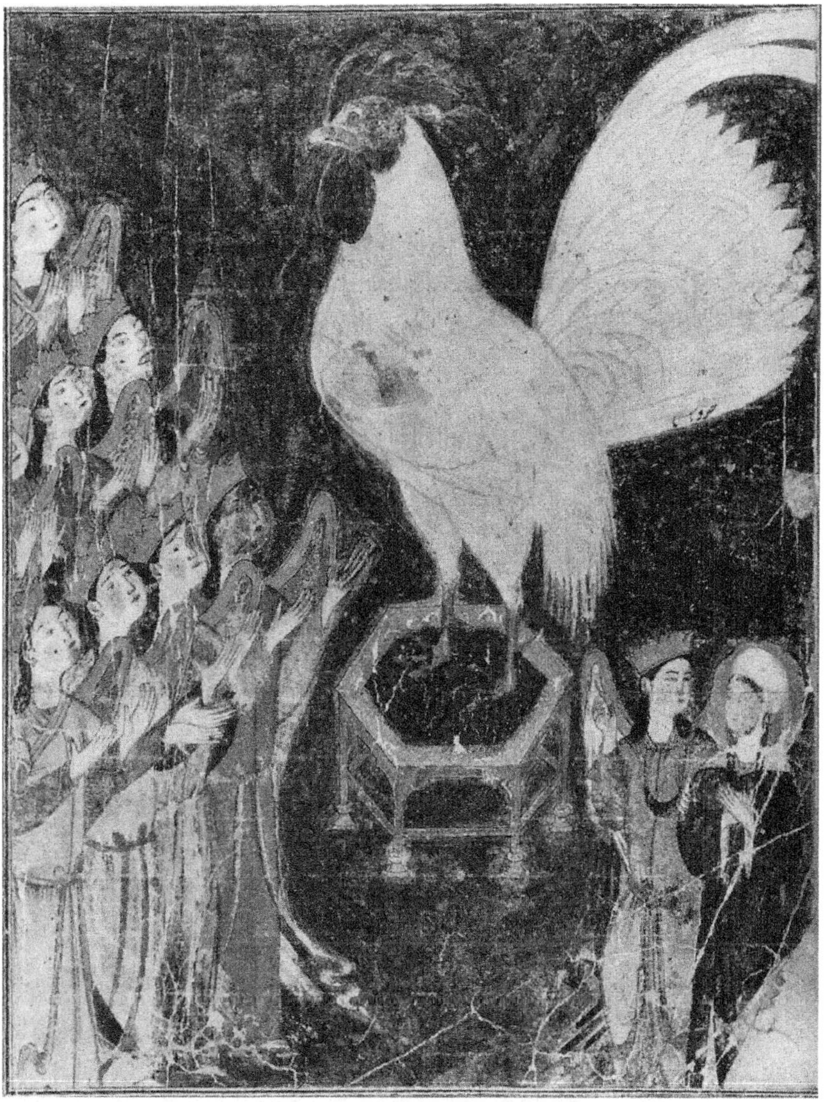

Figure 93. The angel Gabriel showing to Muhammad the cosmic cock Sraosha in a *Mi'rajnameh* "Book of the (Miraculous) Journey" manuscript. Istanbul, Topkapı Sarayi Muzesi [Hazine 2154, fol. 61v] (1317-1335). After: Ipsiroglu, M.S. (1965). *Painting and Culture of the Mongols*. London, fig. 20.

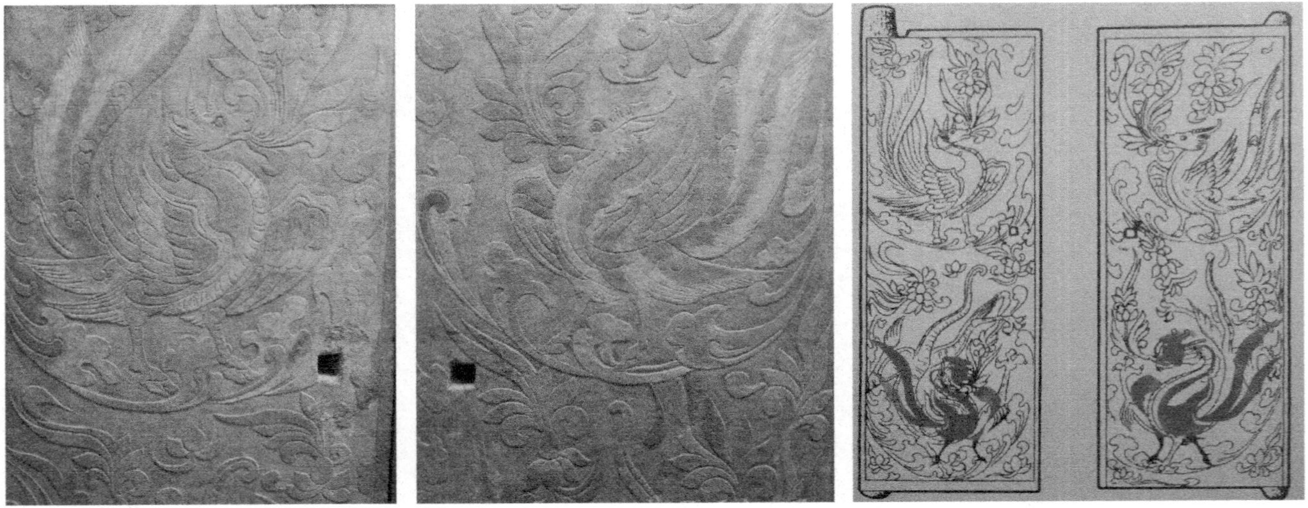

Figure 94a-b. Dragon, *fenghuang* and *feilian* facing each other on the stone door of Xu Xianxiu tomb (571). Taiyuan Museum, Shanxi. Photo: author.

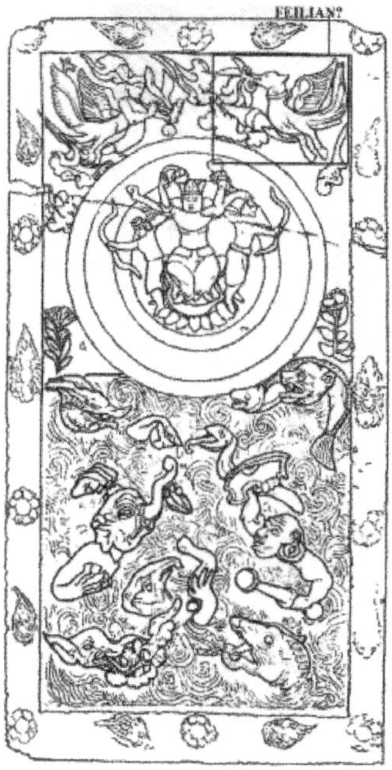

Figure 95. Flying hybrid animals on one panel of the non-excavated Sino-Sogdian "Vahid Kooros" funerary couch. Private collection (sixth century). After: Riboud 2004, fig. 12.

Figure 96a-b. Flying beribboned animals on two panels of the Yidu Sino-Sogdian funerary couch. Qingzhou Museum, Shandong. After: Lerner 2013, figs. 2, 7.

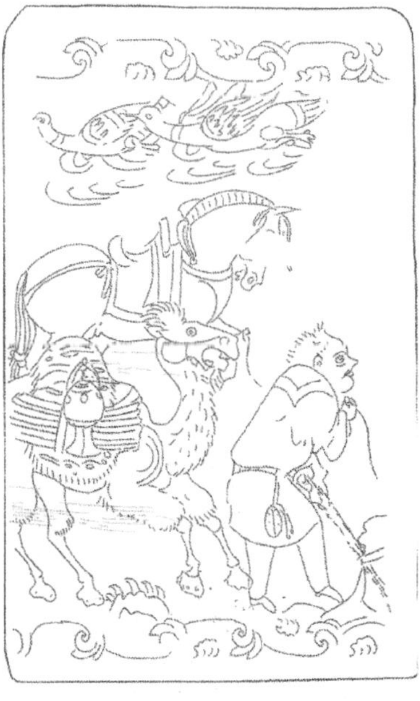

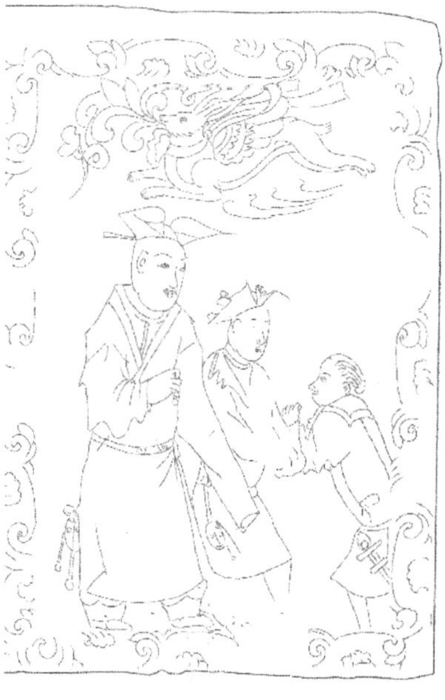

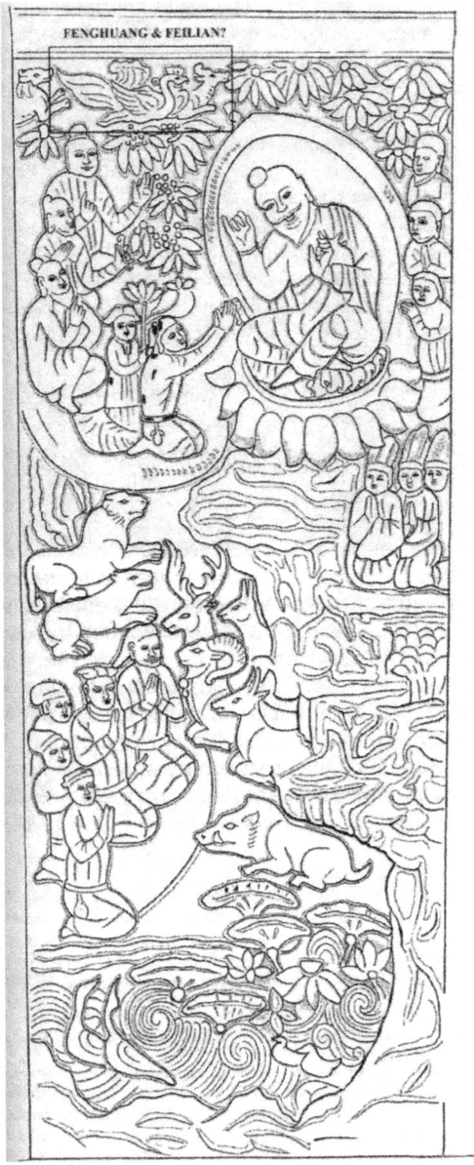

Figure 97. Flying creatures in front of a colossal person in a panel of the Shi Jun Sino-Sogdian stone house (580 CE). Shaanxi History Museum, Xi'an. After: Yang 2014, fig. 104.

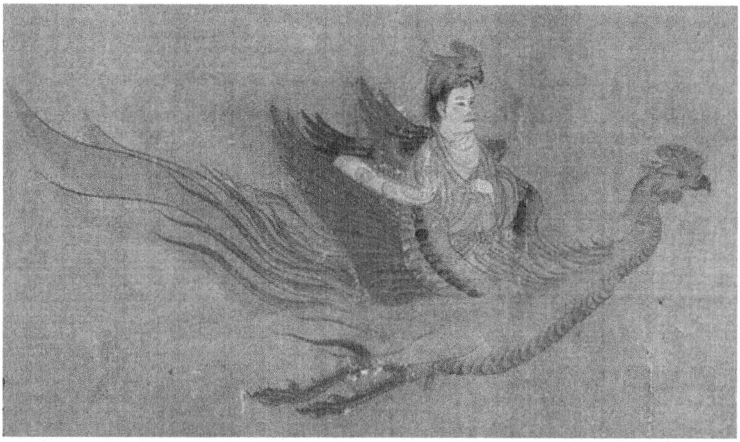

Figure 98. Venus (*Taibai xing*) as a woman riding a *Fenghuang* on a painting on silk copied from an original attributed to Zhang Sengyou (ca. 490-540) (tenth-eleventh century). The Osaka City Museum of Fine Arts, Japan. After: Masterpieces of Chinese Paintings 2013, 146.

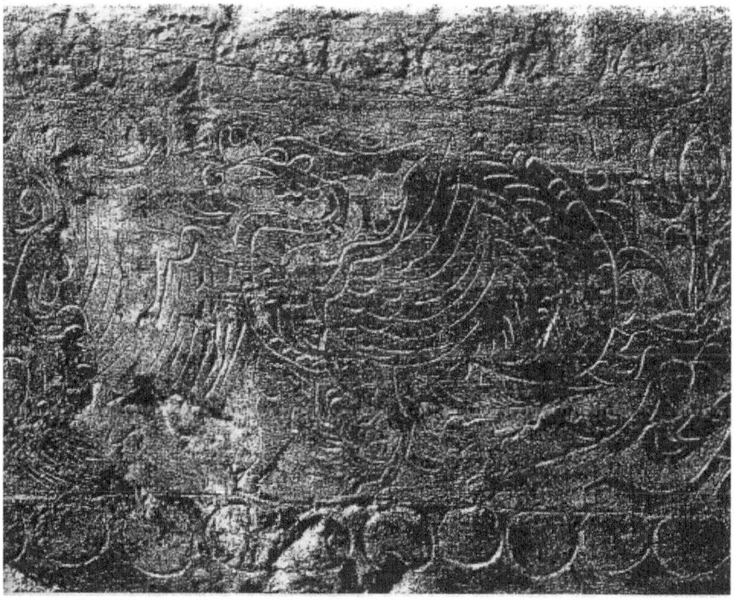

Figure 99. Image of a *fenghuang/zhuniao* bird on the pedestal of the Kang Ye funerary couch (ca. 571). Shaanxi History Museum, Xi'an. After: Xi'an Municipal Institute of Archaeology and Preservation of Cultural Relics 2008, fig. 20.

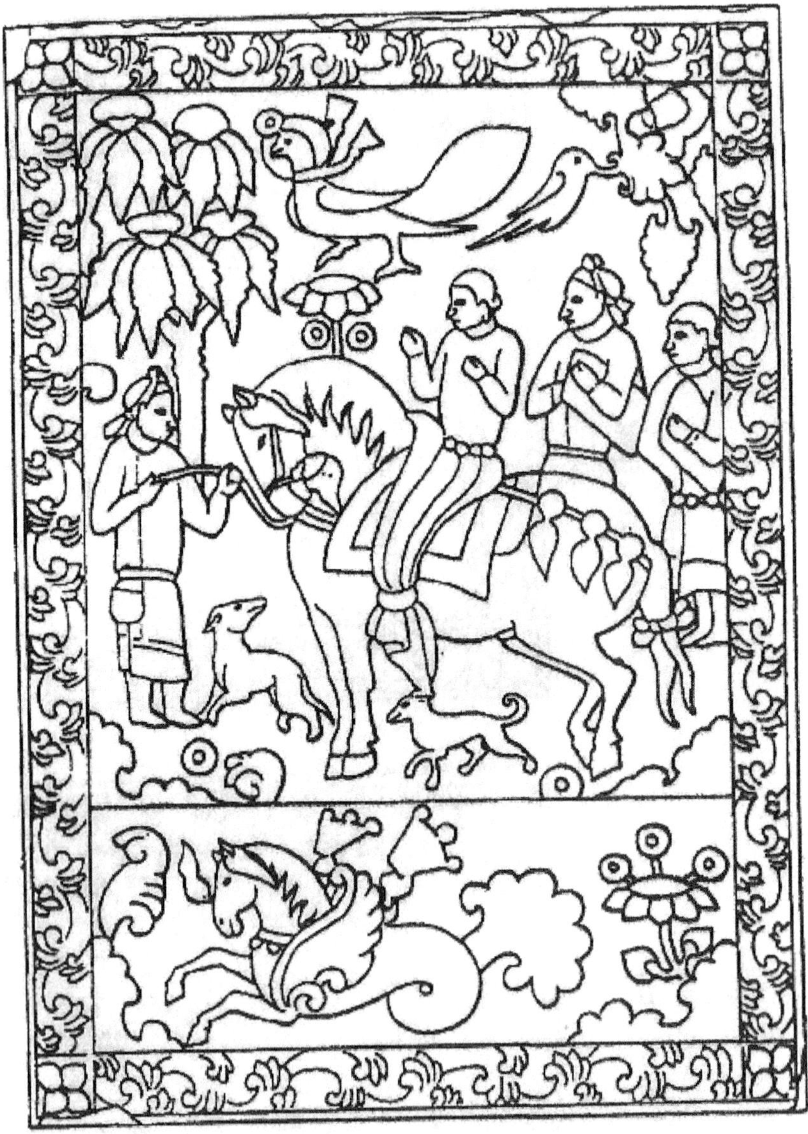

Figure 100. Beribboned peacock with a halo around its head floating in the air above a riderless horse, Yu Hong stone house (592 or 598). Taiyuan Museum, Shanxi. After: Marshak 2001, fig. 22b).

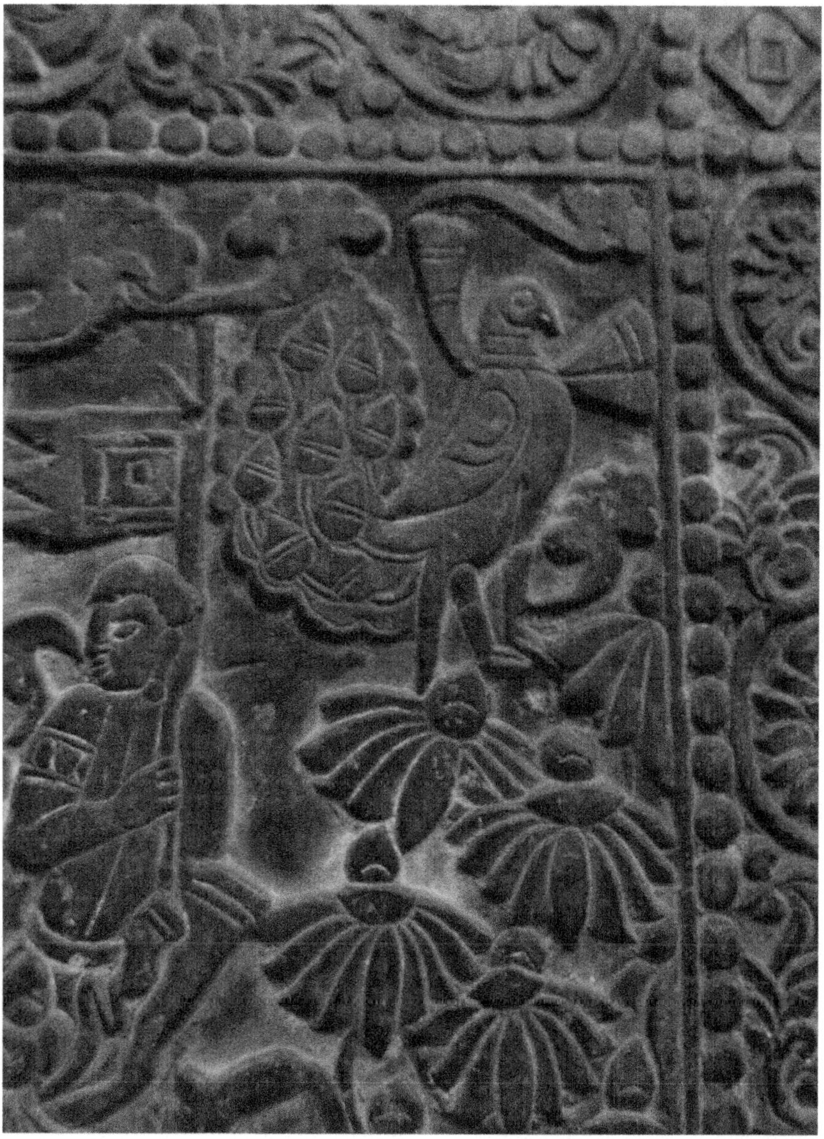

Figure 101. Beribboned bird on the un-excavated Anyang funerary couch (sixth century). Fine Arts Museum, Boston [acquisition 12.589]. Photo: author.

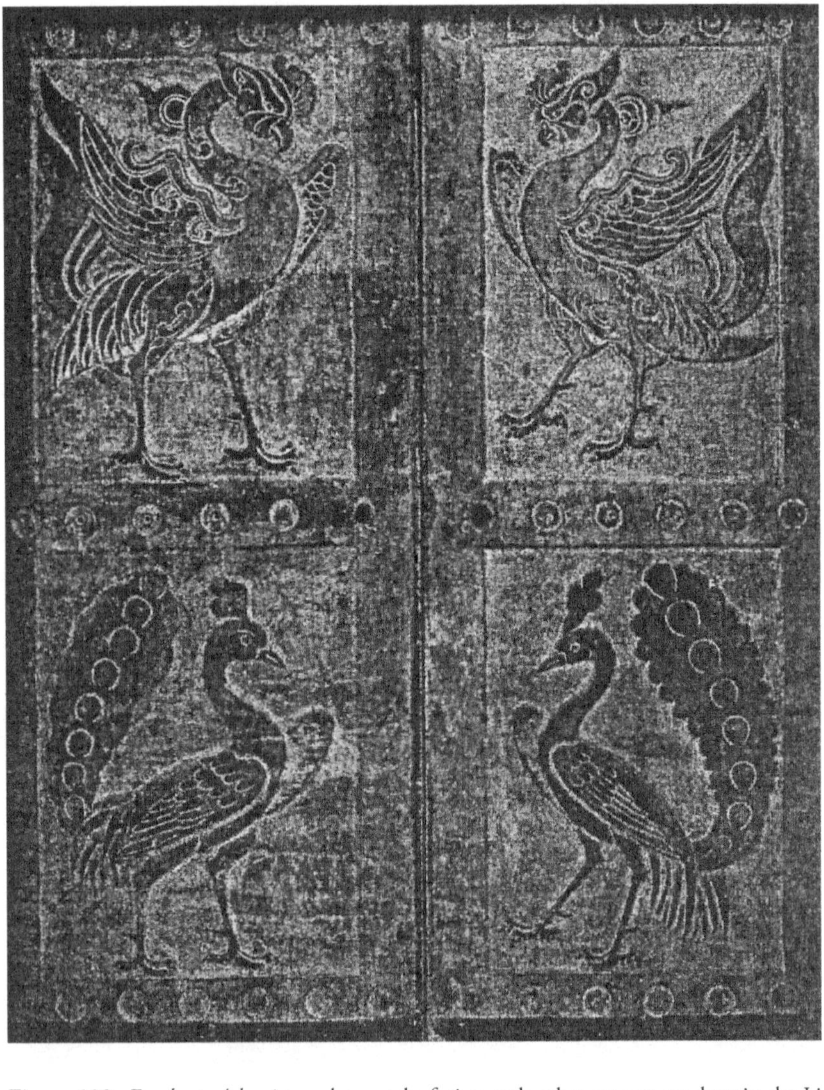

Figure 102. *Fenghuang/zhuniao* and peacocks facing each other on a stone door in the Li Shou tomb (630). After: Asim 1993, 183.

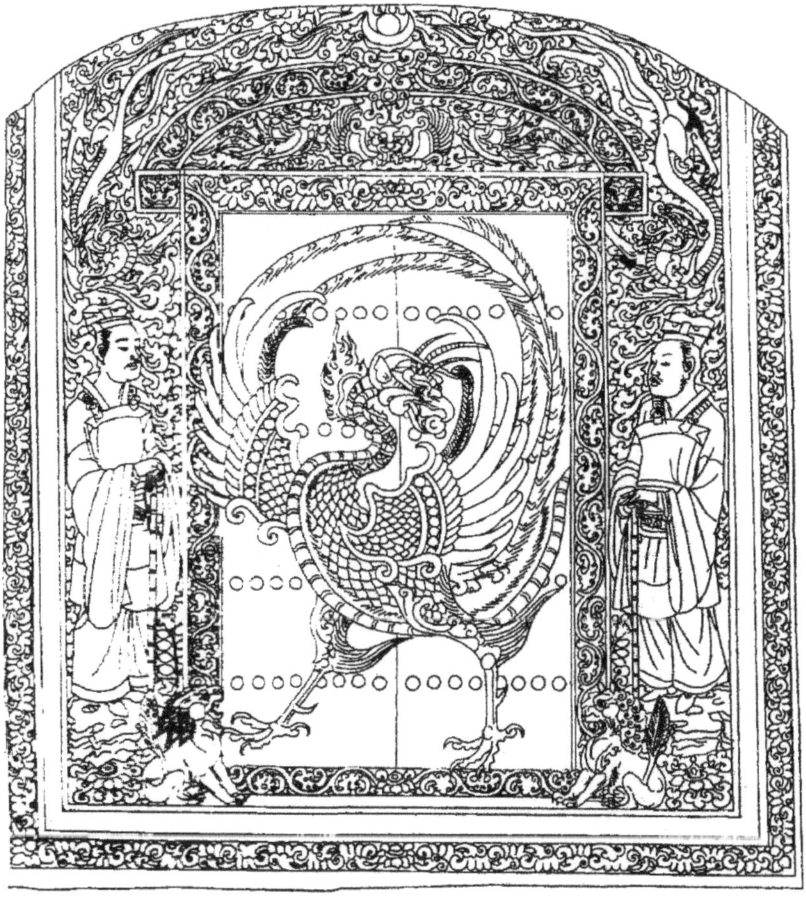

Figure 103. *Fenghuang/zhuniao* on the Sui sarcophagus excavated at Shuicun village, Tongguan County, Shaanxi Province. After: Shaanxi Provincial Institute of Archaeology 2008, fig. 13.

Appendix 2
The construction of Taq-i Bustan according to the anonymous twelfth century Persian Mojmal al-Tawarikh

(French translation after: Mohl 1842, 122-130)

Hormuzd, fils de *Nourschirwan* – Son règne dura douze ans. Aussitôt qu'il fut monté sur le trône, il commença à opprimer ses sujets; il fir périr l'un après l'autre tous les ministres, le grand *mobed*, et tous ceux que son père avait rendus puissants. Saveh, rois de Turcs, entra dans le Khorasan à la tête d'une armée de quatre cent mille cavaliers, et Hormuzd ne puit lui faire face, parce les Romains, les Arabes et le Khazars faisaient de tous côtés entrer des armées dans l'Iran, dont ils convoitaient la conquête. A la fin, il envoya Bahram-Djoubineh [Bahram VI Chubin] contre le roi Saweh, sur l'avis de Mihran-Setad, qui avait entendu les prédictions des astrologues turcs, du temps où il avait amené (du Turkestan) la mère de Hormuzd. Le roi choisit donc Bahram, d'après les indications que Mihran Setad lui avait données, et Babram partit et tua Saweh: c'est une histoire qu'on raconte avec beaucoup de détails. A la fin, Bahram se révolta contre Hormuzd, s'établit, avec son armée à Reï [Rayy], où il fit frapper de la monnaie d'argent portant le nom de Khosrou [Khusraw II Parwiz], et en envoya des pièces à Hormuzd, à Madaïn [Ctesiphon]. Hormuzd conçut le soupçon que Bahram n'agissait que par l'ordre de son fils, et voulut faire périr Khosrou; mais ce dernier s'enfuit dans l'Aderbeidjan [Azerbaijan]. Hormuzd jeta alors Kustehem [Bastam] et Bendoui [Binduya/Bindoe], les oncles maternels de Khosrou, dans les fers. Les Iraniens étaient las de la tyrannie de Hormuzd, se révoltèrent, tirèrent de leur prison Kustehem et Bendoui, et placèrent (Khosrou) sur le trône. Bahram Djoubineh arriva à Nahrwan, et l'armée de Khosrou passa de son côté. Alors ce dernier se décida, d'après l'ordre et avec l'approbation de son père, à se rendre dans le pays de Roum pour demander secours. Kustehem et Bendoui (qui partaient avec lui) s'en retournèrent des portes de Madaïn sans la permission de Khosrou (revinrent au palais), étranglèrent Hormuzd, et repartirent sur-le-champ. Bahram-Djoubineh entra dans Madaïn, s'assit sur le trône, s'empara du gouvernement, et envoya après Khosrou un général nommé Bahram-Siawuschan. Khosrou se reposait dans une église lorsque Bahram et ses troupes arrivèrent; mais, au moment où ils parurent, Bendoui s'avisa d'un ruse. Il prit la robe royale de Khosrou, s'en revêtit, et se plaça sur le toit de l'église pendant que (Khosrou et ses compagnons) s'échappèrent. Les troupes de Bahram voyant Bendoui, n'eurent aucun doute que ce ne fût Khosrou, et entourèrent l'église. Bendoui descendit alors, se revêtit de ses propres habits, et remonta annoncer au nom du roi qu'il demandait se reposer ce jour, et qu'il serait, le lendemain, prêt à partir. Il trompa les troupes de cette manière pendant trois jours. A la fin, quand Khosrou devait avoir atteint la frontière, Bendoui fit connaître la vérité. Bahram l'amena à Madaïn et le jeta en prison. On a beaucoup de détails sur la mort de Bahram, fils de Siawusch, et sur la fuite de Bendoui dans l'Aderbeidjan, où il resta auprès de Moschil l'Arménien jusqu'à ce que Khosrou y arrivât.[582]

Khosrou Parwiz – Son règne dura trente-huit ans. Cette époque comprend le temps pendant le quel Bahram Djoubineh occupa le trône; car on ne peut pas le compter dans la série des rois, parce que Khosrou occupe l'espace pendant lequel Bahram avait usurpé le trône. Maurice, empereur romain, pourvut Khosrou d'une armée, d'armes et d'argent, lui donna en mariage sa fille Mariam, et envoya avec son armée et sa fille son fils Théodose. Après une longue lutte, Bahram fut battu, et s'en fuit chez le *khakan*, où il acquit une grande influence, jusqu'à ce

582 This story is also reported in the Armenian *Episkoposi patmut'iun* "History [of Heraclius] by Bishop Sebeos" (seventh century) and the Arabic *Kitab al-Akhbar al-Tiwal* "The Book of Long Narratives" of Abu Hanifa ibn Dawud al-Dinawari (ninth century): Scarcia 1980, 89-107.

que Khosrou envoyât Khorrad Burzin, qui intrigua contre lui, et finit par le faire tuer par un Turc nommé Kaloun. Selon une autre tradition, Khorrad séduisit la femme du *khakan*, qui chargea un esclave de frapper inopinément Bahram d'un couteau et de le tuer. Dieu connaît la vérité. Ensuite Khosrou fit périr son oncle Bendoui, pour venger la mort de son père. Kustehem, craignant pour sa vie, se révolta et épousa Kordieh [Kurdya], sœur de Bahram Djoubineh. L'armée qu'elle ramenait du Turkestan se réunit à celle de Kustehem; mais à la fin, cette femme, Kordieh, sœur de Babram, assassina son mari par ordre du roi, et épousa Khosrou, qui eut un fils d'elle. Schirin [Shirin] était déjà, antérieurement à ce temps, une des femmes de Khosrou. A partir de cette époque, Khosrou devint extrêmement puissant; aucun roi ne posséda jamais autant de trésors et de choses précieuses et belles que lui. Je parlerai en son lieu, et en détail, de ce que ses trésors contenaient à l'époque de sa mort. Ces richesses étaient telles qu'on n'en a jamais su la valeur; je ne parlerai ici que de quelques objets entre beaucoup d'autres. Il possédait le trône appelé *thakdis*, et c'est lui qui l'acheva. L'histoire de ce trône est fort longue; on dit que Djemschid [Jamshid] commença à le faire exécuter, que Féridoun y ajouta de nouvelles portions, que quelques parties en furent emportées à Roum et dans le Turkestan; que Gustasp le fit reconstruire dans une autre forme, et qu'à la fin Khosrou en fit rapporter les parties de tous les côtés, et le compléta de manière à étonner le monde entier. On dit qu'il y avait en or mille charges d'âne employées à ce trône, sans compter les pierreries, dont la valeur était inestimable. Il y avait dans son harem douze mille femmes, tant esclaves que libres, et parmi elles se trouvaient Mariam, fille du roi de Roum, Bahram-Dokht, Kordieh et Schirin, qui était si belle qu'aucune oeuvre d'art, depuis que le monde existe, n'a pu donner une idée de sa beauté. Le *sipehbed* Ferhad [*spahbed* Farhad] en était amoureux; c'est lui qui a exécuté les travaux à Bisitoun, dont on voit encore les restes. Parwiz avait dix-huit mille chevaux dans ses écuries, parmi lesquels il y en avait qu'il affectionnait particulièrement comme Schebdiz [Shabdiz], que l'on voit sculpté à Kirmanschahan [Kermashah], près d'un bourg appelé Bistham.

Bistham est aussi un nom de Kustehem, oncle de Parwiz.[583] J'ai lu dans le *Firouznameh* que c'est Kitous, fils de Sinnimar le Grec, qui a exécuté ces sculptures sur pierre, le même qui a construit *Khawernak* et *Sedir*. Lui et les autres artistes travaillaient sous les ordres du *sipehbed* Ferhad. On avait bâti, sur l'ordre du roi, au-dessus de la fontaine, une salle d'audience, et au-dessus des sculptures que l'on voit encore, un palais, et quand tout fut achevé, le roi y donna un festin à ses grands et à ses généraux; ensuite il donna (ce lieu) à Ferhad. C'est là qu'on voit encore les figures de Parwiz, de Schebdiz, de Schirin et d'un *mobed*, et la représentation d'une chasse; le tout sculpté dans la pierre.[584] Il avait dans son palais neuf cents éléphants, entre autres un qu'on appelait Kedizad, qui était né dans l'Iran, ce qui était une grande merveille; car, jus qu'alors, jamais éléphant n'avait porté dans ce pays, pas plus qu'une lionne ne porte dans le Roum, une chatte dans la Chine, ou une cavale dans l'Inde. Ce sont là des singularités de ces pays. Parwiz possédait douze mille mulets de bagage. J'ai vu dans le *Firouznameh*, et Dieu sait ce qui en est vrai, que la nourriture de Parwiz coûtait tous les jours douze mille dinars, et que c'était toujours la même somme, parce qu'on mettait tous les jours dans son dîner une pierre fine pilée de cette valeur, ce qui lui était nécessaire, à cause de sa constitution et d'une maladie qu'il avait. Il buvait (par jour) soixante rotls de vin parfumé de roses, et pouvait, dans l'espace d'un jour et d'une nuit, avoir commerce avec soixante femmes. Il consumait tous les jours régulièrement soixante rotls de musc, sans compter les autres parfums. On employa vingt rotls (de ce musc) pour le dîner et la boisson de ses convives, vingt rotls pour l'office et les domestiques, et pour arroser la salle d'audience; dix rotls pour l'eau avec laquelle le roi se lavait, enfin dix pour les femmes du roi.

583 For a very skeptical attitude towards this identification, see: Orsatti 2019, 30.

584 Some Islamic manuscripts illustrated just this popular identification of the sculptures at Taq-i Bustan and not Khusraw Parwiz between Ahura Mazda and Anahita as argued above: Soucek 1974. On the hypothesis of a Zoroastrian magus (*mobad*) playing the role of Ahura Mazda at Taq-i Bustan and other Sasanian rock reliefs, see: Overlaet 2013.

Quand Parwiz allait à la chasse, cinq cents filles se tenaient à sa droite et à sa gauche, brûlant de l'aloës dans des cassolettes d'or, et mille domestiques arrosaient la terre, autour de lui, d'eau musquée, pour que le vent ne soulevât pas de poussière. Mille mulets portaient des litières destinées aux musiciens, dont deux occupaient toujours une litière. Je traiterai plus tard, s'il plaît à Dieu, de son cortège, de ses faucons et des autres détails de sa magnificence, qui était infinie. Parwiz possédait ce qu'aucun roi n'avait possédé, une bouteille de verre dont on pouvait verser autant qu'on voulait de vin, quand même on l'avait remplie d'eau, et sans que la bouteille se vidât jamais. Il possédait aussi une pièce d'étoffe appelée *Aderscheb*, qui était tissée de poils de salamandre; enfin il avait de l'or que l'on pouvait pétrir de la main, et sur lequel on pouvait imprimer un sceau comme sur de la cire. Parmi ses trésors étaient le *Gandji Arous*, le *Gandji Badawerd*, le *Gandji Kaous*, le *Gandji Afrasiab* et le *Dinari Khosrowani*, et il existe sur chacun de ces trésors une histoire, dans laquelle on raconte de quoi il se composait et comment il était tombé entre les mains de Parwiz. Il avait des musiciens comme Sergius le Romain et Barbud. Ce sont eux qui ont fixé toutes les notes et écrit les airs. Jamais il n'y a eu un roi aussi puissant et aussi heureux. Vers la fin de sa vie, il fit tuer Noman, fils de Mondar l'Arabe. La guerre de Dsi Kar eut lieu, et les Arabes vainquirent les Persans au nom du prophète. Parwiz en fut irrité, et lorsque le prophète lui envoya une lettre et des ambassadeurs, il reçut mal leur message, comme je le raconterai plus tard. Avant cela il envoya une armée dans le pays de Roum, parce que son beau-père Maurice avait été tué; mais Héraclius, empereur des Grecs, battit l'armée de Parwiz et la poursuivit jusqu'à Madaïn; et c'est à cela que se rapporte la parole du Koran: "Les Grecs ont été vaincus dans les provinces voisines, etc.". Ensuite Parwiz jeta dans les fers tous les grands de l'empire, et ordonna de les tuer. Leur nombre s'élevait à trente mille personnes, des premières familles de la Perse. A la fin, les Iraniens se révoltèrent, tirèrent, de nuit, Schiroueh, fils du roi, de sa prison, le placèrent sur le trône, et jetèrent le roi dans les fers. Peu après, on le fit périr par la main de Mihr Hormuzd, dont Parwiz avait fait tuer le père dans le même endroit. Il construisit, entre autres, le fort de *Kenkwer* et le château de Schirin sur la route de Bagdad. On voit encore les ruines de ces deux constructions. Ses cuisines étaient dans le district d'Asadabad, là où l'on voit aujourd'hui un bourg nommé Sabakh; mais il passait la saison d'été sur le mont Arwend, près de Hamadan. (On appelle encore dans ces environs un endroit *Dukkani Khosroa*, un autre *Khemi Khosrou*, etc.). Or, j'ai lu dans le *Siar al-Molouk* que, de ces cuisines jusqu'à l'endroit où il se tenait, c'est-à-dire à *Kenkwer* sur l'Arwend, près de Hamadan, les cuisiniers faisaient passer de main en main les mets dans de la vaisselle d'or et des plats ornés de pierreries, de sorte qu'ils arrivaient chauds, tant il y avait d'esclaves employés à cela; ce qui peut donner une idée de ce qu'on raconte de la magnificence de ce règne.

Appendix 3
A Fragment of the Western Wall of the "Blue Hall" of Penjikent

Larisa Yu. Kulakova[585]

The "Blue Hall" is the soubriquet of the large painted reception hall in the south-eastern part of ancient Penjikent (room 41 area VI) which was excavated by Boris Ja. Staviskij in 1956-57. Its murals, datable to the 740ies, the last blossom of Penjikent, are of exceptional artistic quality and preservation. The tiers of murals with illustrations of fairy tales, the epics of Rustam, unidentified epic narratives, and a queue of gods were painted from the floor up. The eastern, better preserved part of the mural was promptly cleaned, conserved, and exhibited and has been published many times since (Marshak 2002b should be referred to as the standard edition).

Another, western half of the mural was until recently known only through tracings of some parts which are however quite generalized, except for a few conserved pieces of fable illustrations from the lower tier on the eastern wall and a fragment with a lion. Over the course of several years prior to 2015, the western half of the Blue Hall was completely cleaned and conserved, and exhibited temporarily in fall 2015. Since then the better-preserved fragment of the combat of Rustam with an elderly knight or a demon was showcased in Delhi and pub-

585 Translated and edited by Pavel B. Lurje. Final revision by Noël Siver.

lished in the catalogue.[586] Other parts are unpublished, and one is described briefly below (fig. 104).[587]

The fragment in question was initially conserved a long time ago but did not call the attention of scholars except Boris I. Marshak.[588] The reason for this neglect was the poor preservation of the mural: the painted surface was significantly deteriorated with serious lacunae. The small and dispersed fragments of painting hindered the "reading" of the scene and the detection of the subject. This part of the mural was apparently not considered worthy of display and that is why it was not cleaned properly then. Careful analysis of the mural however made clear that it possessed interesting details in need of additional cleaning. This cleaning was successfully carried out by the staff of Laboratory for Scientific Restoration of Monumental Painting of the State Hermitage Museum.

This part of the mural, 1,3 by 2,3 m, it was located on the western wall, occupying the space from the south-western corner to the doorway.[589] The plot of the southern wall ended with the group of riders in the corner. They were Rustam and his squad. This is the third time we see this composition in the surviving portions of the murals: the narration starts with it on the western wall to the north of the doorway and a similar riding party occupies the central position on the northern wall.

From the corner onward, a significant portion of the upper part of the tier is washed away; the lines and colours are almost totally lost.

---

586 Kulakova in *The Everlasting Flame. Zoroastrianism in History and Imagination*. Supplement. Delhi, 2016: 26-27; cf. Л. Ю. Кулакова, О.С. Викторова, Р.А. Казимирова. Сцена битвы Рустама с демоном. Фрагмент росписи. // *Возрожденные шедевры. Реставрация в Эрмитаже*, 2015. СПб: Изд. ГЭ, 2015: 16-17.

587 This is part of a general work on the newly restored portions of the Blue Hall that is currently in preparation.

588 Marshak 2002b: 50. He recognized here fragments of two male figures and supposed that a reception scene was depicted.

589 The part of the mural directly attached to the doorway did not survive.

In the lower part we detect a composition of two male figures. On the left-hand side we see a small fragment of blue background and a black strip with protruding white dots. This is a conventional rendering of a dagger handle suspended from the belt, and below it there are tips of boots oriented to the left. This is what remains of a male character sitting on his bent knees.

Another man is posed on the right, standing or stepping towards the sitting character. The upper part of his figure above the waist has not survived. The lower half is dressed in a long red-brown caftan with contrasting fabric at its fringes. The golden scabbard of a sword is attached to his belt. He is holding it with his left hand. It is probable that a dagger with the handle executed identically to that of the sitting character was here too. A small fragment of colour lends support to the supposition that his torso was inclining to the left. The pose of the character and his left hand controlling the scabbard permits the supposition that he holds the sword in his right hand.

Between these two figures there is a large, lobed bowl on a low foot with traces of decoration on its surface, surrounded by the blue background. The unusual size of the vessel (which has a shape similar to well-known Sogdian silver bowls), and the noble metal from which it is made,[590] probably indicate the outstanding role of the bowl in the narrative. Between the bowl and a lower line of pearls, the twisted stem of a plant with a large flower is depicted. In the upper part of the tier, above the standing figure, one can recognize contours of a rectangular object (a carpet?).

The next scene is separated by some object below it, possibly a plant or a hillock. To the right of it one recognizes the galloping horse (only its hindmost part has survived). Its coat and white "socks" on its legs indicate that Rakhsh (Rustam's stallion) is depicted. In some spots we recognize parts of Rustam, maybe he is holding a spear in his hand. The pose of the rider on the "flying" horse, as far as we can

590 Yellow ochre colour conventionally renders gold.

judge from the surviving fragment, mirrors the figure of Rustam on the northern wall where he is fighting Aulād.

The upper part of the register between the first scene and the galloping Rustam is occupied by a giant being in the yellow colour. Behind the back of the standing character one sees large feathers of a tail, to the right of which there are tips of two wings.[591] Other parts of it have not survived; only small patches of yellow colour suggest the dimensions of this figure.

Searching for the literary prototype of the plot of the mural, which has many lacunae in its preservation, we use the items depicted as a kind of "markers" which can be identified with a text of the literary source. In our case, these unusual markers are the golden bowl of large size, the flower next to it, and the giant bird.

There are two episodes in the *Shahnameh* of Firdousi[592] that are worth precise analysis:
The first is the killing of Siyāwush. When his throat was slit, the blood was collected in a bowl. Later this bowl was tipped over, and in the place where the blood was spilled, a grass called "blood of Siyāwush" grew.[593]

If we suppose that the scene of Siyāwush's murder is depicted, the bowl is the one used for his blood and the flower is the plant that grew from it.

Despite the attractiveness of this interpretation, one should notice some considerations that make the validity of this version doubtful.

The person sitting on his bent knees is not weaponless. The dagger is attached to his belt, he is dressed and shod. In medieval miniatures showing Siyāwush's assassination, he is without an upper garment, in underwear, barefoot, with his hands tied behind his back. Perhaps

591 The wings of the flying chariot of demons at the northeastern corner of the hall are depicted in the same manner.

592 We use the Russian translation of the whole text of *Shahnameh* made by Ts. B. Banu-Lahuti (Фердоуси. Шахнаме. т. I-VI М. 1960).

593 *Shahnameh* II: 249-250.

the bloody scene of the murder is omitted and only the bowl and flower are depicted. Consequently the riding and/or fighting Rustam in the next scene could be related to the events known as "Siyāwush's vengeance".

Another consideration concerns the fact that Siyāwush was a beloved and honoured hero. It seems doubtful that only one episode of his story, namely his death, was selected.[594] Moreover, the mural painting being, unlike a miniature, always seen in front of guests' eyes, would forever remind one of Siyāwush's tragedy. We cannot leave unmentioned, however, the record of Narshakhī, saying that Siyāwush was the beloved hero of the Bukhariots, and musicians there composed beautiful songs entitled *kīn-i Siyāwush* "Siyāwush's vengeance" which were also called *girīstan-i mughān* "lamentation of magians".[595]

The second episode in which a noteworthy bowl appears is included in the story of Bīzhan and Manīzha during Kei Khosrow's reign. The son of champion Gīw named Bīzhan gets lost. After unsuccessful searches, the father asks Kei Khosrow for help. The *shah* says that on the coming of Nourūz, he will look into the magical bowl of Jamshīd (*jām-i Jam*). Looking there indeed Kei Khosrow sees Bīzhan taken captive by the Tūrānians.[596] Rustam, having been sent to rescue Bīzhan, freed him.

If we treat the mural as an illustration of this narrative, the male characters are Gīw and Khosrow in front of the magical bowl of Jamshīd. In this case it is not very clear what is in the right hand of

594 Later miniatures for example used to render his trial by fire. If here we have the scene of Siyawush's death, it is included in Rustam's deeds. The penultimate plot on the southern wall comprises his fight against the monster with a lion's head, and we see Rustam riding Rakhsh again after the bowl and flower scene.

595 R.N. Frye (transl.). *The History of Bukhara.* Cambridge, MA, 1954: 17, 23.

596 *Shahnameh* III: 147. The topic of Jamshīd's cup became exceedingly popular in later Persian literature, see M. Omidsalar, Jamšid. II. in Persian literature, in: *Encyclopaedia Iranica*, XIV, 5, 2012: 522-528; also available online https://iranicaonline.org/articles/jamsid-ii (consulted on 26/07/2020).

the standing figure, but hardly his sword. Consequently, perhaps, the flower indicates the season when the events take place – it is spring.[597] One cannot rule out, however, that the flower is painted as an element breaking up the large free space of the background, a device against "*horror vacui*", and does not have any significance in the plot.

The giant winged creature in the next scene is most likely Sīmurgh, the fantastic bird, who rescued and raised Rustam's father, the champion Zāl, and several times came to his aid. In Firdousi's text, Rustam does not meet Sīmurgh. The only episode uniting these two characters is the giant bird advising Zāl how to help Rūdāba, Rustam's mother, in her childbirth labour. One can suggest that by depicting Sīmurgh near Rustam, the painter intended to show that Zāl's kin is under its protection. Alternatively, the encounter of Rustam with Sīmurgh may have been forgotten by the time of Firdousi.[598]

All the versions above have their pro and contra arguments and therefore we had to consider them. Quite possibly the mural illustrates a subject that was not included in Firdousi's masterpiece due for some reasons.

Finally, it is my pleasant duty to thank the conservators, due to whose efforts a part of the mural, where almost nothing was preserved, provided much new and interesting information, the source of new discussions and hypotheses.

597 Unlike the standard Sogdian calendar where *n'wsrδ* fell in mid-Summer in the eighth century, in the folklore the original position of the New Year on the spring equinox might have been preserved.

598 It is worth noting that both the "brave rider *Rustami*" and "wise *Sēnməry*" are attested in the Sogdian "benediction" fragment (Yoshida 2013).

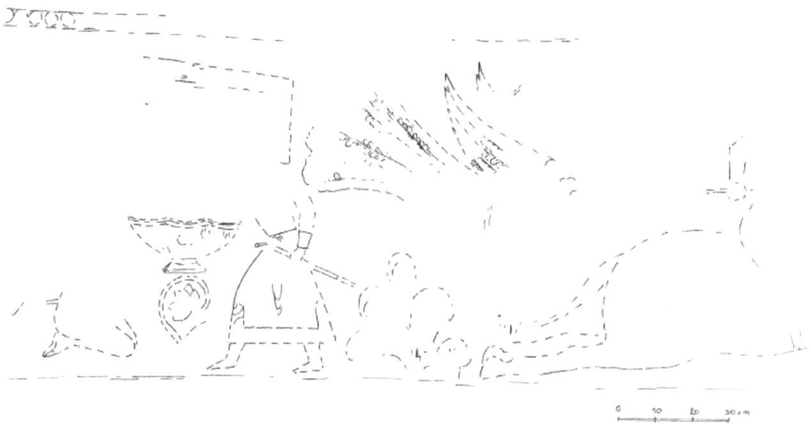

Figure 104. Southern part of the western wall of the Blue Hall. Second tier. Schematic tracing with elements of reconstruction by the author.

Bibliography

Primary sources

Greek and Latin texts

Aeschylus (2009). *Prometheus desmotes*. It. tr. L. Medda. Milano.

Augustine (1982). *De Civitate Dei*. It. tr. C. Carena. Roma.

Claudii Claudiani (1982). *Phoenix. Carmina minora 27*. It. tr. M.L. Ricci. Bari.

Claudius Aelianus (1998). *De Natura Animalium*. It. tr. F. Maspero. Milano.

Herodotus (1956). *Istoriai*. It. tr. L. Annibaletto. Milano.

Homer (1999). *Iliad*. It. tr. G. Cerri. Milano.

Lykophron (1991). *Alexandra*. It. tr. G. Paduano. Milano.

Ovidius (1998). *Fasti*. It. tr. M. Fucecchi. Milano.

Plinius (2000). *Naturalis Historia*. It. tr. F. Maspero. Milano.

Xenophon (1964). *Anabasis*. It. tr. F. Ferrari. Milano.

Xenophon (1997). *Cyropaedia*. It. tr. F. Ferrari. Milano.

Mesopotamian and Anatolian texts

Enuma Elish (1989). Fr. tr. in: Bottéro, J., Kramer, S. (1989). *Lorsque les dieux faisant l'homme*. Paris.

Laroche, E. (1966). *Catalogue des textes hittites*. Paris.

Avestan and Middle Iranian texts

Antia, E.K. (1900). *Kârnâmak-i Artakhshîr Pâpakân*. Bombay.

Avesta (2004). *Avestā*. It. tr. A. Alberti. Torino.

Ayadgar i Zareran (1927). It. tr. in: A. Pagliaro. *Epica e romanzo nel medioevo persiano*. Firenze: 1-20.

Benveniste, E. (1946). *Vessantara Jātaka. Texte sogdien édité, traduit et commenté*. Paris.

Brunner, C.J. (1980). The Fable of the Babylonian Tree. Second Part: Translation. *Journal of Near Eastern Studies* 39, 4: 291-302.

Bundahishn (1880). *Pahlavi Texts Part 1. The Bundahis, Bahman Yast, and Shâyast lâ-Shâyast*. En. tr. E.W. West. The Sacred Books of the East Translated by Various Oriental Scholars, ed. F.M. Müller. Vol. 5. Oxford [Reprint Delhi 2003].

Bundahishn (2020). *The Bundahišn. The Zoroastrian Book of Creation*. En. tr. D. Agostini, S. Thrope. Oxford.

Chunakova, O.M. (1987). *Kniga dejanij Ardashira syna Papaka*. Moskva.

Dînkard (1897). *Pahlavi Texts. Marvels of Zoroastrianism*. En. tr. E.W. West. Oxford [Reprint Delhi 2004]: 1-130.

Grenet, F. (2003). *La geste d'Ardashir fils de Pâbag. Kārnāmag ī Ardaxšēr ī Pābagān*. Die.

Horne C.F. (1917). *The Sacred Books and Early Literature of the East*, vii: *Ancient Persia*. New York.

Humbach, H., Skjærvø, P.O. (1983). *The Sasanian Inscription of Paikuli. Part 3, 1: Restored Text and Translation*. Wiesbaden.

Kârnâmak î Ardashîr î Pâpakân (1927). *Il libro delle gesta di Ardashîr figlio di Pâpak*. It. tr. in: A. Pagliaro, *Epica e romanzo nel medioevo persiano*. Firenze: 21-56.

Lurje, P.B. (2010). *Personal Names in Sogdian Texts*. Wien.

Mihr Yasht. (1959). *The Avestan Hymn to Mithra*. En. tr. I. Gershevitch. Cambridge.

Pirart, É. (1992). *Kayân Yasn (Yasht 19.9-96). L'origine avestique des dynasties mythiques d'Iran*. Barcelona.

Pirart, É. (2006). *Guerriers d'Iran. Traduction annotées des textes avestiques du culte zoroastrien rendu aux dieux Tištriya, Miθra et Vṛθragna*. Paris.

Provasi, E. (2008). Testi medio iranici iii. Parabole. Testi dottrinali, in: *Il Manichesimo. Volume iii. Il mito e la dottrina. Testi manichei dell'Asia centrale e della Cina*, ed. G. Gnoli. Roma: 109-225.

Sanjana, D.D.P. (1896). *The Kârnâmê î Artakhshîr î Pâpakân. Being the Oldest Surviving Records of the Zoroastrian Emperor Ardashîr Bâbakân, the Founder of the Sâsânian Dynasty in Irân*. En. tr. Darab Dastur Peshotan Sanjana. Bombay.

Sims-Williams, N. (1976). The Sogdian Fragments of the British Library. *Indo Iranian Journal* 18: 43-82.

Vendidad (1990). *La legge di abiura dei demoni dell'Avesta zoroastriano*. It. tr. F.A. Cannizzaro, ed. A. Panaino. Milano.

West, E.W. (1880). *Pahlavi Texts Part 1. The Bundahis, Bahman Yast, and Shâyast lâ-Shâyast*. Oxford [Reprint Delhi 2003].

Williams, A.V. (1990). *The Pahlavi Rivāyat Accompanying the Dadestān ī Denīg*. Copenhagen.

Wizidagiha i Zadspram (1897). *Pahlavi Texts. Marvels of Zoroastrianism*. En. tr. E.W. West. Oxford [Reprint Delhi 2004]: 131-170.

The Zend-Avesta (1887). En. tr. J. Darmesteter. Oxford [Reprint Delhi 2000].

Jewish texts

Bible (1991). It. tr. *La Nuova Diodati*. Brindisi.

Ginzberg, L. (1995). *Le leggende degli ebrei. 1. Dalla creazione al diluvio*. Milano [*The Legends of the Jews*. New York 1909].

Islamic texts

Darab nameh. (1977). ed. Z. Safa. Tehran.

Dinawari (1980). Abū Ḥanīfa Aḥmad b. Dāwūd al-Dīnawarī, *Kitāb al-Akhbār al-Ṭiwāl.* It. tr. A. Arioli, in: G. Scarcia, Bastam e la stirpe dei draghi, in: *Transcaucasica II*, ed. G. Scarcia. Venezia: 89-101.

Farid ad-Din Attar (1986). *Manṭiq al-tayr. Il verbo degli uccelli.* It. tr. C. Saccone. Milano.

Halidov, A.B. (1959). Dopolnenija k tekstu "Hronologii" al-Biruni po leningradskoj i stambul'skoj rupokisjam. *Palestinkskij Sbornik* 4: 147-171.

Koran (1955). *Il Corano.* It. tr. A. Bausani. Firenze.

Massé H. (1973). Ibn al-Faqīh al Hamaḏānī. *Abrégé du livre des pays.* Damas.

Mas'udi (1965). *Muruj al-dhahab wa ma'adin al-jawhar. Les prairies d'or.* Fr. tr. C. Pellat. Paris.

Mohl, J. (1842). Extraits du Modjmel al-Tewarikh. *Journal Asiatique* 14: 113-152.

Ruiz Bravo-Villasante, C. (1980). *Manafi'-i hayawan. Libro de las utilidades de los animales.* Madrid.

Shahnameh (1988-2001). ed. D. Khaleghi-Motlagh. Costa Mesa-New York.

Armenian texts

Movses K'orenaci (1993). *Histoire de l'Arménie.* Fr. tr. J.-P. Mahé. Paris.

Sebeos (1980). *Sebeosi episkoposi patmut'iun.* It. tr. C. Gugerotti, in: G. Scarcia, Bastam e la stirpe dei draghi, in: *Transcaucasica II*, ed. G. Scarcia. Venezia: 101-107.

Medieval texts

Jacobus de Varagine (2007). *Legenda Aurea.* It. tr. A. Vitale Brovarone, L. Vitale Brovarone. Torino.

Marco Polo (1981). *Il Milione.* ed. M. Ciccuto. Milano.

Chinese texts

Shanhai Jing (1996). *Libro dei Monti e dei Mari (Shanhai Jing): Cosmografia e mitologia nella Cina antica.* It. tr. R. Fracasso. Venezia.

Indian texts

Kramrisch, S. (1928). *The Vishnudharmottara Part III: A Treatise on Indian Painting and Image-Making.* Calcutta [Reprint New Delhi 2013].

Secondary sources

A

Abdullaev, K. (2011). Parfjanskie motivy v nastennoj rospisi Nahsheba (Erkurgan i ego okruga), in: *Un impaziente desiderio di scorrere il mondo. Studi in onore di Antonio Invernizzi per il suo settantesimo compleanno*, ed. C. Lippolis, S. De Martino. Firenze: 309-320.

Abdullaeva, F. (2009-2010). Kingly Flight: Nimrūd, Kay Kāvūs, Alexander, or why the Angel has the Fish. *Persica* 23: 1-29.

Adamova, A.T. (2008). *Medieval Persian Painting: The Evolution of an Artistic Vision*. New York.

Adamova, A.T., Giuzalyan, L.T. (1985). *Miniatjury rukopisi poemy "Shahname" 1333 goda*. Leningrad.

Aimone, M. (2020). *Byzantine and Sasanian Silver, Enamels and Works of Art*. London.

Ajello, R. (1978). Sulle divinità armene chiamate "Arlez", *Oriente Moderno* LVIII, 7-8: 303-16.

Al-Khamis, U. (1998). An Eary Islamic Bronze Ewer Reexamined. *Muqarnas* 15: 9-19.

A'lam, H. (1989). Būf, in: *Encyclopaedia Iranica*, ed. E. Yarshater, IV, 5: 505-509.

Al'baum, L.I. (1975). *Zhivopis' Afrasiaba*, Tashkent.

Albrile, E. (2000). L'uovo della fenice: aspetti di un sincretismo orfico-gnostico. *Le Muséon* 113: 55-85.

Álvarez-Pedrosa, J.A. (2014). The Reconstruction of the Pre-Christian Slavic Religion and Iranian Lexical Borrowings: A Methodological Review. *Ollodagos* XXX: 61-80.

Amad, G. (1988). *Recherches sur le mythe du phénix dans la mosaïque antique*. Montevideo.

Amoretti Scarcia, B.M. (1968). Un'interpretazione iranistica di Cor. XXV, 38 e L, 12. *Rivista degli Studi Orientali* XLIII,1: 27-52.

Andrés-Toledo, M.Á. (2013). The Dog(s) of the Zoroastrian Afterlife, in: *Le sort des Gâthâs et autres études iraniennes in memoriam Jacques Duchesne-Guillemin*, ed. É. Pirart, Leuven: 13-23.

Angelini, A. (2010). Inghiottiti e inghiottitori: di alcuni mostri nel mito antico, in: *Zoomania. Animali, ibridi, mostri nelle culture umane*, ed. S. Beta, F. Marzari. Firenze: 237-264.

Angelini, A. (2018). *Dal Leviatano al drago. Mostri marini e zoologia antica tra Grecia e Levante*. Bologna.

Angelini, A. (2020). Gryps, in: *Historical and Theological Lexicon of the Septuagint*, ed. E. Bons. Tübingen: 1965-1970.

Arakelyan, B. (1949). *Siuzhetnye rel'efy Armenii IV-VII vekov*. Erevan (in Armenian).

Aro, J. (1976). Anzu and Sīmurgh, in: *Cuneiform Studies in Honor of Samuel Noah Kramer*, ed. B.L. Eichler et al.Neukirchen-Vluyn: 25-28.

Asatryan, G.S., Arakelova, V. (2014). *The Religion of the Peacock Angel. The Yezidis and Their Spirit World*. London.

Asatryan, M. (2005). The Peacock in *Nahj al-Balāgha* and Near East Religious Tradition. *Studies on Persianate Societies* 3: 164-183.

Asim, I. (1993). Die aristokratische Graubkultur des 7. und 8. Jahrhunderts, in: *Chinas Goldenes Zeitalter: Die Tang-Dynastie (618-907 n. Chr.) und das Kulturelle Erbe der Seidenstraße*, ed. D. Kuhn. Heidelberg: 173-219.

Asmussen, J.P. (1990). Sīmurγ in Judeo-Persian Translations of the Hebrew Bible, *Iranica Varia: Papers in Honor of Professor Ehsan Yarshater. Acta Iranica* 30, Leiden: 1-5.

Asutay-Effenberger, N. (2019). Die Theophilos-Türme in den Blachernen und der Senmurw, in: *Sasanian Elements in Byzantine, Caucasian and Islamic Art and Culture*, ed. N. Asutay-Effenberger, F. Daim. Mainz: 143-154.

Aurigemma, M.G. (2004). *Il cielo stellato di Ruggero II. Il soffitto dipinto della cattedrale di Cefalù.* Milano.

Au pied du Mont Ararat. Splendeurs de l'Arménie antique. (2007), ed. C. Sintes, A. Grigorian. Nîmes.

Azarpay, G. (1975). Some Iranian Iconographic Formulae in Sogdian Painting. *Iranica Antiqua* 11: 168-177.

Azarpay, G. (1981). *Sogdian Painting. The Pictorial Epic in Oriental Art.* Berkeley-Los Angeles-London.

Azarpay, G. (1995). A Jataka Tale in a Sasanian Silver Plate. *Bulletin of the Asia Institute* 9: 99-125.

Azarpay, G. (2011). Imagery of the Sogdian Dēn, in: *Florilège offert à Philippe Gignoux pour son 80e anniversaire*, ed. R. Gyselen, C. Julien. Paris: 53-96.

B

Bader, A., Gaibov, V., Koshelenko, G. (1998). Monarchic Ideas in Parthian Margiana as Shown on Seals, in: *The Art and Archaeology of Ancient Persia. New Light on the Parthian and Sasanian Empires*, ed. V.S. Curtis, R. Hillenbrand, J.M. Rogers. London-New York: 24-37.

Bailey, H.W. (1971). *Zoroastrian Problems in the Ninth-Century Books.* Oxford.

Bajpakov, K.M. (1992). Nouvelles données sur la culture sogdienne dans les villes médiévales du Kazakhstan. *Studia Iranica* 21, 1: 33-45.

Bajpakov, K.M. (1998). Medieval Towns in South Kazakhstan and Semireč'e. *Rivista degli Studi Orientali* LXXII, 1-4: 245-261.

Bagnera, A. (1994). Il motivo dei volatili affrontati all'albero della vita nei tessuti islamici, in: M.T. Lucidi. *La Seta e la sua via.* Roma: 151-154.

Barringer, J. (1998). *Divine Escorts. Nereids in Archaic and Classical Greek Art.* Ann Arbor.

Barrucand, M. (1990-1991). The Miniatures of the *Daqā'iq al-Ḥaqā'iq* (Bibliothèque Nationale Pers. 174): A Testimony to the Cultural Diversity of Medieval Anatolia. *Islamic Art* IV: 113-142.

Batto, B.F. (1999). Behemoth, in: *Dictionary of Deities and Demons in the Bible*, ed. K. Von Der Toorn, B. Becking, P.W. Van Der Horst. Grand Rapids MI-Cambridge: 165-169.

Bausani, A. (1978a). Un auspicio armeno di capodanno in una notizia di Iranshahri (Nota ad Ajello). *Oriente Moderno* LVIII, 7-8: 317-319.

Bausani, A. (1978b). Κῆτος fra le stazioni lunari? Considerazioni iconografiche sulla "balena" a proposito di alcuni mss. d'età safavide. *Oriente Moderno* LVIII, 7-8, 275-283.

Begmatov, A., Berdimurodov, A., Bogomolov, G., Murakami, T., Teramura, H., Uno, T., Usami, T. (2020). New Discoveries from Kafir-kala: Coins, Sealings, and Wooden Carvings. *Acta Asiatica* 119, 1: 1-20.

Belenitsky, A. (1975). *Asia Centrale*. Ginevra.

Belenitskii, A.M., Marshak, B.I. (1981). The Paintings of Sogdiana, in: G. Azarpay, *Sogdian Painting*. Berkeley-Los Angeles-London: 11-77.

Belluccio, A. (1987-1988). Le Phénix dans la Nubie chrétiènne. *Nubica* I/II: 475-497.

Berdimuradov, A.E., Bogomolov, G., Daeppen, M., Khushvaktov, N. (2008). A New Discovery of Stamped Ossuaries near Shahr-i Sabz (Uzbekistan). *Bulletin of the Asia Institute* 22: 137-142.

Berlekamp, P. (2007). From Iraq to Fars: Tracking Cultural Transformations in the 1322 Qazwīnī 'Ağā'ib Manuscript, in: *Arab Painting: Text and Image in Illustrated Arabic Manuscripts*, ed. A. Contadini. Leiden-Boston: 73-91.

Berlekamp, P. (2011). *Wonder, Image, and Cosmos in Medieval Islam*. New Haven-London.

Bertel's, A.E. (1997). *Hudožestvennyj obraz v iskusstve Irana IX-XV vv. (Slovo, izobrazhenie)*. Moskva.

Berthier, F. (2001). Le Phénix rouge de la tombe Kitora (Japon). *Arts Asiatiques* 58: 147-148.

Betts, A., Yagodin, V.N., Grenet, F., Kidd, F., Minardi, M., Bonnat, E., Khashimov, S. (2012). The Akchakhan-kala Wall Paintings: New Perspectives on Kingship and Religion in Ancient Chorasmia. *Journal of Inner Asian Art and Archaeology* 7: 125-165.

Bhattacharya, G. (2010). New Element of Fantasy and Rhythm Introduced in Gupta Art, in: *South Asian Archaeology 2007*, ed. P. Callieri, L. Colliva. Oxford: 35-43.

Bhattacharya-Haesner, C. (2004). Some Unique Iconographic Features in Turfan Temple Banners, in: *Turfan Revisited. The First Century of Research into the Arts and Cultures of the Silk Road*, ed. D. Durkin-Meisterernst, S.-C. Raschmann, J. Wilkens, M. Yaldiz, P. Zieme. Berlin: 37-48.

Binyon, L., Wilkinson, J.V.S., Gray. B. (1971). *Persian Miniature Painting*. New York.

Birrell, A. (1999). *The Classic of Mountains and Seas*. London.

Bisconti, F. (1979). Aspetti e significati del simbolo della fenice nella letteratura e nell'arte del Cristianesimo primitivo, *Vetera Christianorum*, 16, 1: 21-40.

Bisheh, G. (1986). Notes on Some Recent Discoveries of Omayyad Cultural Relics. Annual of the Department of Antiquities of Jordan XXX: 7-14 (in Arabic).

Bisheh, G. (1993). From Castellum to Palatium: Umayyad Mosaic Pavements from Qasr al-Hallabat in Jordan. *Muqarnas* 10: 49-56.

Bivar, A.D.H. (1969). *Catalogue of the Western Asiatic Seals in the British Museum. Stamp Seals II: The Sasanian Dynasty*. London.

Bivar, A.D.H. (2006). Sasanian Iconography on Textiles and Seals, in: *Central Asian Textiles and Their Contexts in the Early Middle Ages*, ed. R. Schorta. Riggisberg: 9-21.

Bivar, A.D.H. (2009). The Rukhkh, Giant Eagle of the Southern Seas, in: *Exegisti monumenta. Festschrift in Honour of Nicholas Sims-Williams*, ed. W. Sundermann, A. Hintze, F. de Blois. Wiesbaden: 1-12.

Black, J., Green, A. (1992). *Gods, Demons and Symbols of Ancient Mesopotamia. An Illustrated Dictionary*. London.

Blair, S. (2002). The Religious Art of the Ilkhanids, in: *The Legacy of Genghis Khan. Courtly Art and Culture in Western Asia, 1256-1353*, ed. L. Komaroff, S. Carboni. New York-New Haven-London: 104-133.

Blessing, P. (2019). Silk Road without Fabrics: Ani at the Crossroads of Trade and Textile Motifs in Architecture, in: *Ani at the Crossroads*, ed. Z. Skhirtladze. Tbilisi: 229-254.

Boardman, J. (1983). The Ketos in India, *Bulletin de Correspondance Hellénistique*, supplement XIV, Iconographie classique et identités régionales: 447-453.

Boardman, J. (1987). "Very Like a Whale". Classical Sea Monsters, in: *Monsters and Demons in the Ancient and Medieval Worlds. Papers Presented in Honour of Edith Porada*, ed. A.E. Farkas, P.O. Harper, E.B. Harrison. Mainz: 73-84.

Boardman, J. (1997). Ketos, in: *Lexicon Iconographicum Mythologiae Classicae*, VIII.1, Zürich-Düsseldorf: 731-737.

Boardman, J. (2003). Three Monsters at Tillya Tepe. *Ancient Civilizations from Scythia to Siberia* 9, 1-2: 133-146.

Bogomolov, G. (2020). Zurvanism in Sogd. *Bulletin of the International Institute for Central Asian Studies* 29: 23-32.

Bollók, A. (2015). The Visual Art of the Sāsānian Empire and the Nagyszentmiklós/Sânnicolau Mare Treasure. A Non-Specialist's View, in: *The Treasure of Sânnicolau Mare (Hungarian: Nagyszentmiklós)*, ed. F. Daim, K. Gschwantler, G. Plattner, P. Stadler, Mainz: 43-70.

Borges, J.L., Guerrero M. (1957) *Manual de zoología fantástica. El Libro de los seres imaginarios*. Ciudad de México [It. tr. *Manuale di zoologia fantastica. Il libro degli esseri immaginari*. Milano, 2006].

Borghini, A. (1999). Cane-uccello, cani e uccelli: incomprensione culturale, e recupero del "reale" come retorica, in alcuni passi di Agatia, in: *Prospettive sul Tradoantico*, ed. G. Mazzoli, F. Gasti. Como: 157-165.

Borniotto, V. (2004-2010). "Rex Serpentium": il basilisco in arte e storia naturale, mito e fede. *Studi di Storia delle Arti* 11: 23-47.

Borzsák, L. (1990). Vom zentralsiatischen Xvarənah zur Attilas Bestattung, in: *From Alexander the Great to Kül Tegin. Studies in Bactrian, Pahlavi, Sanskrit, Arabic, Aramaic, Armenian, Chinese, Türk, Greek and Latin Sources for the History of Pre-Islamic Central Asia*, ed. J. Harmatta. Budapest: 55-62.

Boyce, M. (1975). *A History of Zoroastrianism. The Early Period*. Leiden.

Boyce, M., Grenet, F. (1991). *A History of Zoroastrianism. Volume Three. Zoroastrianism under Macedonian and Roman Rule*. Leiden-New York-København-Köln.

Bradford, R.E. (2013). An Egyptian Contribution to a Late 5th-Century Chinese Coffin. *The Silk Road* 11: 93-99.

Bromberg, C.A. (1983). Sasanian Stucco Influence: Sorrento and East-West. *Orientalia Lovaniensia Periodica* 14: 247-267.

Brunner, C.J. (1978). *Sasanian Stamp Seals in the Metropolitan Museum of Art*. New York.

Bunker, E.C. (2001). The Cemetery at Shanpula, Xinjiang. Simple Burials, Complex Textiles, in: *Fabulous Creatures from the Desert Sands. Central Asian Woolen Textiles from the Second Century* BC *to the Second Century* AD, ed. D. Keller, R. Schorta, Riggisberg: 15-45.

Bunker, E.C., Chatwin, C.B., Farkas, A.R. (1970). *"Animal Style" Art from East to West*. New York.

Buyaner, D. (2003). On the Etymology of Middle Persian Baškuč (Winged Monster). *Studia Iranica* 34/1: 19-30.

C

Caiozzo, A. (1999). Le ciel de l'astronome, le ciel de l'astrologue et celui du sorcier, trois conceptions des cieux dans les manuscrits enluminés de l'orient médiéval, in: *La Science des Cieux. Sages, mages, astrologues. Res Orientales* XII, ed. R. Gyselen. Bur-sur-Yvette: 11-51.

Callieri, P. (2014). *Architecture et représentations dans l'Iran sassanide*. Paris.

Callieri, P. (2017). Achaemenid "Ritual Architecture" vs. "Religious Architecture". Reflections on the Elusive Archaeological Evidence of the Religion of the Achaemenids, in: *Persian Religion in the Achaemenid Period*, ed. W.F.M. Henkelman, C. Redard. Wiesbaden: 385-416.

Calmeyer, P. (1979). Fortuna-Tyche-Khvarnah, *Jahrbuch des Deutschen Archäologischen Instituts* 94: 347-365.

Canepa, M/ (2014). Textiles and Elites Tastes between the Mediterranean, Iran and Asia at the End of Antiquity, in: *The Anthology Global Textile Encounters: China, India, Europe*, ed. M.-L. Nosch, Zhao Feng, L. Varadarajan. Oxford-Philadelphia: 1-14.

Carboni, S. (1988). Ricostruzione del ciclo pittorico del *Kitāb al-bulhān* di Oxford: le miniature delle copie ottomane mancanti nell'originale. *Annali di Ca' Foscari* 27, 3: 97-126.

Carboni, S. (1995). The Arabic Manuscript, in: *Pages of Perfection. Islamic Paintings and Calligraphy from the Russian Academy of Sciences, St. Petersburg*, Milan: 77-91.

Carboni, S. (2015). *The Wonders of Creation and the Singularities of Painting. A Study of the Ilkhanid London Qazvīnī*. Edinburgh.

Carile, M.C. (2016). Uccelli paradisiaci e spazio sacro. Note intorno a paradisi terrestri e celesti, in: *"A mari usque ad mare" Cultura visuale e materiale dall'Adriatico all'India. Scritti in memoria di Gianclaudio Macchiarella*, ed. M. Guidetti, S. Mondini. Venezia: 73-88.

Carrega, A., Navone, P. (1983). *Le proprietà degli animali*. Genova.

Carter, M. (2015). *Arts of the Hellenized East. Precious Metalwork and Gems of the Pre-Islamic Era*. London.

Carusi, P. (2007). *Lo zafferano e il geco. Le scienze della vita nella società islamica del Medioevo*. Rome.

Casartelli, L.C. (1891). Çiena-Simurgh-Roc, in: *Compte Rendu du Congrès Scientifique International des Catholique. Sciences Historiques*, VI, Paris: 78-87.

Cassin, E. (1968). *La splendeur divine. Introduction a l'étude de la mentalité mésopotamienne*. Paris.

Cerulli, E. (1971). Intervento sulle relazioni dei proff. G. Pugliese Carratelli e A. Pertusi, in: *La Persia nel Medioevo*. Roma, 629-632.

Charritat, M. (2001). Le Senmurv, in: *L'Étrange et le Merveilleux en terre d'Islam*, ed. M.B. Taylor, C. Jail. Paris: 117.

Childs, W.A.P. (2003). The Human Animal: The Near East and Greece, in: *The Centaur's Smile. The Human Animal in Early Greek Art*, ed. J.M. Padgett, Princeton: 49-70.

Choksy, J.K. (1989). A Sasanian Monarch, His Queen, Crown Prince, and Deities: The Coinage of Wahram II. *American Journal of Numismatics* 1, 117-135.

Christensen, A. (1917). *Le types du premier homme et du premier roi dans l'histoire légendaire des iraniens. Ire partie*. Stockholm.

Christensen, A. (1932). *Les Kayanides*. København.

Christensen, A. (1941). *Essai sur la démonologie iranienne*. København.

Collon, D. (2005). *First Impressions. Cylinder Seals in the Ancient Near East*. London.

Compareti, M. (2004). The Sasanian and the Sogdian "Pearl Roundel" Design: Remarks on an Iranian Decorative Pattern, *The Study of Art History* 6: 259-272.

Compareti, M. (2006). The So-Called *Senmurv* in Iranian Art: A Reconsideration of an Old Theory, in: *Loquentes linguis. Linguistic and Oriental Studies in Honour of Fabrizio A. Pennacchietti*, ed. P.G. Borbone, A. Mengozzi, M. Tosco. Wiesbaden: 185-200.

Compareti, M. (2007). Remarks on the Monstrous Flying Creature in a Northern Dynasty Period Funerary Couch that Belonged to a Sogdian, in: *Fourth-Sixth Century Northern China and the Asian Continent*, ed. Zhang Qingjie, Li Shuji, Li Gong. Beijing: 166-189 (in Chinese).

Compareti, M. (2009a). The Indian Iconography of the Sogdian Divinities and the Role of Buddhism and Hinduism in Its Transmission, *Annali dell'Istituto Orientale di Napoli*, 69/1-4: 175-210.

Compareti, M. (2009b). Sasanians. Textiles: An Iconographical Approach, in: *Encyclopaedia Iranica*, ed. E. Yarshater. Online version: <http://www.iranicaonline.org/articles/sasanian-textiles>.

Compareti, M. (2009c). Sasanian and Sogdian Borrowings in Kashmiri and Tibetan Art, *Transoxiana* 14.

Compareti, M. (2009-2010). "Holy Animals" of Mazdeism in Iranian Arts: Ram, Eagle and Dog. *Nāme-ye Irān-e Bastān* 9, 1/2, 2009-2010: 27-42.

Compareti, M. (2010). The Spread Wings Motif on Armenian Steles: Its Meaning and Parallels in Sasanian Art. *Iran and the Caucasus* 14, 2: 201-232.

Compareti, M. (2011). The Painted Vase of Merv in the Context of Central Asian Pre-Islamic Funerary Tradition. *The Silk Road* 9: 26-41.

Compareti, M. (2014a). A Recently Excavated Image of a Beribboned Ram from Kafir Kala, in: *"My Life is like the Summer Rose". Papers in Honor of Maurizio Tosi for His 70th Birthday*, ed. B.B. Lamberg-Karlovsky, B. Genito, B. Cerasetti. Oxford: 153-162.

Compareti, M. (2014b). Teratologia fantastica in Subcaucasia. La migrazione di motivi decorativi tra l'Iran e il Caucaso, in: *Al crocevia delle civiltà. Ricerche su Caucaso e Asia Centrale*, ed. A. Ferrari, D. Guizzo. Venezia: 11-50.

Compareti, M. (2015). Ancient Iranian Decorative Textiles: New Evidence from Archaeological Investigations and Private Collections. *The Silk Road*, 13: 36-44.

Compareti, M. (2016a). Observations on the Rock Reliefs at Taq-i Bustan: A Late Sasanian Monument along the "Silk Road". *The Silk Road* 14: 71-83.

Compareti, M. (2016b). La Sogdiane et les "Autres". Élements d'emprunts extérieurs dans l'art sogdien pré-islamique, in: *Asie centrale. Transferts culturels le long de la Route de la soie*, ed. M. Espagne, S. Gorshenina, F. Grenet, Sh. Mustafayev, C. Rapin. Paris: 229-239.

Compareti, M. (2016c). *Samarkand the Center of the World. Proposals for the Identification of the Afrāsyāb Paintings*. Santa Ana-CA.

Compareti, M. (2016d). Flying over Boundaries: Auspicious Birds in Sino-Sogdian Funerary Art, in: *Borders Itineraries on the Edges of Iran*, ed. S. Pellò. Venezia: 119-153.

Compareti, M. (2017a). *La raffigurazione di divinità pre-cristiane nella produzione fittile dell'Armenia ellenistica*. Venezia.

Compareti, M. (2017b). Nana and Tish in Sogdiana: The Adoption from Mesopotamia of a Divine Couple, *Dabir* 1, 4: 1-7.

Compareti, M. (2018a). Heroes Fighting Snake Demons: Problems of Identification in Penjikent Paintings. *The Silk Road* 16: 91-99.

Compareti, M. (2018b). Images of the Gorgon in Persian Tradition and Islamic Book Illustrations, in: *Fabulous Creatures and Spirits in Ancient Iranian Culture*, ed. M. Compareti. Bologna: 121-151.

Compareti, M. (2019a). *Simurgh* or *Farr*? On the Representation of Fantastic Creatures in the Sogdian "Rustam Cycle" at Panjikent, in: *New Research on Central Asian, Buddhist and Far Eastern Art and Archaeology. Inner Asian Art and Archaeology II*, ed. J.A. Lerner, A.L. Juliano. Turnhout: 63-90.

Compareti, M. (2019b). Assimilation and Adaptation of Foreign Elements in Late Sasanian Rock Reliefs at Taq-i Bustan, in: *Sasanian Elements in Byzantine, Caucasian and Islamic Art and Culture*, ed. N. Asutay-Effenberger, F. Daim. Mainz: 19-36.

Compareti, M. (2019c). Composite Creatures in Sasanian Art According to Some Numismatic and Sphragistic Evidence. *Journal of Intercultural and Interdisciplinary Archaeology* 3: 15-28 (online version available at PROPYLAEUM-EJOURNALS: <https://journals.ub.uni-heidelberg.de/index.php/jiia/issue/view/4412>).

Compareti, M. (2019d). The "Eight Divinities" in Khotanese Paintings: Local Deities or Sogdian Importation, in: *Proceedings of the Eighth European Conference of Iranian Studies. Vol. I. Studies on Pre-Islamic Iran and on Historical Linguistics*, ed. P.V. Lurje. Saint Petersburg: 117-132.

Compareti, M. (2020a). "Iranian" Decorative Patterns on Enigmatic Central Asian Ceramics. *Journal of Asian Civilizations* 43, 1: 23-40.

Compareti, M. (2020b). Contributions for the Identification of the Human Bust on a Winged Disc in Iranian Arts, in: *The Archaeology of the Historical Period in Iran*, ed. A; Hozhabri, Basel: 157-169.

Compareti, M. (2020c). Recently Unearthed Luxury Art from Qinghai: Iranian Images in the Tubo-Ruled Area, *Dunhuang Research*, 179, 1: 16-22.

Compareti, M. (forthcoming 2021). The So-Called "Pelliot Chinois 4518.24" Illustrated Document from Dunhuang and Sino-Sogdian Iconographical Contacts.

Compareti, M., Cristoforetti, S. (2012). Il fumo iranico della pipa di Perm, in: *Multa et Varia. Studi offerti a Maria Marcella Ferraccioli e Gianfranco Giraudo*, ed. F.C. Ciure, V. Nosilia, A. Pavan. Milano: 239-250.

Compareti, M., Scarcia, G. (2012). Zone d'ombra nell'Est iranico alla vigilia dell'islamizzazione. *Parthica* 14: 207-254.

Contadini, A. (2003). A Bestiary Tale: Text and Image of the Unicorn in the Kitāb na't al-ḥayawān (British Library, Or. 2784). *Muqarnas* 20: 17-33.

Contadini, A. (2005). Musical Beasts: The Swan-Phoenix in the Ibn Bakhtīshū' Bestiaries, in: *The Iconography of Islamic Art. Studies in Honor of Robert Hillenbrand*, ed. B. O'Kane. Cairo: 93-101.

Cornelius I. (2014). Trading Religions' and "Visible Religion" in: *The Ancient Near East Dynamics in the History of Religions: Religions and Trade: Religious Formation, Transformation and Cross-Cultural Exchange between East and West.* Leiden: 141-165.

Cortopassi, R. (1998). Fragment de tenture aux croix ansées, in: *Antinoe cent'anni dopo*, ed. L. Del Francia Barocas. Florence: 137-138.

Cosentino, A. (2013). La divinità dalla testa di gallo e gambe serpentine sulle gemme magico-gnostiche, in: *Monstra. Costruzione e Percezione delle Entità Ibride e Mostruose nel Mediterraneo Antico*, ed. I. Baglioni. Roma: 219-228.

Coulston, J.C.N. (1991). The "Draco" Standard. *Journal of Military Equipment Studies* 2: 101-114.

Creswell, K.A.C. (1940). *Early Muslim Architecture. Umayyads, Early 'Abbasids and Tulunids. Part 2: Early 'Abbasids, Umayyads of Cordova, Aghlabids, Tulunids and Samanids,* A.D. *751-905.* Oxford.

Cristoforetti, S. (2003). *Il Natale della luce. Il* sada *tra Baghdad e Bukhara tra il* IX *e il* XII *secolo.* Milano.

Cristoforetti, S., Scarcia, G. (2013). Talking about Sīmurġ and Tāq-i Bustān with Boris I. Marshak, in: *Sogdians, Their Precursors, Contemporaries and Heirs*, ed. P.B. Lurje, A.I. Torgoev. St. Petersburg: 339-352.

Crone, P. (2012). *The Nativist Prophets of Early Islamic Iran. Rural Revolt and Local Zoroastrianism.* Cambridge-New York.

Cultural Exchange along the Silk Road. Masterpieces of the Tubo Period (7th-9th Century), Dunhuang, 2019.

Cumont, F. (1942). Le coq blanc des Mazdéens et les Pythagoriciens. *Comptes rendus de l'Académie des Inscriptions et Belles-Lettres* 4-6: 284-300.

Curatola, G. (1978). Il "*Vishap*" di Aght'amar: nota sulla diffusione occidentale di un motivo iconografico. *Oriente Moderno* LVIII, 7-8: 285-302.

Curatola, G. (1989). *Draghi.* Venezia.

Curatola, G. (2006). *Ceramiche persiane. Dal IX al XIV secolo.* Milano.

Czuma, S.J. (1986). *Kushan Sculpture: Images from Early India.* New York.

D

Da'adli, T. (2019). Reconstructing the Frescoes of Khirbat al-Mafjar. *Jerusalem Studies in Arabic and Islam* 46: 247-290.

Dahmani, F. (2020). A Reassessment of the Location of the Mural Paintings in the Caliphal Palace of Samarra. *Der Islam* 97, 2: 367-404.

Dalley, S. (2016). Il retaggio della Mesopotamia. Milano [*The Legacy of Mesopotamia.* Oxford. 1998].

Danmanville, J. (1962). Iconographie d'Ištar-Šaušga en Anatolie Ancienne, *Revue d'Assyriologie* 56: 9-29.

Daryaee, T. (2006). The Construction of the Past in Late Antique Persia. *Historia* 55: 493-503.

Daryaee, T. (2013). Sasanian Kingship, Empire and Glory: Aspects of Iranian Imperium, in: *Ranj-o-Ganj. Papers in Honour of Professor Z. Zarshenas*, ed. V. Naddaf, F. Goshtasb, M. Shokhri-Foumeshi. Tehran: 11-22.

Daryaee, Y. (2015). The Xwarrah and the Sēnmurv: Zoroastrian Iconography on Seventh Century Copper Coinage, in: *Faszination Iran. Beiträge zur Religion, Geschichte und Kunst des alten Iran. Gedenkschrift für Klaus Schippmann*, ed. S. Farridnejad, A. Joisten-Pruschke, R. Gyselen. Wiesbaden: 39-50.

Daryaee, T. (2016). Persian Lords and the Umayyads: Cooperation and Coexistence in a Turbulent Time, in: *Christians and Others in the Umayyad State*, ed. A. Borrut, F.M. Donner. Chicago: 73-81.

Davis, D. (2007). Rostam and Zoroastrianism, in: *The Necklace of the Pleiades. Studies in Persian Literature Presented to Heshmat Moayyad on His 80th Birthday*, ed. F. Lewis, S. Sharma. Amsterdam-West Lafayett IN: 49-61.

Day, J. (1985). *God's Conflict with the Dragon and the Sea. Echoes of a Canaanite Myth in the Old Testament.* Cambridge.

de Blois, F.C. (1998). Sīmurgh, in: *Encyclopédie de l'Islam*, ed. C.E. Bosworth. Leiden: 638-639.

de La Vaissière, É. (2005). *Sogdian Traders: A History*. Leiden-Boston.

De' Maffei, F. (1980). Eva e il serpente ovverosia la problematica delle derivazione, o non, delle miniature vetero-testamentarie cristiane da presunti prototipi ebraici. *Rivista di Studi Bizantini e Neoellenici* 17-19: 13-36.

Di Branco, M. (2011). *Alessandro Magno eroe arabo nel Medioevo*. Roma.

Diény, J.P. (1989-1990). Le Fenghuang et le Phénix. *Cahiers d'Extrême-Asie* 5: 1-13.

D'jakonova, N.V., Sorokin, S.S. (1960). *Khotanskie drevnosti*. Leningrad.

Dode, Z. (2016) "Zandanījī Silks": The Story of a Myth. *The Silk Road* 14: 213-222.

Domyo, M. (1984). Costume and Textile Design, in: Sh. Fukai, K. Horiuchi, K. Tanabe, M. Domyo, *Taq-i Bustan IV. Text*. Tokyo: 96-134.

Domyo, M. (1997). Late Sassanian Textile Designs in the Reliefs at Taq-i Bustan. *Bulletin du CIETA* 74: 18-27.

Dorigo, W. (1971). *Late Roman Painting*. London.

Dorudiyan, S. (2016). A Study on a Sasanian Relief in Shahr-e Ray. *Athar* 71: 53-66 (in Persian).

Dozy, R. (1877-1881). *Supplement aux dictionnaires arabes*. Leiden.

Duchesne-Guillemin, J. (1979). La Royauté iranienne et le x^{v}arənah, in: *Iranica*, ed. G. Gnoli, A.V. Rossi. Napoli: 375-386.

Dulaey, M. (2013). Le phénix dans l'iconographie des premiers siècles chrétiens, in: *Le Phénix et son autre: Poétique d'un mythe (des origines au XVIe siècle)*, ed. L. Grosserez. Rennes: 91-118.

Dupont-Sommer, A. (1964). Une plaquette d'argent à inscription araméenne. *Iranica Antiqua* 4/2: 119-132.

During, J. (1988-89). Le mythe du Simorgh dans la musique extatique du Baloutchistan. *Luqman* V, I: 21-38.

Dwyer, E.J. (1973). Augustus and the Capricorn, *Mitteilungen des deutschen archäologischen Instituts Romische Abteilung*, 80: 59-67.

E

Ebanista, C., Fusaro F. (2010). *Cimitile. Guida al complesso basilicale e alla città*. Cimitile.

Ehrenberg, E. (2002). The Rooster in Mesopotamia, in: *Leaving no Stones Unturned. Essays on the Ancient Near East and Egypt in Honor of Donald P. Hansen*, ed. E. Ehrenberg. Winona Lake: 53-62.

Eichert, S. (2018). Griffons and Birds. Mediterranean Motifs on Early Medieval Enamelled Disc Brooches in Central Europe, in: *Lebenswelten zwischen Archäologie und Geschichte. Festschrift für Falko Daim zu seinem 65. Geburtstag*, ed. J. Drauschke, E. Kislinger, K. Kühtreiber, T. Kühtreiber, G. Scharrer-Liška, T. Vida. Mainz: 113-122.

Elikhina, Y.I. (2009). Les textiles Xiongnu de Noïn-Ula, in: *La Route de la Soie. Un voyage à travers la vie et la mort*, ed. S. Whitfield. Bruxelles: 60-63.

Elikhina, Y.I. (2019). Tkani iz kurganov Noin-Uly, hranjashchiesja v Gosudartsvennogo Ermitazhe, i ih izuchenie, in: *Isskustvo drevnego Tekstilja. Metody izuchenija, sohrannost', rekonstrukcija*, ed. Y.I. Elkhina, M. Wagner, P.E. Tarasov. Moskva-Oppenheim am Rhein: 94-107.

Elisseeff, D. (2011). *Hybrides chinois. La quête de tous les possibles.* Paris.

Elliott, J. (1995). The Etruscan Wolfman in Myth and Ritual. *Etruscan Studies* 2: 17-33.

Emelianov, V.V. (2010). On the Early History of *melammu*, in: *Language in the Ancient Near East. Proceedings of the 53e Rencontre assyriologique international.* Winona Lake IN: 1109-1119.

Enderlein, V., Meinecke, M. (1992). Graben-Forschen-Prasentieren. Probleme der Darstellung vergangener Kulturen am Beispiel der Maschatta-Fassade. *Herausgegeben von den Staatlichen Museen zu Berlin*: 137-172.

Erickson, S. (2011). The Han Dynasty Que Pillars of the Central Marchmount Mt. Song in Henan Province. *Oriental Art*, 50, 5: 2-17.

Ettinghausen, R. (1957). Persian Ascension Miniatures of the Fourteenth Century, in: *Oriente e Occidente nel Medioevo*. Roma: 360-383.

F

Faral, E. (1953). La queue de poisson des sirènes. *Romania* 74: 433-506.

Farioli Campanati, R. (1992). Decorazioni di origine tessile nel repertorio del mosaico pavimentale protobizantino del Vicino Oriente e le corrispondenze decorative parietali di Ravenna, Salonicco, Costantinopoli e Qusayr 'Amra. *Corso di cultura sull'arte ravennate e bizantina* XXXIX: 275-295.

Favaro, R. (2008). Teratologia abissale ai confini del mondo, in: *Da Ulisse a... Il viaggio negli abissi marini tra immaginazione e realtà*, ed. G. Revelli, Pisa: 121-133.

Feugère, L. (1995). Oiseau fantastique: fragment de montant de haut-relief, in: *Sérinde, Terre de Bouddha*, ed. J. Giès, M. Cohen. Paris: 152.

Filip, S., Hilgner, A. (2014). *The Lady with the Phoenix Crown. Tang-Period Grave Goods of the Noblewoman Li Chui (711-736).* Mainz.

Fine, S. (2010). *Art and Judaism in the Greco-Roman World. Toward a New Jewish Archaeology.* Cambridge.

Fitzherbert, T. (2001). *"Bal'ami's Tabari". An Illustrated Manuscript of Bal'ami's* Tarjama-yi Tārīkh-i Ṭabarī *in the Freer Gallery of Art, Washington (F59.16, 47.19 and 30.21).* Ph.D. dissertation, University of Edinburgh.

Flood, F.B. (2005). A Royal Drinking Scene from Alchi: Iranian Iconography in the Western Himalayas, in: *Image and Meaning in Islamic Art*, ed. R. Hillenbrand, London: 73-97.

Fontana, M.V. (2002). *La pittura islamica dalle origini alla fine del Trecento.* Roma.

Fontana, M.V. (2012). Su una possibile raffigurazione della storia di Giona a Qusayr 'Amra. *Rivista degli Studi Orientali* LXXXV, 1-4: 279-303.

Fontana, M.V. (2019). Quṣayr ʿAmra, ca 740 CE: amīr al-Walīd Reclining and Dressed in Accordance with Iranian Fashion, in: *Iranian Studies in Honour of Adriano V. Rossi*, ed. S. Badalkhan, G.P. Basello, M. De Chiara. Napoli: 325-342.

Francfort, H.-P. (2008). A Note on the Hasanlu Bowl as Structural Network: Mitanni-Arya and Hurrian? *Bulletin of the Asia Institute* 22: 171-188.

Frothingham, A.L. (1911). Medusa, Apollo and the Great Mother. *American Journal of Archaeology* 15, 3: 349-377.

Fukai, Sh., Horiuchi, K., Tanabe, K., Domyo, M. (1984). *Taq-i Bustan IV. Text.* Tokyo.

G

Gadjiev, M. (2006). Interpretation of a Bronze Figurine of Warrior from Gigatl' (Daghestan), in: *Ērān ud Anērān. Studies Presented to B.I. Maršak on the Occasion of His 70th Birthday*, ed. M. Compareti, G. Scarcia, P. Raffetta. Venezia: 199-212.

Gagetti, E. (2012). Textiles as Iconographic Media between Centres and Peripheries over Time. The Case of the Early Medieval Glass Cameos of the "Atelier of the Oriental Fabrics" on the Cross of Desiderius in Brescia. *Anodos* 12: 89-117.

Galkin, L.L. (1976). Stekljannyj medal'on-amulet s poselenija Ak-Tobe. *Sovetskaja Arheologija* 2: 252-256.

Garrison, M.B. (2013). Royal Achaemenid Iconography, in: *The Oxford Handbook of Ancient Iran*, ed. D.T. Potts, Oxford: 566-595.

Garrison, M.B. (2017). Beyond Ahura Mazda and the Winged Symbol: Imagery of the Divine and Numinous at Persepolis, in: *Persian Religion in the Achaemenid Period*, ed. W.F.M. Henkelman, C. Redard. Wiesbaden: 185-246.

Garsoïan, N. (1976). Prolegomena to a Study of the Iranian Aspects in Arsacid Armenia. *Hande's Amso'reay* 90: 177-234.

Gasparini, M.C. (2014). Woven Mythology. The Textile Encounter of *Makara, Senmurw* and Phoenix, in: *The Anthology Global Textile Encounters: China, India, Europe*, ed. M.-L. Nosch, Zhao Feng, L. Varadarajan. Oxford-Philadelphia: 119-126.

Gasparini, M. (2016). Sino-Iranian Textile Patterns in Trans-Himalayan Areas. *The Silk Road* 14: 84-96.

Gasparini, M. (2020). *Transcending Patterns. Silk Road Cultural and Artistic Interactions through Central Asian Textile Images*. Honolulu.

Gasti, F. (2018). L'immagine della fenice fra "scienza" e simbologia antica. *Eruditio Antiqua* 10: 1-23.

Gazerani, S. (2015). *The Sistani Cycle of Epics and Iran National History. On the Margins of Historiography*. Leiden.

Gelfer-Jørgensen, M. (1986). *Medieval Islamic Symbolism and the Paintings in the Cefalù Cathedral*. Leiden.

Ghirshman, R. (1962). *Iran. Parthes et Sassanides*. Paris.

Gierlichs, J. (1993). *Drache, Phönix, Doppeladler. Fabelwesen in der islamischen Kunst*. Berlin.

Gierlichs, J. (2005). Simurgh-Darstellungen in der islamischen Kunst. *Simurgh* 1: 38-41.

Gignoux, P. (1981). Recension à: H.P. Schmidt, *The Sēnmurv. Of Birds and Dogs and Bats*, Persica 9, 1980. *Abstracta Iranica* 4: 124.

Gignoux, P., Gyselen, R. (1987). *Bulles et sceaux sassanides de diverses collections*. Paris.

Girmond, S. (1993). Die Entfaltung der Pracht im Alltag, in: *Chinas Goldenes Zeitalter: Die Tang-Dynastie (618-907 n. Chr.) und das Kulturelle Erbe der Seidenstraße*, ed. D. Kuhn. Heidelberg: 110-155.

Gnoli, G. (1962). Un particolare aspetto del simbolismo della luce nel Mazdeismo e nel Manicheismo. *Annali dell'Istituto Universitario di Napoli* XII: 95-128.

Gnoli, G. (1982). 'Qut' e le montagne, in: *Studia Turcologica Memoriae Alexii Bombaci Dicata*. Napoli: 251-261.

Gnoli, G. (1984). Note sullo "Xᵛarənah-", in: *Orientalia J. Duchesne-Guillemin Emerito Oblata. Acta Iranica* IX. Leiden: 207-218.

Gnoli, G. (1995). Un emprunt iranien en araméen ignoré jusqu'à présent, in: *Au carrefour des religions. Mélanges offerts à Philippe Gignoux*, ed. R. Gyselen. Bur-sur-Yvette: 87-93.

Gnoli, G. (1999). 'Farr(ah)'. In: *Encyclopaedia Iranica*, IX, ed. E. Yarshater: 312-319.

Gnoli, G. (2002). Nuove note sullo *hu̯arnah-*, in: *Oriente e Occidente. Convegno in ricordo di Mario Bussagli*, ed. C. Silvi Antonini, B.M. Alfieri, A. Santoro. Pisa-Roma: 104-108.

Gnoli, G. (2006). Review of "La geste d'Ardashir fils de Pâbag. Kārnāmag ī Ardaxšēr ī Pābagān" by F. Grenet. *East and West* 4: 467-468.

Göbl, R. (1967). *Dokumente zur Geschichte der Iranischen Hunnen in Baktrien und Indien*. Wiesbaden.

Göbl, R. (1990). *Sasanian Numismatics*. New York.

Godard, A. (1962). *L'art de l'Iran*. Paris.

Gonda, J. (1956). Ancient Indian Kingship from the Religious Point of View. *Numen* 3, 1-2: 35-71, 122-155.

Goodenough, E.R. (1964). *Jewish Symbols in the Greco-Roman Period. Volume Ten. Symbols in the Dura Synagogue*. Toronto.

Grabar, A. (1966a). *Le premier art chrétien (200-395)*. Paris.

Grabar, A. (1966b). *L'âge d'or de Justinien*. Paris.

Grabar, A. (1971). Le rayonnement de l'art sassanide dans le monde chretien, in: *La Persia nel Medioevo*. Roma: 679-707.

Grenet, F. (1986a). Las prácticas funerarias en el Asia central preislámica, in: *Gran Atlas de arquelogia*, ed. C. Flon. Barcelona: 236-237.

Grenet, F. (1986b). Palais ou palais-temple? Remarques sur la publication du monument de Toprak-kala. *Studia Iranica* 15, 1: 123-135.

Grenet, F. (1993a). Trois nouveaux documents d'iconographie religieuse sogdienne. *Studia Iranica* 22, 1: 49-67.

Grenet, F. (1993b). Znanie yashtov Avesty v Sogde i Baktrii po dannym ikonografii. *Vestnik Drevnej Istorii* 4: 149-161.

Grenet, F. (1995). Divinités sogdiennes, in: *Sérinde, Terre de Bouddha. Dix siècles d'art sur la Route de la Soie*, ed. J. Giès, M. Cohen. Paris: 293-294.

Grenet, F. (2010). Iranian Gods in Hindu Garb: The Zoroastrian Pantheon of the Bactrians and Sogdians, Second-Eighth Centuries, *Bulletin of the Asia Institute*, 20: 87-99.

Grenet, F. (2012). Yima en Bactriane et en Sogdiane: nouveaux documents, in: *Yama/Yima: Variations indo-iraniennes sur la geste mythique*, ed. S. Azarnouche, C. Redard, Paris: 83-94.

Grenet, F. (2013). Some Hitherto Unrecognized Mythological Figures on Sasanian Seals: Proposed Identifications, in: *Commentationes Iranicae. Vladimiro F. Aaron Livshits nonagenaris donum natalicium*, ed. S.R. Tokhtas'eva, P.B. Lurje. St. Petersburg: 202-10.

Grenet, F. (2015). Between Written Texts, Oral Performances and Mural Paintings, in: *Orality and Textuality in the Iranian World. Patterns of Interaction across the Centuries*, ed. Julia Rubanovich. Leiden: 422-445.

Grenet, F. (2016). Extracts from a Calendar of Zoroastrian Feasts. A New Interpretation of the "Soltikoff" Bactrian Silver Plate in the Bibliothèque nationale, Paris, in: *The Zoroastrian Flame. Exploring Religion, History and Tradition*, ed. A. Williams, S. Stewart, A. Hintze. London-New York: 205-221.

Grenet, F. (2018). Was Zoroastrian Art Invented in Chorasmia? *Ancient Civilizations from Scythia to Siberia* 24: 68-86.

Grenet, F. (2020). The Wooden Panels from Kafir-kala: A Group Portrait of the Samarkand *nāf* (Civic Body). *Acta Asiatica* 119: 21-42.

Grenet, F., Lee J., Martinez, P., Ory F. (2007). The Sasanian Relief at Rag-i Bibi (Northern Afghanistan), in: *After Alexander. Central Asia before Islam*, ed. J. Cribb, G. Hermann. Oxford: 243-267.

Grossato, A. (2004). La fenice in Oriente, in: F. Zambon, A. Grossato, *Il mito della fenice in Oriente e in Occidente*. Venezia: 82-173.

Grosserez, L. (2013) Le phénix, le temps et l'éternité, in: *Le Phénix et son autre: Poétique d'un mythe (des origines au XVIe siècle)*, ed. L. Grosserez. Rennes: 21-45.

Grube, E. (1978). Persian Painting in the Fourteenth Century: A Research Report. *Annali dell'Istituto Orientale di Napoli. Supplemento* 17, 38. 4.

Grube, E. (2006). Chinese Elements in Islamic Art, Specifically in the Timurid Period, in: *The Phenomenon of "Foreign" in Oriental Art*, ed. A. Hagedorn. Wiesbaden: 71-87.

Guidetti, M. (2017). The "Islamicness" of Some Decorative Patterns in the Church of Tigran Honents in Ani, in: *Architecture and Landscape in Medieval Anatolia, 1100-1500*, ed. P. Blessing, R. Goshgarian. Edinburgh: 155-187.

Guilleux, N. (2001). L'étymologie de "phénix": un état des lieux, in: *Phénix: mythe(s) et signe(s)*, ed. S. Fabrizio-Costa. Bern: 9-23.

Guy, J. (2007). *Indian Temple Sculpture*. Chennai. 2007.

Gyselen, R. (1990). Note sur les "anneaux a trois pendentifs" dans la glyptique sassanide. *Studia Iranica* 19, 2: 205-208.

Gyselen, R. (1995). Les sceaux des mages de l'Iran sassanide, in: *Au carrefour des religions: Mélanges offerts à Philippe Gignoux. Res Orientales* VII, ed. R. Gyselen. Bur-sur-Yvette: 121-150.

Gyselen, R. (2000a). *Arab-Sasanian Copper Coinage.* Wien.

Gyselen, R. (2000b). Un dieu nimbé de flames d'époque sassanide (avec une note additionelle par Ph. Gignoux). *Studia Iranica* XXXV: 291-314.

Gyselen, R. (2005). Vahrām III (293) and the Rock Relief of Naqsh-i Rustam II: A Contribution to the Iconography of Sasanian Crown Princes in the Third Century. *Bulletin of the Asia Institute* 19: 29-36.

Gyselen, R. (2006). Note de glyptique sassanide. 6. Le phénomène des motifs iconographiques communs à l'Iran sassanide et au bassin méditerranéen, in: Ērān ud Anērān. *Studien zu den Beziehungen zwischen dem Sasanidenreich und der Mittelmeerwelt,* ed. J. Wiesehöfer, Ph, Huyse, München: 83-103.

Gyselen, R. (2009). Two Notes on Post-Sasanian Coins, in: *Sources pour l'histoire et la géographie du monde iranien (224-710). Res Orientales,* XVIII, ed. Rika Gyselen, Bur sur-Yvette: 143-172.

Gyselen, R. (2010). "Umayyad" Zāvulistān and Arachosia: Copper Coinage and the Sasanian Monetary Heritage, in: *Coins, Art and Chronology II: The First Milenium* CE *in the Indo-Iranian Borderlands,* ed. M. Alram, D. Klimburg-Salter, M. Inaba, M. Pfisterer. Wien: 219-241.

Gyselen, R. (2016). *Sassanidische Siegelsteine* de P. Horn et G. Steindorff revisité, in: *Words and Symbols: Sasanian Objects and the Tabarestān Archive. Res Orientales* XXIV. Bures-sur-Yvette: 27-106.

H

Hakobyan, Z., L. Mikaelyan (2018). The *Senmurv* and Other Mythical Creatures with Sasanian Iconography in the Medieval Art of Armenia and Transcaucasia, in: *Fabulous Creatures and Spirits in Ancient Iranian Culture,* ed. M. Compareti. Bologna: 39-75.

Halikova, E.A. (1976). Bol'she-Tiganskij mogil'niki. *Sovetaskaja Arhelogija* 2: 158-178.

Hämeen-Anttila, J. (2018). *Khwadāynāmag. The Middle Persian Book of Kings.* Leiden.

Hamilton, R.W. (1959). *Khirbat al Mafjar. An Arabian Mansion in the Jordan Valley.* Oxford.

Hargett, J.M. (1989). Playing Second Fiddle: The *Luan*-Bird in Early and Medieval Chinese Literature. *T'oung Pao* LXXV: 235-262.

Harmatta, J. (1979). Royal Power and Immortality. The Myth of the Two Eagles in Iranian Royal Ideology. *Acta Antiqua Academiae Scientiarum Hungaricae* 27: 305-319.

Harper, P.O. (1961). The Senmurv. *Bulletin of the Metropolitan Museum of Art*: 95-101.

Harper, P.O. (1972). An Eighth Century Silver Plate from Iran with a Mythological Scene, in: *Islamic Art in The Metropolitan Museum of Art,* ed. R. Ettinghausen. New York: 153-168.

Harper, P.O. (1978). *The Royal Hunter. Art of the Sasanian Empire.* New York.

Harper, P.O. (1991). The Sasanian Ewer. Questions of Origin and Influence, in: *Near Eastern Studies Dedicated to H.I.H. Prince Takahito Mikasa on the Occasion of His 75th Birthday*, ed. M. Mori, H. Ogawa, M. Yoshikawa. Wiesbaden: 67-84.

Harper, P.O. (1999). Geographical Location and Significant Imagery: Taq-i Bostan, in: *Coins, Art and Chronology. Essays on the pre-Islamic History of the Indo-Iranian Borderlands*, ed. M. Alram, D.E. Klimburg-Salter. Wien: 315-319.

Harper, P.O. (2000). Sasanian Silver Vessels: The Formation and Study of Early Museum Collection, in: *Mesopotamia and Iran in the Parthian and Sasanian Periods. Rejection and Revival c.238 BC-AD 642*, ed. J. Curtis. London: 46-56.

Harper, P.O. (2006a). La vaiselle précieuse de la deuxième moitié de l'époque sassanide, in: *Les Perses sassanides. Fastes d'un empire oublié* (224-642), ed. F. Demange. Paris: 73-75.

Harper, P.O. (2006b). *In Search of a Cultural Identity. Monuments and Artifacts of the Sasanian Near East, 3rd to 7th Century A.D.* New York.

Harper, P.O. (2015). Golden Ring Set with Garnet Intaglio, in: M. Carter, *Arts of the Hellenized East. Precious Metalwork and Gems of the Pre-Islamic Era*. London: 326-239.

Harper, P.O., Meyer, P. (1981). *Silver Vessels of the Sasanian Period. Volume One: Royal Imagery*. New York.

Hayashi, R. (1975). *The Silk Road and the Shoso-in*. Tokyo.

Hayashi, T. (2000). East-West Exchanges as Seen through the Dissemination of the Griffin Motif, in: *Kontakte zwischen Iran, Byzanz und der Steppe im 6.-7. Jahrhundert*, ed. C. Bálint, Budapest-Napoli-Roma: 253-265.

Heider, G.C. (1999). Tannin, in: *Dictionary of Deities and Demons in the Bible*, ed. K. Von Der Toorn, B. Becking, P.W. Van Der Horst. Grand Rapids MI-Cambridge: 834-836.

Heller, A. (1998). Some Preliminary Remarks on the Excavations at Dulan. *Orientations* 29, 9: 84-92.

Heller, A. (1999). *Arte tibetana. Lo sviluppo della spiritualità e dell'arte in Tibet dal 600 al 2000 d.C.* Milano.

Heller, A. (2003). Archaeological Artefacts from the Tibetan Empire in Central Asia. *Orientations* 34, 4: 55-64.

Heller, A. (2006). Archaeology of Funeral Rituals as Revealed by Tibetan Tombs of the 8th to the 9th Century, in: Ērān *ud Anērān. Studies Presented to Boris Il'ič Maršak on the Occasion of His 70th Birthday*, ed. M. Compareti, P. Raffetta, G. Scarcia. Venezia: 261-274.

Heller, A. (2013). Observations on Painted Coffin Panels of the Tibetan Empire, in: *Tibet after Empire. Culture, Society and Religion between 850-1000*, ed. C. Cüppers, R. Meyer, M. Walter. Lumbini: 117-168.

Heller, A. (2015). Preliminary Remarks on Birds and Deer in Shang shung and Early Tibet, in: *Ancient Civilization of Tibetan Plateau*, ed. Tsering Thar Tongkor, Tsering Dawa Sharshon. Beijing: 3-37.

Henkelman, W.F.M. (2006). The Birth of Gilgameš (Ael. *NA* XII.21): A Case Study in Literary Receptivity, in: *Altertum und Mittelmeerraum: die antike Welt diesseits und jenseits der*

Levante: Festschrift fur Peter W. Heider, zum 60. Geburtstag, ed. R. Rollinger, B. Tuschnegg. Stuttgart: 807-856.

Henning, W.B. (1947). Two Manichæan Magical Texts with an Excursus on the Parthian Ending -ēndēh. *Bulletin of the School of Oriental and African Studies* 12, 1: 39-66.

Heroic Times. A Thousand Years of the Persian Book of Kings (2012). ed. J. Gonnella, C. Rauch. Berlin.

Herzfeld, E. (1920). *Am Tor von Asien*. Berlin.

Herzfeld, E. (1928). La sculpture rupestre de la Perse Sassanide. *Revue des Arts Asiatiques* v, III: 129-142.

Herzfeld, E. (1938). Khusrau Parwēz und der Tāq i Vastān. *Archäologische Mitteilungen aus Iran* IX: 91-158.

Heeßel, N.P. (2011). Evil against Evil. The Demon Pazuzu. *Studi e Materiali di Storia delle Religioni* 77, 2: 357-368.

Hillenbrand, R. (2002). The Arts of the Book in Ilkhanid Iran, in: *The Legacy of Genghis Khan. Courtly Art and Culture in Western Asia, 1256-1353*, ed. L. Komaroff, S. Carboni. New York-New Haven-London: 134-167.

Hillenbrand, R. (2004). *Islamic Art and Architecture*. London.

Hintze, A. (1995). The Saviour and the Dragon in Iranian and Jewish/Christian Eschatology, in: *Irano-Judaica. IV*, ed. S. Shaked, A. Netzer, Jerusalem: 72-90.

Hoffman, E.R. (2008). Between East and West: The Wall Paintings of Samarra and the Construction of Abbasid Princely Culture. *Frontiers of Islamic Art and Architecture: Essays in Celebration of Oleg Grabar's Eightieth Birthday. Muqarnas* 25: 107-132.

Hurwit, J.M. (2006). Lizards, Lions, and the Uncanny in Early Greek Art. *Hesperia* 75: 121-136.

Huff, D. (1998). Formation an Ideology of the Sasanian State in the Context of Archaeological Evidence, in: *The Sasanian Era. The Idea of Iran, vol. 3*, ed. V.S. Curtis, S. Stewart. London: 31-59.

I

Iamanidze, N. (2019).Georgian Reception of Sasanian Art, in: *Sasanian Elements in Byzantine, Caucasian and Islamic Art and Culture*, ed. N. Asutay-Effenberger, F. Daim. Mainz: 93-105.

Ierusalimskaja, A.A. (1995). Shelkovye tkani s "senmurvami" (novye nohodki i starye problem), in: *Ermitazhnye chtenija. Pamjati V.G. Lukonina*. Sankt Peterburg: 62-71.

Institute of History, Archaeology and Ethnography, Academy of Sciences, Tajikistan, National Research Institute for Cultural Properties, Tokyo (2010). *Wall Paintings from the Kakhkakha Site*. Tokyo.

Invernizzi, A. (2007). Les symboles de la royauté arménienne: une introduction à l'Arménie hellénistique, in: *Au pied du Mont Ararat. Splendeurs de l'Arménie antique*, ed. C. Sintes, A. Grigorian. Nîmes: 179-185.

Jeroussalimiskaja [Ierusalimskaja] A.A. (1981). Une soierie récemment trouvée dans le tombeau de Mochtchevaja Balka, Caucase septentrional, in: *Documenta Textilia. Festschrift für Sigrid Müller-Christensen*, ed. M. Flury-Lemberg, K. Stolleis. München: 123-129.

Ierusalimskaja, A.A. (1995). Shelkovye tkani s "senmurvami" (novye nahodki i starye problem), in: *Ermitazhnye Chtenija. Pamjati V.G. Lukonina*. Sankt-Peterburg: 62-71.

Ierusalimskaja, A.A. (2012). *Moshtcevaya Balka. An Unusual Archaeological Site at the North Caucasus Silk Road*. St. Petersburg.

Inner Mongolia Regional Institute of Cultural Relics and Archaeology (2007). *Helingol Han Funerary Wall Paintings*. Beijing (in Chinese).

J

Jacobs, B. (1987). Das Chvarnah. Zum Stand der Forschung. *Mitteilungen der deutschen Orient-Gesellschaft zu Berlin* 119: 215-248.

Jamzadeh, P. (1982). The Winged Ring with Human Bust in Achaemenid Art as a Dynastic Symbol, *Iranica Antiqua*, XVII: 91-99.

Jenkins, M. (1983). *Islamic Pottery: A Brief History*. New York.

Jeon, H. (2005). Documenting the Dreams of the Living and Hopes of the Dead: Goguryeo (Koguryo) Tomb Murals, in: *Art of Ancient Korea*, ed. H. Jeon, J. Choi, Seoul: 164-193.

Johnston, S.I. (1990). *Hekate Soteira. A Study of Hekate's Roles in the Chaldean Oracles and Related Literature*. Atlanta.

Joshi, M.C. (2007). Mithuna, couple d'amoureux, in: *L'âge d'or de l'Inde classique. L'empire des Gupta*, ed. M.C. Joshi, J.-F. Jarrige. Paris: 306.

Juliano, A. (1980). *Teng-Hsien: An Important Six Dynasties Tomb*. Ascona.

Jurković, M. (2015). Un raro motivo iconografico sulla scultura altomedievale. I *senmurv* di Arbe e Nevidane, in: *Scripta in Honorem Igor Fiscović. Festschrift on the Occasion of His 70th Birthday*, ed. M. Jurković, P. Marković. Zagreb: 43-51.

K

Kadoi, Y. (2017). Chinese and Turko-Mongol Elements in Ilkhanid and Timurid Arts. Part 1. The Mongols (c. 1250-1350), in: *A Companion to Islamic Art and Architecture*, ed. F.B. Flood, G. Necipoğlu. Chichester: 636-651.

Kagan, J., Kritt, B. (1995). The Coinage of Kindya. *The Numismatic Chronicle* 155: 261-265.

Kageyama, E. (2006). Use and Production of Silk in Sogdiana, in: Ērān ud Anērān. Studies Presented to Boris *Il'ič Maršak on the Occasion of His 70th Birthday*, ed. M. Compareti, P. Raffetta, G. Scarcia. Venezia: 317-332.

Kalantaryan, A. (1982). *Rannesrednevekovye bully Dvina. Arhelogicheskie pamjatniki Armenii. Vol. 13. Srednevekovye pamjatniki. Vypusk V*. Erevan.

Kalantaryan, A., Karakhanyan, G. et al. (2009). *Armenia in the Cultural Context of East and West. Ceramics and Glass (4th-14th Centuries)*. Yerevan.

Kampouri-Vamvoukou, M. (2014). Le parcours littéraire du Roman d'Alexandre en Orient: son impact sur l'art de l'Islam, in: *Art et civilisations de l'Orient hellénisé. Rencontres et échanges culturels d'Alexandre aux Sassanides*, ed. P. Leriche. Paris: 285-298.

Kapitaikin, L. (2016). Human Flight on a Fabulous Superbird, *Convivium* III, 2: 84-104.

Karamian, G., Farrokh. K. (2017). Sassanian Stucco Decorations from the Ramavand (*Barz Qawaleh)* Excavations in the Lorestan Province of Iran. *Historia i Świat* 6: 69-88.

Karev, Y.M. (2003). Un cycle de peintures murales d'époque qarākhānide (XIIe-XIIIe siècles) à la citadelle de Samarkand: le souverain et le peintre. *Comptes Rendus de l'Académie des Inscriptions et Belles-Lettres* 4: 1685-1731.

Keall, E.J. (2002). Qal'eh-I Yazdigird. *Dossiers d'Archéologie. Les Parthes* 271: 64-71.

Kelly, H.A. (1971). The Metamorphoses of the Eden Serpent during the Middle Ages and Renaissance. *Viator* 2: 301-328.

Khachatryan, Z., Neverov, O. (2008). *Arhivy stolicy drevnej Armenii-Artashata*. Erevan.

Khakimov, A. (2012). Toreutics as a Phenomenon of Artistic Culture, in: *The Artistic Culture of Azerbaijan and Central Asia in the 9th-15th Centuries. Volume II. Toreutics*, ed. K. Baypakov, Sh. Pidaev, A. Khakimov. Samarkand-Tashkent: 6-28.

Kidd, F., Betts, A.V.G. (2010). Entre le fleuve et la steppe: nouvelles perspectives sur le Khorezm ancien. *Comptes Rendus de l'Académie des Inscriptions et Belles-Lettres* II: 637-686.

Kiperwasser, R., Shapira, D.D.Y. (2008). Irano-Talmudica I: The Three-Legged Ass and Ridyā in B. Ta'anith: Some Observations about Mythric Hydrology in the Babylonian Talmud and in Ancient Iran, *Association for Jewish Studies Review* 32, 1: 101-116.

Klimburg-Salter, D. (1989). *The Kingdom of Bāmiyān. Buddhist Art and Culture of the Hindu Kush*. Naples-Rome.

Kotyk, J. (2017). Astrological Iconography of Planetary Deities in Tang China: Near Eastern and Indian Icons in Chinese Buddhism. *Journal of Chinese Buddhist Studies* 30: 33-88.

Kotyk, J. (2018). The Sinicization of Indo-Iranian Astrology in Medieval China. *Sino-Platonic Papers* 282.

Krasnowolska, A. (1998). *Some Figures of the Iranian Calendar Mythology (Winter and Spring)*. Kraków.

Krauskopf, I. (1988). *Gorgo*, in: *Lexicon Iconographicum Mythologiae Classicae (LIMC) IV*. Zürich-Münich: 285-330.

Kröger, J. (1982). *Sasanidischer Stuckdekor*. Mainz.

Kröger, J. (1990). Čāl Tarḵān, in: *Encyclopaedia Iranica*, ed/ E. Yarshater, IV 6. New York: 654-655.

Kuehn, S. (2011). *The Dragon in Medieval East. Christian and Islamic Art*. Leiden-Boston.

Kulakova, L. (2016). Rostam Fights an Adversary, in: *The Everlasting Flame. Zoroastrianism in History and Imagination. Supplement*, ed. S. Stewart, U. Sims-Williams, F.P. Mistree. New Delhi: 19.

Kulik, A. (2009). "The Mysteries of Behemoth and Leviathan" and the Celestial Bestiary of *3 Baruch*. *Le Muséon* 122: 291-329.

L

La Porta, S. (2019). Beyond Image and Text: Armenian Readings of the Old Testament Scenes on the Church at Ałt'amar, in: *The Church of the Holy Cross at Ałt'amar. Politics, Art, Spirituality in the Kingdom of Vaspurakan*, ed. Z. Pogossian, E. Vardanyan. Leiden: 242-252.

Laporte, J.P. (1988). Le tissu aux faisans nimbés de Jouarre description et étude stylistique. *Bulletin du* CIETA 66: 15-25.

Laufer, B. (1915). Asbestos and Salamander. An Essay in Chinese and Hellenistic Folklore. *T'oung Pao* 16, 1: 299-373.

Leclerc, A. (2001). Le Sîmurg, in: *L'Étrange et le Merveilleux en terres d'Islam*, ed. M.B. Taylor, C. Jail. Paris: 120.

Lecocq, F. (2001), L'empereur romain et le phénix, in: *Phénix: mythe(s) et signe(s)*, ed. S.F. Costa. Bern: 27-56.

Lelekov, L.A. (1978). *Iskusstvo drevnej Rusi i Vostok*. Moskva.

Lentz, W. (1962). Yima and Khvarenah in the Avestan Gathas, in: *A Locust's Leg. Studies in Honour of S.H. Taqizadeh*. London: 131-134.

Lentz, W. (1973). Das awestische Chwarenah als magische Kraft des Geistes. *Bulletin of the Iranian Culture Foudantion* I, 2: 9-23.

Lerner, J. (1975). A Note on Sasanian Harpies. *Iran* XIII: 166-171.

Lerner, J. (2013). Yidu: A Sino-Sogdian Tomb?, in: *Sogdians, Their Precursors, Contemporaries and Heirs*, ed. P.B. Lur'je, A.I. Torgoev, St Petersburg: 129-146.

Lerner, J., Sims-Williams, N. (2011). *Seals, Sealings and Tokens from Bactria to Gandhara (4th to 8th Century* CE*)*. Wien.

Li, J. (2014). Indian Grafting Image of Birds and Flowers and Its Development in China. *Dunhuang Research* 3: 93-117 (in Chinese).

Li, S. (forthcoming 2021). A Preliminary Study on the Image of Beribboned Birds Holding a Necklace in the Beak within "Pear Roundels" at Kyzyl, in: *The Hellenistic Legacy along the Silk Road: Cities, Coins, and Arts*. Tianjin.

Litvinskij, B.A., Solov'ev, V.S. (1985). L'art du Toxarlstan à l'époque du Haut Moyen Âge (monuments non bouddhiques). *Arts Asiatiques* XL: 5-17.

Loewe, M. (1979). *Ways to Paradise: The Chinese Quest for Immortality*. London.

Loeschner, H. (2010). Simurgh, Kushan and Sasanian Crowns on AE Coins of the Kushano-Sasanian Ardashir. *Journal of the Oriental Numismatic Society* 203: 12-13.

L'Orange, H.P. (1953). *Studies on the Iconography of Cosmic Kingship in the Ancient World*. Oslo.

Lubotsky, A. (1998). Avestan *x^{v}arənah-*: The Etymology and Concept, in: *Sprache und Kultur der Indogermanen*, ed. W. Meid. Innsbruck: 479-488.

Lucidi, M.T. (1994). *La Seta e la sua via. Exhibition catalogue*. Rome.

Lukonin, V.G. (1976). *Iran II*. Ginevra.

Lukonin, V.G. (1977). *Iskusstvo drevnego Irana*. Moskva.

Luo, F., Rong X. (2016). The Epitaph and Relics found in Western hu-people Di Caoming's Tomb from the Northern Zhou, in: *Sogdians in China: New Evidence in Archaeological Finds and Unearthed Texts*, ed. Rong Xinjiang, Luo Feng. Beijing: 269-299.

Lur'e [Lurje], P.B. (2014). K tolkovaniu syuzhetov i nadpisej pendzhikentskogo zala c Rustamom, *Trudy Gosudarstvennogo Ermitazha* LXXII: 95-102.

Luschey, H. (1996). Taq-i Bostan, in: *Bisutun Ausgrabungen und Forschungen in den Jahren 1963-1967*, ed. W. Kleiss, P. Calmeyer. Berlin: 121-127.

M

Mackintosh, M.C. (1978). Taq-i Bustan and Byzantine Art. A Case for Early Byzantine Influence on the Reliefs of Taq-i Bustan. *Iranica Antiqua* 13: 150-177.

Maciuszak, G. (2006). The Horned Goat versus Demoniac Tree. Some Remarks on Symbolic Meaning of the Pahlavi Text *Draxt ī Āsūrīg*, in: *Proceedings of the 5th Conference of the Societas Iranologica Europæa. Vol. I. Ancient and Middle Iranian Studies*, ed. A. Panaino, A. Piras. Milano: 567-583.

Macuch, M. (2012). The Pre-Islamic Roots of Firdausi's Shahnama, in: *Heroic Times. A Thousand Years of the Persian Book of Kings*, ed. J. Gonnella, C. Rauch. Berlin: 22-27.

Mahé, J.P. (2008). Le mythe d'Ištar dans l'oralité caucasienne, *Comptes Rendus de l'Académie des Inscriptions et Belles-Lettres*, 1: 215-230.

Manassero, N. (2014). Marine monsters in the desert sands. Thoughts on some sealings from Parthian Nisa. *Parthica* 16: 93-109.

Maranci, C. (2008-2009). The Humble Heraclius: Revisiting the North Portal at Mren. *Revue des Études Armeniennes* 31: 167-180.

Marr, N. Ja. (1918). Japhetica I. Fakond – osetinskih skazok i jafeticheskij termin φasqund – "mag", "vestnik", "veshchaja ptica". *Izvestija Rossijskoj Akademii Nauk* 18: 2069-2100.

Marschak [Marshak], B.I. (1986). *Silberschätze des Orients. Metallkunst des 3.-13. Jahrhunderts und ihre Kontinuität*. Leipzig.

Maršak [Marshak], B.I. (1990). Les fouilles de Pendjikent. *Comptes Rendus de l'Académie des Inscriptions et Belles Lettres*: 286-312.

Marshak, B.I. (1998). The Decoration of Some Late Sasanian Silver Vessels and Its Subject-Matter, in: *The Art and Archaeology of Ancient Persia. New Light on the Parthian and Sasanian Empires*, ed. V.S. Curtis, R. Hillenbrand, J.M. Rogers. London-New York: 84-92.

Marshak, B.I. (2000a). Bol orné de l'effigie d'une divinité, in: *L'Asie des steppes. D'Alexandre le Grand à Gengis Khån*, ed. J.-P. Desroches. Paris-Barcelone: 70.

Marshak, B.I. (2000b). Verseuse ornée d'un chameau ailé, in: *L'Asie des steppes. D'Alexandre le Grand à Gengis Khån*, ed. J.-P. Desroches. Paris-Barcelone: 71.

Marshak, B.I. (2001). La thématique sogdienne dans l'art de la Chine de la seconde moitié du VIe siècle. *Comptes Rendus de l'Académie des Inscriptions et Belles Lettres* I: 227-264.

Marshak, B.I. (2002a). Zoroastrian Art in Iran under the Parthians and the Sasanians, in: *A Zoroastrian Tapestry. Art, Religion & Culture*, ed. Ph. J. Godrej, F.P. Mistree. Usmanpure: 134-147.

Marshak, B.I. (2002b). *Legends, Tales, and Fables in the Art of Sogdiana*. New York.

Marshak, B.I. (2004). Plate with Figure of Dionysus, in: *China. Dawn of a Golden Age, 200-750 AD*, ed. J.C.Y. Watt. New York: 184.

Marshak, B.I. (2006a). Le décor de la vaisselle en argent à la fin de la période sassanide a tau début de l'époque islamique, in: *Les Perses sassanides. Fastes d'un empire oublié (224-642)*, ed. F. Demange. Paris: 76-79.

Marshak, B.I. (2006b). The So-Called Zandanījī Silks: Comparisons with the Art of Sogdian, in: *Central Asian Textiles and Their Contexts in the Early Middle Ages*, ed. R. Schorta. Riggisberg: 49-60.

Marshak, B.I. (2006c). Une peinture kouchane sur toile. Suivi d'une note additionnelle par F. Grenet. *Comptes Rendus de l'Académie des Inscriptions et Belles-Lettres* II: 947-963.

Martiniani-Reber, M. (1986). *Soieries sassanides, coptes et byzantines Ve-XIe siècles*. Paris.

Martiniani-Reber, M., Bénazeth, D. (1997). *Textiles et modes sassanides*. Paris.

Masterpieces (2013). *Masterpieces of Chinese Paintings 700 to 1900*. London.

Masuya, T. (2002). Ilkhanid Court Life, in: *The Legacy of Genghis Khan. Courtly Art and Culture in Western Asia, 1256-1353*, ed. L. Komaroff, S. Carboni. New York-New Haven-London: 74-103.

McKenzie, J. (2007). *The Architecture of Alexandria and Egypt ca. 300 BC to AD 700*. New Haven-London.

Meshkeris, V.A. (1989). *Sogdijskaja terrakota*. Dushanbe.

Mazzoleni, D. (1992). Jonah. II. Iconography, in: *Encyclopaedia of the Early Church*, ed. A. Di Berardino. Cambridge: 450-451.

Mayrhöfer, M. (1956-76). *Kurzgefasstes etymologisches Wörterbuch des Altindischen*. Heidelberg.

Meyer, J., Wandel, P. (2016). *Shahnama. The Colorful Epic about Iran's Past*. Copenhagen.

Melikoff, I. (1962). *Abū Muslim: Le 'porte hache' du Khorassan dans la tradition épique turco-iranienne*. Paris.

Miks, C. (2012). Silberschale (XIII. 11), in: *Das Goldene Byzanz un der Orient*, ed. F. Daim. Mainz: 338-339.

Minardi, M. (2016). The Hellenistic Chorasmian *Ketos* of Akchakhan-Kala. *Iranica Antiqua* LI: 165-200.

Minardi, M. (2018). The Oxus Route toward the South Persian Legacy and Hellenistic Innovations in Central Asia. *Ancient Civilization from Scythia to Siberia* 24: 87-154.

Miquel, A. (1980). *La géographie humaine du monde musulman jusqu'au milieu du XIe siècle: Le milieu naturel*. Paris-New York.

Mode, M. (1989). Frühe sogdische Kultbilder. *Archäologische Mitteilungen aus Iran*. 22: 231-251.

Mode, M. (1993). *Sogdien und die Herrscher der Welt. Türken, Sasaniden und Chinesen in Historiengemälden des 7. Jahrhunderts n. Chr. Aus Alt-Samarqand*. Frankfurt am Main - Berlin - Bern - New York - Paris - Wien.

Mode, M. (2006). Art and Ideology at Taq-i Bustan: The Armoured Equestrian, in: *Arms and Armour as Identificators of Cultural Transfer. The Steppes and the Ancient World from Hellenistic Times to the Early Middle Ages*, ed. M. Mode, J. Tubach. Wiesbaden: 393-413.

Mode, M. (2019). In the Heart of the City: On Sogdian Temples and Deities at Penjikent, in: *New Research on Central Asian, Buddhist and Far Eastern Art and Archaeology. Inner Asian Art and Archaeology* II, ed. J.A. Lerner, A.L. Juliano. Turnhout: 91-124.

Mo'in, M. (1964). Sīmurγ (A Fabulous Bird), in: *Dr. J.M. Unvala Memorial Volume*, Bombay: 18-24.

Molè, G. (1970). *The T'u-yü-hun from the Northern Wei to the Time of the Five Dynasties*. Roma.

J. Domela Movassat (2005). *The Large Vault at Taq-i Bustan: A Study in Late Sasanian Royal Art*. New York-Queenston.

Musche, B. (1994). Römische Einflüsse auf den Taq-e Bostan, in: *Beiträge zur Altorientalische Archäologie und Altertumskunde. Festschrift für Barthel Hrouda zum 65. Geburtstag*, ed. P. Calmeyer, K. Hecker, L. Jakob-Rost, C.B.F. Walker. Wiesbaden: 193-199.

N

Naymark, A. (2001). *Sogdiana, Its Christians and Byzantium: A Study of Artistic and Cultural Connections in Late Antiquity and Early Middle Ages*. PhD Submitted at Indiana University, Department of Art History and Central Eurasian Studies.

Nehru, L. (2004). A Fresh Look at the Bone and Ivory, Begram. *Silk Road Art and Archaeology*, X: 97-150.

Neverov, O. (1976). *Antique Intaglios in the Hermitage Collection*. Leningrad.

Nikitin, A.B. (1984). Monnaies d'Arachosie du Haut Moyen-Âge. *Studia Iranica* 13/2: 233-239.

Nikitin, A., Roth, G. (1995). A New Seventh-Century Countermark with a Sogdian Inscription. *The Numismatic Chronicle* 155: 277-279.

Noja, S. (1983). Les chevaux ailés de 'Ā'išah – Dieu soit satisfait avec elle – et les *banāt*. *Annali dell'Istituto Orientale di Napoli* 43, 1: 33-42.

Nöldeke, T. (1930). *The Iranian National Epic or the Shahnamah*. Bombay [reprint Philadelphia, 1979].

Norozi, N. (2017). Le metamorfosi dell'onagro (*gur*) dalle lettere persiane medievali a Balzac. *Quaderni di Meykhane* VII: 1-25.

Nylander, C. (1983). The Standard of the Great King. A Problem in the Alexander Mosaic. *Opuscula Romana* XIV, 2: 19-37.

O

Olivieri, L.M. (2018). Amluk-dara (AKD 1). A Revised Excavation Report. *Journal of Asian Civilization* 41, 1: 1-106.

Ornan, T. (2005a). *The Triumph of the Symbol. Pictorial Representation of Deities in Mesopotamia and the Biblical Image Ban*. Fribourg-Göttingen.

Ornan, T. (2005b). A Complex System of Religious Symbols: The Case of the Winged Disc in Near Eastern Imagery of the First Millenium B.C.E., in: *Crafts and Images in Contact. Studies on Eastern Mediterranean Art of the First Millenium B.C.E.*, ed. C.E. Suter, C. Uehlinger. Fribourg-Göttingen: 207-241.

Orsatti, P. (2019). *Materials for a History of the Persian Narrative Tradition. Two Characters: Farhād and Turandot*. Venezia.

Otavksy, K. (1998a). Zur kunsthistorischen Einordnung der Stoffe, in: *Entlang der Seidenstraße. Frühmittelalterliche Kunst zwischen Persien und China in der Abegg-Stiftung*, Riggisberger Berichte 6, ed. Karel Otavsky. Riggisberg: 119-214.

Otavsky, K. (1998b). Stoffe von der Seidenstraße: Eine neue Sammlungsgruppe in der Abegg-Stiftung, in: *Entlang der Seidenstraße. Frühmittelalterliche Kunst zwischen Persien und China in der Abegg-Stiftung*, Riggisberger Berichte 6, ed. Karel Otavsky. Riggisberg: 13-41.

Ovadiah, R., Ovadiah, A. (1987). *Mosaic Pavements in Israel*. Rome.

Overlaet, B. (2009). A Himyarite Diplomatic Mission to the Sasanian Court of Bahram II Depicted at Bishapur. *Arabian Archaeology and Epigraphy* 20: 218-221.

Overlaet, B. (2013). And Man Created God? Kings, Priests and Gods on Sasanian Investiture Reliefs. *Iranica Antiqua*. XLVIII: 313-354.

Overlaet, B. (2015). Sāsānian, Central Asian and Byzantine Iconography. Patterned Silks and Cross-Cultural Exchange, in: *The Treasure of Sânnicolau Mare (Hungarian: Nagyszentmiklós)*, ed. F. Daim, K. Gschwantler, G. Plattner, P. Stadler, Mainz: 121-133.

P

Panaino, A. (2001). Between Mesopotamia and India: Some Remarks about the Unicorn Cycle in Iran, in: *Melammu Symposia 2*, ed. R.M. Whiting. Helsinki: 149-179.

Panaino A. (2003). The *bayān* of the Fratarakas: Gods or "Divine" Kings, in: *Religious Themes and Texts of Pre-Islamic Iran and Central Asia. Studies in Honour of Professor Gherardo Gnoli on the Occasion of his 65th Birthday*, ed. C.G. Cereti, M. Maggi, E. Provasi. Wiesbaden: 265-288.

Panaino, A. (2019). Symbolic and Ideological Implications of Archery in Achaemenid and Parthian Kingship, in: *Philobiblos. Scritti in onore di Giovanni Geraci*, ed. A. Bencivenni, A. Cristofori, F. Muccioli, C. Salvaterra. Milano: 19-66.

Paribeni, A. (2004). Osservazioni sui mosaici pavimentali dei palazzi omayyadi, in: *Medioevo: arte lombarda*, ed. A.C. Quintavalle. Parma-Milano: 634-642.

Pedone, E. (2001). Falchi e falconeria in Eurasia, in: *Khwuṣhāl Khān Khaṭak. Il libro del falcone*, ed. D. Guizzo, G. Scarcia. Venezia: 75-94.

Pennacchietti, F. (2000). The Queen of Sheba, the Glass Floor and the Floating Tree-Trunk. *Henoch* XXII: 223-245.

Pfister, R. (1938). Coqs Sassanides. *Revue des Arts Asiatiques* XII, 1: 40-47.

Philon, H. (1980). *Benaki Museum. Islamic Art.* Athens.

Piccirillo, M. (1989). *Chiese e mosaici di Madaba.* Jerusalem.

Piemontese, A.M. (1974). Note morfologiche ed etiologiche su al-Būraq. *Annali di Ca' Foscari* 3: 109-133.

Piggott, S. (1949). Sasanian Motifs on Painted Pottery from North-West India. *Bulletin of the Archaeological Survey of India* 5: 31-34.

Pirart, È. (1999). Les métamorphoses de Vṛthragna. *Journal Asiatique* 287, 2: 465-522.

Piras, A. (2004). Sulla gioia e sul diadema. Interazioni culturali fra zoroastrismo, manicheismo e Vicino Oriente, in: *Varia Iranica*, ed. C.G. Cereti, B. Melasecchi, F. Vajifdar. Roma: 183-211.

Pirazzoli-t'Serstevens, M. (1982). *The Han Dynasty.* New York.

Pirtea, A. (2019). From Lunar Nodes to Eclipse Dragons: The Fundaments of the Chaldean Art (CCAG V/2, 131-40) and the Reception of Arabo-Persian Astrology in Byzantium, in: *Savoirs prédictifs et techniques divinatoires de l'Antiquité tardive à Byzance*, ed. P. Magdalino, A. Timotin. Seyssel: 339-365.

Pistoso, M. (1974). L'ipotesi iranistica sul *Vij* gogoliano, in: *Gururājamañjarika. Studi in Onore di Giuseppe Tucci*, ed. G. Gnoli. Napoli, 1974: 313-320.

Pistoso, M. (2007). Di parole e di immagini. Due libri russi sulla civiltà letteraria e artistica dell'Iran medievale, in: *'Uyuṇ al-Akhbar. Studi sul mondo islamico.* Bologna: 101-114.

Polidovich, Yu. B. (2019). Greben' iz Gajmanovoj Mogily i skifskij mif o zmeeborchestve. *Arheologija i davnja istorija Ukraini* 2: 483-492.

Polidovich, Yu. B., Shamina, T.P. (2018). Zobrazhennja skifs'kogo drakona v kolekcii muzeju istorichnih koshtnovnostej Ukraini, in: *Muzejni Chitanija. Materiali naukovoi konferencii "Yuvelirnemistecvo – nogljad kriz' viki".* Kiev: 69-75.

Polos'mak, N.V. (2015). Nouvelles découvertes de tentures polychromes brodées du début de notre ère dans les tumuli no 20 et no 31 de Noin-Ula (République de Mongolie). *Arts Asiatiques* 70: 3-32.

Poulsen, V. (1960). To persiske Kunstværker, in: *Meddelelser Fra Ny Carlsberg Glyptotek.* 17. Kobenhaven: 1-8.

Propp, V.J. (1949). Le radici storiche dei racconti di fiabe. Torino [*Istoricheskie korni volshebnoj skazki.* Leningrad. 1928].

Provasi, E. (2003). Sogdian *Farn*, in: *Religions Themes and Texts of Pre-Islamic Iran and Central Asia. Studies in Honour of Professor G. Gnoli on the Occasion of His 65th Birthday*, ed. C.G. Cereti, M. Maggi, E. Provasi. Wiesbaden: 305-322.

Pugliaro, M. (1998). Il cavaliere sul destriero alato: ipotesi per una "contaminatio" medievale tra il mito di Perseo e il mito di Bellerofonte. *Rivista di Archeologia* XXII: 91-112.

Q

Qi, D. (2013). Grapes, Mythical Birds and Beads: Cultural Absorption and Assimilation in Ancient Chinese Art, in: A Silk Road Saga. The Sarcophagus of Yu Hong, ed. Y. Cao. Sidney: 34-37.

Qi, X., Wang, B. (2016). *The Ancient Culture in Xinjiang along the Silk Road (Continued).* Urumqi.

R

Raggetti, L. (2008). Gli uccelli nel *Kitāb al-Ḥayawān* di al-Ǧāḥiẓ: fonti, tradizione, *adab. Quaderni di studi arabi* 3: 183-200.

Rahimi, F. (2004). Technische Untersuchungen und Herkunftsstudien sassanidiscer Silbergefase von Quri Qaleh, in: *Persiens Antike Pracht. Bergbau-Handwerk-Archaologie. II.* Bochum: 456-461.

Rapoport, Yu. A. (1977). *Kosmogonicheskiy syuzhet na khorezmiyskikh sosudakh*, in: *Srednyaya Aziya v drevnosti i srednevekov'ye.* Moscow: 58-71.

Rapoport, Yu. A., Nerazik, E.E., Levina, L.M. (2000). *V nizov'jah Oksa i Jaksarta. Obrazy drevnego Priaral'ja.* Moskva.

Raspopova, V. (2006). Textiles Represented in Sogdian Murals, in: *Central Asian Textiles and Their Contexts in the Early Middle Ages*, ed. R. Schorta. Riggisberg: 61-73.

Raven, E.M. (1994). *Gupta Gold Coins with a Garuḍa-Banner. Samudragupta-Skandagupta. Volume I.* Groningen.

Rawson, J. (1984). *Chinese Ornament: The Lotus and the Dragon.* London.

Rawson, J. (2001). Creating Universes: Cultural Exchange as Seen in Tombs in Northern China between the Han and Tang Periods, in: *Between Han and Tang: Cultural and artistic Interaction in a Transformative* Period, ed. H. Wu. Beijing: 113-152.

Rempel', L.I. (1978). *Iskusstvo srednego Vostoka.* Moskva.

Rempel', L.I. (1987). *Cep' Vremen. Vekovye obrazy i brodjachie siuzhety v tradicionnom iskusstve Srednej Azii.* Tashkent.

Rezakhani, K. (2017a). *ReOrienting the Sasanians: East Iran in Late Antiquity.* Edinburgh.

Rezakhani, K. (2017b). From the Kushans to the Western Turks, in: *King of the Seven Climes. A History of the Ancient Iranian World (3000 BCE-651 CE)*, ed. T. Daryaee. Irvine: 199-226.

Riboud, K. (1976). A Newly Excavated Caftan from the Northern Caucasus. *Textile Museum Journal* 4/3: 21-40.

Riboud, K. (1977). A Detailed Study of the Figured Silk with Birds, Rocks and Tree from the Han Dynasty. *Bulletin du CIETA* 45, I: 51-60.

Riboud, K. (1983). Brief Comments on the Depiction of the Simurgh. *National Museum Bulletin (New Delhi)* 4, 5 and 6: 107-113.

Riboud, P. (2003). Le cheval sans cavalier dans l'art funéraire sogdien en Chine: à la recherche des sources d'un thème composite. *Arts Asiatiques* 58: 148-161.

Riboud, P. (2004). Description du monument, in: *Lit de pierre, sommeil barbare: Présentation, après restauration et remontage, d'une banquette funéraire ayant appartenu à un aristocrate d'Asie centrale venu s'établir en Chine au VIe siècle*. Paris: 15-31.

Riboud, P. (2005). Réflexions sur les pratiques religieuses désignées sous le nom de *xian*, in: *Les Sogdiens en Chine*, eds. É. de La Vaissière, É. Trombert. Paris: 73-91.

Riboud, P. (2007). Bird-Priests in Central Asian Tombs of Sixth Century China and Their Significance in the Funerary Realm. *Bulletin of the Asia Institute* 21: 1-23.

Riccioni, S. (2016). Dal *kētos* al *sēnmurv*? Mutazioni iconografiche e transizioni simboliche del *kētos* dall'antichità al medioevo (secolo XIII). *Hortus Artium Medievalium* 22: 130-144.

Riccioni, S. (2017). I mosaici altomedievali di Venezia e il monastero di S. Ilario. Orditi "veneto-carolingi" di una *koinè* alto-adriatica, in: *I tempi del consolidamento. Venezia, l'Adriatico e l'entroterra tra IX e X secolo*, ed. S. Gasparri, S. Gelichi. Turnhout: 279-336.

Riccioni, S. (2019). Percorrendo il Bestiario. La rappresentazione del mondo animale nei pavimenti musivi del Medioevo veneziano, in: *Animali figurati. Teoria e rappresentazione del mondo animale dal Medioevo all'Età moderna*, ed. S. Riccioni, L. Perissinotto. Roma: 179-217.

Richard F. (1997). *Splendeurs persanes, Manuscrits du XIIe au XVIIe siècle. Exposition de la Bibliothèque Nationale de France, Galerie Mazarine*. Paris.

Ritter, M. (2019). Eastern Elements in Umayyad Architecture: Audience Hall and Ceremonial Space in Residences, in: *Sasanian Elements in Byzantine, Caucasian and Islamic Art and Culture*, ed. N. Asutay-Effenberger, F. Daim. Mainz: 37-59.

Ritter, N.C. (2010). *Die altorientalischen Traditionen der sasanidischen Glyptik. Form, Gebauch, Ikonographie*. Wien-Berlin.

Róheim, G. (1954). *Hungarian and Vogul Mythology*. Seattle.

Romano, M.C. (1994). Il Senmurv, in: M.T. Lucidi. *La Seta e la sua via*. Rome: 135-137.

Rose, J. (2018). Bird-Men and Other Hybrids: Some Central Asian Representations of Zoroastrian *Yazatas*, in: *Fabulous Creatures and Spirits in Ancient Iranian Culture*, ed. M. Compareti. Bologna: 19-37.

Roux, J.P. (1982). Études d'iconographie islamique. Leuven.

Russell, J. (1986). Arlez, in: *Encyclopaedia Iranica*, ed. E. Yarshater, II, 4, New York: 412.

Russell, J. (1987). *Zoroastrianism in Armenia*. Cambridge MA-London.

Russell, J. (1990-1991). Two Notes on Biblical Tradition and Native Epic in the *Book of Lamentation* of St. Grigor Narekac'i. *Revue des Études Armeniennes* 22: 135-145.

Russell, J. (1990-91). Dragons in Armenia: Some Observations. *Journal of Armenian Studies* V, 1: 3-12.

Russell, J. (1994-1995). Problematic Snake Children of Armenia. *Revue des Études Arméniennes* 25: 77-96.

Russell, J. (2016). Beasts, Real and Imagined, in: *The Everlasting Flame. Zoroastrianism in History and Imagination.* Supplement, ed. S. Stewart, U. Sims-Williams, F.P. Mistree. New Delhi: 28.

S

Saccone, C. (1999). *Viaggi e visioni di re, sufi, profeti.* Milano.

Sáenz López Pérez, S. (2010). El vuelo de Oriente a Occidente del mítico pájaro Rujj y las transformaciones de su leyenda, in: *La creación de la imagen en la Edad Media: de la herencia a la renovación. Anales de Historia del Arte. Volumen extraordinario*, ed. M.V. Chico, L. Fernández: 325-341.

Salviati, F. (1994). La fenice nell'archeologia cinese, in: M.T. Lucidi, *La seta e la sua via.* Rome: 5.

Santi, A. (2020). The Iconography of the of the Pseudo-Sēnmurv in Early Islamic Art: The Case of an Enigmatic Stamped Roundel of the Former Von-Osten Collection, in: Maḥabattnāma. Scritti offerti a Maria Vittoria Fontana dai suoi allievi per il suo settantesimo compleanno, ed. V. Laviola, M. Massullo, Roma: 345-375.

Sarkhosh Curtis, V. (2010). The Frataraka Coins of Persis: Bridging the Gap between Achaemenid and Sasanian Persia, in: *The World of Achaemenid Persia. History, Art and Society in Iran and the Ancient Near East*, ed. J. Curtis, StJ. Simpson. New York: 379-394.

Sarkhosh Curtis, V. (2012). Parthian Coins: Kingship and Divine Glory, in: *The Parthian Empire and Its Religions. Studies in the Dynamics of Religious Diversity*, ed. P. Wick, M. Zehnder: 67-81.

Sasanian Silver (1967). *Late Antique and Early Medieval Arts of Luxury from Iran.* Ann Arbor.

Sbordone, F. (1935). La fenice nel culto di Helios. *Rivista Indo-Greco-Italica* 1-2: 1-46.

Scaglia, G. (1958). Central Asians on a Northern Ch'i Gate Shrine. *Artibus Asiae* 21, 1: 9-28.

Scarcia, G. (1965). Sulla religione di Zabul, *Atti dell'Istituto Orientale di Napoli*, xv: 119-165.

Scarcia, G. (1979). La piaga e la luna, in: *Studi su Harran.* Venezia: 71-122.

Scarcia, G. (1980). Bastam e la stirpe dei draghi, in: *Transcaucasica II*, ed. G. Scarcia. Venezia: 82-107.

Scarcia, G. (1985). Bahr-i ahzar, Muhīt-i islāmī, in: *Studi arabo-islamici in onore di Roberto Rubinacci nel suo settantesimo* compleanno, ed. C. Sarnelli Cerqua. Napoli: 583-592.

Scarcia, G. (1991). Intorno a Noè: simboli armeni fra Oriente e Occidente, in: *Atti del Quinto Simposio Internazionale di Arte Armena*, ed. B.L. Zekiyan, Venezia: 603-612.

Scarcia, G. (2002). Ripensare Zabul, in: *Oriente e Occidente. Convegno in ricordo di Mario Bussagli*, ed. C. Silvi Antonini, B.M. Alfieri, A. Santoro, Pisa-Roma: 236-241.

Scarcia, G. (2003). Sulla fenice dei baluci, in: *Il falcone di Bistam. Intorno all'iranica Fenice/Samand: un progetto di sintesi per il volo del Pegaso iranico tra Ponto, Alessandretta e Insulindia*, ed. M. Compareti, G. Scarcia, Venezia: 7-26.

Scarcia, G. (2010). Montagnes sacrées d'Iran, in: *Montagnes sacrées*, ed. J. Ries, Paris: 102-121.

Scarcia, G. (2017). Alla ricerca di un Ur-Farhâd: Hercules patiens, magnetico signor dottore, scalpellino, feldmaresciallo mecenate?, in: *Studia Philologica Iranica. Gherardo Gnoli Memorial Volume*, ed. E. Morano, E. Provasi, A.V. Rossi. Roma: 395-412.

Scarcia, G. (2018). *Nelle terre dei (sette) dormienti. Sopralluoghi, appunti, spunti*. Perugia.

Scarcia, G., Vercellin, G. (1970). Leucippidi e Dioscuri in Iran. *Annali di Ca' Foscari* IX, 3: 39-50.

Schafer, E. (1963). *The Golden Peaches of Samarkand: A Study of T'ang Exotics*. Berkeley-Los Angeles.

Schiltz, V. (1994). *Les Scythes et les nomades des steppes*. Paris.

Schindel, N. (2013). Sasanian Coinage, in: *The Oxford Handbook of Sasanian Iran*, ed. D.T. Potts. Oxford: 814-839.

Schlumberger, D. (1986). *Qasr el-Heir el Gharbi*. Paris.

Schmidt, H.P. (1980a). The Sēnmurv. Of Birds and Dogs and Bats. *Persica* 9: 1-85.

Schmidt, H.P. (1980b). The Sīmurgh in Sasanian Art and Literature. *The Journal of the K. R. Cama Oriental Institute* 48: 161-178.

Schmidt, H.P. (2002). Simorġ, in: *Encyclopaedia Iranica*, ed. E. Yarshater, online edition: <www.iranica.com>.

Schmitt, G. (1974). Shun als Phönix-ein Schlüssel zu Chinas Vorgeschichte. *Alt-Orientalische Forschungen* I: 309-340.

Schmitz, B. (1997). *Islamic and Indian Manuscripts and Paintings in the Pierpont Morgan Library*. New York.

Schulz, R. (2018). Dionysus Between Sāsānian Iran and Roman Allusions, Art of the Orient 7: 26-45.

Schulz, R. (2019). The Stroganov Bowl in the State Hermitage: Zoroastrian Beliefs between Late Roman and Posthellenistic Iconography in Central Asia, in: *The Age of Empires. Eastern Iran from the Achaemenids to the Sasanians: Arcaheology, History, Culture*, ed. A. Balakhvantsev, N. Makkaveev, Moscow, 2019: 183-194.

Schwartz, M. (2012). On *Aiiehiiā*, Afflictress of Childbirth, and *Pairikā:* Two Avestan Demonesses (with an Appendix on the Indo-Iranian Shipwrecked Seaman), *Bulletin of the Asia Institute*. 22: 95-103.

Semi, F., Rota, L. (1987). I bestiari medievali eguvino e marciano. *Ateneo Veneto* 25, 1-2: 19-51.

Seznec, J. (1953). *The Survival of the Pagan Gods. The Mythological Tradition and Its Place in Renaissance Humanism and Art*. Princeton.

Shaanxi Provincial Institute of Archaeology (2008). The Sarcophagus of a Sui Dynasty Mural Tomb at Shuicun, Tongguan County, Shaanxi Province. *Kaogu yu Wenwu* 3: 33-47 (in Chinese).

Shahbazi, A. Sh. (1980). An Achaemenid Symbol. II Farnah "(God Given) Fortune" Symbolised. *Archäologische Mitteilungen aus Iran* 13: 119-147.

Shahbazi, A. Sh. (1989). Besṭām and Bendōy, in: *Encyclopaedia Iranica* IV, 2, ed. E. Yarshater, London: 180-182.

Shahbazi, A. Sh., Cristoforetti, S. (2009). Zāl, in: *Encyclopaedia Iranica*, ed. E. Yarshater, online edition: <www.iranicaonline.org> (July 20 2009).

Shavarebi, E., Qaemmaqami, S.A.R. (2016). Les mots moyen-perses *XWARRAH* et *FARR*: un nouvel argument onomastique. *Folia Orientalia* LIII: 261-274.

Shayegan, R. (2013). Sasanian Political Ideology, in: *The Oxford Handbook of Ancient Iran*, ed. D.T. Potts, Oxford, 805- 813.

Shenkar, M. (2014). *Intangible Spirits and Graven Images: The Iconography of Deities in the Pre-Islamic Iranian World.* Leiden-Boston.

Shenkar, M. (2017). Royal Regalia and the Divine Kingship in the Pre-Islamic Central Asia. *Parthica* 19: 55-74.

Shenkar, M. (2018). The Coronation of the Early Sasanians, Ctesiphon and the Great Diadem of Paikuli. *Journal of Persianate Studies* 11: 113-139.

Shenkar, M. (2019). The Chorasmian Gad: On the "Colossal" Figure from Akchakhan-kala, in: *New Research on Central Asian, Buddhist and Far Eastern Art and Archaeology. Inner Asian Art and Archaeology II*, ed. J.A. Lerner, A.L. Juliano. Turnhout: 9-30.

Shepard, K. (1940). *The Fish-Tailed Monster in Greek and Etruscan Art.* New York.

Shishkin, V.A. (1963). *Varakhsha.* Moskva.

Silvi Antonini, C. (2006). Ob odnom siuzhete v zhivopis' dvorca Varahshi, in: *Ancient and Mediaeval Culture of the Bukhara Oasis*, ed. C. Silvi Antonini, D.K. Mirzaakhmedov. Rome-Samarkand: 50-54.

Simpson, M.S. (1979). *The Illustration of an Epic. The Earliest* Shahnama *Manuscripts.* New York-London.

Simpson, StJ. (2004). "Baubo" at Merv. *Parthica* 6: 227-233.

Sims, E. (2002). *Peerless Images. Persian paintings and Its* Sources. New Haven-London.

Sims, E. (2012). Five Paintings from Four Dispersed Manuscripts of the Early 14th Century (Edmund de Unger/Keir Collection), in: *Heroic Times. A Thousand Years of the Persian Book of Kings*, ed. J. Gonnella, C. Rauch. Berlin: 96-101.

Sims, E. (2013). The Stephens' Inju *Shahnama* Manuscript: Millennial Thoughts and a Tribute to the Late Boris I. Marshak, in: *Sogdians, Their Precursors, Contemporaries and Heirs*, ed. Pavel B. Lur'e. A.I. Torgoev. St. Petersburg: 450-460.

Sims-Williams, N. (1996). Nouveaux documents sur l'histoire et la langue de la Bactriane *Comptes Rendus de l'Académie des Inscriptions et Belles-Lettres* 2: 633-654.

Sims-Williams, N. (1997). *New light on ancient Afghanistan: The Decipherment of Bactrian.* London.

Sims-Williams, N., Khan, G. (2008). Zandanījī Misidentified. *Bulletin of the Asia Institute. Zoroastrianism and Mary Boyce with Other Studies* 22: 207-213.

Sims-Williams, N., Sims-Williams U. (2015). Rustam and His *zīn-i palang*, in: *From Aṣl to Zā'id: Essays in Honour of Éva M. Jeremiás*, ed. I. Szántó, Piliscsaba: 249-258.

Sinisi, F. (2008). Tyche in Parthia: The Image of the Goddess on Arsacid Tethradrachms. *Numismatische Zeitschrift* 116-117: 231-248.

Sinisi, F. (2017). Royal Imagery on Kushan Coins: Local Tradition and Arsacid Influences. *Journal of the Economic and Social History of the Orient* 60: 818-927.

Sinisi, F. (2019). A Kushan "Scene of Investiture" with Mithra on a Seal Impression from Kafir Qala, near Samarkand, and Its Relation to Kushan Coinage, in: *New Research on Central Asian, Buddhist and Far Eastern Art and Archaeology. Inner and Central Asian Art and Archaeology.* II, ed. J.A. Lerner, A.L. Juliano. Turnhout: 31-48.

Skjærvø, P.O. (1983). Farnah: mot mède en vieux perse? *Bulletin de la Société de linguistique de Paris* 78, 1: 241-259.

Smirnova, O. Ju. (1981). *Svodnyj katalog sogdijskih monet. Bronza.* Moskva.

Sonik, K. (2013). The Monster's Gaze: Vision as Mediator between Time and Space in the Art of Mesopotamia, in: *Time and History in the Ancient Near East*, ed. L. Feliu, J. Llop, A. Millet Albà, J. Sanmartin, Winona Lake-IN: 285-300.

Soucek, P. (1974). Farhād and Tāq-i Būstān: The Growth of a Legend, in: *Studies in Art and Literature of the Near East in Honour of Richard Ettinghausen*, ed. P.J. Chelkowski. Salt Lake City NY: 27-52.

Soudavar, A. (2003). *The Aura of Kings. Legitimacy and Divine Sanction in Iranian Kingship.* Costa Mesa.

Soudavar, A. (2010) Farr(ah). ii. Iconography of Farr(ah)/X^varənah, in: Encyclopaedia Iranica, ed. E. Yarshater, online edition: <www.iranicaonline.org/articles/farr-ii-iconography> (August 24 2010).

Spuhler, F. (2014). *Pre-Islamic Carpets and Textiles from Eastern Lands.* London.

Stančo, L. (2012). *Greek Gods in the East. Hellenistic Iconographic Schemes in Central Asia.* Prague.

Stchoukine, I. (1966). *La peinture turque d'après les manuscrits illustrés. 1er partie de Sulaymān Ier à 'Oṣmān II (1520–1622).* Paris.

Sterckx, R. (2002). *The Animal and the Daemon in Early China.* Albany.

Stewart, S., F.P. Mistree (2013). The Birth of Rostam, in: *The Everlasting Flame. Zoroastrianism in History and Imagination*, ed. S. Stewart. London: 154.

Stricker, B.H. (1964). *Vārəġna*, the Falcon. *Indo-Iranian Journal* VII, 4: 310-317.

Stronach, D. (2018). Notes on the Iconography of the Senmurv, in: *Fabulous Creatures and Spirits in Ancient Iranian Culture*, ed. M. Compareti. Bologna: 77-91.

Subtelny, M. (2011). Zoroastrian Elements in the Islamic Ascension Narrative: The Case of the Cosmic Cock, in: *Medieval and Modern Iranian Studies. Proceedings of the 6th European Conference of Iranian Studies*, ed. M. Szuppe, A. Krasnowolska, C.V. Pedersen, Paris: 193-212.

Sulejmanov, R.H. (2000). *Drevnij Nahshab. Problemy civilizacii Uzbekistana* VII *v. do n.e.*-VII *v. n. e.* Tashkent.

Sun, J. (1996). *The Holy Fire of China: Some Problems about East-West Cultural Interchange and Ancient Chinese Civilization.* Shenyang (in Chinese).

Swietochowski, M.L., Carboni, S. (1994). *Illustrated Poetry and Epic Images. Persian Paintings of the 1330s and 1340s.* New York.

T

Taasob, T. (2020). Representation of Wēś in Early Kushan Coinage: Royal or Local Cult? Afghanistan 3, 1: 83-196.

Tanabe. K. (2006). The Identification of the King of Kings in the Upper Register of the Larger Grotte, Taq-i Bustan: Ardashir III Restated, in: *Ērān ud Anērān. Studies Presented to Boris Il'ič Maršak on the Occasion of His 70th Birthday*, ed. M. Compareti, P. Raffetta, G. Scarcia. Venezia: 583-601.

Tao T. (2013). *The Silk Roads of the Northern Tibetan Plateau during the Early Middle Ages (from the Han to Tang Dynasty) as Reconstructed from Archaeological and Written Sources.* Oxford.

Tao, T., Wertmann, P. (2009). The Coffin Paintings of the Tubo Period from the Northern Tibetan Plateau, in: *Archäologie in China*, 1, ed. M. Wagner, W. Wang, Mainz: 187-213.

Tchukasizian, B.L. (1964). Échos de légendes épiques iraniennes dans les "Lettres" de Grigor Magistros. *Revue des Études Arméniennes* I: 321-329.

Terukazu, A. (1977). *Japanese Painting.* Geneva.

Thierry, N. (1976). Mentalité et formulation iconoclastes en Anatolie. *Journal des Savants* 2: 81-130.

Thompson, D. (1076). *Stucco from Chal Tarkhan-Eshqabad.* Warminster.

Toll, N. (1942). Review of: The Dog-Bird Senmurv-Paskuj, by C. Trever, Pp. 71, figs. In text 11. Leningrad, The Hermitage Museum, 1938. *American Journal of Archaeology* 46, 3: 464-466.

Tottoli, R. (1999). At Cock-Crow: Some Muslim Traditions about the Rooster. *Der Islam* 76: 139-147.

Traina, G. (2010). *La resa di Roma. 9 giugno 53 a.C., Battaglia di Carre.* Roma-Bari.

Trainor, K. (1996). Constructing a Buddhist Ritual Site: Stupa and Monastery Architecture. *Mārg* XLVII, 3: 18-35.

Treadwell, L. (2008). The Copper Coinage of Umayyad Iran. *The Numismatic Chronicle* 168, 331-381.

Treister, M. (2017). Ahemenidskie "importy" na territorjah k severu ot granic Ahemenidskoj derzhavy, in: *Iranica. Iranian Empires and the Greco-Roman Worldfrom the Sixth Century* BC *to the Sixth Century* AD. Kazan: 103-126.

Trésors de l'ancien Iran (1966). Genève.

Trever, K. (1937). *Senmurv-Paskuj Sobaka-Ptica.* Leningrad.

Trever, K.V. (1959). *Ocherki po istorii i kul'ture Kavkazkoj Albanii* IV *v. do n. e.-*VII *v. n.e.* Moskva. Leningrad.

Trever, C.V. (1964). Tête de Senmurv en argent des collections de l'Ermitage. *Iranica Antiqua* 4/2: 162-170.

Trever, C. (2005). The Dog-Bird: Senmurv = Paskuj, in: *A Survey of Persian Art from Prehistoric Times to the Present. Vol.* XVII. *Prehistoric Times to the End of the Sasanian Empire*, ed. A. Daneshvari, J. Glucks. Costa Mesa CA: 161-175.

Trever, K.V., Lukonin, V.G. (1987). *Sasanidskoe serebro. Sobranie Gosudarstvennogo Ermitaža*, Moskva.

Trivedi, S.D. (1998-99). Decorative Elements in Mathurā Art. *Kalā* v: 169-177.

Tuplin, C. (1992). The Persian Bird: An Ornithonymic Conundrum. *Archäologische Mitteilungen aus Iran* 25: 125-129.

Turfan Museum (1992). *Turfan Museum*. Urumqi.

U

Uehlinger, C. (1999). Leviathan, in: *Dictionary of Deities and Demons in the Bible*, ed. K. Von Der Toorn, B. Becking, P.W. Van Der Horst. Grand Rapids MI-Cambridge: 511-515.

Ur Rahman, A., Falk, H. (2011). *Seals, Sealings and Tokens from Gandhāra*. Wiesbaden.

V

Vajnberg, B.I. (1977). *Monety drevnego Horezma*. Moskva.

Van den Broek, R. (1972). *The Myth of the Phoenix, According to Classical and Early Christian Traditions*. Leiden.

Van den Broek, R. (1999). Phoenix, in: *Dictionary of Deities and Demons in the Bible*, ed. K. Von Der Toorn, B. Becking, P.W. Van Der Horst. Grand Rapids MI-Cambridge: 655-657.

Van der Waerden, B.L. (1953). History of the Zodiac, *Archiv für Orientforschung*, XVI, 2: 216-230.

Vanden Berghe, L. (1984). *Reliefs rupestres de l'Iran ancien*. Bruxelles.

Vanden Berghe, L., Schippman, K. (1985). *Les reliefs rupestres d'Elymaïde (Irān) de l'époque parthe*. Gent.

Vanderheyde C. (1994). Réflexions sur l'iconographie du Semourve et sa diffusion dans l'art byzantine. *Revue des Archeologues et Historiens d'Art de Louvain* 27: 35-40.

Vanderheyde, C. (2012). La salamandre: un curieux détail sculpté sur une plaque funéraire trouvée à Andravida dans le Pèloponnèse. *Ktema* 37: 359-372.

van't Haaff, P.A. (2020). *Catalogue of Persis Coinage. Ca. 280* B.C.-A.D. *228. 34 Kings of 5 Dynasties ruled in Iran for 500 Years*. Lancaster (available at: <https://issuu.com/cngcoins/docs/ catalogue_of_persis_coinage?fbclid=IwAR2slrVIJoGB0qafSfDE6ahNnRH8O1b8tlm-lXKhnpLx_92HpKV3WzB7QJBo>).

Vanzan, A. (2012). *Ancient Persia. History and Treasures of an Ancient Civilization*. Vercelli.

Vardanyan, R. (2001). Tendenze culturali e ideologiche nell'impero partico riflesse dalla monetazione. *Parthica* 3: 25-132.

Varenov, A.V., D.V. Cheremisin (2020). Izobrazhenija Senmurvov v naskal'nom iskusstve Srednej Azii, Sibiri i Kitaja, in: *Ancient and Medieval Cultures of Central Asia*, ed. V.P. Nikonorov et al., St. Petersburg: 266-269.

Vercellin, G. (1973). Il monte santuario di Qal-è-Kāh nel Sīstan afghano. *Annali di Ca' Foscari* x, 3: 75-117.

Vernant, J.P. (2014). *La morte negli occhi*. Bologna [*La mort dans les yeux*. Paris. 1985].

Vesel, Ž. (2008). Asie centrale: questions d'iconographie astrale, in: *Islamisation de l'Asie centrale. Processus locaux d'acculturation du VIIe au XIe siècle*, ed. É. de la Vaissière. Paris: 161-173.

Vieira Pinto, O.L. (2020). Birds of Glory: The Falcon (and Its Absence) in Sasanian Art, in: *Raptor on the Fist. Falconry, Its Imagery and Similar Motifs throughout the Millennia on a Global Scale*, ed. O. Grimm. Hamburg: 557-567.

Vitali, R. (2008). A Tentative Classification of the *Bya Ru Can* Kings of Zhang Zhung. *Revue des Études Tibétains* 15: 379-419.

Vitellozzi, P. (2010). *Gemme e magia dalle collezioni del Museo Archeologico Nazionale dell'Umbria*. Perugia.

Vondrovec, K. (2014). *Coinage of the Iranian Huns and Their Successors from Bactria to Gandhara (4th to 8th Century CE)*. Wien.

W

Walker, A. (2008). Patterns of Flight: Middle Byzantine Adoptions of the Chinese *Feng-Huang* Bird. *Ars Orientalis* 38: 189-216.

Walker, A. (2012). *The Emperor and the World: Exotic Elements and the Imaging of Middle Byzantine Imperial Power, Ninth to Thirteenth Centuries CE*. New York.

Wallenfels, R. (1993). Zodiacal Signs among the Seal Impressions from Hellenistic Uruk, in: *The Tablet and the Scroll. Near Eastern Studies in Honor of William W. Hallo*, ed. M.E. Cohen, D.C. Snell, D.V. Weisberg, Bethesda-Maryland: 281-289.

Ward, R. (1993). *Islamic Metalwork*. London.

Weber, D. (2003). Notes of Some Parthian Names from Nisa. *Parthica* 5: 127-129.

Weber, D. (2010). The Pahlavi Script as a Medium of Iranian Identity. Some Paleographical Notes, in: *Iranian Identities in the Course of History*, ed. C. Cereti et al., Rome: 347-356.

Wellesz, E. (1959). An Early al-Ṣūfī Manuscript in the Bodleian Library in Oxford. A Study in Islamic Constellation Images. *Ars Orientalis* 3: 1-26.

Westenholz, J. (2004). *Dragons, Monsters and Fabulous Beasts*. Jerusalem.

Whitehouse, D. (2005). *Sasanian and Post-Sasanian Glass in the Corning Museum of Glass*. New York.

Whitfield, R., Farrer, A. (1990). *Caves of the Thousand Buddhas: Chinese Art from the Silk Road*. London.

Wiesehöfer, J. (2011). The "Accursed" and the "Adventurer": Alexander the Great in Iranian Tradition, in: *A Companion to Alexander Literature in the Middle Ages*, ed. D.Z. Zuwiyya. Leiden: 113-32.

Wikander, S. (1949-1950). *Sur le fonds commun indo-iranien des épopées de la Perse et de l'Inde*. Paris.

Willets, W. (1965). *Origini dell'arte cinese*. Milano [*Chinese Art*. London: 1958].

Wong Pui Yin, M. (2006). Power of Image: A Study of the *Siling* Combinations in Han Tomb Interior. *The Study of Art History* 8: 163-198.

Wood, R. (2017). Identifications: Mihr in Sasanian Iran, in: *Images of Mithra. Visual Conversations in Art and Archaeology*, Oxford-New York: 81-105.

Woodford, S., Spier, J. (1992), Kerberos, in: *Lexicon Iconographicum Mythologiae Classicae*, vi.1, Zürich-Munich: 24-32.

X

Xi'an Municipal Institute of Archaeology and Preservation of Cultural Relics (2008). Tomb of Kang Ye of the Northern Zhou in Xi'an, Shaanxi. *Wenwu* 6: 14-35 (in Chinese).

Xu, X. (2006). The Discovery, Excavation, and Study of Tubo (Tibetan) Tombs in Dulan County, Qinghai, in: *Central Asian Textiles and Their Contexts in the Early Middle Ages*, ed. R. Schorta. Riggisberg: 265-290.

Y

Yang, J. (2014). *Shi Jun Tomb of the Northern Zhou Dynasty*. Beijing (in Chinese).

Yarshater, E. (1998). Esfandīār, in: *Encyclopaedia Iranica*, viii, ed. E. Yarshater, Costa Mesa CA: 584-592.

Yoshida, Y. (2013). Heroes of the Shahnama in a Turfan Sogdian Text. A Sogdian Fragment Found in the Lushun Otani Collection, in: *Sogdians, Their Precursors, Contemporaries and Heirs*, ed. P.B. Lur'je, A.I. Torgoev. St. Petersburg: 201-218.

Z

Zakharia, K. (2002). La 'anqâ'. Quelle place pour le phénix dans le monde arabo-musulman classique?, in: *Le Phénix, mythe(s) et signe(s) = Actes de colloque international organisé à Caen par le Laboratoire d'Études Italiennes, Ibériques et Ibéro-Américaines (leia)*, ed. S. Fabrizio-Costa. Caen: 116-138.

Zambon, F. (2004). Il mito della fenice in Occidente, in: F. Zambon, A. Grossato, *Il mito della fenice in Oriente e in Occidente*. Venezia: 13-81.

Zambon, F. (2018). Introduzione, in: *Bestiari tardoantichi e medievali. I testi fondamentali della zoologia sacra Cristiana*, ed. F. Zambon. Firenze-Milano: xi-xciii.

Zare, S. (2008). Is Eagle a Zoomorphic Symbol of the God Mithra? *Bāstānpazhūhi* 3, 6: 77-92 (in Persian).

Zhang, W., Xu, C., Wu, Z., Qiu, Y. (2013). A Study on the Auspicious Animal Motifs on Han Textiles in Ancient China. *The Silk Road* 11: 100-112.

Zhao, F. (2004). The Evolution of Textiles along the Silk Road, in: *China. Dawn of a Golden Age, 200-750 AD*, ed. J.C.Y. Watt. New York: 66-77.

Zhao, F. (2012). Silks in Sui, Tang, and Five Dynasties, in: *Chinese Silks*, ed. D. Kuhn, Yale: 202-257.

Zhang, H. (1995). *A Collection of China's Tang Dynasty Frescoes.* Shenzhen.

Zheng, Y. (2001). Northern Qi Pictorial Carvings from Qingzhou and Sinicized Sogdian Art: An Observation Inspired by the Yu Hong Sarcophagus and Other New Archaeological Finds, in: *Between Han and Tang: Cultural and artistic Interaction in a Transformative Period*, ed. H. Wu. Beijing: 73-109 (in Chinese).

Index

A

W

X

Y

Z

Questo volume è stato stampato
nel mese di marzo dell’anno 2021
per conto della

Casa Editrice Persiani

Printed in Dunstable, United Kingdom

68355826R00184